Politics and Culture in the Developing World

Fifth Edition

RICHARD J. **Payne**

Illinois State University

JAMAL R. **Nassar**

California State University, San Bernardino

Longman
Boston   Columbus   Indianapolis   New York   San Francisco   Upper Saddle River
Amsterdam   Cape Town   Dubai   London   Madrid   Milan   Munich   Paris   Montreal   Toronto
Delhi   Mexico City   São Paulo   Sydney   Hong Kong   Seoul   Singapore   Taipei   Tokyo

Acquisition Editor: Vikram Mukhija
Senior Editorial Assistant: Beverly Fong
Senior Marketing Manager: Lindsey Prudhomme
Production Manager: Renata Butera
**Project Coordination, Text Design, and Electronic
    Page Makeup:** Chitra Sundarajan / Integra Software Services Pvt. Ltd.
Creative Art Director: Jayne Conte
Cover Designer: Suzanne Behnke
Cover Illustration/Photo: AFP/Getty Images
Manufacturing Manager: Renata Butera
Printer and Binder: Courier Westford
Cover Printer: Moore Langen

Library of Congress Cataloging-in-Publication Data

Payne, Richard J.
    Politics and culture in the developing world/Richard J. Payne, Jamal R.
Nassar.—5th ed.
        p. cm.
    Includes bibliographical references and index.
    ISBN-13: 978-0-205-07591-1 (alk. paper)
    ISBN-10: 0-205-07591-6 (alk. paper)
    1. Developing countries—Politics and government.   2. Globalization.
I. Nassar, Jamal R. (Jamal Raji) II. Title.
JF60.P44 2012
320.9172'4—dc22

                                            2010043433

2 3 4 5 6 7 8 9 10—V013—14 13 12

Longman
is an imprint of

www.pearsonhighered.com

ISBN-13: 978-0-205-07591-1
ISBN-10:   0-205-07591-6

For Sami and Gina Nassar and Josephine and Todd Payne

BRIEF CONTENTS

Detailed Contents   ix

Preface   xiii

Photo Credits   xix

CHAPTER 1   Government, Politics, and Cultures in Africa, Asia, the Middle East, and Latin America   2

CHAPTER 2   Global Interdependence   24

CHAPTER 3   Religion and Politics   42

CHAPTER 4   Nationalism, Colonialism, and Independence   62

CHAPTER 5   Global and Domestic Inequalities   80

CHAPTER 6   Challenges of Development   100

CHAPTER 7   The Costs of Development   124

CHAPTER 8   Women in the Developing World   146

CHAPTER 9   Transitions to Democracy and Human Rights   168

CHAPTER 10   Political Leadership and State Capacity   194

CHAPTER 11   Ethnicity, Ethnic Conflict, and Conflict Resolution   220

CHAPTER 12   Migration   245

CHAPTER 13   Foreign Relations of the Developing Countries   262

Index   286

DETAILED CONTENTS

Preface   xiii
Photo Credits   xix

CHAPTER 1
Government, Politics, and Cultures in Africa, Asia, the Middle East, and Latin America   2

Government, Politics, and Cultures in a Globalized World   3

What Is Globalization?   4

What Is Politics?   4

What Is Government?   5

Forms of Government   6

What Is Culture and Political Culture?   7

What Is a State?   8

What Is a Nation?   9

Africa, Asia, Latin America, and the Middle East   10
> Africa   11
> Asia   13
> Latin America   15
> The Middle East   18

Summary and Review   20

CHAPTER 2
Global Interdependence   22

Globalization and Interdependence   23

The Global Reality   24

Global Interdependence and Your Life   26

Economic Interdependence   26

Environmental Interdependence   29

Cultural Interdependence   30

Globalization   32

Terrorism and Globalization   34
> Case Study: Ghana   35

Summary and Review   37

CHAPTER 3
Religion and Politics   40

Globalization and Religious Revivalism   41

Islam   42
> The Teachings of Islam   44
> Islam and Politics   45

Hinduism   46
> Hinduism and Indian Politics   49

Buddhism   50
> Buddhism and Politics   52

Christianity in Africa, Asia, and Latin America   52
> Case Study: Iran   54

Summary and Review   58

CHAPTER 4
Nationalism, Colonialism, and Independence   60

Globalization and the Nation-State   61

What Is Nationalism?   61

Consequences of Nationalism   64

Colonialism   65
> Case Study: India   68
> Case Study: Algeria   70
> Case Study: Ghana   72
> Case Study: Brazil   74
> Case Study: The Caribbean   75

Summary and Review   76

CHAPTER 5
Global and Domestic Inequalities   78

Globalization and Global and Domestic
  Inequalities   79

Growing Inequality Between the North and
  the South   80
   Enduring Poverty in the South   82
   Economic Inequalities Within Rich Countries   84
   Regional Inequalities   85
   *The Gulf Between the Rich and the Poor in
     the South   85*
   *The Causes of Inequality Between the North and
     the South   86*
   Narrowing the Gaps   90
   Case Study: Brazil   93

Summary and Review   95

CHAPTER 6
Challenges of Development   98

Globalization and Economic Development   99

What Is Development?   100

The Role of Government in Development   101
   *The Classical Economic Model and Free-Market
     Capitalism   102*
   *Non-State Actors, Intergovernmental Organizations,
     and Development   102*
   State Capitalism   103

Theories of Development   104
   Modernization Theory, or Developmentalism   105
   Marxist Theory   106
   Dependency Theory   106
   Third World and African Socialism   107
   Community and Grassroots Development   108
   Feminist Theory   108
   Sustainable Development   108

Factors Facilitating and Impeding
  Development   109
   Values of the Leaders and Citizens   109
   Natural Resources and Natural Disasters   110
   *The International and Regional Economic
     Environment   111*
   Population   112
   Education and Health Care   115
   Political Instability   116
   Corruption and Economic Development   117
   Debt, Foreign Aid, and Development   118
   Case Study: Venezuela   119

Summary and Review   121

CHAPTER 7
The Costs of Development   124

Globalization and the Costs of
  Development   125

Social and Cultural Costs of Development   125
   Child Labor   128
   Sweatshops   130

Economic and Political Costs of
  Development   131
   Consumerism and Development   132
   Urbanization and Development   133
   *The Decline of Agriculture and Economic
     Development   135*
   Environmental Costs of Development   135
   Deforestation   137
   Dam Construction   139
   Case Study: Indonesia   140

Summary and Review   143

CHAPTER 8
Women in the Developing World   146

Globalization and Women   147

The Roles of Women   148

The Status of Women   149

Rape as a Weapon of War   152

Women and Education   153

Women in Development   154

Women in Agriculture   155

Women's Political Participation   157

Women Leaders in the Developing World   160

Empowering Women   162
   Case Study: Turkey   163

Summary and Review   165

CHAPTER 9

Transitions to Democracy and Human Rights   168

Globalization and Democracy and Human Rights   169

Democracy   170
  Political Participation and Democratic Freedoms   *172*
  Factors Conducive to Democracy   *176*
  Transitions to Democracy   *177*
  Democratic Transitions in Latin America   *180*
  Democratic Transitions in Africa   *182*
  Democratic Transitions in Asia   *184*
  Human Rights in the Developing World   *186*
  Case Study: South Africa   *188*

Summary and Review   191

CHAPTER 10

Political Leadership and State Capacity   194

Globalization, Leadership, and State Capacity   195

Patriarchal Leadership   196

Military Leadership   196
  Case Study: Egypt   *197*
  Case Study: Nigeria   *200*
  Case Study: Chile   *201*
  Case Study: Nonmilitary Leadership   *203*
  Case Study: Communist Leaders: The Case of Cuba's Castro   *205*
  Case Study: Leaders in Democracies: The Case of India   *208*
  Leadership and Change   *210*

State Capacity   210

Implementation   211

Regulation   211

The Bureaucracy in Africa, Asia, and Latin America   212
  Structural Uniformity   *212*
  Cultural Variations   *213*
  Shortage of Skilled Staff   *213*
  Corruption   *214*
  Formalism   *214*
  Operational Autonomy   *215*

Case Study: Bureaucracy in the People's Republic of China   *215*
Case Study: Bureaucracy in Mexico   *216*
Case Study: Bureaucracy in South Africa   *216*
Case Study: Bureaucracy in Egypt   *217*

Summary and Review   218

CHAPTER 11

Ethnicity, Ethnic Conflict, and Conflict Resolution   220

Globalization and Ethnic Conflict   221

Ethnicity and Ethnic Identity   222

The Causes of Ethnic Conflict   223

The Costs of Ethnic Conflict   224

Ethnic Conflicts in Africa   226
  Nigeria   *227*
  Liberia   *228*
  The Sudan   *229*
  Rwanda   *230*

Ethnic Conflicts in Asia   231
  India   *231*
  China   *232*
  The Kurds   *233*

Ethnic Conflicts in Latin America   235

Resolving Ethnic Conflicts   236
  Case Study: Sri Lanka   *237*

Summary and Review   240

CHAPTER 12

Migration   244

Globalization and Migration   245

What Is Migration?   246

Causes of Migration   247

Push Factors   248
  Palestinian Refugees   *251*

Pull Factors   251
  The United States   *253*
  France   *253*
  Germany   *254*

The Impact of Migration on Poor Countries   254

The Impact of Migration on Rich Countries   256
  Case Study: Mexico   257

Summary and Review   259

CHAPTER 13
Foreign Relations of the Developing Countries   262

Globalization and Foreign Relations   263

Making Foreign Policy in Developing
  Countries   264

The Developing World and the United States   265
  Afghanistan   265

Economic Globalization and Foreign
  Policies   267

Conflict and Cooperation Among Developing
  Countries   268

Regional Economic and Political
  Integration   270

Foreign Relations of Developing Countries   273
  India   273
  Egypt   276
  Mexico   277
  Cuba   279
  Brazil   280
  Case Study: China   280

Summary and Review   283

Index   286

PREFACE

Addressing shareholders in Fayetteville, Arkansas, in June 2010, Wal-Mart's Chief Executive Michael T. Duke stated that Wal-Mart is committed to becoming a truly global company. Facing sluggish growth in the United States, Wal-Mart decided to concentrate on expanding its operations in developing countries such as Brazil, Mexico, China, India, and Argentina. The developing world is now the engine of global economic growth. By 2010, the Group of 20 leading developed and developing countries had clearly eclipsed the Group of 8 industrialized countries as the principal forum for discussing global economic problems. China, India, Brazil, and other developing countries are growing increasingly confident and assertive about playing more prominent roles in the world and in their relations with the United States and Europe. The rise of China is challenging dominant assumptions about and approaches to economic development and democracy. The global financial crisis and economic recession shifted some power away from the developed world to developing countries. This change in power relations is underscored by major demographic developments that are enhancing the economic power of the developing world relative to that of developed countries. These changes, together with ongoing global challenges, demonstrate the interdependence of rich and poor countries and reinforce our decision to discuss issues in the developing world within the broader context of globalization. The *us versus them* logic is being severely eroded by the forces of globalization.

Our decision to write *Politics and Culture in the Developing World: The Impact of Globalization* grows out of our extensive professional and personal experiences. Our experiences in different parts of the developing world give us not only first-hand knowledge of those countries within it, but also a strong desire to share this knowledge with students. Although our connections to these areas remain strong, we have the additional advantage of being observers from a distance. The problems of developing countries are not abstract concerns for us. An important reason for writing this book is to improve our own understanding of the challenges that poor countries face and to think of possible solutions to some of them. As such, this fifth edition continues in the same spirit as the first, second, third, and fourth editions. The nuclear crisis with North Korea, the war in Iraq, the Israeli–Palestinian conflict, the crisis over nuclear enrichment in Iran, and the constant threat of terrorism are all new reminders of the importance of studying the developing world.

For more than a quarter century, we have been teaching courses on the global South, global issues, international relations, foreign policy, and American government. We have done extensive scholarly research and have published many articles and books on developing countries. For more than a decade, we have shared with our colleagues a strong desire for a comprehensive textbook that is suitable for introductory courses on Africa, Asia, and Latin America. We wanted to write a book that dealt with issues that improve students' understanding of the developing world within the broader context of rapid globalization. Students are increasingly aware of the growing interdependence among countries and the fact that rich and poor countries are being drawn closer together. Rising rates of immigration from Latin America, Asia, and—to a lesser extent—Africa are contributing to profound demographic changes in the United States, Western Europe, Canada, and elsewhere in the industrialized world. These significant changes inspired us to write a text that treats developing countries as integral parts of an increasingly global society.

Globalization, the major theme of the book, makes it more difficult to separate the problems and concerns of rich countries from those of poor societies. Trade officials from the industrialized world are routinely pressured to negotiate agreements that include safeguards for environmental protection and the rights of workers in poor countries. Many of the world's largest corporations, such as Nike, negotiate with advocacy groups in the United States and Europe to develop new codes of conduct for global commerce in which many developing countries participate. Groups, which include many students, have effectively used the threat of protests and boycotts to persuade Starbucks Corporation to pay what they regard as a living wage to coffee bean growers in Central and South America. The anti-sweatshop movements on many American college campuses have influenced companies to make a greater effort to end child labor and oppressive working conditions in their factories in developing countries. Globalization has made these companies vulnerable to pressure from various groups that operate in both rich and poor countries.

We hope that our experiences in the developing world as well as in the classroom have enabled us to write a book that is relevant to our students' lives. We decided to make the text accessible without being simplistic. Based on feedback from our colleagues and students, we believe we have written a book that is intellectually engaging, one that is interesting for students to read, and one that avoids a stereotypical treatment of developing countries. We have relied on carefully selected scholarly literature as well as real-life stories and current events to write this book. We have included pedagogical features that help students to understand the information, to develop critical thinking skills, and to think of ways to solve problems they will encounter beyond college, some of which will undoubtedly involve developing countries.

Consistent with our decision to adopt an accessible writing style, we have included many stories throughout the book. These stories help students develop clearer images of the developing world. They also maintain the students' attention and interest in the material discussed in the chapter. We hope that our stories will encourage students to share their stories with their classmates and teachers.

NEW TO THIS EDITION

- All chapters have been updated to reflect global developments.
- We have added detailed case studies on specific countries (one for each chapter), giving background information on the country and analysis that reflect the content of the specific chapter in a global context.

- Based on feedback from reviewers of the fourth edition, pedagogical features have been changed.
- The impact of the global financial crisis and economic recession is woven into discussions throughout the text.
- There is a sharper focus on how globalization has severely eroded the *us versus them* logic in relations between the developed and developing world.
- We emphasize how power is shifting from the developed world to developing countries such as China, India, and Brazil in light of globalization.
- We stress the decline in the American model of globalization that emphasizes deregulation and privatization and the growing global perception of China as an alternative model of development.
- There is greater emphasis on global crimes such as human trafficking, illegal drugs, and drug-related violence.
- Venezuela and Indonesia receive more coverage.

FEATURES

Politics and Culture in the Developing World emphasizes globalization, and we begin each chapter with a vignette on the impact of globalization on the topics covered in the chapter. These vignettes remind students of the book's main theme. Issues in Africa, Asia, the Middle East, and Latin America are placed within a broader context that is familiar to most students. The vignettes are followed by an introduction to the chapter. The introduction provides a brief overview of the main points in the chapter, tells the students what is covered, and provides examples of controversial issues included in the chapter to stimulate the students' interest in the material.

We have included maps to help put the issues in context and enable students to better grasp essential points discussed in the text. We have carefully selected photographs that portray specific developments, capture the students' attention and imagination, and present an objective and realistic view of developing countries. We have included many different tables in the book. Some tables show the differences between rich and poor countries. These tables contain data on the United States to enable students to see how the United States compares with other countries.

We have made a concerted effort to put definitions, key terms, and concepts in boldface type to draw the students' attention to them. Stressing their importance reinforces the point that they are building blocks of the chapter. The marginal notes are designed to give students a quick reference to basic definitions and concepts. They provide a very brief review for the students. End-of-chapter summaries focus students' attention on the major points of the chapter and assist them in concentrating on the most important information as they review the chapter. Our own students often tell us that review questions focus their attention on the most important information. These questions, concepts, and terms are designed to improve the retention of information, stimulate discussions, and help students prepare for exams. They may also assist teachers in the preparation of their own study guides.

We have included a list of suggested readings at the end of each chapter to familiarize students with the scholarly literature. This section helps students locate additional information on issues in which they are interested. The index allows students to find key terms, concepts, and subjects discussed throughout the book. The index is especially helpful for reviewing for exams. We believe an important aspect of excellent teaching is interaction among students themselves and between students and teachers not only in the classroom but also in more informal settings. Feedback and questions from students are essential for learning and teaching. We encourage you to contact us by e-mail at jnassar@csusb.edu, or write to us at the College of Social and Behavioral Sciences, Office of the Dean, 5500 University Parkway, San Bernardino, California, 92407.

SUPPLEMENTS

Longman is pleased to offer several resources to qualified adopters of *Politics and Culture in the Developing World* and their students that will make teaching and learning from this book even more effective and enjoyable. Several of the supplements for this book are available at the Instructor Resource Center (IRC), an online hub that allows instructors to quickly download book-specific supplements. Please visit the IRC welcome page at www.pearsonhighered.com/irc to register for access.

Passport for Comparative Politics   With Passport, choose the resources you want from MyPoliSciKit and put links to them into your course management system. If there is assessment associated with those resources, it also can be uploaded, allowing the results to feed directly into your course management system's gradebook. With over 150 MyPoliSciKit assets like video case studies, mapping exercises, comparative exercises, simulations, podcasts, *Financial Times* newsfeeds, current events quizzes, politics blog, and much more, Passport is available for any Pearson introductory or upper-level political science book. Use ISBN 0-205-10923-3 to order Passport with this book. To learn more, please contact your Pearson representative.

MySearchLab   Need help with a paper? MySearchLab saves time and improves results by offering start-to-finish guidance on the research/writing process and full-text access to academic journals and periodicals. Use ISBN 0-205-09273-X to order MySearchLab with this book. To learn more, please visit www.mysearchlab.com or contact your Pearson representative.

Test Bank   This resource includes multiple-choice questions, true/false questions, and essay questions for each chapter. Available exclusively on the IRC.

The Economist   Every week, *The Economist* analyzes the important happenings around the globe. From business to politics, to the arts and science, its coverage connects seemingly unrelated events in unexpected ways. Use ISBN 0-205-00261-7 to order a 15-week subscription with this book for a small additional charge. To learn more, please contact your Pearson representative.

The Financial Times   Featuring international news and analysis from journalists in more than 50 countries, *The Financial Times* provides insights and perspectives on political and economic developments around the world. Use ISBN 0-205-00247-1 to order a 15-week subscription with this book for a small additional charge. To learn more, please contact your Pearson representative.

Longman Atlas of World Issues (0-205-78020-2) From population and political systems to energy use and women's rights, the *Longman Atlas of World Issues* features full-color thematic maps that examine the forces shaping the world. Featuring maps from the latest edition of *The Penguin State of the World Atlas*, this excerpt includes critical thinking exercises to promote a deeper understanding of how geography affects many global issues. Available at no additional charge when packaged with this book.

Goode's World Atlas (0-321-65200-2) First published by Rand McNally in 1923, *Goode's World Atlas* has set the standard for college reference atlases. It features hundreds of physical, political, and thematic maps as well as graphs, tables, and a pronouncing index. Available at a discount when packaged with this book.

ACKNOWLEDGMENTS

We are deeply indebted to numerous students and colleagues who made significant contributions to this interdisciplinary project. Because we wanted to make the book accessible to undergraduate students, we solicited feedback from many students over the years and encouraged several of them to assist us. Their questions, insights, suggestions, and research skills were invaluable. We are particularly indebted to Julie Edmunds, Richard Ehlers, Yu Bo, Sherri Replogle, Amentahru Wahlrab, Khalil Marrar, Doug Smith, Michelle Boyer, Aleksandra Malyszko, Sally Kwitkowski, Brennan Berg, and Jennifer Schlemmer. Anthony DiMaggio was extremely helpful in the second edition. Faculty here at Illinois State University and elsewhere were also very helpful, especially Rachitha Dayarante, Conrad Dyer, Marian Ide, Khalil Marrar, Jennifer Ngonga, and Ali Riaz. Dr. Riaz was especially helpful in his suggestions on the forms of government and the section on Islam. Dr. Nancy Lind was of great help as well. Tami Stone and Elaine Graybill did an outstanding job helping us revise and update the fourth and fifth editions, respectively.

   We are grateful to our colleagues, many of whom read parts of the manuscript and made helpful suggestions, based on their experiences teaching both large and small sections of courses on Africa, Asia, Latin America, and global issues. We would like to thank Denis Thornton, Bob Hunt, Carlos Parodi, Ron Pope, and Manfred Steger of the Department of Politics and Government at Illinois State University; Margaret Chapman of Illinois Wesleyan University; Roger Fisher of Harvard Law School; Maria Brisk of Boston University and Boston College; Elizabeth Davis of the Asia Pacific Center for Security Studies in Hawaii; Kelly Keogh of Normal Community High School; Dixie Mills, dean and former dean of the College of Business at Illinois State University; Laura Berk of the Department of Psychology at Illinois State University; Valentine Moghadam, director of Women's Studies at Purdue University; Eleanor Zeff of Drake University; Kenneth Johnson of Eastern Kentucky University; William Crowther of the University of North Carolina–Greensboro; Julio F. Carron, University of Delaware; Earl Conreh-Morgan, University of South Florida; Michael Gold-Bliss, St. Cloud State

University; Carl Lutrin, California Polytechnic State University; Steffen Schmidt, Iowa State University; Shawn Shieh, Marist College; Lionel Ingram, University of New Hampshire; Gardel Feurtado, The Citadel; and Lee Walker of the University of Kentucky.

We would also like to thank a number of reviewers of the previous edition, whose thoughts and comments were incredibly valuable: Nurudeen Akinyemi, Fayetteville State University; Robert Dash, Williamette University; and Tahmineh Entessar, Webster University.

We are especially indebted to Julie Edmunds and Sally Kwitkowski for their excellent research and word-processing skills, to Kay Stultz of Institutional Technology Service, and to Michele Ganschow of the Department of Politics and Government. Robin Bewley of California State University, San Bernardino, and Kate Payne were very helpful with the fourth edition. We are also grateful to Kevin Jones, Roy Horsford, and Violet Hodge for their help with the fifth edition. We would also like to thank Acquisitions Editor Vikram Mukhija and Editorial Assistant Beverly Fong for their patience, hard work, and cooperation throughout the process. Above all, we thank Elaine Graybill and Hanan Nassar for their insights, suggestions, and support.

RICHARD J. PAYNE
JAMAL R. NASSAR

PHOTO CREDITS

Chapter 1   AFP/Getty Images

Chapter 2   Lauren Goodsmith/The Image Works

Chapter 3   Rami Swidan/Landov Media

Chapter 4   Shutterstsock

Chapter 5   Normand Blouin/Landov Media

Chapter 6   Marwan Naamani/AFP/Getty Images

Chapter 7   Reuters/Radu Sigheti/Landov

Chapter 8   Michael Kamber

Chapter 9   Getty Images

Chapter 10   AFP/Getty Images

Chapter 11   Malcom Linton/AFP/Getty Images

Chapter 12   Bloomberg via Getty Images

Chapter 13   Ryan Pyle

Politics and Culture in the Developing World

Government, Politics, and Cultures in Africa, Asia, the Middle East, and Latin America

Government, Politics, and Cultures in a Globalized World

How do we interact in an organized social setting? It is through politics. Our politics are often based on a common culture. But recently, politics and cultures have been going global. What happens in one country is increasingly connected to what happens elsewhere in the world. For example, the government in one country may wish to have a lower price for oil, but that is beyond the control of any single government. Political leaders in one country may want to limit the type of information their citizens receive. That, too, has proven to be largely beyond their control.

In our world, government, politics, and cultures are going through rapid change as a result of globalization. We do not exactly know the shape of future politics or cultures. We do know that our world faces new circumstances whose implications are yet to be fully known. What is obvious is that our interactions in organized social settings have become more complex. This complexity in the midst of a globalized world makes understanding the developing world more important. The recent global recession did not come by accident, it was a result of policies and economics based on an old order that does not fit the current one. Simply put, national solutions to global problems do not work. The developing world represents the overwhelming majority of the people and countries of our world, yet economic policies remain centered on a few countries that are mostly in Europe and North America. It is time for us to learn about the rest of the world.

T he recent great global recession has highlighted the weakness of our old understanding of modern society. Historically, scholars of international politics and economics emphasized European and North American trends as if the developing world did not exist. Today, however, we know that old theories do not fit our modern world. This book focuses on the politics and cultures of Africa, Asia, the Middle East, and Latin America in the era of globalization. These areas make up almost two-thirds of the earth's surface and are inhabited by approximately 80 percent of the world's population. Increasing globalization is creating closer and more complex relationships among the peoples of the developing countries in Africa, Asia, the Middle East, and Latin America and those of the developed countries such as the United States, Canada, Australia, Japan, and Europe. An understanding of the developing world is becoming more important as events there generally have an impact, directly and indirectly, on the lives of people in the more advanced world. September 11, 2001, was a reminder of such an impact as was the recent global recession.

Before driving to a faraway place, most of us look at a map or the Internet to decide which interstate to take to reach our destination; some would simply program their Global Positioning System (GPS) instead. Similarly, before learning about an area that is largely unfamiliar, we need to know the concepts or ideas that constitute the foundation of more complex issues. Concepts are like the interstate. They become the major link between students and their acquisition of a better understanding of the subject. Along the way, we hope that this book will spark a spirit of critical thinking. This chapter focuses on basic concepts, several of which may be familiar to many students. These concepts are used throughout the book. This chapter discusses concepts such as globalization, politics, government, culture, the state, sovereignty, the nation, and the developing world.

WHAT IS GLOBALIZATION?

Globalization ■ The integration of markets, politics, values, and environmental concerns across borders.

This concept will be discussed in detail in Chapter 3. For now, you need to have a brief idea about the notion of globalization. In this book, we define **globalization** as the integration of markets, politics, values, and environmental concerns across borders. This process has been going on throughout history. During recent times, globalization has spread rapidly and its impact has become clear. Today, our global reality is one of interdependence and shared destiny. But globalization has serious consequences. The developing countries cannot live in isolation any longer. Events in other parts of the world affect them more seriously than developed and wealthier states. When the price of oil rises, it takes a greater toll on the poor than it does on the wealthy. When environmental controls are imposed, they have a greater impact on those who depend on the environment more directly. This book will review the impact of globalization in each of its chapters. By the end, you should have a good idea about how globalization affects the developing world.

WHAT IS POLITICS?

If you are a member of a fraternity, sorority, a student organization, or any other group, you know that the group has to have a way to manage its affairs. The group needs some system to decide on activities, to carry out such activities, or to settle disputes. Often, the system allows certain individuals to be in charge. Such individuals take, or are given, a certain amount of power over others in the group. It is this idea of power that is central to the concept of politics.

Politics ■ The means by which a society organizes its affairs.

Politics may be defined as the means by which a society organizes its affairs. In old tribal societies, a chief took charge of organizing the affairs of the tribe. In modern societies, a government is usually formed for that purpose. So, when we study politics or political science, we generally study government. But that is not all, because in essence, what we study is the power relationships in societies. Although governments usually acquire the most power, other entities also have power. Public opinion, for example, is important. Certain groups acquire power on specific issues that relate to them. Labor unions could have a great deal of power when it comes to issues relating to labor. Farmers and farm bureaus are rather powerful on agricultural policies and practices. The so-called gun lobby is powerful on issues of gun control. In the classroom, the teacher has certain powers that students do not. On the job, the manager or the boss has greater power than some of the other workers or employees. But whatever powers an individual or group has, it is usually overshadowed by the greater power of government.

The study of politics, then, is the study of government and the use of power and its allocation in society. When we study national politics, we concentrate on the national government, its powers, and the powers of other groups that can influence the national government and its behavior. Courses on state and local politics look at state governments, and county, city, and township governance. In public administration classes, you learn about governmental administration and the role of civil servants and their organization. The study of international relations, on the other hand, focuses on relations among nations and on international laws and organizations. In comparative politics, you would study other societies and their political forces, processes, institutions, and performances. In political science, you can also study political theory and methodology. Political theory courses try to understand theoretical and ethical notions underlying government and politics. Methodology refers to the methods employed by students, practitioners, and researchers to assess policies and their consequences. Whatever you study in political science, the subject will invariably touch on government.

WHAT IS GOVERNMENT?

Government is one of those concepts that we often use and know but have difficulty explaining. Like the concept of love, we all know what it is, but we can't easily define it. We can see government around us all the time. We see it in the police officer issuing a citation. We see government every time we see a fire engine zooming by or whenever we pay sales tax on the purchases we make. Government seems to be with us all the time. It is in the air we breathe, as government regulates emissions from cars and factories. Government is in the food we eat and the water we drink, as government officials or employees draw guidelines on the permissible. Government builds roads and repairs potholes. It erects bridges and installs traffic lights. It maintains armed forces and police departments. It licenses teachers, doctors, real-estate brokers, and car dealers. Government runs schools and universities. It is, somehow, everywhere. Government was there when we were born, and it will be there when we die. In fact, we are not officially born until a government -certified individual signs a piece of paper called a birth certificate. Similarly, we do not legally die, and no one would dare bury us, until some government-approved individual signs a piece of paper called a death certificate.

So, what is this creature called government? Simply put, **government** comprises the institutions and processes that societies employ to organize their affairs and to protect them from internal or external threats. Often, that mechanism is a complex system of local, regional, and national organizations. Each set of organizations or institutions has particular tasks aiming at organizing and protecting society. Local governments may include a mayor, a city council, a zoning board, a police commission, a health commission, a water authority, a fire commission, and a host of other authorities, each working in a specific sphere to organize and protect people inhabiting that particular community. Regional or state government is even more complex, with a larger web of institutions. The national government is the largest entity and, often, the most complex. Our national government starts with the president, heading a very complex executive branch. Congress in the United States is bicameral (has two houses) and is the legislative branch. The Supreme Court is the highest authority in the judicial branch. Naturally, not all governments are organized in the same way. Some governments do not have such

Government
■ Institutions and processes employed by societies to organize their affairs.

an extensive set of institutions with specialized powers. Some do not even have a president or a congress. Therefore, there are different forms of government.

FORMS OF GOVERNMENT

To simplify matters for our purposes, we can say that there are two basic forms of government: monarchy and republic. A *monarchy* is distinguished by having a monarch. A monarch may be called a king, queen, prince, emir, sultan, emperor, tzar, shah, or even pharaoh. Therefore, any government that is headed by somebody carrying such a title can be referred to as a monarchy. Similarly, a country that has no monarch can be called a *republic*. Therefore, the United Kingdom, having a queen, is a monarchy, whereas the United States, without a monarch, is a republic. This rather simple distinction, however, does not tell us enough. Saudi Arabia, for example, has a king and, therefore, is a monarchy. But the Saudi government is very different from the British government. Cuba does not have a king and is a republic, but we probably know that the Cuban and U.S. governments are not alike. Therefore, there is a need for further distinctions among governments besides those of monarchy and republic (see Figure 1.1).

There are different types of monarchies and republics. The following types can differentiate monarchies: limited, constitutional, and absolute. A **limited monarchy** is a monarchy where the monarch's powers are limited to ceremonial functions. The United Kingdom would be a good example of a limited monarchy. The British queen's functions are ceremonial. Real political power in Britain is in the hands of Parliament and its selected prime minister and cabinet. A **constitutional monarchy,** on the other hand, has a monarch whose powers are allocated in the constitution. In such a case, the monarch has real political power, but remains subject to the law. Other governmental institutions check the monarch's powers. Sweden's monarchy is a good example of a constitutional monarchy. Both limited and constitutional monarchies have democratic practices, and people often call them democracies. A final type of monarchy is the **absolute monarchy,** where the monarch has absolute power. Here, the monarch is above the law and often makes the law. Prior to the Revolution of 1789, France had an absolute monarchy. Some may argue that a state like Saudi Arabia is an absolute monarchy. The Saudi king, however, is likely to disagree, pointing to the system of consultation that exists in the country.

There are different types of republics as well. Some may be said to be dictatorships. A **dictatorship** has absolute power vested in a single person who is not a monarch. Many viewed Chile under Pinochet as a dictatorship. Others saw Iraq

Limited monarchy
■ A type of government where the monarch's powers are limited to ceremonial functions.

Constitutional monarchy ■ A type of monarchy where the monarch's powers are allocated in the constitution.

Absolute monarchy
■ A type of monarchy where the monarch has absolute power.

Dictatorship ■ A government in which a single person, who is not a monarch, has absolute power.

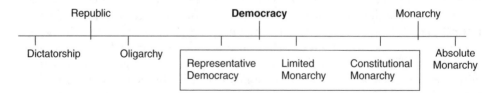

FIGURE 1.1
Forms of Government

under Saddam Hussein as a dictatorship. Another type of a republic can be grouped under the title of oligarchy. An **oligarchy** can be defined as rule by the few. The term *oligarchy* came from the old European feudal systems where the nobility ruled. It is now also applied to military regimes where a **junta,** or a small group of military officers, is in charge of a country. Military officers, as we shall see later, run many countries. Another example of minority rule was the apartheid system that existed in South Africa. Under apartheid, a 15 percent minority of whites ruled the country. It can also be argued that totalitarian governments constitute rule by the few, or an oligarchy. In **totalitarian systems,** all powers are concentrated at the center of government, which is often constitutionally held by the Communist Party, as exemplified by the former Soviet Union, China, Cuba, and North Korea. Naturally, rule by the few is not limited to republics. Sometimes a monarchy may have the nobility or a certain large family share power with the monarch. Similarly, limited or constitutional monarchies may have a democracy. When a republic has majority rule, it is said to be a **democracy;** this is the third type of a republic. Most people like to think of their countries as being democratic, or ruled by the majority.

Another distinction among governments revolves around the distribution of power. Some countries have power **centralized** in the national government. This means that decisions are made at the center of power. Others have **decentralized** systems, meaning power is divided between a national government and smaller provincial or state governments. Often, governments that have a decentralized system also have a federal structure. In **federal structures** smaller political units have certain major powers over their own affairs.

In summary, although all governments are similar in that they have the power to manage society, they can be very different from each other. What form or type of government a people have depends on many factors. Most important among those is the political culture that a group of people shares.

Oligarchy ■ Rule of the few.

Junta ■ A small group of military officers in charge of a country.

Totalitarian system ■ All powers are concentrated at the center of government.

democracy ■ Any system where the majority rules is said to be a democracy.

Decentralized systems ■ Power is divided between a national government and smaller provincial or state governments.

Federal structures ■ Smaller political units that have certain major powers over their own affairs.

Centralized systems ■ Decisions are made at the center of power.

WHAT IS CULTURE AND POLITICAL CULTURE?

On Thanksgiving, many students head home for a family feast with turkey, dressing, and pumpkin pie. When families engage in such practices every Thanksgiving, this becomes part of a family's tradition. Tradition is a portion of culture. **Culture** is a set of traditions, beliefs, and behaviors that a people express and hold. The United Nations Educational, Scientific and Cultural Organization (UNESCO) defines culture as including "the whole complex of distinctive, spiritual, material, intellectual and emotional features that characterize a society or societal groups. It includes not only arts and letters, but also modes of life, the fundamental rights of the human being, value systems, traditions and beliefs."[1] When such traditions, beliefs, and behaviors relate to politics, they are called **political culture.** Many scholars who study political culture focus on attitudes toward politics and government.[2] Attitudes, of course, can also express themselves in beliefs and behaviors and are usually influenced by certain accepted traditions, but often a combination of these political attitudes translates themselves into laws and policies in society. It is the transformation of cultural norms into politics that makes an understanding of political cultures significant to our understanding of a society's politics. In

culture ■ A set of traditions, beliefs, and behaviors that a people express and hold.

Political culture ■ Traditions, values, beliefs, and attitudes that relate to politics and government.

general, every society tries to order its affairs in accordance with its own beliefs and attitudes. In some countries, the belief in the sanctity of human life contributed to banning the death penalty. In others, like the United States, a strong individualistic culture that emphasizes achievement makes it possible for government to enact laws that reward individual achievement.

The starting point of a culture is "its views on creation, the purpose of life and on an after life."[3] Therefore, a community's religious beliefs can be an indication of that community's culture. In theory, societies with religious diversity are likely to be more tolerant of the beliefs of others than a community without such diversity. Tolerance in religious beliefs often spills over to tolerance of other nonreligious beliefs. Naturally, different cultures see the world differently. But whatever cultures a people share, we all live in a rather small world and need to understand each other. Cultural diversity is rapidly becoming a common feature of modern states.

WHAT IS A STATE?

If you have ever traveled to Europe or to other countries, you know that you need a passport. To acquire a passport, you need a proof of citizenship. A birth certificate is usually sufficient to prove your citizenship. But if you were born in another country, a naturalization certificate may be required. Once abroad, your passport serves as your legal identification. Officials who request to see it will know that you are a citizen of your country. Citizenship in a country is equivalent to membership in a state. Today, states are the basic units of world society. Other units do exist, including labor unions, multinational corporations, nonprofit organizations, international and regional organizations, and a host of other professional and issue-oriented groups. Most people in the world live in states, or what many call countries. Legally and politically, a **state** is an internationally recognized, politically organized, populated, geographical area that possesses sovereignty.[4]

State ■ A legal and political unit that must be internationally recognized and politically organized, and must have a populated geographic area that possesses sovereignty.

A state, then, is a legal and political unit that has five basic elements. The first element is *recognition by other states*. Some scholars argue that recognition is not that important. But in international law, recognition by other states bestows legitimacy on a country or state. In northern Cyprus, for example, a Turkish invasion in 1974 led to the creation of a political unit that Turkey called the Turkish Federated State of Cyprus (TFSC). That "state" did not achieve recognition by the other states in the international community. As such, the TFSC was not admitted to the United Nations and was perceived by most other states as a mere extension of Turkey.

A second element of statehood is that of government. We have already seen that people organize their affairs politically by having a government. It would be hard to imagine a country, or state, without a government. In fact, such a thing does not legally exist. *A third element of statehood is population.* You cannot have a state without a people living there. Similarly, you cannot have a state without a geographic area or a territory. *Land, therefore, is the fourth element of statehood.* But these elements of land, people, government, and recognition are not sufficient by themselves. A state must also be sovereign. *Sovereignty is the fifth and final element of statehood.*

Hugo Grotius, a prominent scholar of international law, defined **sovereignty** as the power or authority "whose actions are not subject to the legal control of another, so that they cannot be rendered void by the operation of another human will."[5] What this means is that a state must be independent to be a state. This brings us to an interesting question: Are the 50 states of the United States really states? Given the earlier stipulation that a state must be sovereign or independent, the U.S. states are not considered states under international law. In most countries, such divisions within states are usually called provinces, not states. In the United States, because the 13 original states were actually independent states, the founders saw fit to keep the title of "state" in the Constitution. In international law, however, California or Texas, or any other state in the Union, is called a *province*, not a state. A state is then really what people commonly call *country*. Most people today live in states. Most states today involve a territory or land that has a people who consider themselves to be a nation. Therefore, most states today are nation-states. By now, you have an idea about what a state is. Let us then take a look at the concept of nation.

> **sovereignty** ■ The ability of a state to be independent and free from the control of another state.

WHAT IS A NATION?

Unlike the concept of state, which is concrete or tangible, the concept of nation is intangible. It is not grounded in something as clear as a passport or a birth certificate. A **nation** refers to a group of people who identify with one another as a political community because of common territorial, cultural, and other similar bonds. As such, the concept of nation is more dependent upon a feeling of identity rather than on legal qualifications, as in the case of the state.[6] As we have said before, membership in a state is defined by citizenship. Membership in a nation, on the other hand, is dependent on a feeling of belonging.

> **Nation** ■ A group of people who identify with one another as a political community based upon common territory, culture, and other similar bonds.

Most states today are **nation-states.** This means that nations and states have acquired similar boundaries, with people identifying with the nation and establishing a state for themselves. As such, we can say that most states are **homogeneous,** or have a single nation within their boundaries. Some states, however, are heterogeneous. **Heterogeneous,** or mixed, states have more than one nation inhabiting them. Until recently, the Soviet Union was a heterogeneous state. In the early 1990s, it split in a pattern that goes along with the various nationality groups that inhabited it. Similarly, former Yugoslavia transformed itself, in a bloody conflict, from a single heterogeneous state to a number of new nation-states.

> **Nation-state** ■ Nations and states have similar boundaries where the people identify with the nation and establish a state for themselves.

> **Homogeneous state** ■ A state with a single nation within its boundaries.

Some nations have developed a number of states as well. The Arabs, for example, have found themselves as citizens of many states, even though many of them see themselves as a single nation. The Koreans, the Chinese, the Vietnamese, and the Germans have or have had more than one state. But, in many cases, an eventual reunion between the state and the nation occurred. In most cases, people inhabiting a nation-state have developed over time a strong sense of belonging and pride in their national identity. That sense of belonging is called nationalism. As we will see in Chapter 4, nationalism is a state of mind or a feeling of belonging to a nation. In that chapter, we will discuss nationalism in more detail. For now, it is sufficient to say that nationalism is, perhaps, strongest

> **Heterogeneous state** ■ A state that has more than one nation within its boundaries.

in the developing world. But nationalism today is being challenged by the forces of globalization.

AFRICA, ASIA, LATIN AMERICA, AND THE MIDDLE EAST

The continents of Africa, Asia, and the Vast area Known as Latin America and the region called Middle East are often referred to as the *developing world*. The concept of the developing world is neither precise nor accurate. It includes very large areas of the earth and many peoples. It encompasses more than 160 countries in Latin America, Africa, the Middle East, and Asia. These countries account for three-fourths of the world's population. Even though these developing areas share some common features, they have many differences. Sometimes, the developing world is referred to by other names, including the underdeveloped countries, the Global South, the Third World, and countries that have not industrialized. Essentially, what all such concepts refer to are the peoples and countries outside of Europe and North America with few exceptions.[7]

Societies outside of Europe and North America have many things in common. For the most part, Europeans ruled them for a long time. Also, their economies are largely agricultural based, and their levels of industrialization, while varying widely, are relatively very low. In general, their peoples are poorer than those of Europe and North America. They also have shorter life spans, lower literacy rates, and less urbanization. But even though they have many similarities, they also have differences. As such, generalizations about the developing world must be understood in that context, as generalizations. The many states of the developing world, while sharing some

FIGURE 1.2

Africa, Asia, the Middle East, and Latin America

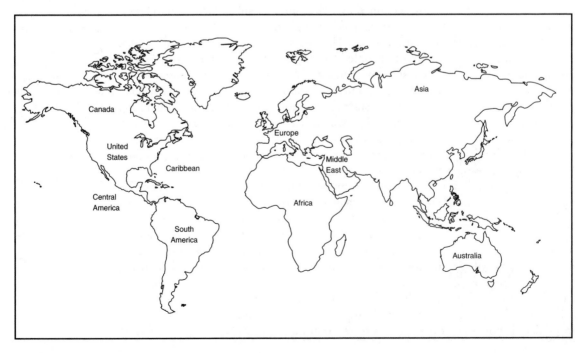

common features, have diverse cultures, political systems, economies, languages, religions, and aspirations. Let us now take a look at each of the continents as well as the region often called the Middle East, which crosses Asia and Africa.

Africa

Africa is a beautiful continent. It is rich in natural beauty, cultures, and minerals. Equally important is the reality that poverty and conflict also plague parts of Africa. Africa is second only to Asia as the world's largest and most populous continent, measuring 11,699,000 square miles and inhabited by a little more than a billion people. Geographically, the Sahara Desert divides Africa into two areas known as North Africa and sub-Saharan Africa. For the most part, the latter contains Africans identifying themselves as adherents to the continent's animist or local religions and Christianity and the former contains Africans identifying themselves as Muslims and sharing an affinity with the Arab-speaking states of the Middle East. However, we must not assume that the predominance of one faith precludes another. For example, North African Egypt has a substantial population of Coptic Christians whereas sub-Saharan African Senegal contains a Muslim majority. Moreover, many African nations—both north and south of the Sahara—speak more than one language. For example, the Moroccans speak Arabic, French, Berber, and Spanish. The Nigerians speak English, Hausa, Yoruba, Ibo, etc.[8]

Africa's diversity, with more than a thousand languages and hundreds of religious and ethnic groups, is unmatched by any other continent. Although groups of 500,000 people or more speak 50 of Africa's languages, groups containing fewer than 500,000 people speak the rest of the languages. Arabic, Swahili, and Hausa are among the most widely spoken languages in Africa. In many governmental and administrative affairs, however, many African states use the languages of the previous colonial empires (e.g., English, French, and Portuguese). This traversing of cultural entities—such as language—along different lines does not end with administration, but also exists among

FIGURE 1.3
Africa

most ethnic groups, cultures, religions, and customs. Thus, for example, a female Nigerian Muslim woman may also ethnically be a Hausa, publicly speak English, pray in Arabic, and perform some rituals of an indigenous African religion. Indeed, many Africans may not identify with a certain group or custom, but rather may incorporate the practices of, and identify with, many different groups and religions. Thus, not only does there exist in Africa an abundance of horizontal diversity (i.e., many different cultures, practices, and customs), but there are many individuals who hold myriad beliefs, which we refer to as *vertical diversity*. This diversity is the result of Africa's rich and proud history, which, most historians, archeologists, and anthropologists argue, is the oldest in the world. Africa holds the earliest human traces, which date back 5 million years. Moreover, traces of the closest ancestry of present-day humans also exist in Africa and date back 2 million years. The first great civilization in Africa dates back 5,000 years. This civilization, dominated by the kingdom of Egypt, was located along the Nile valley and it influenced global civilizations with many of its rich cultural, religious, political, and technological practices. Egypt's strategic Mediterranean location and its rich Afro-Asiatic heritage allowed it to influence the rest of the world in areas of human thought and activity. Ancient Egyptian sophistication led to the apex of ancient material development, of which the pyramids provide an example.

Africa's proud history and civilizations, although exemplified by ancient Egypt, do not stop in Egypt. The kingdom of Ghana is an example of the complex African trade and cultural traditions. Even after its decline by the eleventh century, Ghana passed on to its beneficiaries—North African Muslims and the West African kingdom of Mali—a rich structure of advancement. This intermixing created a combination of many societies, existing and influencing one another through trade routes, which encouraged not only the exchange of goods but also the exchange of cultures and ideologies. This centuries-old process of regional cultural interaction and construction was also influenced by other civilizations, however. During the late eighteenth century, new powers were to play a role in Afro-Asian affairs and forever change the future of Africa.

European colonial posts existed in Africa well before the Berlin Conference of 1884–1885. However, it was at Berlin that the European states of Britain, France, Belgium, Portugal, Germany, and Italy officially carved up African territories and spheres of influence among themselves through the **General Act of Berlin.**[9] The European powers did not invite any Africans to the Berlin Conference, and Africans were not in agreement with the provisions made at Berlin. Although resistance to European conquest was fiercest during the early years subsequent to the Berlin Conference, soon, thereafter, the resistance was co-opted either by European guarantees of enrichment to small elite of Africans or by outright enslavement or murder of members of African resistance movements' leaders and activists. After quelling the African resistance through the destruction of native state structures and turning Africans against one another, European exploitation of humans and resources increased to levels unmatched in the history of the continent, even of the world. This mode of exploitation continued and increased through World War I, when African raw materials such as rubber, grain, and human capital were needed to supply mass armies fighting on the European continent. Between the world wars, the demobilization of those armies, among many other developments in Europe, increased the level of exploitation in Africa to rebuild a shattered Europe. In many

General Act of Berlin
■ A treaty that allowed certain European states to colonize different territories in Africa.

ways, Europe developed and grew its economic power at the expense of Africans among others.

The end of World War II, however, brought new hope for African resistance, which was now growing because of centuries of oppression. African soldiers returned to a lifestyle of misery under the same colonial states that they helped win the war. Exhausted after the horrors of World War II, European colonial powers found it less taxing to decolonize than to hold on to their restless possessions in Africa, where peoples everywhere were yearning to live in freedom from oppression. The overthrow of European colonialism occurred first in North Africa and spread like a chain reaction throughout the continent. Mass parties emerged everywhere that not only called upon European powers to withdraw from their territories—sometimes through force and sometimes through diplomatic dialogue—but also promised their people a better life, free from oppression, exploitation, and economic hardship.

Unfortunately, most of those nationalist visions for a better life did not materialize after the independence of African states. Instead, many of the same nationalist leaders who helped to overthrow the colonial regimes established their own systems of repression or were overthrown because of their failure to bring about an end to corruption, economic deficiency, oppression, etc. Nation building for many of the young African states proved to be the hardest task at hand. This was exacerbated by ethnic conflict, the result of the maintenance and solidification of nineteenth-century borders that often cut across ethnic lines, as well as famine, drought, and diseases such as AIDS.[10] Although most African countries possess the natural resources to overcome such problems, those natural resources are not worth much if they are untapped through technical expertise, adequate infrastructure, and general financial and human capital. Often, when tapped, multinational corporations are the beneficiaries rather than the local population.

Asia

The largest of earth's continents, Asia covers an estimated 17,350,000 square miles and contains three-fifths of the world's population. Asia contains the Dead Sea, which is the lowest point on the earth's surface, and Mount Everest, which is the highest. Asia's diversity lies not only in geography but also in cultures, customs, beliefs, and civilizations. Asia is the center of most major world religions, including Buddhism, Christianity, Hinduism, Islam, and Judaism. It is also in Asia that we find both the Indian and the Chinese civilizations, which are among the oldest in human history. Asian civilizations, including that of old Mesopotamia (today's Iraq), were the first to create systems of governance to manage human affairs. Indeed, the dynamic civilizations that inhabit Asia are among the most diverse in the world.[11] To demonstrate the diversity of Asian peoples, we will turn our attention to comparing some of the present political and economic characteristics of two Asian nation-states, Japan and Bangladesh.

Since 1947, Japan has possessed a democratic limited monarchy, with a bicameral Diet (legislature) as the supreme organ of government. Members of the Diet designate a prime minister to conduct Japan's executive affairs. Although Japan has an emperor, he only has ceremonial powers. Japan's economy is one of the largest in the world, second only to that of the United States. In 2008, Japan's gross domestic product (GDP) totaled $4.4 trillion, which also makes Japan one of

FIGURE 1.4
Asia

Coup d'état

■ Military takeover of government.

the largest producers of goods and services in the world. This economic prosperity stems from Japan's economic engagement in heavy industry—such as the manufacture of steel, motor vehicles, machinery, electronics, and chemicals—and an efficient, hardworking labor force. Because of this economic strength, Japanese citizens enjoy one of the highest standards of living in the world.

In comparison to Japan, Bangladesh is one of the poorest nation-states on earth. Politically, Bangladesh has been plagued by a series of **coup d'états** (military takeover of government) since its conception in 1971. Presently, Bangladesh, like Japan, is a democracy headed by a prime minister. Bangladesh's economy is based on agricultural production. In 2008, the Bangladeshi GDP was estimated at $226 billion, which pales in comparison to Japan's GDP. Because of the poor economic conditions and unstable political atmosphere in Bangladesh, many citizens suffer from a lack of basic necessities such as adequate nutrition, health care, and education. Although the comparison between Japan and Bangladesh may not be a fair one, it serves to demonstrate the diversity of the peoples inhabiting Asia.

Unfortunately, misconceptions about Asia's lack of diversity and major contributions still exist in many areas of our lives—even on our college campuses. A few Americans may not even be able to point to Asia on a map, or if they are able to do that, they may not realize the significance of the timeless contributions that Asians have provided Europeans and Americans. We must not forget that the idea of the very pages that you are reading in this text emerged from Asiatic China. At a time when most people of the world used various inefficient and unrefined materials to write on, such as parchment and papyrus, the Chinese depended on the ingenuity and durability of paper for centuries and introduced it to the rest of the world. Can you imagine where we would be without the luxury of paper? Asian contributions, however, do not stop at the material level. Asians have also provided us with most of our religious beliefs. Jesus, Abraham, Siddhartha, and Mohammad were all born and lived somewhere on the Asian continent. Those great figures of religion have influenced and continue to inspire billions of people. The ideas of those religious figures not only inspire people on a spiritual level but also form the backbone of ethics responsible for the proper treatment of fellow human beings. Most of the religious beliefs in existence today have their origin somewhere in Asia. Thus, almost anywhere you look or anyone you speak to has certainly been influenced in some way by Asian contributions to global civilization.

The first forms of governments in existence developed in Asia. Because of their prehistoric origins, it is nearly impossible to know exactly when governed human settlements in Asia sprang up. For example, although written records did not appear in China until about 1700 B.C.E. under the **Shang Dynasty,** historians roughly place the earliest origins of Chinese civilization at about 3000 B.C.E. The early settlements, which formed the basis of Chinese civilization, were often—as in any other civilization—based on a feature that is of relative importance to human survival. Hence, the earliest traces of Chinese civilization are found along the Huang He or Yellow River, which is one of the most important rivers in China and second in size to the Yangtze. Along with the importance of human cooperation in organized settlements, which depended on elements fundamental to human sustenance such as fertile soil and water, governments were created to manage and ensure that cooperation.

Shang Dynasty ■
Chinese era when written records appeared.

Aside from the study of the origins of Asian civilizations in general and of governments in particular, the study of Asia is crucial to understanding the nature of who we are as a global community. Asia not only provided us with most of the things we identify with our existence, such as religion and organized governance, but also is a model for human diversity, because it is the most diverse continent on earth in terms of geography, political structures, ethnicities, etc. This brief introduction to Asia is not designed to exhaustively inform the student of other global cultures. Instead, it is designed to shed some light on our human origins and what our present is shaped by. Aside from influences of politics, religion, and civilization, Asians have influenced us in many ways beyond the scope of this introduction. They continue to do so until this day.

Latin America

Although the term "Latin America" has raised many controversies in modern scholarship, for the purpose of this work, it will be used to refer to all territories south of the Rio Grande. South America is fourth in size to Asia, Africa, and North America, constituting 6,880,000 square miles, and politically containing 13 countries, including Colombia, Venezuela, Guyana, Suriname, Guiana, Brazil, Uruguay, Paraguay, Argentina, Chile, Bolivia, Peru, and Ecuador. Also, for the purpose of this work, Latin America will subsume the area between the Caribbean Sea and the Atlantic Ocean referred to as the "West Indies," an ambiguous and colonial term employed to describe the island territories of Cuba, Haiti, the Dominican Republic, Puerto Rico, and other smaller islands. Mexico is also considered a part of Latin America even though it is in North America. Although Latin America may appear to be a region composed of homogeneous people, it is instead—like any other region—a very heterogeneous conglomerate of Euro-African and Native American cultures and languages. The **mestizos,** who are the descendants of

Mestizos ■
Descendants of Iberian and Native American ancestry.

Iberian and Native American ancestry, are an example of Latin American diversity. Moreover, Latin America contains other people of mixed ancestry who, although less numerous than the *mestizos*, still compose substantial ethno-national groups. Throughout Latin America, Native Americans are most numerous in the highlands of the central Andean Mountain republics. Argentina and Uruguay hold the largest number of people of Spanish descent in Latin America. Meanwhile, Brazil is predominantly made up of Portuguese descendants, who are the prevailing Iberian element on the continent. In addition, Brazil holds a large number of African and racially mixed groups, while Guyana, Colombia, and Ecuador also contain a large number of people of African ancestry. Latin America also has significant settlements of people who descend from German, Japanese, Indian, Syrian, and Lebanese immigrants.

Between the 1960s and 1996, the Latin American population more than doubled, reaching 488 million. Even though this population increase is mostly attributed to natural phenomena, such as birthrate, some of it is attributed to migrations from, for example, post–World War II Europe. Ninety percent of Latin America's 569 million people are Catholic; however, we must emphasize that the continent also contains many other religious groups, including Protestants, Jews, Hindus, Muslims, Buddhists, and local religions. The reason for the Catholic majority in Latin America is grounded in the turbulent history of the continent. This history included conquest, colonization, and genocide by the European powers, initially by Spain and Portugal, and later by France and Britain. Three of the four European powers—Spain, Portugal, and France—contain a majority Catholic population, hence the Catholic predominance in Latin America. To understand the Latin American past, we now turn to the continent's history.

Earlier, we described the island area between the Caribbean Sea and the Atlantic Ocean by the term *West Indies*. This term is the result of a confusion of its author, Christopher Columbus, who was commissioned by the Spanish and Portuguese governments to find an alternative route to India in 1492. Upon reaching what he thought was India, Christopher Columbus wrongly referred to the area east of the Americas as the "Indies." Since

FIGURE 1.5

Latin America

that time, the term has gained permanent usage and was later simply qualified with the term *West*, which is how we end up with the term *West Indies*. Unfortunately, the historical errors of Europeans toward Latin America did not conclude with confusion of geography or terminology but continued into resource depletion, colonization, slavery, and, ultimately, the genocide of millions of Native Americans and African slaves. After Columbus' landing in the Western Hemisphere, the floodgates opened for other numerous European "explorers," who were always sanctioned by one or more of the European powers to "discover" and ultimately claim, exploit, and colonize territories and peoples of Latin America. One of the best examples of European ruin wreaked upon the inhabitants of Latin America was Francisco Pizzaro, the Spanish conquistador, whose curious explorations led to the subduing and destruction of an entire people, the Inca. In search for personal and national gains and riches for his native Spain, Pizzaro penetrated the gold-rich empire of the Inca in 1531. Within the brief period of five years—through the deadly use of European arms and pestilence—Pizzaro controlled the bulk of the Incan Empire, which included all of the gigantic areas of present-day Peru, Chile, and Bolivia.

The pattern of economic exploitation, colonization, and genocide continued as outlined—with increasing ferocity—for another 300 years. By the nineteenth century, a large part of the Native American population of Latin America was wiped out by disease and warfare. Meanwhile, millions of African slaves who were brought over by European colonizers to work sugar and other agricultural fields perished as a result of exhaustion, disease, and maltreatment. Ironically, it is these conditions of oppression and murder that forced nineteenth-century Latin American colonies to be the first—in what is today referred to as the Third World—to undertake wars of national liberation against European domination. The Latin American struggle for independence—inspired not only by the French and American revolutions but also by the Haitian revolution—occurred in two phases, the first from 1810 to 1816 and the second from 1816 to 1825. Although independence movements promised an improvement in the quality of life, those promises quickly diminished with increasing U.S. hegemony, stagnant economic conditions, the concentration of wealth in the hands of the church and a few wealthy families, and political turmoil.

During the twentieth century, and up to the present, Latin American countries have undergone substantial change, which is part of the global phenomenon of modernization, industrialization, and rapid development.[12] Unfortunately, U.S. policy toward Latin American countries (i.e., dollar diplomacy and the big stick policy, which expanded the U.S. role in Latin America) further added to the economic and political difficulties of Latin American states. The early 1990s brought economic and political rejuvenation to Latin America with the improvement of Latin American markets and the end of the Cold War era and U.S.-sponsored dictatorial regimes, such as that of Augusto Pinochet in Chile. Despite the economic and political stabilization of most Latin American states during the 1990s, problems still remain, such as the growing gap between rich and poor, structural adjustment programs, factionalism of political parties, natural disasters such as the 2010 earthquakes in Haiti and Chile, and ethnic-national and social tensions between groups competing for political and other resources. Such problems contribute to the rise in migration to the north. Many of the migrants cross the border without a visa or other documents.

The Middle East

The term "Middle East" presents scholars with a problem of ambiguity and confusion. Essentially, it is a European concept used to refer to those regions east of Europe. The Far East, the Middle East, and the Near East are all remnants of an old European colonial mind-set, where Europe was viewed as the center of world civilization. Although the other two concepts are slowly disappearing from general usage, the Middle East remains very common. We will use this term in its broad context to refer to the area including modern-day Cyprus, Egypt, Iran, Iraq, Israel, the Palestinian Territories, Jordan, Kuwait, Lebanon, Saudi Arabia, Syria, Turkey, Yemen, and the states along the southern and eastern areas of the Arabian Peninsula, which include Bahrain, Oman, Qatar, and the United Arab Emirates. It was in the Middle East that the earliest civilizations emerged, namely, in Mesopotamia (present-day Iraq), which is often called "the Cradle of Civilization," and in Persia (present-day Iran). Although there is no single defining cultural component of Middle Eastern peoples, a majority of people living in the Middle East identify themselves as Muslims. The reason for this prevalent Islamic identity dates back to events in the seventh century, which we turn to next.

Mohammad ■ The messenger of Islam.

Upon receiving the revelations of an almighty God (Allah), **Mohammad,** an Arab living in Mecca, in present-day Saudi Arabia, declared that he was given the ultimate form of revelation (Islam) to fellow Arabs. Because of Mohammad's revolutionary message, the Meccans banished him to another town, named Yathrib (Medina). This event came to be known as the Hijrah (A.D. 622) in Islamic history, and it became a focal point for all Muslims, marking the beginning of the Islamic calendar. While in Yathrib, Mohammed continued to spread his message, and he gained many followers identifying themselves as Muslims. In a short time, Mohammad returned to Mecca and succeeded in subduing his opposition, gaining political power over the town. By the end of Mohammad's life in 632, many of the old pagan adherents converted to Islam and identified Mohammad as the seal of all prophecy.[13]

Mohammad's sudden death fueled the determination of his followers to spread further his message, and hence that of God, to all peoples surrounding Mecca. Within years, people throughout the Arabian Peninsula had converted to Islam and were as adamant as

FIGURE 1.6

Middle East

Mohammad's initial disciples to spread their beliefs. This became an organized mode of operation under Mohammad's successors (Khalifat al Nabi or Caliph), who not only headed the community of believers, or Muslims, but also worked to export their religion. Taking note of the potential threat posed by Muslims, both the Sassanid Persian and Greek Byzantine empires attempted to eliminate that threat. Both were, however, ailing empires and no match for the emerging Arab-Islamic power; either they were swallowed in whole by the latter (as was Persia) or they lost most of their territory (as did Byzantium).

The rapid Islamic expansion created an empire of universal beliefs rooted in the Judeo-Christian-Islamic tradition, the belief in one God, and stretched from present-day India, China, and Indonesia in Asia to France, Spain, and Portugal in Europe to Nigeria, Morocco, and Somalia in Africa. During the Golden Ages of the Islamic Empire (under the Arabs and later under the Turks), the world gained some of the greatest scientific and cultural contributions ever known, from translations and ultimate preservation of classical Greek works to innovations in mathematics, bureaucracy, and medicine. Indeed, the contributions to civilization made during the expansion of Islam have transformed the Middle East and the rest of the world forever. Thus, today we may read Plato's *Republic* because of its preservation by philosophers (Christians, Jews, and Muslims) living during the height of Islamic power or use the Arabic numerals in mathematics or understand the detrimental effects of germs on humans.

Despite the great advancements made by the Islamic civilization, changes in global affairs forced it to take a lesser place of importance. With the collapse of the Ottoman Empire in 1918, new states emerged in the Middle East, but they were colonized by European powers. The British and French, both victors of World War I, carved up the Middle Eastern remains of the Ottoman Empire, through mandates, between themselves, with the British colonizing the bulk of the Middle East from Iraq to Egypt and the French colonizing territories along the Mediterranean including Syria and Lebanon. One of the main reasons the British and French empires defeated the Ottoman Empire was the use of Arab nationalism against the latter. In return for fighting along with the British and French, Arabs were promised independence after the end of the war. Despite this promise, Arabs were forced to wait for another catastrophic war to gain independence from their colonizers.

World War II not only caused the death of millions around the world, it also destroyed the old empires that participated in it. Hence, by the middle 1950s and early 1960s, most of the Middle Eastern peoples were to gain their independence—except for the Palestinians, most of whose territory was turned into a Jewish state called Israel, and the Kurds, whose lands were carved up among the new states. As Middle Eastern states began to shape their own destinies, they found themselves caught in the middle of a Cold War between the Soviet Union and the United States on the one hand and a Western-centered global economic system on the other. Because of their riches in natural resources and strategic global location, many territories of the Middle East remain coveted by regional powers, such as Iran and Iraq by external powers, such as Russia and the United States. Although the endowments of location and resources may be perceived as a blessing by some, they have mostly brought suffering to the inhabitants of Middle Eastern countries through foreign-supported authoritarian regimes, corruption, arms races, and wars.

Presently, many Middle Eastern countries, like most developing countries, contend with problems of illiteracy, low life expectancy, high infant mortality, exploding populations, economic hardship, and political decay. Some Middle Eastern countries, however, enjoy a high socioeconomic standard of living, such as the oil-producing states of the Gulf (with the exception of Iraq after its devastation in the Gulf War and years of economic sanctions). When compared with other countries in the developing world (e.g., Bangladesh, Afghanistan, Sierra Leone, and Rwanda), Middle Eastern countries appear well off. Nevertheless, like other developing countries, Middle Eastern states, with some exceptions, continue to fall behind. Even oil-rich countries—such as Kuwait—which possess an excess amount of wealth as a result of their petroleum-based economy, still suffer problems such as authoritarian rule, underdevelopment, and disproportionate gaps between the rich and the poor.

SUMMARY AND REVIEW

A people are a group of individuals who make up a community. The way a people organize their affairs is called politics. Essentially, the study of politics is the study of government and power allocation and use in society. Government is a mechanism that people employ to organize their affairs and to protect themselves from threats. In the United States, for example, people employ three branches of government—executive, legislative, and judicial—to enforce, pass, and interpret laws. Although people in the United States live in a republic, many people in other parts of the world live under monarchial forms of government, where a single monarch rules the state. There are different forms of monarchies. A limited monarchy is one in which the monarch's powers are limited to ceremonial functions, whereas a constitutional monarchy has a monarch whose powers are allocated in the constitution. In absolute monarchy, the monarch has absolute power. There are also different forms of republics, including dictatorship and oligarchy. A dictatorship has power vested in a single person who is not a monarch, whereas an oligarchy can be defined as rule by the few. Aside from politics, people also informally manage their affairs through culture. Culture is a set of traditions, beliefs, and behaviors that a people express and hold. Although culture and politics are often interdependent, they can be separated in order to study societies. Throughout the world, different cultural groupings often live under one state. A state is an internationally recognized, politically organized, populated, geographical area that possesses sovereignty. Aside from different cultures, states often possess many different nations, which are distinct from state and culture. A nation refers to a group of people who identify with one another as a political community because of common territorial, cultural, and other similar bonds.

KEY TERMS

globalization 4
politics 4
government 5
limited monarchy 6
constitutional monarchy 6
absolute monarchy 6
dictatorship 6
oligarchy 6
junta 7

totalitarian systems 7
democracy 7
centralized system 7
decentralized systems 7
federal structures 7
culture 7
political culture 7
state 8
sovereignty 9

nation 9
nation-state 9
homogeneous state 9
heterogeneous state 9
General Act of Berlin 12
coup d'états 14
Shang Dynasty 15
Mestizos 16
Mohammad 18

DISCUSSION QUESTIONS

1. How do you define *government*? Explain how your government participates in the activities of your everyday life.
2. Explain the basic forms of government. Give examples of each particular form of government by relating it to a country.
3. Explain the three different forms of monarchies. Give examples of each particular form of monarchy by relating it to a country.
4. What are the basic elements of statehood?
5. What are some of the basic features of the developing world?

SUGGESTED READINGS

Almond, Gabriel, and Sidney Verba. *The Civic Culture.* Princeton, NJ: Princeton University Press, 1963.

Alvarez, Sonia E., Evelina Dagnino, and Arturo Escobar, Eds. *Cultures of Politics, Politics of Cultures: Re-Visioning Latin American Social Movements.* Boulder, CO: Westview Press, 1998.

Dierks, Rosa Gomez. *Introduction to Globalization: Political and Economic Perspectives for the New Century.* Lanham, MD: Roman and Littlefield, 2005.

Hechter, Michael. *Containing Nationalism.* Oxford, UK: Oxford University Press, 2000.

Jacobsen, Michael, and Ole Bruun, Eds. *Human Rights and Asian Values: Contesting National Identities and Cultural Representations in Asia.* Richmond, VA: Curzon, 2000.

Jones, Anny Brooksbank, and Ronaldo Munck, Eds. *Cultural Politics in Latin America.* New York: St. Martin's Press, 2000.

Mason, Colin. *A Short History of Asia: Stone Age to 2000 A.D.* New York: Palgrave, 2000.

Nassar, Jamal. *Globalization and Terrorism: The Migration of Dreams and Nightmares.* Lanham, MD: Roman and Littlefield, 2010.

Payne, Richard. *Global Issues.* New York: Longman, 2011.

Riaz, Ali. *Unfolding State: The Transformation of Bangladesh.* Whitby, ON, Canada: de Sitter Publications, 2005.

Thompson, Lloyd, Dapo Adelugba, and Egbe Ifie, Eds. *Culture and Civilization.* Ibadan, Africa: Afrika-Link Books, 1991.

Weatherby, Joseph J., et al. *The Other World: Issues and Politics of the Developing World.* New York: Longman, 2011.

NOTES

1. *Final Report of the World Conference on Cultural Policies* (Organized by UNESCO in Mexico City, 26 July–6 August, 1982), 41.
2. See, for example, Gabriel Almond and Sidney Verba, *The Civic Culture* (Princeton, NJ: Princeton University Press, 1963).
3. UNESCO, *Culture and Development* (Paris, France: UNESCO, 1994), 16.
4. H. B. Jacobini, *International Law: A Text* (Homewood, IL: The Dorsey Press, 1968), 49.
5. Hugo Grotius, *The Classics of International Law*, trans. F. W. Kelsey, vol. 2 (Oxford, UK: The Clarendon Press, 1925), 102.
6. For an argument against the idea of national belonging being an emotion, see Michael Hechter, *Containing Nationalism* (Oxford, UK: Oxford University Press, 2000).
7. There are many books on the topic. Among those are Howard Handelman, *The Challenge of Third World Development* (Upper Saddle River, NJ: Prentice Hall, 1996); and Joseph J. Weatherby et al., *The Other World: Issues and Politics of the Developing World* (New York: Longman, 1997).
8. See Oxfam, *African Make or Break: Action for Recovery* (London, UK: Oxfam, 1993).
9. See Ali A. Mazrui, *The African: A Triple Heritage* (New York: Little, Brown, 1986).
10. See Kofi Annan, *The Causes of Conflict and the Promotion of Durable Peace and Sustainable Development in Africa* (New York: United Nations, 1998).
11. See Colin Mason, *A Short History of Asia: Stone Age to 2000 A.D.* (New York: Palgrave, 2000).
12. See Thomas E. Skidmore and Peter H. Smith, *Modern Latin America* (Oxford, UK: Oxford University Press, 2000).
13. Richard Bulliet, *Islam: The View from the Edge* (Irvington, NY: Columbia University Press, 1995).

Global Interdependence

Globalization and Interdependence

The recent financial crisis has highlighted the era of interdependence and globalization we live in. In the early 1990s, the then president George H. W. Bush, celebrating the demise of the Soviet Union, declared the dawn of a new world order. Since then, the forces of globalization that contributed to the rise of this new order have been accelerating at a dizzying pace. The new world order, however, should not be an end in itself; rather, it should be a means to an end. The end ought to be an improvement in the human condition globally. Have we arrived there? Sadly, the answer is no. Although some people in this interdependent and globalized world have reaped the benefits of this new world order, others have suffered its negative consequences. It is hoped that, in time, globalization will lead to improved standards of living for everyone. The United States likes to view itself as the world leader, the captain of the global ship, so to speak. But, although the captain of the ship gets the luxury of the captain's cabin, the captain also gets the responsibility for the well-being of the whole ship. Many Americans, somehow, want the luxury without the responsibility. This interdependent global community of ours needs caring and globally minded leadership, not a parochial or self-centered one. Some day, perhaps, the majority of Americans will be up to the task of providing the world with the required new world leadership.

Imagine, for a moment, that as you leave the classroom and exit the building, you see strange creatures descending to earth and aiming their destructive beams upon structures and peoples all over the world. Clearly, these aliens are trying to conquer the earth. If that were to happen, it is feasible to expect soldiers everywhere to aim their guns and missiles toward the invading aliens and engage them in battle. Soldiers—American, Cuban, Iraqi, Indian, Pakistani, Arab, Israeli, North and South Korean, and of every state—would suddenly forget their own state enemies and become instant allies in their struggle against the alien invaders. Should such a scenario ever occur, people everywhere would realize that we share one planet and a common destiny. You, as an educated college student, need not wait for such an invasion to reach this realization. Although our planet Earth is divided into independent states, it is also becoming increasingly interdependent. The growing interdependence of our global community is slowly changing the relationships of states and individuals. Simply put, local concerns have become global in implication. National problems are now global problems. Whether it is inflation, recession, environmental pollution, terrorism, monetary fluctuation, communicable diseases, drug trafficking, religious revivalism, or a host of other troubles, local or national solutions would not solve them. Global problems require global solutions. Our world of nation-states can offer mainly national solutions to global concerns. So far, the nation-state system has failed to solve many contemporary global problems.

THE GLOBAL REALITY

Scientists and space explorers have, so far, been unable to produce evidence that human life is viable anywhere in the universe outside of planet Earth. We have no options and no place to inhabit other than cohabiting this planet. There was a time on this planet when people lived independently of one another. Subsistence living, by definition, meant independent living where people produced a sufficient amount of food for their survival as an independent family unit. In time, people slowly became interdependent through the division of labor. Some food was produced, other food was traded, and service became a new trade item. Soon thereafter, society became so interdependent that individuals served only specialized functions—such as teaching, secretarial, construction, plumbing, etc.—while others produced their food or their other needs for survival. Today, our planet has become a web of global interdependence, linked together in ways that our forbearers could not have imagined. Like individuals and families, peoples, nations, and states are all spinning this web while at the same time they are suspended in it. No state can any longer sustain its standard of living if it chooses to isolate itself from the rest of the world. Actions of one state have ramifications that go beyond its borders. Nor can states today escape the impact of developments outside their borders. In sum, the world we inhabit has become seamless and indivisible despite the borders that divide its many states.

Economically, the world is so interwoven that the livelihood of one depends upon the production of many others. When you go to visit a nearby mall, you are, in effect, entering a global marketplace rather than a mere local shopping center. Even in a single store you are likely to encounter merchandise from many parts of the world. The shoes may come from Italy, the sweater may say "made in Malaysia," the jeans are likely to be made in the United States, and the coffeemaker may come from Germany or Sweden. Even the single item that may say it was made in a specific country is likely to have many more sources outside of that country where it was produced. Take, for example, a dress that proclaims Singapore as the state where it was fabricated. The material for the dress is partly cotton and partly synthetic. The cotton, perhaps, came from Egypt or India. The petroleum for the synthetic may have originated in Iran or Saudi Arabia and been manufactured in England or South Korea. The lace on the dress may have come from Italy. The zipper made of a copper pull and plastic material might have started as copper ore in Chile and the plastic zipper in Mexico or Ecuador. Once cut and sewn in Singapore, the dress may have been hung on a Chinese-made hanger and placed in a Malaysian-made nylon bag. Once packaged, the dress could have been shipped on a Liberian-licensed cargo ship to Miami or Los Angeles for distribution to stores around the country. The increasing **globalization** of economic activity is most visible in the areas of production, trade, and finance. Electronic trading has opened the way for massive movements of funds. This weakened the effectiveness of governmental policy decisions in the areas of currency values and international trade. In the areas of production and trade, global interdependence is a visible fact of life. The production and trade of a dress, similar to the one mentioned earlier, can be an example of globalization in this area.

Interdependence is also evident in the area of minerals and other natural resources. Consumption of critical minerals has been on the rise and known reserves

globalization ■ The integration of markets, politics, values, and environmental concerns across borders.

are concentrated in a few areas of the world. The reality is that no country is endowed with all the raw materials that it consumes. Some countries are rich in some minerals but lack others. Some lack most. Even a rich and large country like Germany can be poor in some resources vital to its economic activity. The United States, for example, is totally dependent upon others for its needs in chromium, manganese, and tin. All three materials are vital for the industrial economy of the country. The United States is also poor in its resources of many other minerals, including aluminum, copper, iron, lead, nickel, potassium, tungsten, and zinc. In the area of energy, global interdependence manifests itself in the realm of politics. The Arab oil embargo of the early 1970s was a striking wake-up call to all nation-states. It highlighted the emergence of petroleum as a tool of foreign policy. The ramifications of the embargo were felt not only by the targeted states but also by many other countries.

Interdependence is, perhaps, most evident in technology and communications. A technological or scientific breakthrough in the United States benefits not only Americans but also people everywhere. If, for example, a cure for cancer is found somewhere, cancer patients could benefit everywhere. As Lester Brown reported in 1972, "more and more, the new technology used in any given country originates outside that country."[1] His conclusion is even truer today. In communications, global interdependence is evident every time you turn on your television set or radio, log on to a computer network server, or read a newspaper. Fax machines, universal telephone service (including cellular), and low-cost and high-speed computers enable us to communicate globally and instantly. Environmentally, we inhabit a planet with a delicate ecological balance. In this planetary environment, there was a day when people could and did pursue their survival in isolation. We no longer can do so. Our numbers and our progress have made our fate as a species and as inhabitants of one ecological system interlocked and interdependent. An environmental disaster in one part of the planet is a disaster for the whole planet.

Food and agricultural interdependence is also evident every time you drink soda, order a hamburger, or have a cup of coffee. Some areas of the planet have an abundance of certain foods or agricultural products, whereas others have different ones. Even though the United States may be called the breadbasket of the world, it certainly is not the world's food basket. Although the United States exports a large amount of grain, it imports many other agricultural products, including beef, coffee, bananas, and other fruits and vegetables. Other areas of global interdependence include our own health when viruses and diseases travel beyond borders and infect people of all races and nationalities. Even our own neighbors may be the products of global interdependence. Migration now has become so common and easy with air transportation. No longer do we live in the same community of our birth. Today people are continuously on the move. Consequently, our modern societies are rapidly becoming multicultural and sometimes even multilingual. In sum, global interdependence has become a reality no state or individual can escape. No people can shut themselves off from "foreign" influences. When imperial China tried to do that some 500 years ago, it went quickly from "being the world's most advanced and powerful nation to becoming a poor backwater of the globe."[2] No nation can do that anymore. Perhaps, by now, some of you are thinking, "What do I care?" It is true that world affairs seem too far beyond your immediate interests. At this point in your life, you just want to finish college and get a decent job. You may have many other concerns. Some may be financial; others may relate to your circle of friends, your club, or your family. In sum, the world beyond seems too distant to worry about. This may be a good time to take a look at how events and developments that seem far may be very significant in determining the rest of your life.

GLOBAL INTERDEPENDENCE AND YOUR LIFE

Many of us know very little about the rest of the world. All of us, however, are influenced by what happens there. Some are impacted in a drastic way. Take, for example, the story of a college student. Her name was Cindy. Cindy Marie Beaudoin was a first-year student at the University of Connecticut in September 1990. Just a month before Cindy went to college, Iraq had invaded Kuwait. As a soldier in the 142nd Medical Company of her state's National Guard, Cindy was called to active duty on November 17, 1990. Cindy had a month to go toward completing her first semester in college. In January 1991, Cindy and company were sent to Saudi Arabia. As the war began, Cindy and her unit moved into Iraq behind advancing combat units and later entered Kuwait. A few days later, the Iraqi army had been defeated and former president Bush declared a cease-fire. But wars are not totally over with declarations. About 3:00 P.M. on February 28, Cindy's convoy was rocked by an explosion. Falling from her truck, she shouted, "They're firing at us." Moments later, she realized that she had been hit. We still do not know the cause of the explosion, but we do know that Cindy's abdomen was torn and her leg was gone. A medical helicopter picked her up, but Cindy couldn't wait. She died during the flight. Cindy Marie Beaudoin was dead at the age of 19, without even completing her first semester in college.[3]

Few months before her death in Kuwait, Cindy may have not known much or cared much about places like Kuwait, Saudi Arabia, or Iraq. Maybe Cindy didn't even know where these places were on a map. Yet, Cindy's life ended prematurely in Kuwait. You may now say that Cindy was in the National Guard, and because you are not, what happens in the world does not affect you. If so, you are wrong. When you turned 18, if you are a male, you were required to stop at a post office to register yourself in the Selective Service System. Should there be a major crisis, it is possible that you could be drafted into a branch of the military and, after a short boot camp experience, be sent to some faraway place to fight. If the draft is restored in an emergency, it is likely that it will also include females as well. In many other countries, military service is required of all those who are within a specific age group and are physically able to serve.

Military service is not the only way in which global interdependence may touch your life. We all know about our military and political interdependence. Economically, environmentally, and even culturally we are all dependent on each other on this planet of ours. Let us now take a detailed look at each of these areas.

ECONOMIC INTERDEPENDENCE

In the days of the old American West, many people went west and found a nice piece of land and settled on it. There, the family built its own log home and raised cows, pigs, and chickens. They planted and harvested their own vegetables and grains. The mother taught the children to read and write. In sum, in those days, the American family was independent or self-sufficient. Today, however, the average family in the United States, or anywhere in the world, has become interdependent. We now live in a world where specialization has replaced self-reliance. Our society today is similar to an assembly line where each person performs a specific function and countless others provide for the rest of that individual's needs. Just like people, states are no longer economically self-sufficient. All must engage in international trade in goods, services, and financial resources. Whether a state is rich or poor, whether it is capitalist or socialist, every state is interlinked to the rest of the world. The United States is at the center of this global economic interdependence. Americans now own more than $2.5 trillion in shares and other assets located outside the United States. It is likely that some of the money paying for your college expenses comes from such assets. Foreigners also own plenty of shares and assets located in the United States. Today, more than $1.5 trillion in currency exchanges occur every single day. In more ways than we realize, our lives have become very dependent on a global economic system. Even here, the food we eat reflects different cultures. The car you may buy may be a better example of interdependency. You may think that you are buying an American-made car when you purchase a General Motors product. The reality is that General Motors makes or assembles its cars in about 34 countries. The one you buy could be made in Finland, Kenya, or Brazil. Trade boomed in the twentieth century, and the boom promises to continue in the twenty-first century.[4] The flow of goods and services has witnessed a tremendous jump in the last three decades. But the institutions regulating the globalized and very interdependent economy remained localized in national governments. Eventually, the imbalance contributed to the first global recession in history. Table 2.1 shows the extent of such a financial stress and provides an economic outlook.

What could such rise in global financial stress mean to you? What impact would this global economic downturn have on you? Why should you care about world trade? As a student, you are a consumer. Purchasing is a major activity in your life. To a small child, milk does not come from cows, it comes from stores. Most small children have never seen a cow being milked, so in their world, milk comes from stores. What if there is to be a crisis of some sort that will prevent that child's parent or you from being able to purchase the barest of daily necessities

TABLE 2.1				
World Economic Outlook				
	Percent Change			
World Economic Outlook	2006	2007	2008	2009
Imports				
Advanced Economies	7.5	4.5	1.9	1.3
Developing Economies	14.7	14.2	11.7	8.9
Exports				
Advanced Economies	8.4	5.9	4.3	1.8
Developing Economies	11.0	9.5	6.3	4.4

Source: IMF, *Global Prospects and Policies* (2010), http://www.imf.org

such as milk, toothpaste, cereal, bread, toilet paper, or soap? That would be a very unsettling experience. Trade does not occur in the exchange of goods alone. It also involves services. Even though students generally are not producers of goods, many are producers of services that make a large part of trade. If you work at the library, deliver pizza, or stock the shelves at a nearby grocery store, you are involved in a service activity. Today's trade activities involve services of architects, computer specialists, financial advisors, teachers, bankers, hotel managers, and a host of other services that people need. Almost half of U.S. exports are in services.

International investment is another form of global economic activity that is seeing rapid growth. Americans invest abroad often. Whenever an individual has stocks in some foreign company, or when foreigners own stocks in U.S. companies, they are involved in international investment. Multinational corporations (MNCs) are at the forefront of the flow of international investments. They not only buy and sell stocks but also have subsidiaries all over the world. Global monetary relations have also contributed to the growing global interdependence. The growth in economic activity may seem wonderful to many people. Governments and businesses usually encourage such activities and see them as signs of economic vitality as well as sources of profit, employment, and economic well-being. Economic growth has serious consequences to other areas of global interdependence. Clearly, the economic downturn in the United States and Europe almost immediately became a global recession. Another consequence is the well-being of the environment. We simply cannot afford to keep the global economy on a collision course with our earth's ecosystem. Economic progress and environmental concerns are interlocked in a cycle of interdependence.

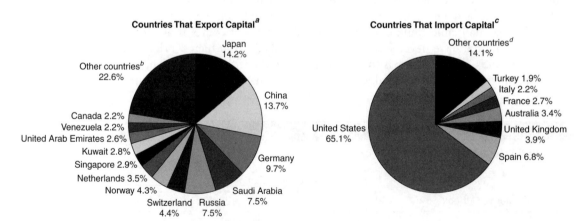

FIGURE 2.1

Major Net Exporters and Importers of Capital in 2005

[a] As measured by countries' current account surplus (assuming errors and omissions are part of the capital and financial accounts).

[b] Other countries include all countries with shares of total surplus less than 2.2 percent.

[c] As measured by countries' current account deficit (assuming errors and omissions are part of the capital and financial accounts).

[d] The rest of the world.

Source: International Monetary Fund, World Economic Outlook database as of March 27, 2006.

ENVIRONMENTAL INTERDEPENDENCE

In the 1990s, developers in Houston drew up plans to build a new airport on a 200,000-acre wetland that is home to many species of birds. The Sierra Club attempted to block the new development. To do so, the Sierra Club joined forces with its nemesis, the National Rifle Association (NRA). The two strange bedfellows came together in 1995, when Marge Hanselman, a Sierra Club activist, set up a booth at a Houston gun show. After hearing ridicule from some visitors, she was asked by an NRA director why she was there. She made her case to the director, citing a long list of game birds that would be displaced if the airport were approved. The impressed director then introduced Hanselman to Sue King, a very active NRA member and a proud hunter of game birds. The two women soon became friends and put aside their differences for the common interest of protecting the wetland. The coalition of Sierra Club and NRA members proved too strong for the developers. Consequently, the city council recommended that the area be made a protected wetland.[5]

Environmental issues may sound local in some instances. Their ramifications, however, are usually global.[6] Air pollution, global warming, nuclear waste, and acid rain have become a part of our common vocabulary. What they all denote is much more than preserving some species of game birds. Pollution of any sort in one place is invariably pollution in other places. The loss of the ozone layer affects not only people in the United States, but life on earth. Just like the NRA and the Sierra Club worked together to save game bird habitat in Houston, countries of the world must work together on a large scale to preserve our planet's health and well-being.

Economic growth that states seek in order to enhance the well-being of their people often leads to environmental degradation and loss of biodiversity that endanger all of us. A balance between economic growth and environmental protection is needed. To do so, countries must cooperate and plan together. The good news is that there has been progress made in this area. In 1972, the United Nations began the process of global discussions when it hosted the Conference on the Human Environment in Stockholm, Sweden. The result was the creation of a permanent program known as the United Nations Environmental Programme (UNEP). Since then, many international trade agreements incorporated environmental protection into their clauses. In 1987, the UNEP held a conference in Montreal, Canada, on the protection of the ozone layer. In time, countries committed themselves to reduce the emission of chlorofluorocarbons (CFCs). CFCs are used as a refrigerant but contribute to the depletion of the ozone layer. In 1992, the **Earth Summit** in Rio de Janeiro, Brazil, addressed the issue of global warming and many countries signed on to reduce the emissions of gases that contribute to it.[7] On December 12, 2008, the European leaders approved a climate change pact that is designed to cut greenhouse gas emissions by 20 percent by the year 2020. In January 2009, transportation ministers meeting in Japan agreed to combat climate change and air pollution in the transport sector. In December 2009, another Earth Summit, held in Copenhagen, affirmed the need to control rising world temperatures. Such agreements give hope that the world finally is paying attention to the environment.

Earth Summit ■ Addressed the issue of global warming.

There has also been progress on a range of other environmental concerns including the dumping of hazardous wastes and toxic materials. But the progress so far falls far short of the needed drastic changes in the way we do things. Economic progress, sometimes seen as corporate interests, seems to outweigh global environmental well-being. This disparity was highlighted in 1999, when the World Trade Organization held its meeting in Seattle, Washington. That meeting drew 35,000 demonstrators and activists from environmental and labor groups concerned about the corporate role in the era of globalization. Since then, many attempts have been made at improving the quality of life by minimizing the impact on the environment. Action on environmental issues has gone global, in part, because of the dramatic revolution in global communication. This revolution in communication has contributed to greater cultural interaction at the global level.

CULTURAL INTERDEPENDENCE

Cultural globalization is, perhaps, the most familiar form of interdependence to most people. Almost everyone on earth knows the sports stars, the icons of popular culture, and the commercials for Coca Cola. This was not the way it was 50 or so years ago. During the first part of the twentieth century, most people lived in remote villages that had never seen a television and were amazed at the sounds of the radio. Most were illiterate. Today, their grandchildren are on the move. They listen to music, watch television, and many participate in chat rooms and play games on the Internet.

Even the aspirations and dreams of children are becoming more alike as they become more exposed to the same television shows, news stories, and songs. Be

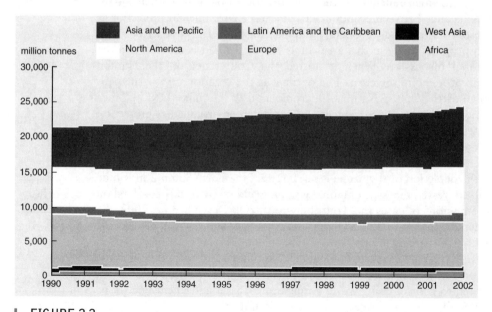

FIGURE 2.2
Carbon Dioxide Emissions by Region

Source: UNEP, GEO Year Book 2006, http://www.unep.org/geo/yearbook/yb2006/022.asp. GEO Data Portal based on United Nations 2005. The United Nations is the author of the original material.

it Kobe Bryant, Ricky Martin, Leonardo DiCaprio, or Britney Spears, children and teenagers throughout the world over look up to them. You could walk on the streets of Accra or Jakarta and see images of such idols on clothing, in magazines, and on billboards. If you play Internet games, you may join a table with someone from Australia or Japan or South Africa. In sum, the world has become as interconnected in the area of cultural symbols and values as it has in other areas. The dominant culture is sweeping the world and sending messages that neither governments nor families abroad are able to control. American culture, with its emphasis on consumption, market economy, and individualism, has gone global. Of course, this dominance is not without opposition. Some intellectuals in Africa, Asia, and Latin America argue that their societies are now victims of "**cultural colonialism.**" Some countries have tried to close their borders to outside cultural influences. Iran, for example, tried to do so in vain during the early years of its Islamic Revolution and more recently after their contested election of 2009. Afghanistan, Saudi Arabia, China, and others have made similar attempts. In 1980, the majority of states at the United Nations meeting in Belgrade at the UNESCO General Conference even adopted a resolution that aimed at regulating the flow of information. Known as the **New World Information and Communication Order**, this resolution advocated respect for each people's cultural identity. Needless to say, resolutions do not necessarily translate into actions. This one did not.

cultural colonialism
■ The penetration of local cultures by the powerful states.

New World Information and Communication Order
■ An attempt by the poorer states to regulate the dominant media in the world.

The fact remains that information crosses borders without any regard to political divisions. If leaders try to stop the spread of such technologies, they endanger their societies of falling farther behind. If they allow the spread, they risk unwanted consequences. Take, for example, a remote village in Yemen. People there still live in a traditional setting. Their homes are made of clay and they have no running water or electricity. The village has no school and most adults are illiterate. Imagine if one day the village elder comes back from the city with a battery-operated television set and a satellite dish to go with it. In the evening, when villagers usually sit around together to discuss their crops or livestock, the village elder now turns on the television. People watch the magic of seeing a new world unfold in front of their eyes as they view programs such as Desperate Housewives, Two and a Half Men, or some French or Italian movie. They see cars, streets, modern buildings, indoor plumbing, and a way of life they never imagined could exist. When the village elder clicks on the remote and removes the television set, everybody goes home to sleep on his or her dirt floors in their mud-and-clay homes. As they go to sleep, the villagers are likely to dream of having a car or installing an amazing faucet that brings water inside a home. We would like to call this process **migration of dreams**, which follows the dissemination of information technologies. The wealthy and advanced countries are, in essence, encroaching on the dreams of the poor.

migration of dreams
■ The impact on the poor of television programs emanating from wealthier societies.

Migration of dreams is something that happens every day in every society. As the poor villagers begin to have greater dreams for themselves and their families, their level of expectation is sure to grow as well. Now, the villager may expect running water, roads, and even a car. The government of the country may be so poor that it cannot afford to provide running water or roads to every small village. That government may have greater priorities of providing for infrastructure in the capital or in other cities. Or, perhaps, the government needs to put its limited resources into education or health care rather than bringing water or roads to such a remote place with very few people.

Social scientists tell us that the gap between expectations and achievement is a significant contributor to violence. They call this theory **relative deprivation**. Social scientists define relative deprivation as the gap between what a person gets and what that person thinks he or she should get. They tell us that the greater the gap between the two, the more likely an individual is to turn to violence.[8] If this popular theory is accurate, then it would be fair to conclude that the rising expectations of the poor in the Yemeni village or elsewhere could contribute to rising violence. That violence may be directed against a spouse, the children, the neighbors, or even the government. If some opposition group comes to the village to recruit fighters, arguing that the government is not doing its job well, more villagers are now likely to agree and, perhaps, join the opposition. Someone may argue that governments should do something to stop the migration of dreams. In fact, some governments, such as Saudi Arabia and China, have attempted to regulate the Internet. But the reality is that information technology has forged ahead of governmental abilities to control. Even in the United States, the government is scrambling to keep up with the speed by which information technology is developing. Moreover, governments in the poorer countries are being pushed to open up their markets to the world market. Most people refer to this as globalization, which is a subject deserving more detailed discussion.

relative deprivation
■ The gap between what a person gets and what that person thinks he or she should get.

GLOBALIZATION

At the start of the twenty-first century, globalization has become a powerful concept in governmental, business, and even scholarly circles.[9] Governments often blame their failing economies on globalization. Corporations downsize or cut back on the number of workers, arguing that they need to be able to compete in the new global market. Scholars argue the merit of globalization and its direction. But globalization is not a totally new phenomenon. It has been around in some form or another for a long time. The whole process of interdependence is a process of globalization. What is new about globalization is its unchallenged spread during the past two decades. Prior to the fall of the Berlin Wall, globalization was checked by a strong Soviet presence. After the demise of the Soviet Union, the challenge to globalization was left to some weak and barely organized nongovernmental organizations that are practically helpless to stop the momentum.

Globalization is the integration of markets, politics, values, and environmental concerns across borders. This process of integration is driven by the desire for higher profits and hopes of greater world economic prosperity or a better future for the earth and its inhabitants. Those who oppose it fear greater economic disparities between rich and poor, loss of cultural distinctiveness, and environmental degradation. MNCs see it as opening new markets to their products and services. Governments support it as the only available course to eliminate an inevitable isolation and economic disaster if they opposed it or as a means to enhance their economic positions. Labor unions fear it because it diverts jobs away to distant places where cheap labor and sweatshops could replace union work. Environmentalists fear the potentially unregulated production of goods for the sake of profit-producing environmental disasters. Investors in financial institutions and stock markets support it as a means for growth of their portfolios. In sum, globalization has become an extremely contentious issue. Scholars too have entered the debate on globalization. Benjamin Barber argues that globalization is leading to a homogenized **"McWorld"** in which American popular culture and consumerism are overtaking the globe. Rejecting such American and consumerist domination, other cultures are producing movements of resistance, which Barber refers to as "Jihad."[10] Whether it is Barber or some other scholar, the critics of globalization warn against unrestricted capitalism at the global level. One such scholar, Manfred Steger, refers to globalization as an ideology of market economy and calls it globalism.[11] It is also clear that globalization has highlighted concerns of human rights. Such concerns are discussed in more detail in Chapter 9.

> **McWorld** ■ Term used to sum up Benjamin Barber's argument that American popular culture and consumerism is taking over the world.

Capitalism at the global level has, on occasion, had some serious ramifications. Take, for example, the case of a California billionaire who has paid $2 million to clone his dog, Missy. As CNN reported the story on March 22, 2000, some poor fellow in some remote African village may have questioned this decision as unsustainable. A student or an executive corporate officer in New York or London, on the other hand, may have seen this as the billionaire's natural right to clone his dog. After all, he is using his own money to do so. To the average African, spending so much money on cloning a dog when people die from starvation on a daily basis would be seen as going too far. The CNN story may not have significant ramifications, other than engendering some resentment by the poor toward the rich.

How the rich sometimes make their money, though, could have serious consequences for the poor.[12] An example of such consequences would be the sweatshops that generate wealth for the rich and perpetuate poverty for the workers. Take, for example, the story of a young Pakistani boy named Iqbal Masih. Iqbal was one of the thousands of children in Pakistan who worked full-time, weaving "oriental" carpets. People around the world value such carpets. They fetch very high prices in countries like the United States. Pakistan is a major producer of "oriental" carpets, and the United States is its largest market. Pakistani carpets are often produced using child labor. Between 500,000 and 1,000,000 children aged between 4 and 14 work 14 hours a day, 6 days a week, to make these beautiful carpets. Children as young as four are often chained to looms in carpet factories in Pakistan. These children are usually sent by their parents to work in the factories to help support the family. They are often thin and malnourished. Their size is small for their age, and their backs are curved from constant bending in front of the loom. Their hands are scarred, and they have difficulty breathing from the constant inhaling of cotton dust. In 1992, Pakistan adopted a law under international pressure outlawing the practice of making payments to parents to bond children in labor. A Pakistani human rights group, the **Bonded Labor Liberation Front (BLLF)**, began to visit factories to inform the

> **BLLF** ■ Bonded Labor Liberation Front.

children of the new law. Iqbal was one of those children freed from bonded labor by the BLLF. At age four, his parents had bonded him to a carpet manufacturer, where he stayed until the age of 10 in 1992.

Under the tutelage of the founder of the BLLF, Iqbal became an outspoken activist on behalf of other bonded children. He even traveled to Europe and the United States to expose the practice to potential buyers of Pakistani carpets. The energy, enthusiasm, and unique personality of Iqbal made him a very successful spokesperson for all bonded children of Pakistan. Between 1992 and 1994, Pakistan's carpet sales fell for the first time and the pressure on the country to enforce the law on bonded children mounted.

On April 16, 1995, a gunman shot Iqbal to death. The 13-year-old boy's death was blamed on what the founder of the BLLF called the "carpet Mafia." The practice of bonding children continues in Pakistan until this day. So does the pressure to end it. What this story tells us is that demand for "oriental" carpets in rich countries contributes to bad production practices in other countries. Although the carpet manufacturers become wealthy, children suffer. Unless the buyers of the product are aware of such practices and are willing to boycott products produced by such means, exploitation of the underprivileged is likely to continue. Chapter 5 explores the gap between the rich and the poor. Now, let us take a brief look at globalization of terrorism, which some see as a consequence of exploitation, poverty, and injustice.

TERRORISM AND GLOBALIZATION

On the morning of September 11, 2001, two passenger planes plunged into the World Trade Center leading to its collapse and the death of almost 3,000 innocent civilians. Another plane destroyed a section of the Pentagon, and a fourth plane went down into a field in Pennsylvania. For days the world seemed to stand still. The shock of the terror was too grave for most people to take. Terrorism from abroad had reached the shores of the United States in a deadly fashion.

Those who engage in terrorism come from all colors and from all cultures. Terrorism is a symptom rather than a disease. It has many causes. Most definitions of the concept, however, seem to focus on the symptom and avoid any reference to its causes. What is clear after hundreds of years is that terrorism is a societal, rather than genetic, disease. Terrorist acts are not merely the acts of fanatics but are committed for clear purposes by people with clear agendas. Terrorism may be traced back to two fundamental underlying motivations: the struggle for power and domination, and acts of desperation in response to this power struggle.

Terror has been global for a long time. The threats of nuclear, biological, and chemical attacks by terrorists are ominous. The "War on Terrorism" declared by former president George W. Bush received an early positive global reaction. His war on Iraq, however, reversed that attitude in a short time. President Barack Obama has vowed to continue the fight against terrorism. That fight against terrorism must include not only military and intelligence global cooperation but also rethinking of policies and activities. When the question of "why terrorism" is posed, issues of poverty, ignorance, injustice, and despair are often part of the answer. We address these issues in Chapter 5. Interdependence and globalization have highlighted such disparities. Let us now take a look at a case study to see the impact of both interdependence and globalization on one specific country.

▶ CASE STUDY: Ghana

Ghana, on the west coast of Africa, is a state that experienced colonialism and a struggle to achieve its independence. Ghana represents an old civilization that had a thriving history. Archaeological remains indicate human inhabitance going back to the Bronze Age (4000 B.C.E.). In the ninth century, a famous Arab writer, Al Yaqubi, referred to Ghana as one of the three most-organized states in Africa. While ancient Ghana was to the west of modern-day Ghana, the region had a glorious history. Its rulers were known for their wealth and skills. They were masters of trade and had lots of gold. In fact, Ghana was rich in gold and diamonds.[13]

Our image of precolonial Africa is rich in ignorance and stereotypes. Many in the United States and Europe still view Africa as "primitive," "tribal," and "backward." This is what one could call the "Hollywood Africa" or the "TV Land Africa." With movies like *Tarzan*, the image of the so-called Dark Continent is maintained. A similar phenomenon in Europe or the United States may be called a forest or a national park, but in Africa it is often referred to as a jungle. This condescending attitude toward Africa is being challenged. The term *tribe* is often applied to small villages as well as to large empires and, in most cases, in conjunction with the adjective *primitive*. Are the Yorubas of Nigeria, with almost 40 million people, more of a tribe than the Swedes, Norwegians, or Irish? If not, then why not use the term to describe the less numerous European groups? If ethnic conflict in Africa is tribal, why not describe the conflict in Northern Ireland or Yugoslavia as tribal as well? In other words, it is time that we begin to diagnose our usage of terms to become consistent in applying them to peoples and cultures all over the world. When it comes to Africa, Western society has been unfair. We cannot afford to continue to stereotype so many in this era of globalization.

The dominant group of people in what came to make up Ghana is the Ashanti. Under a series of activist leaders, the Ashanti people expanded their rule and established a confederacy that became one of the most powerful kingdoms in the region. Within their empire, the conquered territories were allowed to retain their own customs, and their leaders were given a seat on the Ashanti State Council. Each territory exercised a form of internal self-rule. Such a state of affairs existed when Europeans began their encroachment on Ghana. The first Europeans to arrive were the Portuguese. Prince Henry the Navigator arrived with his crew in 1471 and began to trade for gold, ivory, and pepper. He called this area the Gold Coast because of its abundance in that precious mineral. In 1482, the Portuguese built a trading post, the Elmina Castle, which still stands today. Today, however, the Elmina Castle stands as a reminder of European trade in African slaves. Within few decades, as gold and ivory resources began to dwindle, slave trade became the major export of the area. Forced human globalization was, therefore, in place in Ghana some centuries ago.

The British made their way into the Gold Coast by creating the British African Company of Merchants in 1750. This company built and manned its installations, carried out trade, and defended its authority over areas under its jurisdiction. By 1875, the British became the dominant European power on the Gold Coast. In the 1880s, the British began to penetrate the northern areas of the region, and by 1902, the Northern Territories were declared a British protectorate—meaning, in practice, a colony. The Ghanaians resisted European encroachment all along. By the 1890s, they had formed an organized opposition with the establishment of the Aborigines' Rights Protection Society, which protested unfair land laws that violated traditional land tenure practices in the society. In 1920, a British West Africa Council was formed, which demanded elected representation for all of the peoples of the region. Although such pressure seemed of little value at the time, it actually paid off in the years following World War II. The British were drained from that destructive war and soon thereafter their empire began to break away. The first sign of British acquiescence to Ghanaian demands came in 1946, when the British governor issued the Gold Coast Constitution. This constitution created a new legislative council that included elected members. Even though the council was only advisory to the British governor, it still was a bold move that gave Ghana a level of political participation not found anywhere else in colonial Africa.

With elections, political parties began to form. The first such group was formed in 1947 by a group of British-educated Ghanaians with the objective of achieving self-government. The United Gold Coast Convention (UGCC) wanted self-government "in the shortest possible time." Its leaders were arrested in March 1948 for political activism. Among those arrested was Kwame Nkrumah, who later broke with the UGCC to form his own party, the Convention People's Party (CPP), in 1949.[14] The CPP demanded "self-government now" and identified itself with the working classes rather than the intellectual circles. Nkrumah's charisma and the slogans adopted by his party made the CPP very popular and worried the British administration. In 1950, the CPP started a campaign of "positive action" aiming at general strikes, boycotts, and other nonviolent resistance. But violence did occur. Consequently, the British arrested Nkrumah. His arrest, however, gave him more popularity among his people and made his party the undisputed winner of the colony's first national elections. The British governor had no choice but to release Nkrumah and offer him the job of "leader of government business," a position similar to that of prime minister. Using his political skills and popular support, Nkrumah was able to convince the British authorities to give him more power and, in time, to create a complete political system managed mostly by elected officials. Having effectively lost political power to Nkrumah's government, the British wanted to maintain some economic advantages. Therefore, at the request of the government of the Gold Coast, the British gave the country independence on March 6, 1956, so long as the new state remains a member of the British Commonwealth. The name adopted for the new country was Ghana, an old name used by the people of the area more than a century earlier.[15]

The economy of Ghana has a rich base in agriculture and minerals, but the country remains dependent on support from the international community. The major agricultural product of Ghana is cocoa. If you liked chocolate milk as a child, you are likely to have been using Ghanaian cocoa as a child. If you like cola, you are likely to still be using Ghanaian cocoa today. Consumers of chocolate may not know how important Ghana is for their sweet delicacy. Individuals who wear gold and diamonds may very well be wearing Ghanaian products. Just as Ghana exports its products to the world, it also imports products from others throughout the world. It imports capital products, petroleum, and food items.

Ghana's very language is imported as well. Because the country has 47 ethnic languages, the main language used in official and educational circles is English. While many features of African religious practices remain, most people in Ghana practice Christianity. About a third is Muslim. As such, globalization of culture and theology has been a part of Ghana's interdependence for some time. The former Secretary General of the United Nations, Kofi Anan, is a Ghanaian as well. When you visit Ghana and turn on a television set, you are likely to see American programs and news. European programs are also common. TV3 actually has more global programming than it has local. Just like other states in the world, Ghana is interdependent and part of our globalized planet.

SUMMARY AND REVIEW

The growing interdependence of our global community is slowly changing the relationships of states and individuals. Economically, the world is so interwoven that the livelihood of one depends on the production of many others. This relationship of interdependence transcends the economic sphere and includes environmental and political interests. In addition, the world has become smaller through efficient and low-cost traveling and the electronic media, such as the World Wide Web. Other areas of global interdependence include our own health when viruses and diseases travel beyond borders and infect people of all races and nationalities. AIDS, for example, does not discriminate on the basis of race, religion, nationality, sexual orientation, or any other human characteristic, immutable or otherwise. Indeed, global interdependence affects all of us, from the clothes we wear and the air we breathe to the food we eat and any forms of technology we use. Interdependence has yielded many positive as well as negative influences upon human life. Hence, for example, although jeans and baseball have become global cultural icons, many critics brand this trend as cultural colonialism, whereby American culture has spread to engulf a world where there exists no global minimum wage or labor laws to protect ordinary people from the exploitative tendencies of mass production. As seen in the case study, countries today are very interdependent. Ghana is simply a part of that global interdependence.

KEY TERMS

globalization   24
Earth Summit   29
cultural colonialism   31
New World Information and
   Communication Order   31

migration of dreams   31
relative deprivation   32
McWorld   33
Bonded Labor Liberation Front
   (BLFF)   33

DISCUSSION QUESTIONS

1. What are the characteristics of subsistence living? Is subsistence living possible in today's world? Why or why not?
2. What are the attributes of globalization?
3. How does the saying, "one person's mess is another person's catastrophe," apply to contemporary environmental conditions?
4. Is there any truth to the argument against cultural colonialism? Why or why not?
5. Discuss how television and other media play a role in migration of dreams and relative deprivation.

SUGGESTED READINGS

Anderson, Terry L., and Donald Leal. *Free Market Environmentalism Today*. New York: Palgrave, 2000.

Biel, Robert. *The New Imperialism: Crisis and Contradiction in North/South Relations*. London, UK: Zed Books, 2000.

Cohn, Theodore H., Stephen McBride, and John Wiseman, Eds. *Power in the Global Era: Grounding Globalization*. New York: St. Martin's Press, 2000.

Giddens, Anthony. *Runaway World: How Globalization Is Reshaping Our Lives*. New York: Routledge, 2000.

Jones, R. J. Barry. *The World Turned Upside Down? Globalization and the Future of the State*. New York: Palgrave, 2000.

Lane, Jan-Erik. *Globalization and Politics: Promises and Dangers*. Burlington, VT: Ashgate, 2006.

Lutz, James M., and Brenda J. Lutz. *Global Terrorism*. New York: Routledge, 2004.

Nassar, Jamal R., *Globalization and Terrorism: The Migration of Dreams and Nightmares*, 2nd Ed. Lanham, Maryland: Rowman & Littlefield, 2010.

Nye Jr., Joseph S. *Power in the Global Information Age: From Realism to Globalization*. New York: Routledge, 2004.

Sjursen, Katrin, Ed. *Globalization*. New York: H. W. Wilson, 2000.

Steger, Manfred. *Globalism: The New Market Ideology*. Lanham, MD: Rowman and Littlefield, 2001.

Steger, Manfred B. *The Rise of the Global Imaginary: Political Ideologies from the French Revolution to the Global War on Terror*. Oxford, UK: Oxford University Press, 2008.

Stott, Philip, and Sian Sullivan, Eds. *Political Ecology: Science, Myth and Power*. Oxford, UK: Oxford University Press, 2000.

Zakaria, Fareed. *The Post-American World*. New York: W.W. Norton, 2008.

NOTES

1. Lester R. Brown, *World Without Borders* (New York: Vintage Books, 1972), 192.
2. Murray Weidenbaum, "No Way Out of Global Markets," *The Christian Science Monitor*, 19 October 1995, 20.
3. John T. Rourke, *International Politics on the World Stage* (Sluice Dock, Guilford, CT: Dushkin/McGraw-Hill, 1999), 11.
4. See Jan Aart Scholte, *Globalization: A Critical Introduction* (New York: M. E. Sharpe, 2000).
5. "For the Birds," *Mother Jones*, February 2000, 22.
6. See Terry L. Anderson and Donald Leal, *Free Market Environmentalism Today* (New York: Palgrave, 2000).
7. For an excellent discussion of environmental politics, see Philip Stott and Sian Sullivan, Eds., *Political Ecology: Science, Myth and Power* (Oxford, UK: Oxford University Press, 2000).
8. See, for example, Ted Robert Gurr, *Why Men Rebel* (Princeton, NJ: Princeton University Press, 1970).

9. See R. J. Barry Jones, *The World Turned Upside Down? Globalization and the Future of the State* (New York: Palgrave, 2000).

10. Benjamin Barber, *Jihad vs. McWorld* (New York: Times Books, 1995).

11. Manfred Steger, *Globalism: The New Market Ideology* (Lanham, MD: Rowman and Littlefield, 2001).

12. See Robert Biel, *The New Imperialism: Crisis and Contradiction in North/South Relations* (London, UK: Zed Books, 2000).

13. For more details on Ghana's civilization, see Basil Davidson, F. K. Buah, and Ade Ajayi, *The Growth of African Civilisation* (New York: Longman, 1965).

14. For a good book on Africa's view of colonialism, see A. Adu Boahen, *African Perspectives on Colonialism* (Baltimore, MD: Johns Hopkins University Press, 1987).

15. For more details on Ghana's struggle for independence, see Kwame Nkrumah, *Ghana: The Autobiography of Kwame Nkrumah* (New York: International Publishers, 1957).

Religion and Politics

Globalization and Religious Revivalism

Religion has been a globalizing force throughout history. The spread of religion from its place of origin to other parts of the world has contributed to globalizing values and culture. In some cases, religion has been a source of peace, nonviolence, and humanitarian concerns. In other cases, religion has been used to incite violence, wars, and hatred. In some cases religion has been suppressed, whereas in other cases promoted. In all situations, religion continues to play a pivotal role in the values societies hold.

The last quarter of the twentieth century witnessed a revival of religious fervor in many parts of the world. This revival of religion is often called fundamentalism. Fundamentalists usually hold rather conservative values that they want to incorporate into political life. Be it on abortion, gay and lesbian rights, gender roles, or religious nationalism, fundamentalists usually hold strong views rooted in some divinely ordained belief system. Fundamentalist groups normally cross the borders of states and are transnational. Whether it is Jewish, Christian, Islamic, Hindu, or Buddhist fundamentalism, the phenomenon remains similar in that its adherents are true believers in the righteousness of their own beliefs. In this global era, religion is now a force that can unify or divide people all over the world. It has the power to create harmony as well as tensions. As our world moves deeper into globalization, the impact of religion also becomes more global. It is increasingly imperative that an educated person be familiar with the religious cultures of others. No more can we survive on stereotypes. The consequences could be grave.

The countries in Africa, Asia, the Middle East, and Latin America are incredibly diverse in their cultures. Each region has a wealth of cultural diversity within itself. They defy easy generalizations. People in Africa, for example, not only have almost 60 countries, but also have a large variety of languages, customs, traditions, and religions. Very often many people who live in the United States do not fully understand the cultures of others who live in distant places. Given the global nature of our existence, we all need to have a better understanding of each other. There are many reasons for that lack of understanding. One of them may have to do with an educational system that was originally designed to Americanize an immigrant population. More than 200 years later, the educational system still holds to the ideal of Americanizing a population that has become rather parochial. Another reason for lack of understanding may have to do with the media that depend too heavily on the sound bite. News of great events and peoples abroad is usually reduced to few seconds' or few lines' coverage where the adjective replaces real content. Therefore, major actors are often reduced to warlords, tribal leaders, terrorists, fundamentalists, extremists, drug kingpins, or some other adjective leading to generalizations about other peoples and their cultures. There are many other reasons for the incomplete understanding of the cultures of others. The task here, however, is to introduce you to such cultures.

The last few decades have witnessed a religious revivalism in a variety of forms. This phenomenon is global. Religious revivalism is not limited to a specific region or religion. In the United States, for example, religious revivalism could be seen in the rise of the "Christian Coalition," or the demonstrations in front of abortion clinics, or even the killing of abortion clinic doctors and nurses. Similar revivalism can be found in the ranks of other religions including Judaism, Islam, Hinduism, and Buddhism. Four great religions dominate the regions under discussion. Almost a billion and a half people in Asia, the Middle East, and Africa are adherents of Islam. The majority of those who inhabit the Indian subcontinent are Hindu, whereas East Asia is mostly Buddhist. Most people in Latin America are Roman Catholic. Many others throughout adhere to some Christian denomination. Others are Jews, Sikhs, Baha'is, Zoroastrians, or animists.

This book cannot provide you with the needed in-depth information about the many cultures of the world. What this chapter can do is try to introduce you to the major religious cultures of some of the peoples of the vast areas being covered. The interaction between religion and politics is rather obvious. This chapter discusses that interaction especially as it relates to the politics of development and change.

ISLAM

The brief introduction in Chapter 1 discussed the Middle East region and presented a historical overview of the region's Islamic culture. Islam, however, is practiced in countries outside of the Middle East. In fact, one of the more common misperceptions is the one that equates Islam with Arabs. Contrary to this misperception, Arabs are a small minority among **Muslims,** or followers of Islam. Only one of every eight Muslims in the world is an **Arab.** Moreover, many Arabs are Christian and some are Jewish. The most populous Islamic country is not even in the Middle East. That country is Indonesia, which is in Southeast Asia. Today, Islam is the fastest growing religion in the world. It is also the fastest growing religion in the United States. Yet, the perception most Americans have of Islam is often colored by stereotypes such as the one on the Arabs. A rather common image of Islam in the United States is that of a faith prone to fanaticism, extremism, and violence. As we already learned, all religions have some elements that are extremist, fanatic, and violent. Islam is not an exception. It is in the same boat as all other religions.

Islam is the product of the seventh-century Arabian Peninsula. The history of its origin is a success story. It produced an outstanding civilization that made major contributions to human development and progress. When the messenger of Islam, **Mohammad** (A.D. 570–632), was born, his native lands were in turmoil. For many decades Arabia had suffered an economic depression resulting from the decline of trade with Europe. Most people of the Arabian Peninsula were pagan and prayed to many gods. Mohammad preached to the people, seeking to replace their paganism with loyalty to God, or Allah in Arabic. As other religious teachers before him, Mohammad lived simply and taught justice, love, and kindness.

When Mohammad was born, his father had already passed away. His mother died six years after his birth. He was raised and cared for by his grandfather and later his uncle. According to the Islamic holy book, the **Quran,** Mohammad grew up in poverty (Sura 93, v, 6f). He originally practiced the religious beliefs of his community. The community worshiped the gods of Hubal and al-Uzza and believed in spirits, a Satan, good, and evil. Mohammad, however, was disturbed by the wars

Muslim ■ A person who belongs to the Islamic faith.

Arab ■ Individual whose native language is Arabic.

Mohammad ■ Messenger of Islam.

Quran ■ Islamic holy book.

FIGURE 3.1
Muslims in the World

that the tribes waged against each other. He reportedly was outraged at the practices of gambling, drinking, and the burial alive of unwanted infant daughters. As he matured, Mohammad learned about the Christian and Jewish monotheistic beliefs and seems to have been impressed by them. According to Islamic tradition, the angel Gabriel appeared to Mohammad in a cave at the base of Mount Hira, near Mecca, and revealed to him God's final revelation, The Quran. Shortly thereafter, Mohammad began to preach the message of God to the people of Mecca. The Quran recognizes the divine origin of the Old and New Testaments and that Mohammad received from God the final revelations as the last and greatest of the prophets. Many of the stories that appear in the Jewish Torah and the Christian Bible reappear in the Quran. The story of creation and the stories of Noah, Abraham, Moses, and Jesus are all told in the Muslim Holy Book as well.

The doctrines and rites of Islam not only embodied features of the older revealed religions but also carried over and modified certain of their elements. It is such modifications that gave Islam a unique and, perhaps, an Arab character. One such modification had to do with the geographic center of the faith. Older monotheistic religions look toward Jerusalem in prayer. Even though Jerusalem remained important to Islam, Muslims look toward Mecca in prayer. Mecca, as you already know, was already an important center of Arab pagan worship. Islam also retained the idea of a holy day but changed the day to Friday. It was on a Friday that Mohammad brought on his first convert to Islam. Unlike Christianity and Judaism, Islam, however, did not make the entire day holy, but only that part of it spent in prayer.

The Teachings of Islam

The basic teachings of Islam could be found in the name itself.[1] *Islam* is a noun formed from the infinitive of a verb meaning to submit or to surrender. A *Muslim* is one who has submitted or surrendered to God. A good practicing Muslim, therefore, is one who surrenders his or her soul to God. A Muslim does that act of submission by living in accordance to the scriptures of Islam found in the Quran. Most important among those are five duties known as the **Pillars of Islam.** The five duties or pillars are as follows:

Pillars of Islam
■ The five duties of a Muslim.

1. *Shahada, or profession of faith:* A good Muslim must profess that there are no Gods but God and that Mohammad is God's messenger. Acceptance of this profession of faith and its faithful repetition constitute the first step in being a Muslim. These simple words are heard often among the Muslims. They are broadcast on loudspeakers from minarets throughout the Islamic world when the faithful are called to prayer.
2. *Salat, or prayer:* A practicing Muslim must pray five times every day. The first is at sunrise, the second is at midday, and then at mid-afternoon, sunset, and the fall of darkness. Muslims go through this ritual regularly. At prayer they recite praise of God and reaffirm their submission to His will. As mentioned earlier, Muslims look toward Mecca whenever they are praying.
3. *Zakat, or almsgiving:* An important duty for Muslims is to give to those who are less fortunate. Almsgiving is a voluntary obligation for every Muslim to help those in need. Most Muslims either give direct gifts to the poor or make contributions to various charities.
4. *Sawm, or fasting during Ramadan:* A practicing Muslim who is not sick, pregnant, or a child needs to fast during the holy month of Ramadan. A fasting Muslim does not eat, drink, smoke, or engage in sexual activity from sunrise to sunset. Ramadan is the month during which the Quran was revealed to Mohammad. Because Muslims use a lunar calendar, Ramadan varies on the Western calendars from year to year. As you probably know, Western calendars are solar ones with slightly longer years than those of the Muslim or Jewish calendars. The act of fasting gives Muslims the opportunity to feel the hunger of those who are hungry and the thirst of those who are thirsty. Whether you are a king or a factory worker, Ramadan allows you to become a more understanding human being as you feel the suffering of those who are less fortunate than you are.
5. *Hajj, or pilgrimage:* Once in a lifetime, a Muslim is expected to make a pilgrimage to Mecca. It is also recommended that a Muslim complete the pilgrimage by visiting holy mosques in Medina and Jerusalem. The pilgrimage to Mecca is conditioned on its feasibility to a person. A person who is unable to do so because of financial difficulty, illness, or other similar reasons is excused from this duty.

Many Muslims around the world abide by these five duties. They are often committed to living a life of virtue and submission to what they believe to be the will of God. There are times, however, that interpretations of Islamic teachings clash with modern political and civic practices.

Islam and Politics

Strictly speaking, there is no independent political theory in Islam. Everything related to governance falls within the domain of religion. Unlike Christianity, which proposed giving to "Caesar what is Caesar's and to God what is God's," Islam does not have a distinction between what is secular and what is religious. It may very well be this factor more than any other that has transferred the basis of loyalty in Islamic societies. The Muslim, who professes belief in God and the message of the Quran, is a member of the Muslim community not on the basis of kinship, language, race, or nationality but only on that of religion.

Politically, a strict Muslim community or state could be characterized by four main features:

1. The sole head of the community is God.
2. God's teachings as revealed in the Quran are the law and constitution of the Muslim community.
3. The function, form, and constitution of the community are eternal and cannot be changed regardless of time and place.
4. The purpose of the community or state is to uphold the faith.

It is clear from the characteristics listed here that the Quran and the totality of God's teachings, known as the **shari'a,** are to be the law for every Muslim. This makes Islam more than just a religion as known in modern Western society. Islam is rather an infallible doctrine of ethics, prescribing the rules of conduct for an entire Muslim's life. This includes not only religious life but also a person's political, social, domestic, and private domains. Similar to the other great religions of our day, Islam is being rocked and battered by the revolutionary changes of today's world. Adherents of all major religions, including Christianity, Judaism, Hinduism, Buddhism, and Islam, are in the same boat. But the anguish and pain are in many ways greater for Muslims than they are for others. This is because Muslims more than any of the others are committed to the establishment of the Kingdom of God on earth. For them, there should be no separation between what is secular and what is religious, national and religious community, or civic and private duties. The advent of the modern nation-state and its incorporation of Western ideals have resulted in the dislocation of traditional Islamic political and cultural life. Islamic history did not prepare Muslims well for this fate. Their great history of success even during the life of the messenger of the religion made their current subservient role very hard to accept.

As mentioned in Chapter 1, Islamic history is rather glorious and full of major contributions to world civilization. Students in the West study the Dark Ages and its practices of feudalism, serfdom, and witchcraft, and yet Islam of that same era had established a great empire that reached distant Spain on the west and central

shari'a ■ The totality of God's teachings in Islam.

Asia to the east. As Muslims conquered the Byzantine Empire, they absorbed rather than destroyed. In the process, they were able to transform old knowledge into a distinctive civilization. At the height of the Islamic Empire in the ninth and tenth centuries, Muslims contributed much to our knowledge. At the time Europe was practicing witchcraft in medicine, Muslims had hospitals and were practicing surgery. Many contributions in mathematics are still with us today as we use the decimal point, Arabic numerals, algebra, and the zero. When the Crusaders of Europe went to the Holy Land in the eleventh century, they found a civilization far more advanced than the Europe they left behind.

This glorious history, clearly, did not prepare Muslims for their current secondary role in global civilization. Consequently, some Muslim intellectuals began to ponder the fate of their people at various times in modern history. Some of those have argued that Islam should be adapted to fit modern technology. Others insisted that it is the people and not the religion that were the cause of their own downfall. Such intellectuals called for returning to Islamic scriptures and living by them. Yet others have proposed a separation between religion and modern political society. It is this last group that came to dominate most Islamic countries in the twentieth century. As a result, most Islamic states today have modern constitutions that are based on secular rather than religious principles. Some have developed well-managed democratic structures. A few have even elected women to executive roles. Bangladesh, Pakistan, and Turkey have all elected women to the position of prime minister. Indonesia, the largest Islamic country, had a woman president. Other Islamic countries are still struggling to find an accommodation between religion and politics.

Muslim states
■ States with Muslim majorities and secular governments

Islamic states
■ States with Muslim majorities that use Islam for guidance.

Islamist states
■ States with Muslim majorities using Islamic law in governance.

Essentially, there are three types of regimes in Islamic states: **Muslim states, Islamic states,** and **Islamist states.** Muslim states have Muslim majorities, but a secular system of government where religion is separated from government. Turkey would be an example of such a state. Islamic states have a Muslim majority and a system of government that uses Islam for guidance in political affairs. Egypt and Indonesia are examples of such states. Islamist states, on the other hand, depend on Islamic law or Shari'a for governance. Saudi Arabia and Iran are such examples. Most countries with Muslim majorities are considered Islamic states where Islam guides political process rather than direct it. Few are Muslim states and only a couple are Islamist states. As such, it is time to abandon the generalizations and stereotypes about Islamic societies. Similarly, stereotypes need to be abandoned when it comes to other religious cultures such as Hinduism.

HINDUISM

Hinduism is a very old and diverse religion. Some of its doctrines date back to 3000 B.C.E. Hindus have a very wide selection of beliefs and practices. It is perhaps the most complicated of all religions in the world. Some have even argued that Hinduism is more than one religion. Today, Hinduism is the dominant religion in India and has more than 700 million followers. One of the reasons that Hinduism is complicated is that it has no founding figure like in most other religions. It developed over a long period and has incorporated many rituals and legends from many eras.

To simplify a complex set of beliefs, we will emphasize those features common to Hindus regardless of the strain they may believe in. Most significant among those is the notion of Karma.[2] **Karma** refers to actions or deeds. Basically, it is the belief or law that a person's thoughts, words, and deeds have an ethical consequence fixing his or her lot in future existences. You could simply view this Hindu law as essentially the same as the statement, "as you have sown you shall reap."

Although the idea of retribution for our actions is not unique to monotheistic religions, Karma goes beyond the notion of souls going to heaven or hell. Hinduism firmly believes in the notion of **Samsara,** or rebirth. It is their belief that the soul of a person who dies does not (except in a single case) die, but rather is reborn into another existence that will terminate in due time and necessitate yet another birth. Rebirth follows rebirth with a single exception, which will be explained later, in an endless chain. The successive births do not have to be on the same plane of being. It may occur in any of a series of heavens or hells. Or, it could occur on earth in any of the forms of life. Most Hindus believe that a person's soul could be reborn as a vegetable, animal, or human. What determines the nature of the rebirth is the law of Karma.

Hindu teachings are directed to humans only. They emphasize the need to live a virtuous way of life similar to that taught by Christianity, Islam, and Judaism. But Hinduism does not insist on extreme virtue in one life. Because souls are reborn, salvation could be achieved over many existences. Therefore, Hinduism is, perhaps, more tolerant of deviations than the other religions, as it does not insist on salvation in a single life. A person could live his or her entire life in a single existence seeking any of the following **Four Permissible Goals in Life:**

1. *Kama:* The desire for pleasure, especially through love, is an acceptable goal in life for a Hindu. It is seen as a sacred duty for a person to experience fulfillment in his or her own love life, as well as the fulfillment of that person's partner. Lust, pleasure, and love represent acceptable behavior provided the person remains within the bounds set by general social rules. It is understood, however, that this person will, in this life or in a future existence, come to the realization that pleasure alone is not enough. Eventually, that individual would want and would pursue a more deeply satisfying goal in life.

2. *Artha:* Power and substance are the essence of Artha. It refers to material possessions or high social status. Seeking wealth and other forms of materialism, or aspiring to positions of authority, is a legitimate aspiration for a Hindu. But here again, it is understood that the person will eventually learn that a deeper satisfaction comes from following a greater path in life.

3. *Dharma:* Righteousness and discipline are more satisfying goals than either of the first two. Dharma is considered, in a strict sense, as a religious and moral law that sets the standard for a worthier and more deeply satisfying life. A person who chooses to follow Dharma is a disciplined individual who will renounce his or her personal desires and social success and seek the good of all. That person would do his or her duty toward others in the community, including family, caste, or the larger community. But again, the joy, however great, is not ultimate. There is one ultimate satisfaction that could be achieved by successfully following the fourth permissible goal in life.

Karma ■ The most significant belief in Hinduism that refers to actions or deeds.

Samsara ■ The Hindu belief of rebirth.

Four Permissible Goals in Life
■ Goals in the Hindu faith that include Kama, or the desire for pleasure; Artha, or seeking wealth and positions of authority; Dharma, or righteousness and discipline; and Moksha, or liberation or salvation.

4. *Moksha:* Liberation or salvation is the ultimate goal of a Hindu. It represents the final release of the soul from the cycle of rebirths. Moksha is the highest and only truly satisfying goal in life. To make Moksha your goal in life means living a life dedicated to work, knowledge, and devotion to Hindu teachings. Once liberated, the soul is forever satisfied. Although not all Hindus are in agreement on this, many later Hindus have come to accept the notion that when a soul achieves Moksha or liberation, it achieves Nirvana. Nirvana is mainly used in Buddhist teachings, but has been employed in Hindu texts. It refers to the ultimate state of liberation from rebirth. Hindu texts seem to have accepted the Buddhist definition of **Nirvana** as the fullness of being, which no human words can describe.

Nirvana ■ The fullness of being, which no human words can describe.

Even though Hinduism argues that a person's Karma determines his or her future rebirth into any of the forms of life, it also has a well-articulated division among humans. Rebirth as a human can occur into any of the castes or even at a lower level. That rebirth into a caste or out of it is determined by a person's Karma as well. It is not proper to define the Hindu castes as classes because classes represent economic divisions whereas castes represent broader ones. Many authors, however, have made a linkage between the two because the **caste system** seems to also follow economic distinctions such as those between laborers, professionals, and aristocrats. The Hindu caste system has four castes of people grouped on the basis of their birth:

caste system ■ A Hindu differentiation among people based on rebirth.

Brahmin: This is the highest of all castes and includes the priesthood. They are the people who are supposed to be devoted to the teaching of the religion.

Brahmin ■ The highest caste in Hinduism, which includes the priesthood.

Ksatriya: This caste includes the aristocratic nobility and the warriors or knights. In essence, the Ksatriya represent the ruling elite of society.

Ksatriya ■ The second caste in Hinduism, which includes the aristocratic nobility, warriors, or knights.

Vaisya: This caste is usually the largest and includes the peasants, the merchants, and the professionals. It could be referred to as the caste of the common people.

Shudra: This caste includes all non-Aryans or those who are not of Indo-European origin. Such people included blacks, Semites, slaves, servants, and even some prisoners of war. Further divisions came about over the centuries. But the most noted group is that of the **outcastes, or the untouchables.** The outcastes are considered the dregs of society whose mere touch pollutes a caste. Such individuals have no hope of rising in the social scale. For centuries, the outcastes were stigmatized by Hindu society. Many were left to live in the misery of poverty and starvation.

Vaisya ■ The third and largest caste in Hinduism, which includes the peasants, merchants, and professionals.

Shudra ■ The fourth caste in Hinduism, which includes all non-Aryans or those who are not of Indo-European origin.

outcastes or untouchables ■ Outsiders who are considered the dregs of society.

For a long time the caste system was practiced as the norm in Hindu society. Even when the British dominated India for centuries, they left the practice intact. Just like there was a time when feudalism seemed inseparable from Christianity, the caste system also came to be seen as an integral part of Hinduism. When Indian independence became a reality in 1947, the new leaders of the independence movement did not hesitate to abolish it. But as we know from our experiences in the United States, ending slavery did not mean an end to prejudice and discrimination.

The legal termination of the caste system in India did not fully terminate the long tradition of social prejudice. Its abolition, however, has signified that the caste system is not an essential feature of Hinduism.

Hinduism and Indian Politics

The new post-independence leaders of India found themselves clashing with religion over the caste system. Long before independence, however, the struggle they waged for independence found a way to accommodate itself to religion. India's struggle for independence benefited from the ideas of Mohandas Karamchand Gandhi, known as the Mahatma Gandhi. Gandhi was not a religious or spiritual leader as much as he was a political leader. However, he used the concept of **Satyagraha,** meaning holding fast to truth, and set out to entice his people to employ self-sacrifice in their struggle to liberate their homeland. Gandhi argued that his approach of "Satyagraha and its off-shoots, non-cooperation and civil resistance, are nothing but new names for the law of suffering."[3] Gandhi was born in India, studied law in Britain, and worked briefly in South Africa. There, he resisted the discriminatory practices of the white South African government. In 1915, he went back to India and began a campaign to oust the British from his homeland. Drawing on Hindu principles of Dharma, the third permissible goal in life, Gandhi advocated the use of righteousness and virtue in a disciplined way to force the British colonists to leave India. In his own way, Gandhi was able to combine Hindu principles and nationalist ideals that, in time, came to symbolize India's struggle for independence.[4]

Satyagraha ■ The Hindu concept for rebirth.

Although Gandhi accepted most Hindu traditions, including the principle of a caste system, he modified some of them. For example, Gandhi did not like the limitations imposed on the outcastes, or the untouchables. He called the untouchables the **Harijans,** or the children of God. He attempted to integrate them into India's society and sought their participation in the struggle for independence. Working with India's Congress Party, Gandhi practiced nonviolent civil disobedience and was able to move hundreds of thousands of people into joining his cause. His many incarcerations and hunger strikes made him even more popular. Gandhi reasoned that the British continued to colonize India because they made a profit out of it. Therefore, he set out to take away that incentive. He urged his fellow Indians not to buy British-made clothing. Instead, he wanted them to make their own with the cotton they produced. Gandhi took on the loom as a symbol of his struggle and started weaving his own clothing. His famous Salt March marked a turning point in India's struggle for independence and showed that suffering and self-sacrifice could achieve positive results.

Harijans ■ The name Gandhi gave to the untouchables, meaning the children of God.

Even though Gandhi's approach of passive resistance did force the British to the negotiating table and out of India, India's partition into two states, India and Pakistan, resulted in mass murders and a massive refugee problem for both new states. Hindu extremists did not like Gandhi's stance against their atrocities. On January 30, 1948, one such extremist assassinated the Mahatma Gandhi. Today, many Indians refer to Gandhi as the Father of India. His legacy, however, went beyond the borders of India. Dr. Martin Luther King, Jr., often referred to Gandhi's teachings in his struggle for civil rights in the United States. Other leaders struggling for justice from Burma to South Africa also were inspired by the work of Gandhi.

Recent Indian politics, however, have taken more religious tones as religious nationalists came to dominate recent elections. Consequently, tensions between the Hindu majority and the Muslim minority have, on occasion, escalated into bloody conflicts. The 2008 attacks on several places in Mumbai illustrate the level of tensions between adherents of the two faiths. The use of Hindu icons in politics is now a common feature of some political parties. Islamic violence has also increased in some parts of the country, as seen in December 2008 in Mumbai.

BUDDHISM

Buddhism arose in India as a direct challenge to the rigid caste system inherent in Hinduism. Its founder, Siddhartha Gautama (500 B.C.E.), known as the Buddha (the Enlightened One), was the son of an Indian king. He grew to adulthood under conditions of great comfort and splendor. Living on the palace grounds, the young Siddhartha had servants and slaves caring for his needs. At age 19, he was married to a beautiful princess, who bore him a son. It was at this time that Siddhartha began to take chariot rides into the city. Here, for the first time in his life, he came into contact with poverty, crippling diseases, old age, and death. One night, after a palace feast, Gautama left his sleeping wife and newborn son and ran away seeking enlightenment. He wandered for many years, living the life of a beggar, hoping to understand the meaning of life. He wandered from one village to another, one town to another, begging for food and seeking spiritual truth. He wandered for six years. One time, after 49 days of meditation, enlightenment came upon him. Siddhartha Gautama became a Buddha, or an enlightened one, and began preaching.

Early Buddhism was an outgrowth of Hinduism, and both religions have several significant beliefs in common. Among them is the idea that all living things are reborn into new lives (Samsara) and that all actions in this life will be compensated in the next (Karma). The main ideas of Buddhism are contained in the statements known as the **Four Noble Truths:**

Four Noble Truths

■ These truths include that life is suffering, suffering is caused by ignorance, sorrow ends when a person is enlightened, and enlightenment is achieved by a course of disciplined and moral conduct.

1. *Life is suffering:* Life, according to the Buddha, is full of suffering. It is a sorrowful state of existence. It should be the objective of every person to end the cycle of rebirth and the suffering that it brings.
2. *Suffering is caused by ignorance:* The most fundamental cause of the painful rebirth of every individual is ignorance. This ignorance leads to craving for life and its seeming pleasures. Our thirst to live and our desires to have a life based on pleasure and prosperity cause our rebirth, which continues the cycle of suffering.
3. *Sorrow ends when a person is enlightened:* Suffering ends when a person overcomes ignorance and becomes emancipated from "the-will-to-live-and-have." Once a person is enlightened, that individual becomes exempt from evil desire and their Karma expires. Upon the end of that individual's current existence,

he or she would achieve Nirvana. Nirvana is explained in Buddhist literature as "the fullness of being which no human words can describe."

4. *Enlightenment is achieved by a course of disciplined and moral conduct:* The life that concludes in the attainment of Nirvana requires a full understanding of the Four Noble Truths. The path to Nirvana is called the Noble Path of Buddhism (**Ariyamagga**). This path represents the essence of the Buddhist system of ethics. It presents eight specific means for achieving Nirvana. Those center on virtuous practice, mental composure, and wisdom.[5]

Ariyamagga ■ The Noble Path of Buddhism, which is the path to Nirvana.

Buddhist writings are contained in the **Tripitaka,** or Three Baskets. In the Tripitaka, there is a great discussion of these concepts and an explanation of the Noble Path of Buddhism. Sometimes called the Noble Eightfold Path of Buddhism, it gives a clear picture of the ethical norms accepted in Buddhist literature.

Tripitaka ■ Buddhist holy books.

The first norm of this Path is Right View, or Right Understanding. This involves an understanding of the power of the individual. Individuals have choices, and their future position is determined by their behavior and not predetermined by some supreme god or even by past action. Fate and determinism, therefore, are rejected in Buddhism.

Right Thought is the second norm of the Noble Path. This path bridges thought and action. It preaches the importance of having thoughts that are free from lustful relations or greed, free from hatred, and free from violent intentions. Thoughts, it is believed, lead to actions. Therefore, a good Buddhist must be free of improper thoughts.

The third step in the Buddhist Path is Right Speech. It involves avoiding false speech, slanderous speech, harsh speech, and frivolous talk. A Buddhist, therefore, must at all times seek to cultivate truthfulness and trustworthiness. He or she must also promote unity among those who are divided. A good Buddhist speaks in a pleasant and delightful manner. Finally, a Buddhist needs to cultivate meaningful, purposeful, and timely speech.

Right Conduct or Right Action is the fourth step in the Buddhist Path. It suggests avoidance of bodily harm to oneself or to others. Violence against all living things is warned against. Right Action means a life full of love, compassion, and abstention from wrongful gratification of your senses, especially in terms of sexual misbehavior.

Right Occupation or Livelihood is the fifth step and suggests a morally acceptable means of livelihood. Occupations that are materially rewarding but morally wrong must be avoided. Engaging in any occupation that could result in harming others is considered unacceptable in Buddhism. Such occupations include making or trading weapons, poisons, or animal flesh. A Buddhist monk has much more stringent conditions.

The sixth step in the Eightfold Path is Right Effort. The emphasis on effort is significant in Buddhism. Effort is the most important factor for the victory of morality over temptations within every individual. Individuals must be determined to prevent evil within themselves and to choose the moral alternative.

Right Mindfulness is the seventh step. This guides a person's mental, verbal, and bodily behavior toward a moral direction. Some may describe this path as the need to remain alert at all times in order to prevent any evil thoughts or actions.

The final step is Right Concentration or Meditation. This step requires clear and composed mental condition that helps in achieving wisdom and avoiding evil. Meditation is considered as a form of mental training for an ethical life of the Buddhist.

In his own way, Siddhartha Gautama introduced major ideas and suggested a way of life that is based on morality and ethics. Although Buddhism began in India, it did not last there for long. Soon it spread to other parts of Asia. Today, Buddhism and its variations are the dominant religion in Sri Lanka, Burma, Tibet, Thailand, Japan, North and South Korea, Mongolia, Cambodia, and even China. Buddhist universal ethics have influenced not only the cultures of such societies but also their politics.

Buddhism and Politics

The image of Buddhism in Western society may be that of a religion of withdrawal. The reality of modern Buddhist societies is, however, very different. Buddhism in contemporary Asian society seems to stand for active engagement in social and political life. Two recent Nobel Peace prizes went to Buddhist activists. One was awarded to the **Dalai Lama** of Tibet and the other to San Suu Kyi of Myanmar or Burma. Buddhist monks throughout Asia advocate social change. Buddhists have also contributed a great deal to the conceptualization of nonviolent action for social justice in many corners of the world.[6] Although Buddhism is returning to China, it is still not accurate to call China a Buddhist country. After all, the People's Republic of China is a state run on the basis of communist ideology. Buddhist revival in China, however, is showing its impact on the country's politics as well.

Dalai Lama ■
A Tibet Buddhist leader who won a Nobel Peace Prize.

CHRISTIANITY IN AFRICA, ASIA, AND LATIN AMERICA

As you are well aware, Christianity began in the Middle East. Even though Christianity took root in Europe and the Americas, it also penetrated Africa and Asia. China, for example, has more than 10 million Christians, India has more than 2 million, and Japan has almost 1.5 million. A number of countries in Africa and Asia have Christian majorities. Ethiopia, Nigeria, the Central African Republic, the Philippines, and others are mostly Christian. Latin America is overwhelmingly Christian. Similar to other religions, Christianity in Africa, Asia, and Latin America has experienced religious revivalism. American and European missionaries and evangelical groups have established a foothold in many countries in Africa and Asia. They started schools where there were none and worked on projects designed to improve the physical well-being of the people there. Food and health projects are also among the many contributions of missionaries and evangelical activists. Regardless of motive, such projects tend to improve living standards of the poorest people in many parts of Africa, Asia, and Latin America. Christianity, therefore, is also used to achieve greater communal objectives. Local Christians even developed activist Christian doctrines to achieve justice for the less fortunate and the oppressed. Most prominent among those are the doctrines of **liberation theology.**

Liberation theology is rooted in the thoughts and actions of a number of Catholic priests and nuns working with the poor and oppressed. Although advocated only by a few, liberation theology has become an essential component of political life in many parts of Latin America. It has contributed to serious changes in Nicaragua, El Salvador, and Haiti. It even contributed to the rise of "people power" in the Philippines. Even though the Roman Catholic Church has historically taught conservative doctrines that advocated acceptance of authority, the experiences of Latin America in the last half of the twentieth century gave birth to new ideas of activism and rebellion. Some Latin American theologians attempted to make the Gospel of Jesus Christ relevant to the social, economic, and political situations in which many of the continent's poor found themselves. In a direct challenge to the established church doctrines, liberation theologians embarked on an interpretation of the scriptures that supported the poor and oppressed majority of Latin America.

One of the early advocates of liberation theology was a priest from Peru. **Gustavo Gutierrez** argued that poverty which dehumanizes people is an evil and an offence against God. Gutierrez lives and works among the poor in Lima, the capital of Peru. In 1971, he published a book that came to influence other theologians in Latin America.[7] In this book, Gutierrez argues that God takes the side of the poor and that poverty is the result of human failure to construct a world of justice. The Bible, then, has a promise of liberation not only from individual sin but also from oppressive systems that keep the majority of the people in Latin America in poverty. He insists that the practice of Christians should match their beliefs. Therefore, the church should be involved to correct injustices and to bring about a more equitable social, economic, and political system. In sum, liberation theologians like Gutierrez attempted to explain the relationship between the Christian faith and justice in the world.

The work of Gutierrez and others like him has emphasized the relationship between Christianity and justice. Latin American theology of liberation has influenced many people. Many Latin Americans found it justifiable to join revolutionary movements in countries such as El Salvador, Nicaragua, Colombia, and others. Even priests and nuns became active in revolutionary struggles. Government agents or troops murdered a number of them. Many of those were in El Salvador, where even the archbishop was murdered.

Archbishop Oscar Romero was gunned down in 1980 for his open criticism of injustices in his homeland. After the Sandinista Revolution in Nicaragua overthrew the repressive government, a number of liberation theologians who supported the revolutionaries took government posts in the new regime. In Haiti, the first democratically elected president was a former priest and liberation theologian, Jean-Bertrand Aristide. Latin American doctrines of liberation theology have influenced others beyond Latin America. African and Asian theologians developed similar arguments and organized for social justice. Even in the United States, black and feminist liberation thought developed along the lines of Latin American ideas of linking Christianity to a person's social experiences. Informal as well as formal contacts have developed among such theologians to the dislike of the Church's leadership in Rome.

liberation theology
■ A Latin American movement connecting Catholic theology to social justice.

Gustavo Gutierrez
■ Liberation Theology advocate.

Case Study: Iran

Iran is the embodiment of a very old civilization. One of its early pioneers was Cyrus the Great, who created a major empire around 533 B.C.E. known as the Persian Empire, which spread its wings into many parts of the modern Middle East. With the rise of Islam, Iran became a major cornerstone of the Islamic Empire, and its people made major contributions to Islamic civilization. After the death of Mohammad, however, many in Iran disagreed with other Muslims over the issue of succession to leadership. That disagreement contributed to a split among the Muslims, dividing them into Sunnites and Shi'ites. The Sunnites are today the large majority of Muslims, and they dominate among the Arab countries. Iran, on the other hand, which is not an Arab country, became the leader among the Shi'ites. In time, certain traditions and practices separated the two groups even further. Although Iran has a long and significant history, our concern in this chapter is with modern Iranian politics and its interaction with religion.

Shah ■ King of Iran.

By the turn of the twentieth century, Persia, now known as Iran, was a monarchy ruled by a **Shah,** or king. Historically, the country had an agricultural society in which few landlords owned most lands. As an urban class began to develop, resentment to the aristocracy grew. By 1906, the frustrated urban elements revolted and demanded a constitution giving them a share in power. In 1908, oil was discovered. The discovery of oil intensified a European rivalry over domination of Iran. With World War I

FIGURE 3.2
Iran

breaking out in 1914, the British and Russian governments occupied the country. In 1917, the Russians withdrew after their revolution at home. The British, on the other hand, placed the country under their protection and attempted to maintain control over it.

The Shah of Iran naturally resented British meddling in his country's affairs. Consequently, his relationship with the British "protectors" deteriorated. In 1921, the British, working with elements in Iran's military, engineered a coup d'état, or military takeover, of the government. One of those collaborators with the British, Reza Khan, soon emerged as the next leader of Iran. He was crowned shah-n-shah, or king of kings, in 1925. His crowning marked the start of the Pahlavi Dynasty, which came to rule the country for a good part of the twentieth century. The new Shah proceeded to implement major domestic programs that aimed at modernizing the country. His flirting with Germany during World War II, however, brought on another occupation by British and Soviet forces in 1941. The British forced Shah Reza Khan to abdicate in favor of his young son, Muhammad Reza. The new Shah was too young to rule, and a Board of Regents was appointed to rule on his behalf. Feeling betrayed by Shah Reza Khan, the British pressured the Board of Regents to allow more participation and create a system of government that would be more like that of Britain itself. They encouraged the formation of political parties, elections, and greater empowerment of the prime minister. By 1951, the leader of the National Front, Dr. Muhammad Mossadeg, was elected prime minister on a platform that promised to nationalize Iran's oil.

U.S. Involvement

The nationalization of Iran's oil that followed Mossadeg's election brought on the involvement of the United States. Fearing the spread of such policies of oil nationalization, the U.S. government initiated a very secretive operation to be implemented by the Central Intelligence Agency (CIA). In collaboration with the seven major oil companies, known as the **Seven Sisters**, that used to operate in Iran, a boycott of Iranian oil was declared. The aim of the boycott was to bring oil production in the country to a halt. Without the expertise of the oil companies, their shipping fleets, and pipelines, Iran could not drill, refine, or sell its oil. The consequence of such action was to drive Iran into an economic recession. The oil companies were hoping that the economic crisis would weaken Mossadeg. Instead, it strengthened him. Nationalism gripped the Iranian public and turned their anger on foreign powers and corporations trying to undo the nationalization decision. Iranians took to the streets chanting anti-Western slogans and showing their support of Mossadeg. In time, some elements in Iran's parliament (the Majlis) began to question the prime minister's actions. In the summer of 1953, the prime minister dissolved the Parliament. In August 1953, the Shah fled the country under pressure from the prime minister's supporters.

Having failed to unseat the prime minister by the boycott, the CIA sent Kermit Roosevelt, director of its Near East operations, to the country with the objective of overthrowing Mossadeg's government. Within six days of the Shah's departure, military units took over the government and imprisoned Mossadeg and many of his allies. They called upon the Shah to return to his throne. The Shah returned to Iran triumphantly. It was not until 25 years later, in the summer of 1978, that the CIA declassified documents showing its central role in that operation.[8] By then the Shah

Seven Sisters
■ Seven large oil companies that had monopolized the world's oil market.

Savak ■ The Shah's secret service agency.

had smashed all opposition and created an autocratic regime dependent upon his wishes. With the help of his secret service agency, the **Savak**, the Shah consolidated his power and attempted to create a staunchly pro-Western regional force in Iran. His equating of Westernization with modernization, however, created new problems for the country. Severe poverty existed next to tremendous wealth, and corruption by the Shah and members of his family irritated many Iranians. In time, many people were ready to do the unthinkable—revolt.

The Iranian Revolution

Shortly after the declassification of U.S. government documents about the CIA involvement in 1953, Iranian college students took to the streets to denounce the United States and the Shah's close relationship with it. The Shah ordered his troops to stop the demonstrators. In doing so, some students were shot and killed. Their funerals turned into larger demonstrations that included many other segments of the society. More troops were dispatched, leading to more deaths. Demonstrations spread to many parts of the country, and the cycle of deaths followed by more demonstrations continued until early 1979. This is not meant to say that the Iranian Revolution was caused by the American announcement. Discontent with the Shah and his government had been mounting for many years. Social, economic, and political pressure had been building within the country for more than two decades. Opposition to the Shah came from very diverse groups that included religious elements, intellectuals, the middle class, urban poor, and political parties, including the communist **Tudeh Party**.[9]

Tudeh Party ■ The Communist Party of Iran.

Although the Shah envisioned a strong Iran that would be a major regional power, his attempt at doing so backfired. Aside from irritating his neighbors, his spending on arms purchases diverted his attention from solving problems of poverty at home. Even though they knew that their country was rich in oil, the poor saw no oil money filtering down to their backward and impoverished villages. Consequently, Iran's poor resented the regime and joined the demonstrators. The Shah also managed to offend the religious elements in his society. Those people were upset with his Westernization of the culture and his 1961 land reform and the later exile of Ayatollah Khomeini. Although the revolution itself would later be called the Islamic Revolution, the fact remains that real revolutionary activities were not limited to the religious elements in the country. Instead, Iran's revolution started spontaneously and incorporated many segments of the society. The religious leaders, however, became more significant in time as they eventually managed to take over the revolution. The leftists of Iran were also significant participants in the revolution. Led by the Tudeh Party, this communist underground force was vehemently opposed to the Shah's close relationship to the United States, a country they viewed as imperialist. Communist Party members were also determined to end the Shah's secret police, the Savak, and their torture chambers. After all, they were the target of the Savak. Other political parties in the country were also unhappy that they lost all power after the return of the Shah in 1953. The Iranian middle class, represented by the shopkeepers and others, were willing participants in the revolution. Corruption, mismanagement, and the feeling that they had no voice in government alienated them. Their children in colleges were the ones who started the cycle of demonstrations. This new educated youth had learned to question, and they demanded a better form of government for their society.

Together, these segments of Iran's society proved stronger than the Shah's armed forces. But they lacked common leadership. In time, many began to look to the **Ayatollah Khomeini,** who was exiled by the Shah more than a decade earlier, as the symbolic leader of their rebellion. The Ayatollah was now in his late seventies and had suffered one and a half decades of exile for his opposition to the Shah. Through the years, the Ayatollah continued to speak, advocating the overthrow of the monarchy in Iran. Audio recordings of his sermons were often smuggled into the country for his followers to hear. Soon after the Shah fled the country in January 1979, the Ayatollah came back to a hero's welcome. The Ayatollah's return gave the revolutionaries a common leader. However, many in the revolution were not thrilled about that leadership and argued for a modern secular political system. The transition that followed was characterized by a great deal of euphoria mixed with anxiety about the future. The Ayatollah's followers demanded the formation of an Islamic political system and the secularists expected an open and more democratic system.

Ayatollah Khomeini
■ Religious leader of Iran after the revolution of 1979.

The Constitutional Compromise

—A compromise was soon reached. A new constitution was adopted that seemed to bridge the gap between the secularist and religious elements. The constitution created a republic that incorporated separation of powers and Islamic ideals. It declared Ayatollah Khomeini as the country's "leader" and allowed for popular elections and representation. The leader became the supreme commander of the armed forces, appointed significant judicial figures, and approved the credentials of presidential candidates. The first presidential election was won by **Dr. Abulhassan Bani-Sadr,** a French-educated economist. Parliamentary elections brought together a mixture of religious and nonreligious elements. To ensure that the **Majlis,** or parliament, would not enact laws that violate the teachings of Islam, the constitution set up a **Guardian Council** of 12 members. Their task was to scrutinize all legislation to ensure compliance with Islam. Thus the Islamic Republic of Iran was born.

Dr. Abulhassan Bani-Sadr ■ Iran's first elected president.

Majlis ■ Iran's parliament.

Guardian Council ■ Ensures that Iranian laws comply with the teachings of Islam.

Although the Iranian constitution remained the same, the collaboration between the religious elements and the secularists did not last long. In July 1981, President Bani-Sadr fled the country under pressure from the religious elements. Islamic Revolutionary Guards had executed some of his close associates and cabinet ministers, and his leadership had come into question as the country was losing battles in its recent war with Iraq. Bani-Sadr also became the target of ridicule by Islamic elements that held American diplomats hostage at the American Embassy compound in Tehran. Bani-Sadr clearly wanted to end the hostage crisis, while his opponents wanted to drag it on.[10]

Soon after the United States admitted the deposed Shah into the country for cancer treatment, some Iranian students, demonstrating in front of the American Embassy, climbed the walls of the compound and took over the embassy. They feared that the Shah's entry to the United States was a part of a plot with the CIA to bring the Shah back to Iran. They called the diplomats *spies* and the embassy *the nest of spies.* Such terms were in clear reference to the 1953 coup engineered by Kermit Roosevelt. Even after the Shah died of cancer, the American diplomats were not released. They remained there for a total of 444 days, before their eventual release in January 1981. Relations between Iran and the United States remained strained into the early part of the twenty-first century. Former president George W. Bush even referred to Iran as an "axis of evil" state. The wars in Afghanistan to the east and Iraq to the west have placed U.S. troops on both sides of the country. Many Iranians feel that the United States plans to invade or attack their country in the near future, especially after Iran began to develop a nuclear program. Iran's president, Mahmoud Ahmadinejad, has not helped U.S.-Iranian relations either. His constant verbal attacks on the United States and Israel make matters worse. Although Islam found its expression in Iran, it still has a long way to go before it can be the dominant political force in most other countries with Islamic majorities. Most of those have opted for systems that allow for some separation between religion and politics.

SUMMARY AND REVIEW

As we have seen in this chapter, religion has been used for good and for bad. Throughout history, religion was used for political purposes. Today, that trend continues. In Iran, Islam was used to rid the country of an oppressive absolute monarchy. Once in power, Islamic leaders attempted to use Islam to suppress opposition to their leadership. In India, Hinduism was also employed in the struggle for liberation. Gandhi's approach borrowed from the Hindu notion of self-sacrifice and Dharma in order to move a population to struggle against British colonialism. Soon after the British withdrew, the Hindu caste system caused India much suffering, and it is now used as a political tool by some. Buddhism was also used to bring about freedom from poverty. But, as took place in Sri Lanka, it also contributed to the rise of extremist nationalism and a bloody conflict with a Hindu minority. Christianity has often been used to suppress others. In Latin America, Christianity was partly responsible for oppression against the native populations. The Catholic Church there has historically been identified with repressive regimes as well. But the Catholic Church also produced a brand of theology that contributed to the betterment of the region and its peoples. Religious revivalism is a phenomenon of our times. Some resent it; others praise it. In the areas we are looking at in this book, religion clearly had both effects. Although religion can be a tool for oppression, it also can be one for liberation. What matters here is that you have a better idea about the religious cultures of those regions and that you understand that all religions are in the same boat. They are all being rocked and battered by the revolutionary changes in today's world. As a result, religious leaders occasionally fight back. Some do so by rejecting modern practices; others do so by reinterpreting their scriptures to lead the process of change. That religion and politics relate is a simple fact. That religion is a globalizing force is also a simple fact, for better or for worse.

KEY TERMS

Muslims 42
Arab 42
Mohammad 42
Quran 42
Pillars of Islam 44
Shari'a 45
Muslim states 46
Islamic states 46
Islamist states 46
Karma 47
Samsara 47
Four Permissible Goals in Life 47

caste system 48
Nirvana 48
Brahmin 48
Ksatriya 48
Vaisya 48
Shudra 48
outcastes or the untouchables 48
Satyagraha 49
Harijans 49
Four Noble Truths 50
Ariyamagga 51
Tripitaka 51

Dalai Lama 52
liberation theology 53
Gustavo Gutierrez 53
Shah 54
Seven Sisters 55
Savak 56
Tudeh Party 56
Ayatollah Khomeini 57
Dr. Abulhassan Bani-Sadr 57
Majlis 57
Guardian Council 57

DISCUSSION QUESTIONS

1. Is the separation of religion and state possible under Islamic beliefs?
2. What is the Shari'a? How is the Shari'a affected by the Five Pillars of Islam?
3. How do you think the caste system affects Indian democracy?
4. What role do you suggest that adherents of Buddhism play in politics?

SUGGESTED READINGS

Brown, L. Carl. *Religion and State: The Muslim Approach to Politics*. New York: Columbia University Press, 2000.

Diamond, Larry Jay, Marc F. Plattner, and Daniel Brumberg, Eds. *Islam and Democracy in the Middle East*. Baltimore, MD: Johns Hopkins University Press, 2003.

Esposito, John L. *Islam: The Straight Path*. New York: Oxford University Press, 1991.

Harris, Ian, Ed. *Buddhism and Politics in Twentieth-Century Asia*. London, New York: Pinter, 1999.

Jain, Girilal. *The Hindu Phenomenon*. New Delhi, India: UBS Publishers' Distributors, 1994.

Kamitsuka, David G. *Theology and Contemporary Culture: Liberation, Postliberal, and Revisionary Perspectives*. New York: Cambridge University Press, 1999.

Krishna Iyer, V. R. *Religion and Politics*. Delhi, India: Konark Publishers, 1991.

Lane, Jan-Erik, and Hamadi Redissi. *Religion and Politics: Islam and Muslim Civilization*. Burlington, VT: Ashgate, 2004.

Primasiri, P. D. "Ethics of the Theravada Buddhist Tradition," in S. Cromwell Crawford, Ed. *World Religions and Global Ethics*. New York: Paragon House, 1989.

Ratnapala, Nandasena. *Buddhist Democratic Political Theory and Practice*. Colombo, Sri Lanka: Sarvodaya Vishva Lekha Publishers, 1997.

Riaz, Ali. *God Willing: Islam in Bangladesh*. Lanham, MD: Rowman and Littlefield, 2004.

NOTES

1. For more detailed information on Islam, see John L. Esposito, *Islam: The Straight Path* (New York: Oxford University Press, 1991).
2. For an excellent dictionary of Hindu concepts, see Karel Werner, *A Popular Dictionary of Hinduism* (Lincolnwood, IL: NTC/Contemporary Publishing Company, 1994).
3. Mohandas K. Gandhi, "Excerpts from *The Essential Writings of Mahatma Gandhi*," in Manfred B. Steger and Nancy S. Lind, Eds., *Violence and Its Alternatives* (New York: St. Martin's Press, 1999), 294.
4. For an excellent discussion of Gandhi's discourse on nationalism, see Manfred B. Steger, *Gandhi's Dilemma: Non-Violent Principles and Nationalist Power* (New York: St. Martin's Press, 2000).
5. P. D. Primasiri, "Ethics of the Theravada Buddhist Tradition," in S. Cromwell Crawford, Ed., *World Religions and Global Ethics* (New York: Paragon House, 1989), 40.
6. For a good survey of Buddhist engagement, see Christopher S. Queen and Sallie B. King, Eds., *Engaged Buddhism: Buddhist Liberation Movements in Asia* (New York: SUNY Press, 1996).
7. Gustavo Gutierrez, *A Theology of Liberation*, Ed. and trans. Sister Caridad Inda and John Eagleson (Maryknoll, NY: Orbis Books, 1988).
8. For more details on this CIA operation, see Kermit Roosevelt, *Countercoup: The Struggle for the Control of Iran* (New York: McGraw-Hill, 1979).
9. For details, see Eric Hoogland, *Reform and Revolution in Rural Iran* (Austin, TX: Texas University Press, 1982).
10. See Gary Sick, *All Fall Down: America's Tragic Encounter with Iran* (New York: Random House, 1985).

Nationalism, Colonialism, and Independence

Globalization and the Nation-State

Empire by definition is a globalizing force. Europeans created empires as they colonized most of Africa, Asia, and Latin America in previous centuries. Colonization, in turn, sowed the seeds for nationalism and independence. Today, the new wave of globalization is creating new challenges for nation-states and contributing to an emergence of new forms of nationalism and universalism.

Today, there are more than 27,000 nongovernmental organizations (NGOs) that advocate global reforms. Whether it is Greenpeace, which wants to protect the environment, or Amnesty International, which aims at protecting the individual, such NGOs are slowly changing the way governments behave and creating a world system much more complex than any in the past. The information revolution has made us all uneasy neighbors on our shrinking planet.

When we take a look at the world, we find that it is divided into countries, or states. There are about 200 states in the world today. Some states are large and have large populations—such as the United States, China, or Russia. Others are small and have small populations—such as Kuwait or Singapore. Most states are nation-states. Because of that, many people have come to use the concepts of nation and state interchangeably. As discussed in Chapter 1, however, state and nation do not denote the same thing. *Nation* refers to a people who share common bonds. *State*, on the other hand, refers to a political unit commonly known as a country. As a result of colonialism, mass migrations, and natural disasters, among many other factors, many states throughout Africa, Asia, and Latin America do not possess one single nation. To understand both the concepts of state and nation, let us begin by looking at nationalism.

WHAT IS NATIONALISM?

In his book *In Retrospect: The Tragedy and Lessons of Vietnam*, the late U.S. Secretary of Defense Robert S. McNamara argued that a major lesson to be learned from the Vietnam War is not to underestimate the power of nationalism. He went on to point out that his own Department of Defense, under both the Kennedy and Johnson administrations, did not understand the North Vietnamese and Viet Cong's ability to motivate people to fight and die for their beliefs and values. McNamara asserted that the United States continues to underestimate the power of nationalism in many parts of the world.[1] U.S. troubles in Iraq and Afghanistan may be such cases.

What is this power that McNamara was blaming for America's defeat in the Vietnam War? **Nationalism,** then, as briefly mentioned in Chapter 1, is a state of mind or a feeling based on belonging to a nation. Sometimes the attachment may be to an ethnic group or even a religious one. The intensity of that feeling can, sometimes, be so strong as to drive a person to extremes. Under intense

nationalism
■ A state of mind or feeling based on belonging to a nation.

bonds of nationalism
■ Common territory;
common language;
common culture;
common enemies.

nationalism, a person who may never be able to slaughter a chicken for food may not hesitate to shoot and kill another human being in the name of a nation. People tend to become attached to a nation for many reasons. Among them is what has been called the **bonds of nationalism.** Scholars argue that these bonds give people a sense of identification and belonging. Although many scholars have discussed such bonds, their listing and order change from one scholar to another. In this book, we will list only the most significant ones. They are as follows:

1. *Common territory:* Let us say that this is time for spring break and you are now in Florida, basking in the sun. You have left cold New York behind for a week in the sun. Right next to you, a group of other college students spread their blanket on the beach while drinking cans of cold cola. As they sit down, one of them says to the others, "Isn't it great to be here in the sun rather than back in cold New York?" As soon as you hear *New York* mentioned, you are likely to raise your head and ask, "Are you from New York? I am from there too. Where in New York do you come from?" A conversation is likely to start and you may end up with new friends for the week. On the other hand, if that same person in the group had remarked that he or she was from Iowa, perhaps you would not have started a conversation. Being from the same area provided you with an instant bond with the group. Coming from the same territory makes both you and the group feel closer to each other than with someone from Iowa. Common territory, then, is a bond that gives people inhabiting that territory a sense of identification, belonging, and attachment to the territory and its inhabitants.

2. *Common language:* Say it is summer now. This summer you decide to tour Europe. While lost in Rome or touring the Vatican, you overhear a couple conversing in English. You are likely to approach them, asking where they are from and introducing yourself as an American or Canadian. "We are from Australia," one of the couple responds. Although Australia is much farther from North America than Italy is, you are likely to feel closer to this couple than you would to most Italians. You may complete the tour with them, or you may even join them for lunch or on a tour the following day. Language, then, works to bond people or to give them a sense of mutual belonging.

3. *Common culture:* Students on your campus socialize in different ways with a variety of other students. If you pay attention to foreign students, you may discover that European students tend to socialize more with other European students. They may even have a European Student Association. Muslim students are also likely to display similar processes of socialization. Even though Muslim students, or European students, speak different languages and come from different countries, they tend to feel closer to one another because of their common cultural bonds. Culture, then, whether in the form of religion, tradition, historical experiences, or general outlook, also works to bond people together.

4. *Common enemies:* Nationalism thrives on external crisis. It is strongest when the nation is perceived to be threatened. People tend to unite and work together more in crisis. When the common enemy is seen as evil, people join

in their hatred of that enemy. In the United States, as elsewhere, the popularity of a leader soars in the presence of an "evil" common enemy. Such was the case in the aftermath of the September 11, 2001, attacks on the United States. People everywhere raised the flag and joined together in their hatred of the evil terrorists. When the Soviet Union existed, the perceived threat of "the imperialist West" was a major ingredient of its people's solidarity with their leaders. Similarly, the perceived communist threat played a unifying role in states like the United States. At times in the history of nations, nationalist fervor gets so strong as to see "the enemy" in less than human terms. Nazi nationalism, for example, reached the peak of bigotry and racism to the point where "the other" was perceived to be biologically inferior—a perception culminating in an attempt to exterminate the inferior other. Thus, during Nazi rule, German nationalism engaged in the ultimate expression of bigotry—genocide. Similarly, American frontier nationalism presumed a superior heritage of the white European over the native population and the African slaves. Therefore, nationalism can contribute to racist attitudes and practices.

To distinguish one nation from others, nations have created symbols that stand for its glory. The **symbols of nationalism** include the following:

symbols of nationalism
■ The flag, national anthem, slogans, legends, and historical sites.

1. *A flag:* Every nation has a flag, and people are usually proud of the flag because it stands as a symbol of the nation. Many nations that have no states also have a flag. The Kurds or the Palestinians have flags but no states.
2. *A national anthem:* Just like a flag, every nation has a national anthem that glorifies the nation, its people, leaders, and lands. If you ever thought that the United States was the only "Land of the Free and Home of the Brave," you were wrong. Almost every national anthem praises its people as being free and brave.
3. *Popular slogans and legends:* You must have heard the statement so eloquently spoken by President Kennedy: "Ask not what your country can do for you, ask what you can do for your country." Statements like this or many others— such as "America: Love it or leave it," "The sun never sets on the British flag," or "My country, right or wrong"—are slogans that symbolize pride in one's nation-state. They are symbols of nationalism that develop over time. Similarly, notions symbolizing pride in the nation are stories and legends about the nation's great leaders or founding elders. In the United States, the story of George Washington and the cherry tree is just one example of this symbol of nationalism. In China, the legend of Pan-Ku, the creator-god whose remains formed the five sacred mountains of China, was another example until the end of the empire in that state.[2]
4. *Historical sites:* Nations also preserve certain buildings and erect monuments glorifying the nation, its leaders, or its beliefs. The home of George Washington is a well-preserved and visited site in the United States. Why would anyone want to preserve and visit a 200-year-old home if it was not for the fact that the country's first president and one of the founding fathers lived there? Other countries have similar sites that they maintain and visit.

CONSEQUENCES OF NATIONALISM

competition ■ Aids in the development and growth of nations.

Nationalism is an important ingredient in the creation and maintenance of nation-states. It helps to maintain cohesion within nation-states. **Competition** among nations helps drive each to develop, grow, and excel; nationalism is a significant force. Nationalism could be credited for the competition that sparked the Industrial Revolution and the age of Renaissance in Europe. Nationalism is also credited for the rise of the new developing countries into **independence.** Among the landmarks of nationalism are the American and the French revolutions. The Declaration of Independence in what became the United States advocated a brand of nationalism that is based on equality, liberty, and secularism. French nationalism sparked revivals in many societies when its ideals were carried to faraway lands by Napoleon's invasions.

independence

■ Occurs when a country is no longer subject to another country's rule.

There were times when nationalism took on racist tones. Nazi German nationalism, American frontier nationalism, and white South African nationalism all presumed a superior biological heritage of one people over others. In Nazi nationalism, the nation was perceived to be more important than the individual. Consequently, racial purity became a Nazi obsession and those who didn't fit became targets of a genocide campaign. Nationalism is seldom as extreme and full of hate as in Nazi Germany, but the role of nationalism is rarely absent in modern nation-states. It is because of nationalism that each nation-state has become the center of its own universe. As a result, international morality has often become an extension of national morality. What is right for a nation is perceived by that nation to be right for all nations. Americans, for example, "take it for granted that democracy is a noble ideal."[3] It is hard for Americans to imagine that any people would choose communism over democracy. Should people choose communism, it would be assumed that coercion was used to force people into accepting communism. Little do Americans know that, even though the rights to vote or freedom of speech are noble ideals, they may be secondary luxuries to others in the world. The communist promise of right to shelter, food, and health care may legitimately be more appealing to those who are homeless, starving, or lacking health care provisions.

wars of national liberation ■ Battles of independence fought by colonized peoples.

homogeneous
■ States that include a single nation.

international wars
■ Wars in which numerous countries fight, such as the World Wars.

Early Western nationalism also contributed to the rise of colonialism. In their quest to be the best, most powerful, and greatest nation, European nation-states sought raw materials and new markets on other continents. In the process, Europeans came to rule peoples all over the world. In time, those ruled by the Europeans learned from their European masters many new ideas and practices. One of those was the idea of nationalism. Empowered with nationalist sentiments, the colonized peoples began to agitate for independence. **Wars of national liberation** ensued, and eventually the colonies began to emerge as new independent states. Many of those new states, however, did not have a **homogeneous** population. Ethnic strife developed in some states, leading to internal conflicts and civil wars. Sudan, Rwanda, and Nigeria provide good examples of ethnic divisions that contributed to domestic violence within the newly independent states. Nationalism also contributed to many **international wars.** World War I, for example, originated with ethnic nationalism in the Balkans.[4] World War II was, in part, a consequence of the rise of Nazi German nationalism. Similarly, the recent conflict in the former Yugoslavia between Bosnians, Serbs, and Croats (or Albanians) is rooted in competing ethnic nationalism.

Nationalism, then, can be a force for good or bad. Recently, however, nationalism has been challenged by new developments in our world. Advances in military technology are making the nation-state more vulnerable. The rise of multinational corporations and international organizations is widely regarded as weakening national sovereignty. Transnational ideological and political movements are also challenging nationalism. In fact, global interdependence, the subject of Chapter 2, is a serious challenge not only to nationalism but also to the life of every individual inhabiting the earth. In the past few centuries, however, nationalism was a defining phenomenon that shaped our modern world. As Europeans developed their own sense of nationalism and gained military superiority over the rest of the world, they went beyond Europe to colonize other parts of the globe.

COLONIALISM

Cecil Rhodes, one of Britain's most famous advocates of colonialism, once said that Britain "must find new lands from which we can easily obtain raw materials and at the same time exploit the cheap slave labor that is available from the natives of the colonies. The colonies also provide a dumping ground for the surplus goods produced in our factories."[5] With that objective, Europeans set out to colonize the rest of the world. Both nationalism and economic interests motivated colonialism. In some cases, the spread of Christianity was a motivation. **Colonialism** has often been defined as a country's control of areas outside of its territory. By 1921, for example, Britain had controlled more than 25 percent of the land and population on earth. However, colonialism, in some form or another, had existed long before European dominance. Even Europeans were subject to non-European domination. The Huns, the Mongols, and the Turks had themselves dominated parts of Europe at various times in history. Therefore, the history of colonialism is not limited to the past 500 years when Europeans became dominant.

colonialism ■
A country's control of areas outside of its territory.

It will not be surprising if future historians look at the period from the sixteenth to the twentieth centuries as being the most significant time in human history. It was during that period that Europeans expanded beyond their continent to explore, dominate, and exploit peoples all over the globe. Now, as we moved into the twenty-first century, colonialism in its traditional mode is over. Today, new forms of indirect domination and exploitation are common. Those are sometimes called imperialism, or neocolonialism, which we will learn about in later chapters.

The legacy of colonialism is permanent. European conquest of the rest of the world transformed the colonized societies forever. Most of them were deprived of their major resources when Europeans exploited the silver, gold, diamonds, or other natural resources they came across. Many lost their own languages when Europeans imposed their own language upon those under their control. It is no surprise that South Americans communicate in Spanish or Portuguese, or North Americans in English. Similarly, the official languages of most of Africa's states are European ones. In some parts of South Asia, the official language is English.

With the language went the culture, as European cultures came to be the dominant cultural norms for many of the elite of the colonized societies. Also lost were many of the historical artifacts and treasures of those ruled by Europeans. Egyptian artifacts and mummies, for example, are more abundant in European and American museums than they are in Egyptian ones. In some cases, even many of the peoples who were ruled by Europeans were transferred to other parts of the world via the slave market. Some were exterminated. Also, very importantly, the economies of the colonized areas became permanently dependent upon those of Europe and North America. Their local precolonial economies were devastated and their new ones were tied to those of the powerful motherlands. In many cases also, Christianity replaced native religions in the colonies. The colonists did achieve prestige, acquisition of resources, control over sea routes, and global trade.

Colonialism also brought some advances. Education, health care, and transportation were improved with the advent of colonialism. Of course, the educational vision the Europeans had was a Euro-centered one that contributed to the devastation of local cultures. The enhancement of transportation was also essentially designed to facilitate European trade interests. For example, railway lines connected areas where mineral wealth was extracted to the ports, from where it was transported to Europe and elsewhere. In time, colonialism also led to the rise of nationalism among the indigenous peoples who were colonized. The development of nationalism brought with it aspirations for independence. The European colonizers initially resisted the nationalist agendas of those they ruled. Such resistance by the colonizers pushed many of the new nationalists into declaring wars of national liberation.

Table 4.1

From Colonialism to Independence: Sample States

Country	Colonizing Country	Year of Independence
Algeria	France	1962
Argentina	Spain	1854
Bahrain	Britain	1971
Brazil	Portugal	1822
Chile	Spain	1810
Djibouti	France	1977
Haiti	France	1801
India	Britain	1947
Indonesia	Netherlands	1945
Jordan	Britain	1945
Lebanon	France	1945
Nigeria	Britain	1961
Syria	France	1945
Tunisia	France	1956

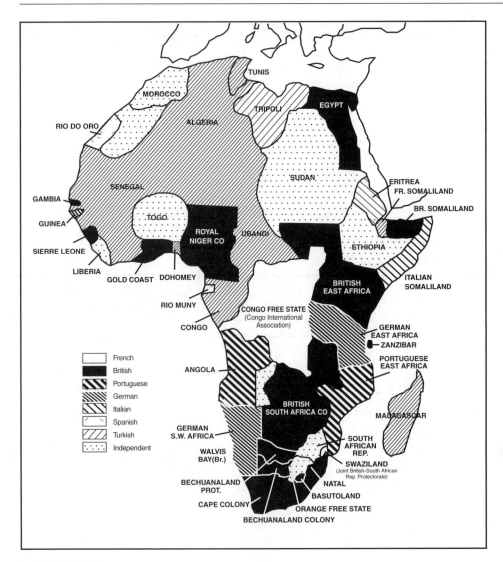

FIGURE 4.1
European Colonization in Africa, 1895

Colonialism in time led to the rise of those colonized against the colonial rulers. As nationalism developed among the colonized, they began to agitate for independence. Often, the struggle for independence was long, cruel, and very costly in lives and material possessions. For some of the luckier states, that struggle was brief and less confrontational. Let us now take a look at some examples of the colonized states and their struggle for national liberation or independence.

Case Study: India

When India became independent in 1947, it emerged as one of the "New States." It is ironic that a society as old as India's would be called a "New State." India is the home of great civilizations that spanned more than 5,000 years. That culture's contributions to human progress are significant. Yet, by the year 1600, Europeans were able to penetrate that great society and, in time, dominate it for centuries.

Trade in ancient times between Europe, India, and China had been carried on through the ports of Alexandria and Constantinople (Istanbul) in the Middle East. But shortly after the rise of Islam in the Middle East, Europeans started the Crusades against the Muslims. This created tensions that effectively blocked European access to the luxury goods and spices of Asia. The European explorations that followed were spurred on by the need to find new routes to Asia. You probably know that Christopher Columbus discovered the Americas while looking for a new route to India. In fact, when he landed on the shores of the New World, he thought that he was in India. Consequently, he called the inhabitants of the newly found lands "Indians."

Among the earliest European adventurers in India were the Portuguese, who established settlements on the Indian subcontinent and used them as trading centers. The British first approached to trade with India after Queen Elizabeth granted a charter to

FIGURE 4.2
India National Liberation

establish the **East India Company** in 1600. The East India Company set up its major trading centers in major cities. Later, the largest Portuguese settlement on the island of Bombay was given to the English monarch, Charles II, by the king of Portugal as part of a dowry. This made Bombay a British possession, which was used by the East India Company. The East India Company made its way toward political control of India by constructing large-scale forts to protect its employees from the counter activities of the local rulers. Some local rulers naturally saw the East India Company as a threat to their society and to their own authority. The forts, once established, required armed forces to maintain and defend. The East India Company brought into India its own armed forces that, by 1760, had military supremacy over the country. Thus, a British company came to rule a country many times larger than Britain. In 1773, the British Parliament passed a law placing the military arm of the company under government administration, and in 1858 the British Crown totally abolished the East India Company and took direct control of India. As such, trade had turned into colonialism by the mere passage of a law in London.

Prior to British control, India had had a thriving industry and a prosperous agriculture. India's cotton production was highest in the world and its textile industry was the envy of many Europeans. By the time the British left India in 1947, the country was in economic ruin. The British were successful in making the country dependent upon the import of many European products for its basic necessities. Local industry was discouraged by the imposition of laws limiting production or giving British companies monopoly over the sale of many products, and agriculture was turned into the production of raw materials for British industries. Those who watched the movie *Gandhi* may remember that Indians were deprived of the right to collect salt from the ocean and were required to purchase their salt and other needed supplies from British companies that had monopoly power over the Indian market. Discontent with the British was evident from the beginning. As the British began to dominate India, the local population's resistance became more organized and more persistent. In 1857, there was a major rebellion that the British refer to as the Mutiny of 1857, also known as the Sepoy Mutiny. Later attempts at getting rid of British rule were crushed. In the twentieth century, nationalist groups had emerged with the objective of achieving independence. Most significant among those were the **Congress Party** and the Muslim League. Often, these two nationalist groups worked together to achieve their common objective of ridding the country of British domination.

As you already know, nationalism can be a very powerful force in society. British oppression contributed to the rise of Indian nationalism. A great nationalist Indian leader was a charismatic and spiritual man named **Mohandas Gandhi.** As discussed in Chapter 3, Gandhi returned to his native India in 1919 from South Africa, where he witnessed the oppression of apartheid. In India, Gandhi saw his native lands colonized and ruled in a fashion similar to South Africa's apartheid. He became determined to rid India of its foreign rulers. To do so, Gandhi articulated a philosophy for nationalists resisting oppression. His philosophy of nonviolent resistance aimed at making colonialism expensive for Europeans to maintain. Soon after, Gandhi joined the Congress Party and began to preach and practice his philosophy known as **Satyagraha.** Satyagraha literally means holding fast to truth. Practically, it is a philosophy of nonviolent civil disobedience. Gandhi called for a boycott of British products and laws

East India Company
■ The British company that came to dominate India.

Congress Party
■ The major party that led the Indian struggle for independence.

Mohandas Gandhi
■ Charismatic leader of the Indian struggle to gain independence from Britain.

Satyagraha ■ The philosophy of nonviolent civil disobedience.

depriving Indians of their own resources. He argued that for Indians to fight the British while their clothes are made by them would be self-defeating. He took the loom and began to weave his own clothes. In time, millions of Indians followed suit, and the loom became a national symbol for India's struggle. Gandhi led Indians in the famous Salt March, defying unjust British laws. When arrested, Gandhi never resisted and often went on long hunger strikes to mobilize the nation and the world behind the cause of justice to his people. In sum, Satyagraha was an active means of resistance that brought world attention to the injustice of colonialism. In the words of the Mahatma Gandhi, "non-violence is infinitely superior to violence; forgiveness is manlier than punishment."[6] Gandhi led a simple lifestyle which earned him the respect of the people. Even when invited to London to negotiate India's independence, Gandhi got the attention of the British people by his modest dress and simple lifestyle. Consequently, many in Britain were drawn to support Gandhi's struggle against their own country.

Pakistan ■ A country created out of India prior to independence.

Severely weakened by the devastation of World War II, the British were unable or unwilling to put up with the costs of controlling a defiant India. In August 1947, India gained its independence. A day before the country became free, **Pakistan** was declared independent. Pakistan was carved out of India in order to give India's Muslims a country of their own. The northeast and northwest regions of India, separated by a thousand miles, became a new country called Pakistan. These were areas where Muslims constituted a majority. In 1971, the eastern part of Pakistan split and declared itself an independent state called **Bangladesh.** Therefore, what used to be India under the British became three independent states: India, Pakistan, and Bangladesh.

Bangladesh ■ Split from Pakistan in 1971.

When the British drew the borders between India and Pakistan, they left many Muslims in India and many Hindus in Pakistan. Fearing for their lives as minorities in new states, most left their homes seeking refuge in their new "homelands." This created a massive refugee problem for both countries, when more than 12 million people were on the move. Violence, starvation, and exhaustion killed about a million refugees. In one area between the two newly independent countries is the region of **Kashmir.** There, the population is mostly Muslim, but when the British were drawing the border in 1947, the governor was a Hindu. Pakistan wanted Kashmir to be part of its country. The Hindu governor preferred to be with India. Since then, three major wars have taken place between India and Pakistan over the fate of Kashmir. In 1998, both countries tested nuclear weapons. Some people fear that the conflict over Kashmir may someday lead to a nuclear war between the two countries. As such, the consequences of colonialism remain with us and continue to contribute to conflict not only in what was India, but also in many places around the world.

Kashmir ■ A disputed region between India and Pakistan.

Case Study: Algeria

In the early nineteenth century, Algeria was a rural society that found it possible to manage its own affairs. Algeria even exported grain and other products to the European market. It is said that it was this export of grain that eventually brought to Algeria the French colonizers. Historians tell the story of a French army purchase of wheat from two merchants in the capital city of Algiers in the 1790s. The French army, however, failed to pay for the purchase. The Algerian ruler, Husayn Dey (1818–1830), demanded payment to the two merchants. Instead of making payments, French merchants armed their factories in Algeria in violation of business agreements with the Algerian government. It is reported that at a meeting between the Algerian leader and the French Consul on April 29, 1827, the Algerian leader struck the French Consul with a flyswatter.[7] This insult, it is said, provoked a serious crisis that eventually led to the French occupation of Algeria in 1830.

The people of Algeria resisted French occupation from the start. The French, however, suppressed Algerian resistance to their occupation mercilessly. French settlers soon followed the occupation of Algeria. The settlers had little respect for the Algerians and their culture. They desecrated Muslim mosques and treated the local population very harshly. They soon confiscated the best agricultural land and distributed it to settlers and French corporations. This, in time, brought more settlers from France. By the 1850s, more than 180,000 Europeans, mostly French, had settled in Algeria. The settlers concentrated on growing grapes and wheat for French consumption. French wines, after all, require plenty of good quality grapes. In time, the French declared the colony a district of France. Although Algerian resistance to French rule was continuous, it was not until 1954 that the Algerian War of Independence was declared. In that year, the **National Liberation Front (FLN)** was created with the stated objectives of achieving independence and establishing a democratic and socialist state. The FLN trained its fighters in the mountains and employed guerrilla tactics, attacking French interests and running to safety. The French response was to send 400,000 troops to Algeria to achieve total victory.

The French army's method of uprooting the Algerian fighters included torture, population resettlement, and major attacks on guerrilla bases. Many of the FLN's leaders were arrested and tortured. Those included Ahmed **Ben Bella**, who later became the country's first president. The French resolve to keep control of Algeria became solidified after the 1956 discovery of oil in the southern part of the country. With that resolve came greater atrocities. Stories of torture and ill-treatment of the Algerian population gained the sympathy and support of many people in Africa and the Middle East and even in Europe. The story of **Jamila** Buhrayd, for example, was later produced in an Egyptian film and published in French in a book. Jamila was a young educated woman who had joined

FLN ■ The National Liberation Front of Algeria.

Ben Bella ■ Algeria's first president after independence.

Jamila ■ Algerian woman independence fighter tortured by French occupiers.

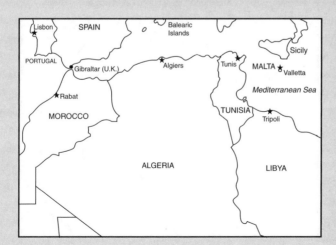

FIGURE 4.3
Algeria

the FLN. She was arrested by the French and subjected to brutal torture. Torture did not make Jamila confess about her comrades, but, with the film and the book, it made the French authorities look bad and generated worldwide support for the struggle of the people of Algeria. In 1962, France concluded the Evian Agreement with the leaders of the FLN, which gave Algeria its independence. By then more than 1 million Algerians had been killed (out of a population of 9 million), 800 villages were destroyed, and more than 3 million peasants were dislocated. Algerian independence came at a heavy cost to the country and its people. Such was not the story of independence in some other parts of Africa.

Case Study: Ghana

Ghana, on the west coast of Africa, is another state that experienced colonialism and a struggle to achieve its independence. Just like India and Algeria, Ghana represents an old civilization that had a thriving history. Archaeological remains indicate human inhabitance going back to the Bronze Age (4000 B.C.E.). In the ninth century, a famous Arab writer, Al Yaqubi, referred to Ghana as one of the three most-organized states in Africa. While ancient Ghana was to the west of modern-day Ghana, the region had a glorious history. Its rulers were known for their wealth and skills. They were masters of trade and had lots of gold. In fact, Ghana was rich in gold and diamonds.[8]

Our image of precolonial Africa is rich in ignorance and stereotypes. Many in the United States and Europe still view Africa as "primitive," "tribal," and "backward." This

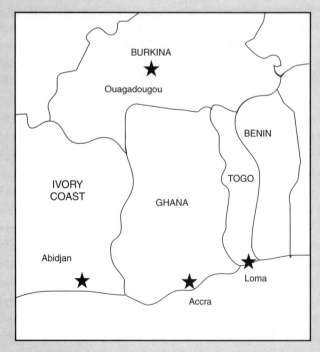

FIGURE 4.4
Ghana

is what one could call the "Hollywood Africa" or the "TV Land Africa." With movies like *Tarzan, The Lion King,* and *The Last King of Scotland,* the image of the so-called Dark Continent is maintained. A similar phenomenon in Europe or the United States may be called a forest or a national park, but in Africa it is often referred to as a jungle. This condescending attitude toward Africa is being challenged. The term *tribe* is often applied to small villages as well as to large empires and, in most cases, in conjunction with the adjective *primitive.* Are the Yorubas of Nigeria, with almost 40 million people, more of a tribe than the Swedes, Norwegians, or Irish? If not, then why not use the term to describe the less numerous European groups? If ethnic conflict in Africa is tribal, why not describe the conflict in Northern Ireland or former Yugoslavia as tribal as well? Somehow, Western media continue to insult the people of Africa. It is time for us in Western countries to diagnose our language and correct faulty dominant images.

The largest group of people in what came to make up Ghana is the **Ashanti.** Under a series of militant leaders, the Ashanti people expanded their rule and established a confederacy that became one of the most powerful kingdoms in the region. Within their empire, the conquered territories were allowed to retain their own customs, and their leaders were given a seat on the Ashanti State Council. Each territory exercised a form of internal self-rule. Such a state of affairs existed when Europeans began their encroachment on Ghana. The first Europeans to arrive were the Portuguese. Prince Henry the Navigator arrived with his crew in 1471 and began to trade for gold, ivory, and pepper. He called this area the **Gold Coast** because of its abundance in that precious mineral. In 1482, the Portuguese built a trading post, the Elmina Castle, which still stands today. Today, however, the Elmina Castle stands as a reminder of European trade in African slaves. Within few decades, as gold and ivory resources began to dwindle, slave trade became the major export of the area. Locals were captured, chained, and transported across the ocean to the colonies in the New World in return for silver and gold coins. There is no doubt that many African Americans would have roots in what was called the Gold Coast.

The British made their way into the Gold Coast by creating the **British African Company of Merchants** in 1750. This company built and manned its installations, carried out trade, and defended its authority over areas under its jurisdiction. By 1875, the British became the dominant European power on the Gold Coast. In the 1880s, the British began to penetrate the northern areas of the region, and by 1902, the Northern Territories were declared a British protectorate—meaning, in practice, a colony. The Ghanaians resisted European encroachment all along. By the 1890s, they had formed an organized opposition with the establishment of the Aborigines' Rights Protection Society, which protested unfair land laws that violated traditional land tenure practices in the society. In 1920, a British West Africa Council was formed, which demanded elected representation for all of the peoples of the region. Although such pressure seemed of little value at the time, it actually paid off in the years following World War II. The British were drained from that destructive war and soon thereafter their empire began to break away. The first sign of British acquiescence to Ghanaian demands came in 1946, when the British governor issued the Gold Coast Constitution. This constitution created a new legislative council that included elected members. Even though the council was only advisory to the British governor, it still was a bold move that gave Ghana a level of political participation not found anywhere else in colonial Africa.

Ashanti ■ The dominant ethnic group of Ghana.

Gold Coast ■ The name of Ghana prior to independence.

British African Company of Merchants ■ A company that dominated the Gold Coast.

UGCC ■ United Gold Coast Convention.

Nkrumah ■ Ghana's first prime minister.

CPP ■ Convention People's Party of Ghana.

With elections, political parties began to form. The first such group was formed in 1947 by a group of British-educated Ghanaians with the objective of achieving self-government. The **United Gold Coast Convention (UGCC)** wanted self-government "in the shortest possible time." Its leaders were arrested in March 1948 for political activism. Among those arrested was Kwame **Nkrumah,** who later broke with the UGCC to form his own party, the **Convention People's Party (CPP)** in 1949.[9] The CPP demanded "self-government now" and identified itself with the working classes rather than the intellectual circles. Nkrumah's charisma and the slogans adopted by his party made the CPP very popular and worried the British administration. In 1950, the CPP started a campaign of "positive action" aiming at general strikes, boycotts, and other nonviolent resistance. But violence did occur. Consequently, the British arrested Nkrumah. His arrest, however, gave him more popularity among his people and made his party the undisputed winner of the colony's first national elections. The British governor had no choice but to release Nkrumah and offer him the job of "leader of government business," a position similar to that of prime minister. Using his political skills and popular support, Nkrumah was able to convince the British authorities to give him more power and, in time, to create a complete political system managed mostly by elected officials. Having effectively lost political power to Nkrumah's government, the British wanted to maintain some economic advantages. Therefore, at the request of the government of the Gold Coast, the British gave the country independence on March 6, 1956, so long as the new state remains a member of the British Commonwealth. The name adopted for the new country was Ghana, an old name used by the people of the area more than a century earlier.[10] By that time, Ghana's natural resources had been almost completely depleted and many of its able-bodied people had been transported to the New World.

Case Study: Brazil

It can be argued that Brazil does not belong in this section because it had no struggle for national liberation. Brazil is the largest state in South America and its only Portuguese-speaking nation. But unlike many other parts of Latin America, Brazil's independence was relatively peaceful. Even though South America experienced colonialism before Africa and Asia, it had similar struggles for independence. Revolutionaries fought hard to achieve an end to the mostly Spanish colonialism. Most prominent among the revolutionaries was Simon Bolivar, who led the struggle in many parts of the continent.

Brazil was colonized by Portugal in 1500. It was ruled by the Portuguese crown as a colony until 1808, when the royal family established its seat of power in Rio de Janeiro. The royal family did so when it escaped Napoleon's invasion of Portugal. Thus, the Portuguese government came to directly rule Brazil as a kingdom. When the Portuguese king returned home in 1821, his son declared himself emperor over an independent Brazil on September 7, 1822. The monarchy remained until 1889, when the marshal of the army took over the government and declared it a federal republic. Brazil remains a federal republic until this day.

Brazil covers nearly half of South America and is slightly smaller than the United States. With a population of more than 193 million, Brazil has few native inhabitants

FIGURE 4.5
Brazil

left (less than 1 percent of the population). The native inhabitants are mostly Tupi and Guarani Indians. Many Brazilians are of African or mixed origin. The majority of Brazil's population today is of white European origin. Most (more than 80 percent) are Roman Catholic. The United States imports coffee, cocoa, citrus, and beef from Brazil. Many Latin American and Caribbean states had similar experiences while dealing with colonialism and its ramifications.

Case Study: The Caribbean

The Caribbean comprises more than 7,000 islands, islets, reefs, and cays. These islands are known as the West Indies. They are called the West Indies because when Christopher Columbus first landed there in 1492, he somehow thought that he reached India. The native population in the Caribbean is believed to have been close to 750,000 people before the arrival of the Europeans. Most of them perished with war and disease after the advent of European colonialism. Various European countries came to colonize the islands. The British took Anguilla, Antigua, the Bahamas, Barbados, Bay Islands, British Virgin Islands, Cayman Islands, Dominica, Grenada, Jamaica, and a host of other smaller islands. Today's Virgin Islands of the United States were then colonized by the Danish.

The Dutch took over Antilles and Aruba. The French dominated Dominica, Haiti, Saint Croix, and few other islands. The Portuguese took over Barbados for few decades. The Spanish ruled Cuba, the Dominican Republic (until 1609), Puerto Rico, Jamaica (until 1655), Trinidad, and Bay Islands. Even the Swedes ruled Saint-Barthelemy and Guadeloupe.

European rule over the Caribbean was based on regional groupings for the domains of the European motherlands. The struggle for independence was violent in some cases and peaceful in others. As you probably know, some of the islands are yet to achieve full independence, such as Puerto Rico, Anguilla, Aruba, Martinique, and others. Like other areas in the developing world, the islands of the Caribbean continue to deal with the ramifications of colonialism.

heterogeneous
■ States that include more than a single nation.

SUMMARY AND REVIEW

As discussed in Chapter 1, nation and state do not denote the same thing. Nation refers to a people who share common bonds. State, on the other hand, refers to a political unit commonly known as a country. Even though most states today include a single nation, some do not. States that include a single nation are known as homogeneous states, whereas states that include many nations are known as **heterogeneous** states. All persons identifying with a nation exhibit some form of nationalism or a state of mind in which loyalty is given to the nation they belong to. Most nations possess common territory, language, culture, and enemies. Symbols of nationalism include a flag, national anthem, popular slogans and legends, and historical sites. Nationalism has many different consequences, some positive and others negative. Thus, although nationalism may promote competition among nations that produces growth and development, that competition may spawn wars and genocide. Nationalism did also lead to colonialism or the expansion of a nation beyond its territories. It was also nationalism that led to wars of national liberation, such as the American and the Indian revolutions from the British monarchy. Despite wars of national liberation, the legacy of colonialism on all countries that were either colonizers or colonized is permanent. Hence, Britain's riches extracted from overseas colonies remain a major source of wealth among Britons and in the British economy. Conversely, many territories possessed by Britain, such as Ghana, are still recovering from years of exploitation and enslavement, both of which directly resulted from British domination. Although the transfer of wealth under colonial enterprises has always been lopsided, the transfer of ideas has been more equal because Europeans and the people they colonized equally acquired many advances in civilization. Of course, such advances came at a cost.

KEY TERMS

nationalism   61
bonds of nationalism   62
symbols of nationalism   63
competition   64
independence   64
wars of national liberation   64

homogeneous   64
international wars   64
colonialism   65
East India Company   69
Congress Party   69
Mohandas Gandhi   69

Satyagraha   69
Pakistan   70
Bangladesh   70
Kashmir   70
National Liberation Front
   (FLN)   71

Ben Bella   71
Jamila   71
Ashanti   73
Gold Coast   73

British African Company of
  Merchants   73
United Gold Coast Convention
  (UGCC)   74

Nkrumah   74
Convention People's Party
  (CPP)   74
heterogeneous   76

DISCUSSION QUESTIONS

1. Describe the differences among a nation, a state, and a nation-state.
2. Name the bonds of nationalism and describe each.
3. Describe an extreme example of nationalism.
4. Discuss some consequences of nationalism, and describe how they have affected the world.
5. Describe colonialism and the cultural, social, and economic impacts it had and still has on civilizations.

SUGGESTED READINGS

Boahen, A. Adu. *African Perspectives on Colonialism*. Baltimore, MD: Johns Hopkins University Press, 1987.

Davidson, Basil, F. K. Buah, and Ade Ajayi. *The Growth of African Civilisation*. New York: Longman, 1965.

Martin, Meredith. *The Fate of Africa: The Hopes of Freedom to the Hearts of Despair*. Cambridge, MA: Perseus Books Group, 2005.

Nkrumah, Kwame. *Ghana: The Autobiography of Kwame Nkrumah*. New York: International Publishers, 1957.

Rodney, Walter. *How Europe Underdeveloped Africa*. Washington, DC: Howard University Press, 1981.

Zeigler, Harmon. *The Political Community: A Comparative Introduction to Political Systems and Society*. New York: Longman, 1990.

NOTES

1. Robert S. McNamara, *In Retrospect: The Lessons of Vietnam* (New York: Times Books, 1995).
2. John B. Noss, *Man's Religions*, 4th Ed. (London: Macmillan, 1969), 249.
3. Harmon Zeigler, *The Political Community: A Comparative Introduction to Political Systems and Society* (New York: Longman, 1990), 61.
4. See James Joll, *The Origins of the First World War* (Princeton, NJ: Princeton University Press, 1991).
5. Quoted in Edward Goldsmith, "Development as Colonialism," *The Ecologist* 27, No. 2 (March–April 1997): 70.
6. Mahatma Gandhi, "Excerpts from *The Essential Writings of Mahatma Gandhi*," in Manfred B. Steger and Nancy S. Lind, Eds., *The Violence and Its Alternatives* (New York: St. Martin's Press, 1999), 293.
7. Lois A. Aroian and Richard P. Mitchell, *The Modern Middle East and North Africa* (New York: Macmillan, 1984), 133–134.
8. For more details on Ghana's civilization, see Basil Davidson, F. K. Buah, and Ade Ajayi, *The Growth of African Civilisation* (New York: Longman, 1965).
9. For a good book on Africa's view of colonialism, see A. Adu Boahen, *African Perspectives on Colonialism* (Baltimore, MD: Johns Hopkins University Press, 1987).
10. For more details on Ghana's struggle for independence, see Kwame Nkrumah, *Ghana: The Autobiography of Kwame Nkrumah* (New York: International Publishers, 1957).

Global and Domestic Inequalities

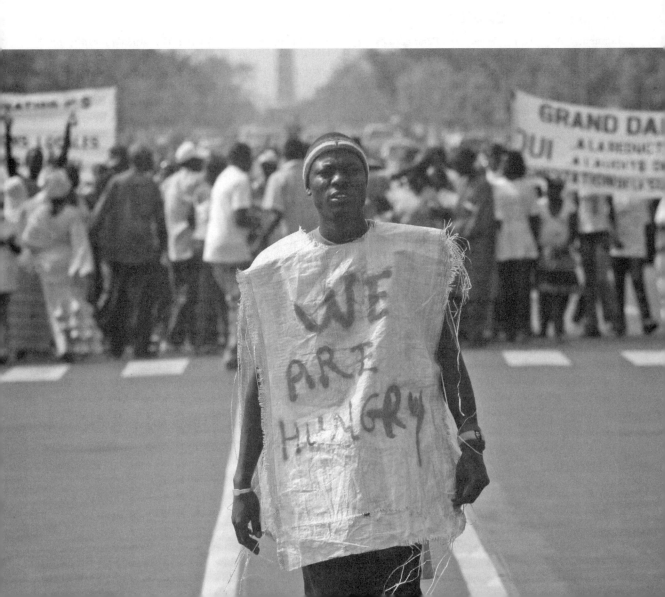

Globalization and Global and Domestic Inequalities

The global financial and economic crises of 2008 and 2009 increased attention to economic inequality in both rich and poor countries. Globalization, which encourages the growth of free trade, open markets, and competition in the world economy, is viewed as contributing to both equality and inequality among as well as within countries. Globalization offers opportunities to states and individuals. By making national borders less significant and more porous, globalization challenges the prevailing tendency to view the world almost exclusively in terms of rich nations versus poor nations. Economic inequalities among and within countries have always existed and cannot be attributed primarily to globalization. Global economic interdependence means that major economic problems spread from one country to another, thereby heightening the sense of economic insecurity as well as widening the gap between the rich and the poor. But globalization also holds the promise of greater opportunities for the poor to improve their economic positions. Countries that are more involved in the global economy tend to have less poverty and greater income equality.

D iscussions about wealth and poverty are as old as humankind. Individuals, groups, and governments throughout the world have, at one time or another, wrestled with the issue of economic inequality and income distributions. Despite many efforts to narrow the gap between rich and poor individuals, groups, and countries, the adage that the rich get richer and the poor get children seems to be supported by continuing global and domestic inequalities. The fact that inequality exists is not in and of itself the major problem, especially if the standard of living for those on the bottom is improving. In a wealthy society, such as the United States, inequality is mitigated by access to social services, training, and education. Wide economic disparities are often narrowed in a growing economy and the possibility of upward mobility creates hope among the poor. However, financial and economic crises in 2008 and 2009 challenged this view. Extreme and relatively permanent economic inequality within as well as among countries is widely regarded as detrimental to political stability and economic development. Extreme inequality, especially in societies with a weak middle class, often leads to the concentration of social and political power and the stifling of competition. As Chapter 9 shows, the existence and healthy functioning of democracy depends to a large extent on a significant degree of social and economic equality. Furthermore, extreme inequality generally negatively affects relations between the developing world and industrialized countries. Given the increasing levels of globalization, inequality among and within countries spills over into virtually all areas, from democratization and human rights to migration and ethnic conflicts. Following the attacks on the United States on September 11, 2001, poverty in the developing world was widely viewed as a major contributor to terrorism. The growth of the Taliban in Pakistan is directly linked to wide economic disparities between the elite and the majority.

This chapter examines the widening economic gap between the rich countries of the industrialized North and the poor countries of the less-developed South, inequality within both rich and poor countries, the causes of unequal income distribution, and attempts to reduce poverty. The number of poor people continues to grow, partly because the population in the poorest societies steadily increases. Colonialism and its legacies are widely believed to also contribute to the growing gap between rich and poor countries. Most poor countries, just as they did during colonialism, continue to be exporters of primary products and importers of manufactured goods and technology from rich countries. However, globalization is changing this relationship, as companies in the industrial world locate manufacturing and production operations in many developing countries in an attempt to reduce costs and be competitive. Detrimental governmental policies, natural disasters, low literacy rates, widespread hunger and malnutrition, inadequate health care, and the rapid spread of AIDS and other infectious diseases in most parts of the developing world combine to reinforce inequality between the North and the South. This chapter points out that many developing states are the most unequal societies in the world. In both rich and poor countries, women are likely to be the poorest of the poor. Instead of just concentrating on the problems, this chapter also stresses that attempts to reduce poverty are as persistent as poverty itself.

GROWING INEQUALITY BETWEEN THE NORTH AND THE SOUTH

Although living standards have improved significantly in many countries over the past century, global inequalities have risen steadily. The vast majority, approximately 80 percent, of the world's population lives on about 20 percent of the world's income. The United States alone, which has 5 percent of the world's population, consumes 30 percent of the world's resources. Historic trends indicate that the richest countries will maintain their lead over the poorest countries for a long time. The gap between the richest country and the poorest country was 3 to 1 in 1820, 11 to 1 in 1913, 35 to 1 in 1950, 44 to 1 in 1973, and 72 to 1 in 1992. By the end of the twentieth century the richest 20 percent of the world's population had 86 times as much income as the poorest 20 percent.[1] To understand this income disparity between rich and poor countries, assume that Thomas Proctor lived in Britain in 1820 and Yusuf Kebede lives in Ethiopia today. Thomas's income in 1820 would be about six times that of Yusuf's in 2009, 189 years later. Table 5.1 indicates such income gaps.

Economic development throughout Asia, Latin America, and, to a lesser extent, Africa has not significantly closed the gap between the North and the South, despite rising incomes in the developing countries. In fact, the rich countries have experienced higher rates of economic growth than poor countries over the past 20 years. Per capita income actually declined in more than 100 poor countries, many of them in Africa. In other words, these societies have less income than they did 20 years ago. This economic polarization contradicts predictions by many economists, political scientists, development specialists, and others that developing countries as a whole would eventually catch up with industrialized nations.

Table 5.1	
Income Gaps Between Rich and Poor Countries	
	GDP Per Capita (US $) 2008
Rich Countries	
Luxembourg	111,743
Norway	94,791
Switzerland	65,200
United States	45,230
Denmark	62,520
Japan	38,578
Ireland	61,314
Iceland	52,490
Sweden	52,035
United Arab Emirates	63,966
United Kingdom	43,544
Poor Countries	
Ethiopia	319
Burundi	138
Congo, Dem. Rep.	2,934
Guinea-Bissau	257
Sierra Leone	418
Malawi	278
Niger	354
Mozambique	440
Rwanda	458
Nepal	465

Source: United Nations Statistics Division, National Accounts Section, available from the National Accounts Main Aggregates Database website, http://unstats.un.org/unsd/snaama/Introduction.asp.

However, despite this gap, economic conditions for many individuals in the developing world have greatly improved. People are generally better off now than they were 20 years ago. Both China and India, the two most populous states in the world, illustrate the ever-widening income gap between the North and the South. Since 1985, both China and India have experienced faster income growth than most rich countries, especially following the global financial crisis and economic recession of 2008–2009. It was estimated that it would take approximately 100 years of constant growth at rates higher than those now experienced by industrialized states just to reach current American income levels.[2] However, the economic recession in 2009 led to significant declines in economic growth in the industrialized world, including the United States. Given the extremely high standard of living in the United States, both India and China would be relatively prosperous if they achieved half the income level of Americans. Singapore and Kuwait, two high-income states, demonstrate that some formerly poor states have managed to achieve high rates of economic prosperity through the implementation of astute political, social, and economic policies (in the case of Singapore) and the possession of valuable natural resources such as petroleum (in the case of Kuwait).

Enduring Poverty in the South

Disparities in per capita income underscore significant economic differences between the North and the South. For more than two-thirds of humanity, poverty is an enduring reality, one that is only being slightly altered by the growing economies in the South. Although living standards are improving in the developing world and the middle class is growing, the number of poor people continues to grow, partly because the population in the poorest societies steadily increases, thereby making the possibility of escaping poverty more difficult. In 2008, the World Bank changed the criteria for measuring extreme poverty. Given growing inflation, it estimated that $1.25 a day, instead of $1, was essential to escape **absolute poverty**. There were 1.4 billion people living in extreme poverty.[3] However, with the exception of sub-Saharan Africa, most developing countries are reducing poverty.

Another measure of poverty in the South is **low literacy rates**, especially among females. The connection between illiteracy and poverty is very strong. Industrialized societies are also very well-educated societies. Without high levels of education, these societies would not function effectively and would soon deteriorate economically. Just as education is essential to upward mobility for individuals, high literacy rates are an important part of any attempt to lessen poverty in developing countries in Africa, Asia, and Latin America. But poverty contains many vicious circles. Having few resources to allocate to literacy programs, poor countries often find themselves in a downward spiral of poverty. Those countries that manage to increase literacy rates are likely to attract foreign investments, reduce population growth, improve health care and various public services, and, ultimately, create more wealth for the majority of their citizens. In Haiti, for example, almost half of all school-age children have never attended school. The same proportion of Haitians are illiterate, and these problems became more severe after the 2010 earthquake. In India, where females have limited access to education, less than half of all women are literate. African countries not only are the poorest in the world but also have the lowest literacy rates.

Hunger and **malnutrition** are generally regarded as even more obvious and important indicators of poverty than low literacy rates. Seriously malnourished children and adults are unable to function effectively. Chronic hunger and malnutrition are integral components of poverty and contribute to its perpetuation. Malnutrition causes impaired vision, an inability to concentrate and to learn, greater vulnerability to disease and poor health, and a shorter life expectancy. It is estimated that almost one-sixth (840 million) of the world's population is malnourished. This number represents a decline from the 1969–1971 period, when almost 1 billion people were undernourished. Conditions have improved in China, Southeast Asia, Latin America, and the Caribbean. In Africa, however, malnutrition, especially among children, has increased.[4] But South Asia is the region with

absolute poverty
■ World Bank 2008 definition of people living on less than $1.25 per day.

low literacy rates
■ Used as a measure of poverty because illiteracy and poverty are strongly connected.

malnutrition
■ An indicator of poverty that causes impaired vision, shorter life expectancies, and increased vulnerability to disease.

the highest rate of malnutrition and where more than half of all the malnourished children live, despite greater agricultural production.

Two decades ago, every day 40,000 people died of malnutrition and related preventable disease. By 1990, the number declined to 35,000. Today, approximately 24,000 people die from hunger and hunger-related disease daily. The vast majority of the victims are children under five years of age. Where poverty is extreme, the youngest members of society tend to be the most vulnerable. Access to food is often determined by sex, control of resources, and social status. In some societies, girls and women have lower status and generally receive less food. However, when women are the head of the household, they not only allocate more money to food, but also tend to favor a more equal distribution of food.[5]

In countries where ethnic conflicts are widespread and prolonged, famine usually results. **Famine** is generally defined as a situation in which food supplies are suddenly reduced, which causes a large number of deaths. Many people are severely malnourished, even when food is provided by international relief organizations and governments. This is partly due to the tendency of factions in civil wars to use food as a weapon. They deliberately restrict the availability of food supplies in order to starve the population associated with a rival faction into submission. This strategy has been used in Ethiopia, Somalia, Angola, Sudan, and elsewhere. Conflicts also create hunger and starvation by diverting scarce resources away from food and other basic needs to weapons and general supplies for combatants. Furthermore, conflicts disrupt agriculture, livestock production, markets, transportation, and other activities related to growing and distributing food. In the southern part of the Sudan, famine and conflict, over a period of 15 years, have claimed the lives of about 2.5 million people. Another 3 million Sudanese are starving. Without the cooperation of the warring factions or the government, attempts to diminish starvation are often only marginally successful. A combination of controlling prices for food, fuel, and commodities created a global crisis in 2008. Riots and demonstrations erupted in several developing countries. In 2009–2010, there was an increased availability of food due to higher production, the termination of trade bans on food exports, and lower energy costs.[6]

Another indicator of the gap between the North and the South, one that cannot be separated from poverty, is the **inadequate health care** in less-developed countries. The vicious circles of poverty cannot be neatly isolated and analyzed. Malnourished children and adults are vulnerable to diseases, which, in turn, rob them of nutrients and their appetites. Chronic poor health drains individuals of energy needed to take care of their selves and their families, find and keep employment, and protect their environment. These problems are usually made worse by the government's inability or unwillingness to provide adequate sanitation and access to clean water and health care. Infectious diseases thrive in unsanitary conditions.

The AIDS epidemic clearly demonstrates inequality between the North and the South. With modern health care services and access to sophisticated drugs, Americans infected with HIV live with the disease for a relatively long time. Although their families' resources are severely strained, it is unlikely that they will be reduced to poverty. In Africa, by contrast, where there are few safety nets, AIDS has devastating consequences for the society and for families. When a man or woman is sick, agricultural productivity declines, more resources are allocated to

famine ■ A situation in which food supplies are suddenly reduced, which causes a large number of deaths.

inadequate health care ■ An indicator of the economic gap between the North and the South.

medicines and hospital expenses, and family members must take care of the sick person. In many cases, grandparents look after grandchildren whose parents died of AIDS. Those countries most affected by AIDS are usually the poorest, and have many other diseases. These diseases reinforce each other and become more deadly. Many of those who have HIV/AIDS also suffer from tuberculosis and malaria.[7]

Economic Inequalities Within Rich Countries

Economic prosperity in the industrialized countries often masks the reality of large income disparities among different groups of citizens. Although much of the focus is on the gap between rich and poor countries, it is increasingly obvious that economic inequality within societies, both North and South, demands greater emphasis. The globalization of the economy and the interdependence that characterizes the international system are challenging not only our national boundaries but also our perception of issues such as poverty and income distribution. Within the United States, the gap between rich and poor Americans has widened since 1977. In 1999, the richest 2.7 million Americans, or 1 percent of the population, earned as much money as the poorest 100 million citizens, or 37 percent of all Americans. Although robust economic growth in the United States has benefited most income groups, the richest 1 percent of Americans received about 90 percent of the economic gains. In fact, since 1977, the gap has widened into a chasm. In 1977, the top 1 percent had as much as the bottom 20 percent, or 49 million Americans.[8] In 1979, the top 1 percent received 7.5 percent of the national income, compared with 15.5 percent in 2000. During this period, the share received by the poorest 40 percent declined from 19.1 percent of the national income to 14.6 percent. In 2000, the top 1 percent earned an average of $862,000, compared with $21,350 for the bottom 40 percent. In other words, the top 1 percent earned 40 times as much as the bottom 40 percent. By 2000, the top 10 percent of households in America had 44 percent of the total household income. In 2003, the top 1 percent owned roughly 57 percent of the country's wealth, which includes stocks, bonds, real estate, business, savings, insurance, and other assets. Incomes in the top 1 percent of households ranged from $237,000 to several billion dollars. By 2006, the top 0.1 percent of Americans earned 77 times the income of the bottom 90 percent. The financial and economic crises of 2009 underscored inequality in America.

The gap between the rich and the poor has been widening in Europe. In Germany, for example, the rich got richer and the poor became poorer. In 1998, a single person in the poorest income bracket earned $912 a month, compared to $864 a month in 2008. By contrast, the average monthly income for Germans in higher income brackets rose from $3,216 in 1998 to $3,618 in 2008.[9]

The increase in income enjoyed by the wealthiest Americans is matched by losses among some groups, especially those with limited education. High school graduates lost approximately 15 percent in wages between 1973 and 1993. As most students know, educational achievement determines income levels to a much greater extent now than previously. But a college education is more expensive and beyond the reach of an increasing number of Americans. Americans with higher family incomes have greater access to higher education, which, in turn, reinforces their economic advantage. The poor are generally at a disadvantage in a global economy.[10] Roughly 37.3 million Americans, including 20 million children, are in the low-income category and struggle to survive financially. The 2009 global financial and housing crisis, together with an economic recession, made life very difficult for many Americans, including many in the middle class. For the poorest Americans, life resembles that in many less-developed countries.

Regional Inequalities

An emphasis on North–South economic disparities often obscures major differences among countries that are classified as part of the South. Whereas some parts of the Middle East have abundant petroleum supplies, many African and Latin American countries import petroleum. However, countries in the same region and with approximately equal natural resources often experience different rates of economic growth and development, and countries with few natural resources may develop faster than countries with many resources.

Although Asia, Africa, and many countries in Latin America were in a similar economic position four decades ago, *there are now huge income gaps among them.* Countries in Asia, especially East Asia, occupy the top position in the developing world, with Latin America in the middle and Africa on the bottom. Even though Asia and Latin America achieved significant industrialization and reduced their dependency on primary products such as oil, copper, bauxite, coffee, bananas, and cocoa, Africa's economic conditions essentially remained the same. Most African countries are marginal players in international markets, and their per capita income remains extremely low. Almost 90 percent of Africa's export earnings come from primary commodities, compared with about 30 percent for East Asia.[11] Unlike Asia and Latin America, where population growth has slowed and agricultural productivity has increased, Africa's population continues to grow faster than its food supply.

The Gulf Between the Rich and the Poor in the South

On June 9, 1998, a cyclone with winds of more than 100 miles per hour created a wall of water, about eight feet high, that inundated the vast low-lying tidal mudflats of Kandla, on the west coast of India. These mudflats or salt pans produce sea salt that is harvested by some of India's poorest people. As many as 10,000 workers died when their shacks were swept away by the water. In a country with more than 1 billion people, the vast majority of whom live in poverty, such tragedies are common. What is also common is the general disregard for the poor. Drivers who hit a cow on the streets of New Delhi face the very real threat of being attacked by a mob, furious over the death of a sacred animal. But when thousands of people from society's bottom rung die, there is a collective shrug of resignation. Workers in India are generally treated as slaves.[12] In most countries of Africa, Asia, and Latin America, there are two distinct worlds, one inhabited by the middle and upper classes and the other by the poor masses. Rich people in the developing world live like rich people in the North and are integrated in the world's economic and social system. The poor, by contrast, live in slums and marginal housing. They struggle to survive as agricultural workers, subsistence farmers, and manual laborers. Some regions are more prosperous than others. In Mexico, for example, most living in extreme poverty are concentrated in the south, in places such as Chiapas, Oaxaca, and Guerrero. There are sharp disparities between urban and rural areas, between men and women, and among castes and ethnic groups. With assets worth more than $60 billion, Mexico's Carlos Slim Helu is the world's richest person. Similarly, the Indian state of Bihar has an absolute poverty rate of 64 percent, compared to 25 percent for the states of Punjab and Haryana. In Swaziland, Southern Africa, King Mswati III, the last absolute monarch in sub-Saharan Africa, drives between his various palaces in a $500,000 Maybach 62 luxury sedan. Two-thirds of Swazis live below the UN poverty line, 20 percent receive international food aid, 40 percent are unemployed, and the elderly survive on $13 a month. In Lagos, Nigeria, where the average person lives on roughly $2 a day, the very wealthy have multimillion-dollar yachts and expensive cars. Just as countries in the North are generally fearful of an invasion of poor migrants from the South, rich people within the South are fearful of the poor at home. Walls guarding the homes of the wealthy and gated communities are common throughout the developing world. Afraid of crime, especially kidnapping and car robberies, many elite armor their cars to protect themselves. But armoring cars is also another way of displaying status and the gulf between the rich and the poor.[13]

The Caste System: Structured Inequality   The gap between the rich and the poor within countries is rooted in cultural beliefs, attitudes, and values. Just as countries of the North are viewed as having unfair advantages by many leaders in the South, certain groups within developing societies are disadvantaged because of ethnicity or social class. When South Africa was governed by **apartheid laws,** the rigid social segregation of blacks, whites, Asians, and mixed-race groups was required. Apartheid also preserved a privileged position for "whites only." But India's caste system is the most obvious and pervasive example of structural inequality. As we saw, the **caste system** is a rigid hierarchical system of social classes in Hinduism, which determines the status, rights, privileges, occupations, and social interaction of each person from birth. As seen in Chapter 2, even though discrimination on the basis of caste was outlawed in India, old practices continue.

Women: The Poorest of the Poor   Women in most societies, both in the North and the South, generally have fewer resources and opportunities than men. In many societies, the inequality of women is enshrined in both laws and customs, as we will see in Chapter 8. The inferior status of women plays a major role in their access to employment, the kind of work they perform, and their compensation. Equally important is the impact of how women are treated on their self-perception, their ability to provide for their children, their opportunity to obtain education, and their attempts to help break the cycle of poverty. It is clear from discussions throughout this book that narrowing the gap between the North and the South depends to a large extent on closing the gap between men and women.

The Causes of Inequality Between the North and the South

One of the issues debated most passionately by the international community is the cause for the persistent and growing economic disparity between rich and poor

apartheid laws
■ South Africa's practice of rigid social segregation based on skin color.

caste system ■ A rigid hierarchical system of social classes in Hinduism.

countries. There are many causes of inequality within countries and among them. These include (1) colonialism and its legacies, (2) the structure of the world economy that perpetuates the status of poor countries as exporters of primary products to rich countries and importers of manufactured goods and technology from rich countries, (3) increasing globalization of the economy, (4) overpopulation in the developing world, (5) ineffective and detrimental government policies or decisions, (6) political and economic instability, and (7) natural disasters.

Colonization, it is generally argued, laid the foundation for the economic gap between rich and poor countries. Inequality breeds inequality because wealth tends to perpetuate wealth and poverty tends to perpetuate poverty. As we have seen, countries that were rich a hundred years ago, due partly to their colonization of the developing world, are generally still rich today. However, the ability of poor countries that were colonized to acquire wealth clearly demonstrates that these positions can change. Kuwait, Saudi Arabia, Singapore, and South Korea, now relatively rich, were considered poor until fairly recently. Nonetheless, it is widely argued that colonization has made it difficult for poor countries to close the North–South economic divide and to reduce the economic inequality within countries that began during colonization.

Structure of the World Economy   Colonialism and historical experiences, as well as current practices, are seen as creating an unfair global economy that keeps poor nations poor and rich nations rich. The Scottish economist Adam Smith, who wrote *An Inquiry Into the Nature and Causes of the Wealth of Nations*, believed that governments should not interfere with the functioning of markets and that businesspersons would be led as by an invisible hand to do the best for society. However, many leaders of developing nations argue that governments and businesses in the rich countries work together to maintain an unfair world economy. They generally subscribe to what is called **dependency theory**, which holds that the South's reliance on exports of primary commodities, many of which were developed during colonization for the benefit of Europeans, puts it at an economic disadvantage. The prices obtained from their exports decline relative to the prices of manufactured imports. Many poor countries depend on one or two products for most of their income. Botswana depends on diamonds for almost 80 percent of its revenues, Nigeria receives 90 percent of its income from petroleum, and El Salvador relies on coffee exports for more than half its money. When commodity prices decline, developing states' revenues plunge.

An increasing number of developing countries are exporting manufactured goods to industrialized countries. Many of their citizens are experiencing greater prosperity as a result. The movement of assembly production out of the United States, Western Europe, and Japan to the developing world means that making clear distinctions between the economies of rich and poor countries is increasingly difficult. Developing countries effectively compete with technologically advanced countries as multinational corporations (MNCs) transfer machinery, skill-intensive technologies, management techniques, and capital to them and provide access to global markets for finished products. Many developing nations have an advantage due to the low wages workers get, despite their high rates of productivity. Another development that challenges the dependency theory is the opening of new markets

dependency theory
■ The South's reliance on exports of primary commodities puts it at an economic disadvantage.

in other developing countries for goods and services produced by MNCs based in the South. Many developing countries cooperate with one another to produce manufactured products.[14]

economic globalization ■ Free trade, open markets, and competition in the world economy.

Increasing Globalization **Economic globalization** is defined as free trade, open markets, and competition in the world economy and is viewed as causing both inequality and equality among and within nations. Globalization blurs distinctions between economic activities within countries and international economic activities. By making national borders less significant and more porous, *globalization* challenges the tendency to view the world exclusively in terms of rich countries versus poor countries. By heightening competition among as well as within states, globalization helps engender economic success or failure for groups in both rich and poor nations.

Despite the gap between rich and poor countries, many citizens of developing countries are experiencing significant economic gains and enjoy a standard of living that is increasingly indistinguishable from that of middle-class Americans. Overall, globalization has produced many benefits for a large number of the inhabitants of the developing world. Most governments have implemented *free-trade policies*, competition, and other aspects of globalization. But to compete effectively, governments are forced to adopt some policies that are seen as promoting greater inequality within their societies. For example, governments often reduce spending on social services, health care, subsidized food, and programs that benefit the poor, especially women and children, thereby increasing poverty for the most vulnerable citizens. To attract investment capital, it is argued, many governments further weaken the poor by engaging in what is seen as a race to the bottom in relation to wages. On the other hand, *foreign investment* contributes significantly to economic development, a process that is generally beneficial to the poor.

Skilled workers generally fare better than unskilled workers in both rich and poor countries. In India, for example, programmers and other computer experts, like their counterparts in rich countries, have enjoyed great financial success. Many are recruited to work for multinational companies such as IBM, Motorola, and Honeywell, which have branches in India. Global competition and free trade generally benefit most of the population by increasing job opportunities, weakening monopolies, and reducing consumer prices. Although wages in some industries also decline in rich countries and jobs are lost because of weakened labor unions, the relocation of industries from rich to poor countries, corporate restructuring, and cheaper imports from the developing world benefit American consumers and diminish inflation.[15] When General Motors or Eureka Company moves factories from the United States to Mexico, U.S. workers lose jobs, but Mexicans gain jobs, improve their standard of living, and help narrow the gap between the rich and the poor within Mexico and between Mexicans and U.S. citizens. *Globalization contributes to both inequality and greater equality.*

Overpopulation is one of the most important causes of inequality. As we have seen, the economic chasm that separates rich countries from poor countries has widened over time. We have also seen that although population growth has decreased in the North, it has exploded in the South. Since 1950, the population in rich countries has grown by about 50 percent, compared to 250 percent in poor countries. As will be discussed in Chapter 7, overpopulation results in part from deliberate personal choices. Poorer people generally have larger families. *Children are widely regarded as a source of social security* for aging parents and as contributors to the family income. Large families perpetuate poverty in most cases. Usually if children having access to education are malnourished, they will be unable to learn because hunger destroys brain cells and retards development. Forced to work at menial jobs to help support the family, children fail to acquire skills essential to escape poverty. Their own children will probably face similar circumstances, thus ensuring the continuation of poverty. Lester C. Thurow contends "people who are poor in poor countries with rapid rates of population growth are going to die in poor countries. Whatever one believes about the world's ability to provide enough food, huge income gaps will emerge not just with the first world but between those parts of the third world that have their populations under control and those that do not."[16]

Government policies play a key role in making global and domestic economic divisions. When Korea was divided into North Korea and South Korea in 1948, South Korea adopted capitalist policies that fostered economic success. North Korea, by contrast, decided to isolate itself from most of the world and to adopt a communist system of government based on norms of economic and social equality. When communism collapsed with the disintegration of the Soviet Union in the late 1980s, North Korea lost its external support and descended into famine, which took the lives of 2–3 million of that country's 24 million citizens. Government policies in North Korea produced and reinforced poverty. Accused by South Korea of sinking one of its warships in 2010, North Korea faced increased hardships as relations deteriorated between the two countries. But decisions by governments that lead to prosperity can also spawn inequality, which demonstrates that inequality is a complex issue. People can actually be better off despite growing inequality. The People's Republic of China, for example, has gradually modified communist economic policies in favor of creating free-enterprise zones. China has experienced tremendous economic growth and prosperity, especially in coastal areas. As a result of China's economic policies, some Chinese are very prosperous—and yet the majority is less well off. In a sense, these policies created greater inequality. These inequalities led to strikes by workers across China. Workers at a Honda auto parts plant in Zhongshan went on strike in an effort to double their wages. The government also supported wage increases to reduce inequality and is developing the interior of the country. In many East Asian countries, governments pursued policies to ensure both rapid economic growth and equality in the distribution of income. Latin America, by contrast, has focused less on the poor and more on the rich and middle class. Instead of investing in the education of the poor, governments in Latin America allocate resources to disproportionately benefit the higher education of the wealthy. With limited education, the poor have remained trapped in the cycle of poverty. Brazil, as we see in the case study, has made a concerted effort to reduce poverty and to narrow the gap between the rich and the poor.[17]

Civil wars, political and economic instability, and ethnic conflicts, which have plagued many parts of the developing world, directly contribute to economic disparities between the North and the South. Even though stability is not always conducive to development, as was shown in the case of North Korea, those societies torn by civil war and ethnic conflict have little hope of getting out of poverty. In many cases, economic disadvantages suffered by ethnic groups cause conflicts that send poor countries into a downward spiral. For example, in Sudan the Islamic government's unequal treatment of the country's Christians and **animists** (people who worship animals, stones, plants, and other objects) fuels civil wars that have made the country even poorer. As Chapter 11 shows, civil wars, ethnic conflicts, and political instability not only discourage foreign investment but also influence the best educated, most talented, and most financially successful citizens to flee or to invest their money outside the country. Instability reinforces the vicious cycle of poverty.

Natural disasters, such as drought, earthquakes, volcanic eruptions, and hurricanes, help perpetuate economic inequality among nations. These natural disasters destroy important economic sectors, create serious infrastructural problems, force the relocation of a large number of people, and lead to greater impoverishment. As population increases and land becomes scarce, unsafe areas are inhabited, making more people vulnerable to natural disasters. In many parts of Africa, both droughts and floods cause severe economic hardships and widespread starvation and famine, thus weakening governments and creating political and economic instability. The cyclones that regularly plague many parts of Asia, especially Bangladesh, the Philippines, and India, help perpetuate inequality by eliminating much of the progress achieved through economic development. The unprecedented flooding in Pakistan in July and August 2010 was predicted to have a long-term negative effect on the nation's economy, food supply, and political stability. Hurricanes frequently destroy major parts of the economies of the Caribbean that depend on tourism and the export of primary products such as bananas. In many ways, *geography contributes to North–South economic inequality*.

Narrowing the Gaps

Attempts to decrease the rich–poor divide are as persistent as the chasm between the rich and the poor is durable. As long as there are obvious economic disparities among people, it is likely that there will be efforts to bridge those gaps. Despite overwhelming evidence to support the adage that the rich get richer and the poor get poorer, there is also sufficient evidence to suggest that fortunes change, and that many poor individuals are able to overcome poverty and become middle class, or even join the ranks of the rich. A poor person who lives in a rich country generally has a much greater chance of overcoming poverty than a poor person who lives in a poor country. But globalization and the interdependence of states hold the promise of more opportunities for the poor of the South to improve their economic position by giving them access to education, technology, and jobs. Governments and **nongovernmental organizations (NGOs)**, organizations that are not part of the government of a nation, can reduce poverty by investing in social and economic programs that uplift and empower the poor. In 2000, the United Nations issued the **Millennium Declaration**, which advocated the achievement of the Millennium Development Goals. These include cutting extreme poverty and hunger in half, reducing child mortality by two-thirds, providing universal primary education, and achieving equality for women by 2015. It was clear that these goals

animists ■ People who worship animals, stones, plants, and other objects.

NGOs
■ Organizations that are not part of a government.

Millennium Declaration ■ Aims to dramatically reduce poverty, hunger, and infant mortality and to secure greater equality for women.

are elusive. Rich countries, facing serious economic problems, have not made the financial contributions essential for achieving them. Ultimately, however, many solutions to the problem of global and domestic inequality must be found at the grassroots level by groups and individuals. Personal choices that reinforce poverty within families will eventually reinforce national poverty. As we have seen, there are many causes of inequality. This section offers some suggestions for narrowing the gap between the rich and the poor.

Education and Family Planning   One of the most effective ways to reduce inequality is through education and family planning. Education, especially for women, has a direct impact on the number of children a woman has and their level of education and quality of life. Educated women are more likely than uneducated women to use birth control, thereby reducing overpopulation, which is a major cause of inequality. Education for the society as a whole contributes directly to economic development, as shown in Chapter 6. Countries that make education and family planning priorities usually have smaller, healthier, more productive, and more economically and technologically competitive populations. These countries, such as Taiwan, Singapore, and South Korea, have effectively reduced domestic inequality as well as narrowed the gap between themselves and industrialized countries.

Democracy May Help   Democratic governments, by definition, are generally responsive to the demands of voters and are less likely to engage in conflicts with other democracies. The poor, who are the majority in developing countries, can reward their political leaders for promoting their interests and the general welfare and punish leaders who ignore or damage their interests or are incompetent, corrupt, or irresponsible. However, when President Cristina Fernandez de Kirchner of Argentina decided to increase taxes on grain exports to redistribute resources to the poor, she engendered widespread protests and her plans were rejected. Democracy reduces domestic conflict by providing greater access, representation, and institutionalized avenues of bargaining and compromise among competing ethnic groups. Democratic governments may be pressured to reduce economic inequalities by grassroots social movements, interest groups that represent the poor, and political parties that want the votes of the poor. For example, the untouchables of India have used their political power to influence their government to implement equal opportunity programs that reserve a percentage of all public service jobs for them.[18]

Building and Promoting Grassroots Organizations   The Grameen Bank, founded by Muhammad Yunus in Bangladesh, is one of the most successful grassroots efforts to alleviate poverty. By granting small loans to women to start businesses, the Grameen Bank enables the poor to improve their lives. This bottom-up approach is now practiced around the world.

The Green Revolution   Norman Borlaug and the Rockefeller Foundation worked together to increase food supplies by developing new varieties of wheat, rice, corn, and other grains. Through experimentation with different plant hybrids, Borlaug and his colleagues were able to develop a variety of wheat in Mexico that increased

Green Revolution

■ Dramatic growth in food supplies due to agricultural advancements.

the average yield of 11 bushels per acre to 39 bushels per acre. The new plants grew faster, produced more grain, and absorbed large quantities of fertilizer, while remaining short and sturdy. This dramatic growth in food supplies is known as the **Green Revolution.** India was an early beneficiary of the development of high-yielding hybrids. Between 1965 and 1972, India's wheat production grew by 165 percent and its rice production grew by 35 percent. This revolution in farming enabled India to reduce widespread starvation by becoming self-sufficient in food grains.[19]

Even though the Green Revolution helped countries end their dependence on grain imports and become food exporters in some cases, it has been widely criticized for also creating inequalities within countries. The high-yielding varieties of grain require more fertilizer, irrigation, herbicides, pesticides, larger farms, and farm machinery. It is argued that smaller farmers lost their land as richer farmers expanded their farms. Furthermore, many small farmers could not obtain money to purchase expensive seed, machinery, fertilizers, etc. Many were unable to read and follow instructions to implement this agricultural breakthrough. Forced from their land, or staying on as agricultural workers for the new owners, these small farmers generally became poorer than they were before the Green Revolution. On the other hand, increased food supplies around the world contributed to lower food prices for many poor people. The Green Revolution also mitigates some of the major causes of inequality, such as overpopulation, natural disasters, and the unequal structure of the global economy. For example, the Green Revolution addresses the issue of overpopulation by helping feed rapidly growing populations and lessening the need for more hands to provide labor to produce crops. The Green Revolution helps with the problem of natural disasters by providing crops that are more resilient to droughts and pests. Rising food prices and the global food crisis in 2008 renewed interest in improving agricultural productivity.[20]

Diminishing Poverty Through Debt Reduction   Debt reduction can be achieved through debt forgiveness and through restructuring and rescheduling debt. Debt reduction could stimulate economic growth and foster stability. It could also influence governments to abandon excuses for poor performance and to implement social, political, and economic reforms. More money would be available to spend on programs to reduce infant mortality and malnutrition, improve educational opportunities for the poor, and build modern infrastructure to facilitate economic development and enhance the quality of life.

Government Policies and Free Trade Could Make a Difference   Decisions made by governments in poor countries have been responsible for growing inequality both within and among states. Governments that make population control, access to education for males and females, health care, and free enterprise their priorities improve their societies' chances of reducing poverty. By implementing far-reaching economic reforms, China has attracted foreign investment, encouraged domestic entrepreneurship, and reduced population growth. As a result, China has a rapidly growing middle class and fewer poor people. By promoting free trade and foreign investments, Mexico has attracted many companies from the United States. These companies have significantly increased the number of middle-class Mexicans.

However, economic prosperity for Mexicans is often seen as coming at the expense of American workers.

Development Assistance   Economic aid can help diminish poverty and enhance the quality of life in developing countries. To achieve these objectives, the cooperation of government is essential. In many cases, aid never reaches the poor. In fact, aid has declined due partly to the financial problems of rich countries.[21] Countries with free-market policies, institutions and values that discourage corruption and hold leaders accountable, and commitment to social and economic equality are generally better able to use financial assistance to help the poor. Often, however, aid from rich countries goes to serve the national interest of the giving state rather than the needs of the poor. Remittances that go directly to individuals, as we discuss in Chapter 12, are far more effective than aid in diminishing inequality.

Case Study: Brazil

Slightly smaller than the United States, Brazil occupies the eastern half of South America and borders all the South American countries except Chile and Ecuador. With a population of 200 million people and a gross domestic product (GDP) of $10,200, abundant resources, and a growth rate of around 5 percent (despite the global financial crisis and economic recession), Brazil is an emerging global power. Its global cities, São Paulo and Rio de Janeiro, are among the 10 largest in the world. Roughly 86 percent of the population is urbanized and life expectancy is 74 years for females and 68.43 years for males. Brazil is a global leader in income inequality. The richest 20 percent of the population received 64 percent of the wealth, and the poorest 20 percent obtained 2.2 percent.

During an earlier period of globalization, when Portugal was a leading power, Pedro Alvares Cabral, a Portuguese navigator, landed in Brazil (in 1500). Portuguese colonists pushed into the interior with large numbers of enslaved Africans and subdued many of the indigenous peoples. Slavery was not abolished until 1888. Brazil's transition from colonial rule to independence was relatively peaceful. Fleeing Portugal during Napoleon Bonaparte's invasion and occupation in 1808, the king, Dom Joao VI, transferred the seat of government to Brazil. Following his return to Portugal, his son Pedro declared Brazil's independence in 1822. Led primarily by military dictators and coffee exporters for most of its history, Brazil made a relatively peaceful transition to democracy in 1985.

Brazil's ability to reduce income inequalities is related to a large extent to its fast-growing economy. Brazil has the world's largest supplies of fresh water, is home to one-third of the world's rainforests, and has such fertile land that farmers often harvest crops three times a year. Brazil is the world's leading producer and exporter of sugar-based ethanol, coffee, beef, orange juice, and poultry. Its commercial forests produce much of the world's pulp, and the discovery of huge offshore oil deposits in 2007 and 2008 made it a leading petroleum producer. By the 1970s, Brazil was Latin America's largest industrial economy. It has large and well-developed agricultural, mining, manufacturing, and service sectors. Under the leadership of Fernando Henrique Cardoso

(1995–2003) Brazil experienced lower inflation and a stable predictable macroeconomic environment in which business could flourish.[22] Economic liberalization opened Brazil's economy to foreign trade and investments. Many state industries were privatized. Brazil's vast resources, stable democracy, and a market that is rapidly expanding due to a growing middle class are attracting investments from China and other countries. Brazil's companies are also expanding and consolidating their global operations. Both productivity gains and a surge in commodity prices have contributed to rising agricultural exports.

Elected as president in 2003, Luiz Inacio Lula da Silva, a son of sharecroppers, a grade school dropout, and a union leader, made reducing searing income inequality, ending hunger, creating jobs, and addressing the needs of the poorest Brazilians national priorities. Widespread poverty in the northeast of the country challenged successive governments. Under Lula da Silva, the public sector employment grew, the arid farmland was irrigated to improve fruit and grain production, and the region benefited from increased industrialization. These developments have led to a sharp decline in poverty in the region. Since 2004, the percentage of people who are classified as middle class increased from 42 percent to 52 percent. A 100 percent increase in the minimum wage and government programs such as Bolsa Familia, or Family Fund, have contributed to significant declines in income inequality. Under Bolsa Familia, which is a model for other countries, more than 12 million families receive financial assistance and are encouraged to send their children to school and give them medical care. Partly due to this program, extreme poverty has declined by more than 50 percent since 2003.[23] Equally important, poor people in Brazil help others even poorer than themselves by volunteering in soup kitchens, homeless shelters, legal aid clinics, and antiviolence organizations. Brazil also has implemented various forms of affirmative action programs to diminish inequality. Lula da Silva decided to address inequality by "democratizing" land titles and expanding poor people's access to credit. Granting property rights to millions of slum dwellers is viewed as a way of creating greater economic opportunities for the poor.

Despite important gains toward diminishing poverty and reducing income inequalities, Brazil remains a highly unequal society with economic globalization contributing to an increase in the wealthy, including a growing number of billionaires. Roughly 31 percent of the population remains below the poverty line and 45 million people live on less than $2 a day. About 17 percent of the homes lack electricity and running water, and many families live in homemade shacks by highway bridges. Violence is widespread and the sound of gunfire is a daily experience for many Brazilians. Violence by police is common, and they sometimes summarily execute suspects. Individuals who are convicted of serious crimes often are unpunished, and those in prison live out a brutalized existence.[24] Lula da Silva's efforts to distribute land to the poor have been violently resisted by large landowners. Consequently, the government has achieved little more than half its target of helping 400,000 families obtain land. However, Brazil's extraordinary economic performance and commitment to reducing poverty and inequality are contributing to rapidly expanding the middle class and greater income equality. On October 31, 2010, Brazilians voted strongly to continue da Silva's programs when they elected his chosen successor, Dilma Rousseff, as Brazil's first female president.

SUMMARY AND REVIEW

In many ways, globalization has widened the gap between the rich and the poor within countries, including those in the developing world. Although living standards have improved significantly in many countries over the past century, global inequalities have risen steadily. The vast majority, approximately 80 percent, of the world's population live on about 20 percent of the world's income. Historic trends indicate that the richest countries will maintain their lead over the poorest countries for a long time. The gap between the richest country and the poorest country was 3 to 1 in 1820, 11 to 1 in 1913, 35 to 1 in 1950, 44 to 1 in 1973, and 72 to 1 in 1992. By the end of the twentieth century, the richest 20 percent of the world's population had 86 times as much income as the poorest 20 percent. Although the gulf between the rich and the poor varies along the North–South divide, on a country-by-country basis, the gap between the rich and the poor is greatest in Asia, Africa, and Latin America. Moreover, women in the South appear to be the poorest, least literate, group. Along with great income gaps, malnutrition and famine are rampant. Approximately 24,000 people die from hunger and hunger-related disease daily. The vast majority of the victims are children under five years of age. Where poverty is extreme, the youngest members of society tend to be the most vulnerable. Access to food is often determined by sex, control of resources, and social status. In some societies girls and women have lower status and generally receive less food. The contemporary quandaries of inadequate health care, malnutrition, and poverty are attributable to natural disasters, personal decisions, colonialism and its legacy of inequality, wars, lack of equitable distribution, government decisions, and overpopulation. Ways to solve those problems include democracy, Green Revolution, debt reduction, free trade, development assistance, and nongovernmental organizations (NGOs). Integration in the global economy also helps.

KEY TERMS

absolute poverty   82
low literacy rates   82
malnutrition   82
famine   83
inadequate health care   83

apartheid laws   86
caste system   86
dependency theory   87
economic globalization   88
animists   90

nongovernmental
   organizations   90
Millennium Declaration   90
Green Revolution   92

DISCUSSION QUESTIONS

1. Discuss the reasons behind the gap between the rich and the poor. Why does it vary along lines of, for example, class and gender?
2. Does globalization contribute to the growing gap between the rich and the poor or does it diminish it? Why or why not?
3. Discuss how dependency theories explain global inequalities. According to dependency theorists, what sort of future should most poor countries in Asia, Africa, and Latin America expect, given the present condition of global systems? Will it be a future of prosperity and equality or one of failure and inequality?
4. Would government action be effective in inducing a trend toward equality? How or why not?
5. What forms should development assistance take? Should it only include South–South development assistance or strictly North–South?

SUGGESTED READINGS

Collier, Paul. *The Bottom Billion*. New York: Oxford University Press, 2008.

Douste-Blazy, Philippe, and Daniel Altman. "A Few Dollars at a Time: How to Tap Consumers for Development." *Foreign Affairs* 89, No. 1 (January/February 2010): 2–7.

Hubbard, Glenn R., and William Duggan. *The Aid Trap: Hard Truths About Ending Poverty*. New York: Columbia Business School Publishing, 2010.

Nissanke, Michiko, and Erik Thorbecke, Eds. *The Poor Under Globalization*. New York: Oxford University Press, 2010.

Perlman, Janice. *Favela: Four Decades of Living on the Edge in Rio de Janeiro*. New York: Oxford University Press, 2010.

Sachs, Jeffrey D. *Common Wealth: Economics for a Crowded Planet*. New York: Penguin Press, 2008.

Yunus, Muhammad. *Creating a World Without Poverty*. New York: Public Affairs, 2008.

NOTES

1. U.N. Development Program, *Human Development Report 1999* (New York: Oxford University Press, 1999), 38.

2. Jeffrey D. Sachs, *The End of Poverty* (New York: Penguin, 2006).

3. "World Bank Finds That Adjustment Places More in Steep Poverty," *The New York Times*, 27 August 2008, A7.

4. Phillip Nel, *The Politics of Inequality in Developing Countries* (New York: Palgrave Macmillan, 2008).

5. Isobel Coleman, "The Better Half: Helping Women Help the World," *Foreign Affairs* 89, No. 1 (January/February 2010), 126.

6. "Whatever Happened to the Food Crisis?" *The Economist*, 4 July 2009, 57.

7. Philippe Douste-Blazy and Daniel Altman, "A Few Dollars at a Time," *Foreign Affairs* 89, No. 1 (January/February 2010), 2.

8. Laura D' Andrea Tyson, "How Bush Widened the Wealth Gap," *BusinessWeek*, 1 November 2004, 44.

9. "Income Inequality Rising in Germany," *Daily Herald*, 16 June 2010, 35.

10. Kenneth F. Scheve and Matthew J. Slaughter, "A New Deal for Globalization," *Foreign Affairs* 86, No. 4 (July/August 2007): 34.

11. Michael T. Rock, "Twenty-Five Years of Economic Development," *World Development* 21, No. 11 (November 1993): 179.

12. Kevin Sullivan, "That's the Way It Is, the Indians Say," *Washington Post National Weekly Edition*, 13 July 1998, 16; and Anand Giridharadas, "Exploring the Fringes of India's Prosperity Through the Eyes of the Invisible Men," *The New York Times*, 15 August 2008, A7.

13. Will Connors, "Affluences and Chaos Meet in an African Boomtown," *The New York Times*, 13 August 2008, A9; and Alexei Barrionuevo, "Strong Economy Propels Brazil to World Stage," *The New York Times*, 31 July 2008, A1.

14. "No strings: Why Developing Countries Like Doing Business with China," *The Economist*, 15 March 2008, 14.

15. Ethan B. Kapstein, "Africa's Capitalist Revolution," *Foreign Affairs* 88, No. 4 (July/August 2009), 121.

16. Lester C. Thurow, *The Future of Capitalism* (New York: William Morrow, 1996), 91.

17. Alexei Barrionuevo, "Strong Economy Propels Brazil to World Stage," *The New York Times*, 31 July 2008, A1; and Keith Bradsher, "A Labor Movement Stirs in China," *Miami Herald*, 12 June 2010, 3B.

18. Blanca Morena-Dodsen and Quentin Wodon, *Public Finance for Poverty Reduction* (Washington, DC: World Bank, 2008).

19. Allen Kornmesser, "Changing Indian Agriculture," in C. Steven La Rue, Ed., *The India Handbook* (Chicago, IL: Fitzroy Dearborn Publishers, 1997), 123.

20. Andrew Pollack, "Mousanto Seeks Big Increase in Crop Yields," *The New York Times*, 5 June 2008, A10; and Catherine Bertini and Dan Glickman, "Farm Futures," *Foreign Affairs* 88, No. 3 (May/June 2009): 94–95.

21. André-Michel Essoungou, "Millennium Development Goals: Time to Step Up," *Africa Renewal*, April 2010, 5.

22. "Brazil Takes Off," *The Economist*, 14 November 2009, 15.

23. "Brazil Growing Middle Class Wants the Good Life Right Now," *The Economist*, 14 November 2009, 16.

24. "Two Americas," *The Economist*, 14 November 2009, 18.

Challenges of Development

Globalization and Economic Development

Globalization accentuates the need for economic development. Because human beings share a desire to improve their standard of living and acquire more material possessions, governments are pressured to embrace economic changes.

People in poor countries become more aware of the benefits of economic development enjoyed by people in the developed world. Globalization directly affects economic development because it spreads technology, managerial skills, and investment essential for economic prosperity. It also requires governments to play a diminished role in the economy and to reward private entrepreneurial activities. Privatization of public enterprises becomes commonplace. Fewer subsidies, including those that benefit the poor, are provided by governments that embrace free markets as the path to economic development. The growing ties across global markets increase the likelihood that economic difficulties will spread from one country to another. Globalization makes it more difficult for individual governments to determine economic development. However, non-state actors have considerable influence on the process of economic change.

Throughout history, human beings have attempted to have better lives. They have advocated change, and they have resisted change. The idea of progress, which is generally accepted in the United States and Western Europe, is not always viewed positively by everyone in Western societies or in other parts of the world. Even when most citizens agree on the need for improvements, they may disagree about the pace of change, about the degree of change, on how to accomplish change, and on how to deal with the positive and negative results of change. Who should benefit from change? Who should pay the cost of change? Because new ways of doing things and new ideas and values usually threaten those who benefit from the status quo, change is not only an economic issue but also a political one. Both proponents of change and those who resist it often utilize politics to achieve their economic and social objectives. Consequently, the study of development, which is essentially about change to improve economic and social conditions, focuses on politics, economics, psychology, sociology, and other academic disciplines. Values, ideologies, institutions, resources, and technology play a crucial role in efforts to achieve and manage change. Development is an uneven process. There are different levels of development not only among countries but also within countries. As we have seen in Chapter 5, the economic and social gaps between citizens within many developing societies are often wider than those between rich and poor countries. However, development is generally beneficial to most citizens. This is demonstrated in part by the Millennium Development Goals set by the global community. This chapter discusses the nature of economic development; the role of governments, non-state actors, and intergovernmental organizations in the process; and the factors that facilitate and impede development, such as cultural values, government policies, access to natural resources, and political instability. It concentrates primarily on the positive aspects of development.

WHAT IS DEVELOPMENT?

development
■ Significant and measurable economic growth and the emergence of social, economic, and political institutions.

growth
■ Quantitative increases in economic activities, including a larger economy and more money.

economic development
■ Encompasses growth and equity or human development.

infrastructure
■ Items such as roads and bridges that aid in the effective use of resources.

gross national product (GNP) ■ Total market value of all goods and services produced by citizens of a state regardless of where they are located.

gross domestic product (GDP)
■ Total market value of all goods and services produced within a country.

Development is usually defined as significant and measurable economic growth, and the emergence of social, economic, and political institutions. The emphasis on economic growth leads some political scientists, economists, and others to equate development with industrialization. In response to the narrow focus on economic growth, others argue that a distinction should be made between growth and development. For them, development is about the quality of life, environmental sustainability, and human development. **Growth** is seen as quantitative increases in economic activities, a larger economy, and more money. Development, on the other hand, is viewed as more equitable distribution of economic resources. But it is difficult to separate growth from development. A growing economy is more likely to produce greater benefits for more people than a stagnant or declining one. A more useful definition of **economic development** encompasses growth, sustainability, equity, and human development.

Growth is usually associated with the development of natural resources and the construction of an **infrastructure** to effectively utilize those resources. As countries mine copper, produce petroleum, manufacture steel, grow and process agricultural products, and make automobiles, they also build roads, bridges, ports, airports, railways, and lighthouses; develop communication networks; generate electricity; and provide reliable mail service, water, and medical services. The infrastructure—roads, bridges, etc.—is essential to development. Countries lacking a developed infrastructure attract little investment in manufacturing or services and generally suffer from low levels of economic growth and productivity. Computers are not very useful if countries do not have a reliable supply of electricity; factories cannot function efficiently without electricity and water; and products cannot be shipped on time without good roads, bridges, railways, reliable telecommunications systems, and ports.

Growth is also seen in terms of a country's **gross national product (GNP)** or its **gross domestic product (GDP).** Most measures of economic development focus on either the total market value of all goods and services produced within a country (GDP) or the total market value of all goods and services produced by resources supplied by residents and businesses of a particular country, regardless of where the residents and businesses are located (GNP). Most countries prefer to use their GDP to measure economic performance. In an industrialized society, such as the United States, it is relatively easy to measure the market value of goods and services because of the availability of relevant information and resources to analyze the information. It is much more difficult to determine the GDP of most developing countries because of the poor quality of information and self-sufficiency. Many people in poor countries produce much of what they consume, and many economic transactions occur informally and are not recorded. Another problem with determining a country's GDP is deciding what to include. For example, the government of Colombia began to include money earned from the growth of illegal drugs within the country as part of the GDP. Although Colombian officials do not have precise measurements of drug production, they estimate that the illegal trade is worth $4 billion a year, or about one-third of the country's legal exports. Government economists argue that by including revenues from growing cocaine and other narcotics in the GDP, they are able to more accurately measure the total value of all economic activities in the country. However, they do not include money earned from the processing and trafficking of cocaine, marijuana, and heroin.[1] Such calculations ignore the equity and human development components of development.

The equity and human development aspects of development recognize that economic growth is essential to achieve greater equality in society. Instead of measuring development in terms of GDP or GNP, the equity and human development components of development measure improvements in the quality of life for all citizens.[2] This means that basic needs should be satisfied. People should have access to adequate health care, housing, education, proper nutrition, a safe environment, an overall improved quality of life, and the enjoyment of freedoms associated with democratic governments. The United Nations Development Programme (UNDP) developed a **human development index (HDI)** to measure the quality of life people experience in different countries. The HDI is based on a formula that takes into account life expectancy at birth, income, literacy, and access to education, measured by the average years of schooling. The **gender-related development index (GDI)** includes the same measures of the HDI, but concentrates on inequalities between women and men.

human development index ■ Measures the quality of life people experience.

gender-related development index ■ Index including the same measures as the human development index, but concentrating on inequality between women and men.

THE ROLE OF GOVERNMENT IN DEVELOPMENT

As the discussion of theories and strategies for development indicates, governments may promote or impede development by implementing particular policies. There is a close relationship between economic development and political development. **Government institutions**—legislatures, judicial organizations, executive bodies, and bureaucracies—provide the essential framework within which development occurs. Institutions help structure social, economic, legal, and political behavior. They provide a great degree of certainty and stability. Institutions determine the rules of the game, protect property rights, and inspire investor confidence. Banks and other financial institutions can make investment capital available to entrepreneurs without fearing that they will be unable to secure repayment of the loans. Entrepreneurs can take financial risks without fearing the imposition of arbitrary government decisions that would deprive them of their property. For example, Ghana's growth rate of 6.5 percent in 2010 during the global recession was attributed to discoveries of large oil reserves as well as its political stability and good governance.

government institutions ■ Provide the essential framework within which development occurs.

Many developing societies fail to make significant economic progress because they are unable to maintain order, collect revenues, enforce laws, and provide essential public services such as education and health care. Governments are primarily responsible for building the infrastructure to facilitate development. Many Asian countries, as will be discussed, developed the infrastructure and adopted policies to promote industrialization. The Mexican government initiated the **maquiladora program,** which encouraged U.S. manufacturing companies to locate their factories along the 2,000-mile border between the United States and Mexico to take advantage of the lower wages in Mexico.[3] The Mexican government provided subsidies to encourage American companies to move to the border,

maquiladora program ■ A program initiated by Mexico that encouraged U.S. companies to locate on the Mexican–American border.

North American Free
Trade Agreement
(NAFTA)
■ Designed to lower
trade barriers among
Mexico, Canada, and
the United States.

passed laws to allow them to import machinery and raw materials without paying duties, and negotiated the **North American Free Trade Agreement (NAFTA)** to lower trade barriers among Mexico, the United States, and Canada. However, escalating drug-related violence and the global financial and economic crisis have significantly reduced economic growth.

The Classical Economic Model and Free-Market Capitalism

**law of supply and
demand**
■ Determines the
price of goods and
services.

As discussed in Chapter 5, some scholars argue that individuals are primarily concerned with maximizing their economic interests. The prices of goods and services are believed to be determined by **the law of supply and demand.** The classical economic model emphasizes competition among producers, the growth of production, the efficient allocation of resources, and relatively little governmental involvement in the market. Instead of government regulations and excessive taxation, the invisible hand of economic forces would regulate the market. The economic rationality of human beings would ultimately produce greater economic growth and enhanced living standards. Free-market capitalism or neoclassical economic theory is essentially an updated version of the classical economic theory. The neoclassical economists and free-market advocates favor low taxes, strong national currencies, the prohibition of monopolies in order to maximize economic competition, and minimum government regulations. The main economic role of government is to facilitate free-market competition.[4] Both domestic and international barriers to trade should be removed to build a global economic system. In essence, they advocate economic liberalization. **Trade barriers** prevent the free exchange of goods and services and are therefore seen by some as an impediment to economic development.

trade barriers
■ Prevents the free
exchange of goods and
services.

privatization ■ The
reduction of
government
involvement in
economic activities,
and the increase in
private influences on
the economy.

Privatization increased rapidly in the developing world in the 1980s, especially after the fall of communism in the Soviet Union and Eastern Europe. The inefficiency and corruption often associated with government-controlled companies helped to strengthen the argument for privatization. On the other side of the issue of privatization are those who benefit from government monopolies and subsidized services and products, especially food. In Nigeria, for example, trade union members view privatization as a direct threat to their job security. Who controls the new privatized economic activities also becomes a significant political issue in an ethnically divided country such as Nigeria. From the free-market perspective, the gains achieved by removing trade barriers and restricting government involvement in economic affairs clearly outweigh the costs for countries that want to develop. However, the rapid rise of China as a global economic power and the severe economic problems that the United States, Britain, Greece, Spain, and other European countries are facing due to the global financial and economic crisis are challenging the dominance of free-market capitalism.[5]

Non-State Actors, Intergovernmental Organizations, and Development

Economic liberalization, which is an integral component of economic globalization, has reinforced and significantly expanded the role of non-state actors in economic development. Privatization of numerous activities that were traditionally conducted by governments has created an increasing need for non-state actors to assume greater responsibilities for many aspects of development. In both developing and developed countries, governments embrace non-state actors as partners in development. Globalization, as we saw in Chapter 2, has profoundly altered the traditional roles and power of states. Revolutions in technology, communication, and transportation have combined to weaken states and strengthen non-state actors. Multinational corporations (MNCs) have been historically powerful non-state actors. Today we see a proliferation of nongovernmental organizations (NGOs), ranging from large foundations to grassroots groups, participating in development. It is obvious that few governments have the capability to effectively deal with the challenges of development. Non-state actors provide infrastructure, education, health care, employment, clean water, and other essential services. For example, the Bill and Melinda Gates Foundation, working with the World Cocoa Foundation, provides 60,000 Ghanaian cocoa farmers with money for training in new farming techniques, business skills, and crop diversification. In many cases, the survival of governments is intertwined with the activities of non-state actors.

Intergovernmental organizations such as the **International Monetary Fund** (**IMF**) and the World Bank (also known as The International Bank for Reconstruction and Development) play a crucial and often controversial role in development and economic globalization. Both the IMF and the World Bank stress promoting trade liberalization, privatization of state-owned enterprises, opening up developing countries to foreign investment, and deregulating labor markets. The IMF and the World Bank try to influence governments to adopt policies that enhance good governance and provide a political and legal environment that is conducive to economic development. The UNDP takes a broader and more comprehensive approach to development. Leading the effort to achieve the Millennium Development Goals, UNDP coordinates the development activities of various agencies of the United Nations, such as the Food and Agriculture Organization, the United Nations Children's Fund (UNICEF), and the World Food Program. It also promotes partnerships between intergovernmental organizations and private corporations such as Cisco, Coca-Cola, Google, Microsoft, Pfizer, and Visa.[6]

International Monetary Fund
■ An organization created to encourage world trade and international cooperation.

State Capitalism

State capitalism stresses the importance of economic competition to secure growth. Private entrepreneurs, as in the case in free-market capitalism, are primarily responsible for promoting economic activities. Unlike free-market capitalism, state capitalism rejects the idea of the invisible hand as the regulator of the marketplace and gives the government a central role in economic development. Countries such as Japan, Singapore, Taiwan, South Korea, Vietnam, and China, which have enjoyed rapid growth and equity, are leading proponents of state capitalism. State capitalists believe that individuals, driven by self-interest, cannot be relied on to do what is best for the society as a whole or to support national interests. Consequently, governments must decide national priorities, and must assist industries that will help secure those national objectives. Furthermore, in addition to emphasizing the need for economic growth, state capitalists view equity as an

state capitalism
■ Gives the government a central role in economic development.

equally important goal. In other words, they believe that both growth and equity are essential elements for development, and that industrialization and urbanization should not result in the neglect of agriculture and rural communities.

Under state capitalism, the government makes resources and financial assistance available to selected industries and invests in education, especially technical education, health care, housing, and infrastructure; it also invests, initially, in labor-intensive, low-skill manufacturing industries to produce shoes, apparel, and other consumer products for export. The abundance of cheap labor in these countries has enabled these exports to effectively compete with goods produced in the United States and Western Europe prior to the implementation of global trade rules. As the Asian economies developed, the governments supported the building of larger and more technologically advanced industries. These included ship building, steel, automobile manufacturing, home appliances, and electronics. The global financial and economic crisis made the model more attractive, especially to the developing world. China's steady economic growth and America's economic decline are changing perceptions of state capitalism.

THEORIES OF DEVELOPMENT

theory ■ Predicts how humans behave, or how things work in the world under certain circumstances.

development theory ■ Explains how countries achieve economic improvements.

Human beings develop theories as they deal with ordinary as well as not so ordinary problems and challenges in life. Parents and psychologists develop theories on how to raise children, and financial analysts develop theories about the stock market. The general purpose of a **theory** is to describe, explain, and predict how humans behave or how things work in the real world under specific circumstances. A theory is an orderly, logical, integrated set of ideas or statements regarding the natural environment, human behavior, and so on. All theories tend to simplify more complex realities. **Development theory** tries to explain how countries achieve specific economic and political improvements.

Even though we try to find the one best theory, the complexity of reality demands the applications of several theories. Consequently, theories tend not only to compete but also overlap. Most scholars reject the view that there is a single theory of development. A theory often contains a strategy, or strategies, of how to make things work, and how to achieve the desired results. The theory and practice of economic development vary from one period of history to another and from place to place. Medieval thinkers in Europe examined economic issues through the lens of Catholicism. Later, Protestants, especially the Calvinists and Puritans, equated discipline, hard work, and high-quality work with honoring God. Economic theories such as mercantilism focused on economic development as an essential ingredient of national power. Theories change to take into account new developments, changing values and assumptions, and new social, economic, technological, and political realities. Some scholars distinguish between individualist and structural theories. Individualism focuses on individuals as determinants of a country's economic performance, whereas structuralism views the structures of society and the global system as governing individual responses.[7]

Modernization Theory, or Developmentalism

As many developing countries gained their independence after World War II, many advocates of economic development believed that the former colonies should emulate the capitalist, industrialized countries to achieve economic growth and build modern political institutions. A central belief was that all societies go through similar stages of development. Britain and France, for example, were once agrarian societies in which most of the inhabitants produced enough food for themselves. As technology improved, industrialization increased and more people found jobs making things for the rest of society. Improvements in agricultural methods resulted in greater agricultural productivity, which led to an increase in migration of people previously employed in farming from rural areas to the newly emerging urban centers where most manufacturing jobs were located. Ultimately, these societies became highly industrialized, technologically sophisticated, and predominately urban and service oriented. Subsistence agriculture gave way to mass production and consumerism.

Modernization theory, or developmentalism, embraces the classical economic model and free-market capitalism. It was strongly influenced by the **naturalistic theories** in sociology and geography, which stressed the role of environmental factors in development, by Max Weber's emphasis on cultural aspects of development, and by structural functionalism, which combined naturalism with rationalism, stressed by Weber. It argues that all countries go through stages of development, from traditional through transitional to modern. These stages are also identified as (1) underdevelopment, (2) take-off, and (3) modernity. The leading proponent of the stages of development was **Walt W. Rostow**.[8] Traditional societies are characterized by ascription, fatalism, self-sufficiency, an emphasis on the present, loyalty to the family, strong kinship and ethnic groups, weak institutions, low levels of literacy and technology, and widespread superstition. These characteristics are believed to be barriers to development. Transitional societies contain both traditional and modern characteristics. They are far less focused on subsistence agriculture, and literacy increases. Village values are not as pervasive, and new social, economic, and political institutions emerge to challenge traditional norms and behavior. Modern societies are essentially Westernized. They are achievement oriented, increasingly urban, and literate, and they have a high quality of life and a great degree of personal and political freedom. The modernization theory holds that developing societies would have to change their values; adopt Western technology, economics, and political institutions; and create a climate that would attract foreign investment for industrialization.[9] Industrialization and modernization are largely perceived as synonymous. Modernization was the dominant theory for much of the 1950s and 1960s. Its emphasis on Western Europe and the United States as models of development for the rest of the world and on free-market capitalism was viewed as ethnocentric. It often ignored specific problems and conditions in developing countries and tended to treat African, Asian, and Latin American societies as a monolithic group, despite these areas' historical, cultural, economic, and political differences. Very little effort was made to understand or respect the values and cultures of the developing world.

naturalistic theories
■ Stress cultural and environmental influences on development.

Walt W. Rostow
■ The leading proponent of stages of development.

Marxist Theory

Karl Marx (1818–1883), a German economist, philosopher, and revolutionary, and Friedrich Engels (1820–1895), a German socialist and a successful industrialist in Manchester, England, articulated a philosophy of scientific socialism, which became known as Marxism. Marx and Engels developed their theory in numerous books, most notably *The Communist Manifesto* and *Das Kapital*. **Marxism** is based on the philosophical method known as dialectical materialism, which emphasizes the dominance or primacy of economic determinants of history. The essence of dialectical materialism is that change occurs through the struggle of opposites. From the Marxist perspective, the history of society is essentially the history of class struggle, with those who control the means of production or wealth occupying the dominant political and social positions. A specific class would rule as long as it represented the economically productive forces in society, but it would be challenged by another class and eventually replaced. Marx and Engels believed that dialectical materialism explained the movement of society away from agrarianism and feudalism to capitalism and ultimately to socialism and communism.

Marxism holds that when human beings lived in agrarian societies, they were dominated by large landowners, or feudalists. A class of artisans and merchants evolved to satisfy the demand of the feudalists for goods and services. When the artisans and merchants acquired wealth, they challenged the feudalists, resulting in a class struggle that gave rise to capitalism. Capitalism led to the expansion of the Industrial Revolution, which drew people from the countryside into the growing urban industrial centers. These industrial workers, or proletarians, were exploited by the owners of capital, or the bourgeoisie. Capitalism, by its competitive nature, demanded more sacrifices from the workers to increase profits. From the Marxist view, capitalism led to unprecedented economic development on a global scale. However, it produced high levels of unemployment, subsistence wages, successively more serious economic crises, and other conditions that eventually influenced the workers to unite and overthrow the capitalist system. The workers would create a socialist society, in which the state would own and operate the economy. According to Marxist theory, economic development is determined and controlled by the government. Ultimately, after the economy is developed to the point where it can provide for everyone, the state will wither away because there will be no need for government.

Dependency Theory

Dependency theory, developed by Latin American intellectuals, students, and some religious leaders, is influenced by the Marxist emphasis on class conflict. It is closely related to **world systems theory**, articulated by Immanuel Wallerstein, which views the division of the world into economic groups as originating in the world capitalist economy developed in Western Europe in the sixteenth century. **Dependency theory** sees three classes of countries in the international system: (1) countries at the industrial core, (2) countries of the semiperiphery, and (3) countries at the periphery. The first group is composed of the industrial countries in Western Europe and North America and their MNCs. The second

Marxism ■ Stresses the dominance of economic determinants of history and the inevitability of class conflicts.

world systems theory ■ Stresses the role of European capitalism in creating economic groups of countries.

dependency theory ■ Stresses the relationships among three classes of countries.

group consists of developing countries that have achieved significant levels of economic growth. The third class, the periphery, is the poorest developing countries. The relationship between the core and the periphery was established by colonialism for the benefit of industrial powers. Developing countries, formerly colonies, continue to be largely suppliers of raw materials to, and importers of manufactured products from, rich industrial countries. Instead of working to the benefit of all, capitalism reinforces dependency and economic inequalities among countries. Dependency theorists believe that economic development can occur primarily by restructuring the global economic and political system in a way that gives the poor a greater share of the world's resources. This view was at the heart of efforts in the United Nations and elsewhere by the **Group of 77** developing countries to create a **New International Economic Order (NIEO).** Dependency theory also advocates cooperation among poor countries in order to diminish their reliance on rich countries. One strategy suggested to accomplish this is the development of domestic industries for domestic consumption. This is also known as **import substitution.** Instead of importing finished products from industrialized countries, poor countries would make their own manufactured goods. From the dependency theory viewpoint, development is accomplished by a mixture of free-market capitalism and state capitalism.

Third World and African Socialism

Many developing countries adopted variations of what is generally called Third World socialism to distinguish themselves from communist societies. Unlike state capitalism, in which private entrepreneurs are the main economic actors, **Third World socialism** called for less private enterprise and a greater role for government in determining economic priorities and in running industries. The most important features of Third World socialism include (1) industrialization through import substitution, (2) protectionism, (3) fixed exchange rates, (4) the development of state-owned companies, and (5) government control of agricultural prices.[10]

Import substitution was widely perceived as a strategy for stimulating economic growth through industrialization. Starting with the manufacture of textiles, shoes, and other basic consumer goods, governments later supported the manufacturing of construction materials, farm machinery, and the assembly of automobiles for the domestic market. Import substitution gave rise to protectionism because many of the new industries were inefficient, produced poor-quality products, and could not effectively compete with foreign companies. Governments, to protect their industries, violated almost all the rules of free-market capitalism. They imposed high tariffs, restricted how much of a particular product could be imported, and prevented the importation of other goods. Lacking competition, domestic firms had no incentive to become more efficient. Furthermore, even though they made imported goods, including raw materials and machinery needed for industry, cheaper, fixed exchange rates and overvalued currencies also made it more difficult for local producers of agricultural products to compete. In an effort to restrain imports, governments required importers to obtain special licenses, and imposed high duties on imports.

A more specific variation of Third World socialism was **African socialism.** In 1967 the leader of Tanzania, Julius K. Nyerere, issued the Arusha Declaration,

Group of 77 ■ A group created by the developing nations that demanded that global wealth be redistributed.

New International Economic Order (NIEO) ■ An international platform for nations of the South to challenge the comparative strength of Northern countries to exploit weaker countries.

import substitution ■ The development of domestic industries for domestic consumption.

Third World socialism ■ Calls for less private enterprise and a greater role for government in the economy.

African socialism ■ A theory that opposes Marxism and capitalism and draws upon African traditions of communalism and humanism.

Ujamaa
■ Traditional African concept of familyhood.

which called for greater self-reliance and egalitarianism. African socialism, based on the concept of **Ujamaa,** or familyhood, opposed both Marxism and capitalism. Instead, it drew upon African traditions of communalism and humanism. The government controlled many major economic activities.

Community and Grassroots Development

Community development and grassroots development are essentially interchangeable. Other theories stress the role of government and multinational companies in development, whereas community development and grassroots development assume that the people most affected by poverty are able to improve their standard of living by using their own resources and adopting strategies that are consistent with their values and local conditions. This is a bottom-up approach to development. Traditional values, rather than being impediments to development, are utilized to promote economic growth and equity. Community development is based on the concept that people with common concerns can work together to deal with those concerns. It attempts to bring responsibility for development back to those who want to escape poverty.[11] An example of this strategy is the **Grameen Bank** in Bangladesh. The Grameen Bank is a small-scale credit program designed to help the poor, especially women, become microentrepreneurs. Grameen's founder, Muhammad Yunus, won the Nobel Peace Prize in 2006. This is discussed in greater detail in Chapter 8.

Grameen Bank ■
A small-scale credit program designed to help the poor, especially women, become microentrepreneurs.

Feminist Theory

Feminist theory emanates from the long struggle to achieve equal rights for women in Western Europe, the United States, New Zealand, Australia, and many parts of the developing world. Feminist theory, the essence of which is change, concentrates on inequality, poverty, and gender relations. It challenges traditional approaches to development, perceptions of women, and accepted views of women's roles in relation to economic development. Influenced by globalization, feminist theories broadened to include more of the concerns of women in the developing world. By the early 1980s, women were advocating the formulation and recognition of new theories of development that embraced feminism. Feminist theories focus on women's empowerment, active participation in economic development, and improved social, economic, and political conditions.

Sustainable Development

Believing that earth's resources were inexhaustible, and viewing development as almost synonymous with the destruction of the natural environment, advocates of development, whether they applied the capitalist or socialist theory, were largely unconcerned with protecting the environment and preserving natural resources for future generations. In the 1960s and 1970s, students, environmental activists, and others challenged the idea of the inevitability of pollution and the destruction of the natural environment. The energy crisis of 1973–1974, which resulted from the oil embargo imposed on the Western industrial economies by the Organization of Arab Petroleum Exporting Countries (OAPEC), underscored the need to rethink the idea of inexhaustible and readily available energy supplies. The disappearance of some animals and plants drew attention to the need to preserve endangered species and to safeguard biodiversity. The destruction of the rain forests of the Amazon and the onset of global warming motivated individuals, groups, governments, and international organizations to treat environmental problems seriously. Out of this new awareness and shifting values came the theory of sustainable development. **Sustainable development** holds that growth can be consistent with using resources in such a way that future generations will have access to them and continue to experience both an adequate standard of living and equity. Sustainable development is, essentially, about recognizing the limits of natural resources and redefining development to reflect this reality.

> **sustainable development**
> ■ Favors both growth and conserving natural resources.

FACTORS FACILITATING AND IMPEDING DEVELOPMENT

Major factors influencing development include (1) the values of the leaders and citizens, (2) natural resources and natural disasters, (3) the international and regional economic environment, (4) population, (5) education and health care, (6) political instability, (7) corruption and economic development, and (8) debt and foreign aid.

Values of the Leaders and Citizens

At the heart of the various theories of development is culture. **Culture** is composed of beliefs, attitudes, values, moral codes, and institutions. Because culture is socially constructed, it is essentially subjective. Both positive and negative factors, which impinge on development, are found within any given culture. Values, which are widely shared assumptions about what is right and wrong, desirable or undesirable, good and bad, or just and unjust, influence how countries develop. The values of leaders are usually viewed as the main determinants of development. If leaders are committed to change, development is much more likely than when they want to perpetuate traditions that reject change.

> **culture** ■ A social construct composed of beliefs, attitudes, values, moral codes, and institutions.

In Iran, for example, prior to the revolution of 1979, which created an Islamic Republic, the leaders embraced modernization, and Iran experienced significant economic growth. When Ayatollah Khomeini and other religious leaders seized power, Westernization was rejected and tradition was strictly enforced. The values of the new rulers, coupled with a war with Iraq, reversed the economic gains made prior to 1979. Asian values have been seen as the major reason for the economic success of Japan, Taiwan, South Korea, Singapore, and now China. These countries, it is argued, follow **Confucianism.** Confucian values spread from China to other parts of Asia. They include social harmony, adherence to a social hierarchy, obedience, loyalty, respect, strict morals, thrift, hard work, collective discipline, trust, and honesty. Japan, for example, stressed ethnic homogeneity and a powerful bureaucracy as important elements of Confucianism. However, these values are found in all societies to greater or lesser degrees. The United States is ethnically diverse and remains the world's leading economic power.

> **Confucianism** ■ Belief in values that include social harmony, adherence to a social hierarchy, obedience, loyalty, respect, strict morals, trust, and honesty.

Natural Resources and Natural Disasters

Natural resources play a crucial role in the initial stages of development. The United States, with an abundance of natural resources, developed rapidly. Many countries in the developing world have also achieved rapid growth because of their ownership of gold, petroleum, copper, and other raw materials. South Africa's economy was built on gold, diamonds, and other valuable minerals. Saudi Arabia and many other countries in the Middle East used oil revenues to modernize their economies. Places such as Dubai in the United Arab Emirates are using their vast wealth, derived from petroleum and natural gas, to construct some of the world's tallest buildings and to become leading global financial centers. Botswana also benefited from its diamonds and other resources. In 2010, when the United States discovered nearly $1 trillion in untapped mineral deposits in Afghanistan, officials predicted those new resources would fundamentally change the country's economy for the better.

Access to resources alone does not determine development. Without effective leadership, entrepreneurship, adequate infrastructure, access to international and regional markets, values that are conducive to development, and government policies that are designed to encourage economic growth, development is unlikely to occur even in countries with abundant resources. As will be discussed, poor management, corruption, political violence and instability, and weak institutions have combined to prevent resource-rich countries such as Nigeria, Zambia, and Zaire from achieving significant growth and greater equality. Abundant oil resources are often seen as a curse rather than a blessing. Discovery in Zimbabwe in 2010 of one of the largest diamond deposits in the world brought cautious predictions that the new wealth could be used to subvert attempts to bring democracy to the country that has long been under authoritarian rule.

Natural disasters can also impede or reverse development. Drought, desertification, and floods, caused in part by disregard for sustainable development, overpopulation, and urbanization, often have devastating consequences in the poorest parts of the world and the most economically vulnerable countries. In 1999, Indonesia experienced its worst drought in 50 years. This natural disaster, together with the forest fires caused by farmers and others, resulted in a sharp decline in agricultural productivity and an increase in food imports. This also contributed to wider political and social problems, which escalated into food riots and political violence, and instability in Indonesia. In 2010, Thailand lost more than half its rice crop due to a severe drought and a rising demand for water.[12] In 1998, Hurricane Mitch caused extensive damage, an estimated $20 billion, to the

FIGURE 6.1
Central America

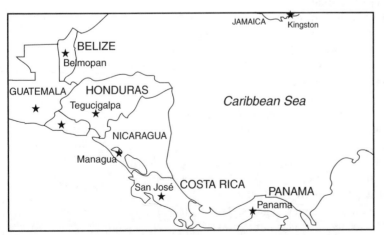

fragile economies of Central America, a high-risk zone for earthquakes, hurricanes, floods, landslides, and volcanoes. In addition to destroying homes, businesses, and infrastructure, the hurricane destroyed much of the region's agriculture. Honduras lost much of its banana industry. Chiquita and Dole, two major producers of bananas, were forced to reduce their workforce by more than 70 percent, which further weakened the economy that depended heavily on banana exports. Just before the beginning of the tourist season in 1999, Hurricane Lenny destroyed many crops, businesses, hotels, and the infrastructure in much of the Caribbean. In 2008, Hurricanes Gustav and Ike caused extensive damage in the Caribbean. Flooding in Haiti caused many deaths. On January 12, 2010, an earthquake in Haiti killed roughly 250,000 people and left an estimated 1.5 million homeless. Another devastating natural disaster was the earthquake and tsunami that occurred in Asia on December 26, 2004. More than 165,000 lives were lost, and property damage was unprecedented.

The International and Regional Economic Environment

An important component of the international and regional economic environment is **ideology,** or a system of values, beliefs, and ideas. These values, beliefs, and ideas influence economic, social, and political activities.[13] During the period of colonialism, the prevailing ideology justified the economic arrangement between the colonies and the colonial powers. When the Cold War, an ideological struggle between the Soviet Union and the West—the United States in particular—began after World War II, the international environment was instrumental in both facilitating and stifling development. The United States and the Soviet Union assisted development efforts to demonstrate the superiority of their ideology. Countries such as Taiwan and South Korea benefited from this competition. However, many African countries suffered economically and politically as leaders focused on their own interests and used the East–West rivalry to advance their own interests.

ideology ■ A system of values, beliefs, and ideas.

The economic development of a major country or a group of countries usually benefits other countries in the region. A strong American economy contributes to the growth of Mexico's economy, and a prosperous South Africa benefits Botswana, Lesotho, and other countries in southern Africa. People from poorer neighboring states migrate to richer countries to find employment. The money sent home by migrant workers can help stimulate development. **Regional economic development banks,** which provide loans for various economic projects and regional economic integration, often increase the development prospects of the member-states. Regional groupings, as well as individual countries, achieve greater economic growth and equity when the global economy is strong. Rich countries are more likely to grant poor countries greater access to their markets. On the other hand, a strong global economy may depend on the availability of inexpensive natural resources, thereby making exporters of these resources more vulnerable. Declining oil prices, for example, are widely viewed as a positive development for oil-importing countries but are usually a disaster for members of the Organization of Petroleum Exporting Countries.[14]

regional economic development banks ■ Banks that provide loans for various projects and regional economic integration.

Although a strong international economy stimulates demand for some raw materials, it also reduces demand for others. For example, the strength of the U.S. currency and the American economy diminished the need of investors to protect their assets by buying and keeping gold. As the demand for gold decreased, prices also declined. The decision of Britain to sell gold further reduced prices. The implications of this international economic development were serious for South Africa, the world's largest producer of gold, and poor countries such as Mali, Tanzania, Uganda, and Ghana. Many of them had planned to expand gold production as an important component of their effort to further their development. Between 1997 and 1999, the price of gold fell from $325 an ounce to $255 an ounce. Approximately 103,000 gold-mining jobs were lost in South Africa. Mozambique and other neighboring countries that depend on gold mining in South Africa for employment were seriously affected by low gold prices.[15] However, the price of gold climbed to more than $1,360 an ounce in 2010 due to concerns about the global recession.

Globalization profoundly affects development. Globalization has changed the way countries, as well as non-state actors, interact. It has also diminished the ability of governments to exercise control over economic, political, and social developments within countries. Economic globalization also means that a crisis in one region usually affects other regions. For example, the Asian economic crisis of the late 1990s negatively affected Africa, Latin America, and other parts of the world.

However, between 2002 and 2010, developing economies grew two and a half times as fast as developed economies. Globalization makes it easier for countries to develop if they have the essential technology and skills. Industries, or divisions of industries, can be located virtually anywhere and, contrary to the view of dependency theorists, the hierarchy of core and periphery is becoming less meaningful. Companies from rich countries transfer assembly plants and information technology to developing countries that have the necessary infrastructure and skills. India, for example, is fast becoming an important center in the computer-dominated world. Location is largely irrelevant in the new global society. Companies reduce data-processing and other computer-related costs by moving their operations to India.[16]

Population

The size and growth rate of a country's population directly affect its development. A small population can impede development. Fewer consumers generally influence businesses to increase prices so as to cover their basic operating costs. A small population is also likely to discourage most investments, partly because of the inability of a country with fewer people to provide the infrastructure essential for industries to operate. Educational, health, recreational, and shopping facilities require a sufficient number of users to make them economical. In other words, small populations may prevent the realization of **economies of scale.** Economies of scale deal with the relationship between output and costs. Industries and organizations that are larger generally have a greater output and lower production costs. Most countries solve problems associated with small populations by pooling their resources and cooperating to achieve economies of scale. Inexpensive transportation and the revolution in communications technology have enabled places with small populations to diminish their disadvantages.

economies of scale
■ Theory concerned with the relationship between output and costs.

Overpopulated countries are generally poor. Most of the societies with the largest populations and the highest growth rates are in the developing world. Roughly 97 percent of the growth of the world's population is occurring in Africa, Asia, and Latin America. Industrialized countries, such as Japan and countries in Western Europe, are experiencing declining growth rates and an aging population, which also have implications for development. An older population generally requires more expensive care than a younger population, but the strength of industrial economies and controlled immigration from the developing countries reduce the likelihood of serious economic problems arising in rich societies. The demographic differences between rich and poor countries are shown in Table 6.1.

Table 6.1

Demographic Trends

	Total Population (Million)			Annual Population Growth Rate (%)		Population Aged 65 and Above (as % of Total)	
	1975	2009	2015	1975–2005	2009	2005	2009
United States	220.2	307	329.7	1.0	0.98	12.2	12.8
Japan	111.5	127.1	126.6	0.5	−0.19	19.7	22.2
Sweden	8.2	9.1	9.4	0.3	0.2	17.2	18.8
United Kingdom	56.2	61.1	62.8	0.2	0.3	16.1	16.2
France	52.7	62.1	63.7	0.5	0.5	16.3	16.4
Germany	78.7	82.3	81.8	0.2	−0.1	18.8	20.3
Italy	55.4	58.1	59.0	0.2	−0.05	19.7	20.2
Venezuela	12.7	26.8	31.3	2.5	1.5	5.0	5.2
Mexico	60.7	111.2	115.8	1.8	1.1	5.8	6.2
Thailand	42.2	65.9	66.8	1.3	0.6	7.8	8.7
Philippines	42.0	97.9	101.1	2.3	1.9	3.8	4.1
Saudi Arabia	7.3	28.6	29.3	3.9	1.8	2.8	2.5
Brazil	108.1	198.7	210.0	1.8	1.2	6.1	6.4
China	927.8	1338.6	1388.6	1.2	0.7	7.7	8.1
Indonesia	135.4	240.3	251.6	1.7	1.1	5.5	6.0
Egypt	39.2	83.1	86.2	2.1	1.6	4.8	4.8
India	613.8	1166.1	1302.5	2.0	1.5	5.0	5.3
Ghana	10.3	23.8	27.3	2.6	1.9	3.6	3.6
Pakistan	68.3	176.2	190.7	2.8	1.9	3.9	4.2
Nigeria	61.2	149.2	175.7	2.8	2.0	2.9	3.1
Bangladesh	79.0	156.1	180.1	2.2	1.3	3.5	4.0
Zambia	5.0	11.9	13.8	2.7	1.6	2.9	2.3
Ethiopia	34.2	85.2	101.0	2.9	3.2	2.8	2.7

Source: United Nations Development Programme, *Human Development Report 2009* (New York: Palgrave Macmillan, 2009); and Central Intelligence Agency, *The CIA World Factbook 2010* (New York: Skyhorse Publishing, 2009).

In India, where roughly 360 million people live in dire poverty and 400 million people are illiterate, the population grows by about 33 persons a minute, 2,000 an hour, or 48,000 per day. By 2025, India will surpass China as the world's most populous country, with about 1.5 billion people, compared with China's 1.4 billion people. Asia alone, with the world's highest poverty rates, will account for more than half of the increase in the world's population in the next 50 years. China and India alone account for one out of every three children added to the global population. Africa is also growing rapidly, despite the devastating effects of AIDS. Comparing Europe and Africa illustrates the problem. Europe's population was three times larger than Africa's in 1900. By 2050, Africa will have more than three times the population of Europe.[17]

carrying capacity
■ The maximum number of humans and animals a given area can support without creating irreversible destruction.

The rate of population change threatens the earth's carrying capacity. **Carrying capacity** refers to the maximum number of humans or animals a given area can support without creating irreversible destruction of the environment and, ultimately, of humans and animals themselves. Carrying capacity depends not just on the amount of available resources but also on the values of the population. This means that overpopulation is a problem for rich countries as well as poor countries, depending on how they utilize their resources. Because rich countries consume more than poor countries, rich countries overtax the world's resources despite their smaller populations. Education, especially for women, plays a crucial role in reducing fertility rates. It helps to determine other factors affecting population growth rates such as contraceptive usage, the age of marriage and childbearing, social status, employment opportunities outside the home, and residence. Educated women usually postpone childbearing, acquire information about their societies and cultures, become more aware of both employment opportunities and social options, are less constrained by traditional values, are more likely to use effective contraceptives, and exercise greater control over their economic and reproductive lives. Educated women have fewer children because they realize that in order to provide their offspring with a standard of living similar to or higher than their own they will have to budget their resources carefully and concentrate them on a small family. Urban residents have fewer children, whereas women who work in agriculture in rural areas have larger families. Apart from the constraints of tradition, women in rural areas are likely to be less educated than women who live in cities.[18]

one child policy
■ Deng Xiao Ping's policy that limited couples to having one child.

Government policies also promote population control in order to accelerate economic development. Although most countries rely on education to convince women in particular to have fewer children, India and China have adopted more aggressive approaches to control population growth. During the 1970s, Prime Minister Indira Gandhi of India implemented policies that allowed forced mass sterilization, an approach that Indians violently rejected. When Deng Xiao Ping decided to reform China's economy in 1979, he implemented the **one child policy.** China established a State Family Planning Bureau to formulate policies and procedures for enforcing the one child policy. Family planning committees at the local level are responsible for rewarding those who comply and punishing those who violate the One Child Pledge. However, although the one child policy is still officially in place, it has in practice been virtually abandoned because it is largely unenforceable in the cities and about 100 million Chinese are constantly migrating. Under the one child policy, a couple can have only one child, except in the following cases: (1) The first child has a defect. (2) In the case of remarriage, one partner does not have a child. (3) The couple is involved in a job such as mining. (4) Both partners come from families with one child. Women are encouraged, and sometimes forced, to be sterilized, especially after the birth of a second child. Women are often pressured to have abortions. Failure to comply with the one child policy may result in loss of benefits for the first child, fines, loss of state employment, and seizure of property. Those who comply receive a monthly stipend until the child is 14 years old; get preferential treatment when applying for housing, education, and health benefits for the child; and are granted a pension when they are old. In rural areas, where the one child policy is less rigidly enforced and often ignored, those who comply may receive a larger allocation of land, which is owned and controlled by the government.[19] China is concerned about a shortage of girls and a rapidly aging population.

Education and Health Care

As discussed in Chapter 5, rich societies are distinguished from poor not only by measures such as per capita income and GDP but also by the number of physicians and nurses, access to clean water, sanitation, and literacy rates. Education is an essential foundation of development. Advances in agricultural productivity, the invention of industrial technologies and labor-saving devices, the growth of entrepreneurship, and the development of a productive labor force depend on access to information and training. Education challenges traditional values and social arrangements, empowers both women and men, and helps individuals actively participate in shaping their societies. Basic education allows farmers to read instructions for using modern agricultural techniques, enables them to develop effective marketing strategies, and improves their ability to obtain more resources from the government. American farmers are extremely successful partly because of their educational achievements, whereas African farmers are the least productive.[20]

Many developing countries are caught in a vicious cycle of poor health and widespread poverty. Poor health reduces productivity, impedes access to education, limits mobility, diminishes employment opportunities, and places a severe economic and social burden on families and on the society as a whole. Countries in Asia that have experienced rapid industrialization have heavily subsidized health care. They realized that an unhealthy population is detrimental to achieving economic development. Africa, the least developed continent, is plagued by diseases that have impeded both agricultural growth and industrialization. Africa's poverty reinforces its health problems. Few Africans can afford to buy drugs to treat diseases. Throughout the developing world, AIDS is severely undermining economic development efforts. India, Cambodia, China, Thailand, Brazil, Haiti, and most countries in Africa are seriously affected by the AIDS epidemic. Cultural values, inadequate medical resources, and low levels of education contribute to the rapid spread of AIDS in poor countries in general and in Africa in particular. Of the 34 million people with AIDS worldwide, 25 million are in Africa. More than 5,000 people with AIDS die each day in Africa. It is estimated that by 2007 more people in Africa had died from AIDS than from the bubonic plague that killed 20 million people in Europe in the fourteenth century.[21]

AIDS is undoubtedly one of the most serious threats to Africa's development. It reduces valuable human resources, increases health and welfare costs, diverts resources away from productive investments, destroys communities, and further contributes to the economic and social marginalization of Africa. Asia, where AIDS is growing the fastest, will soon face many of the economic problems now confronting Africa. At Zambia's largest cement company, absenteeism has increased dramatically since 1992. Uganda's railroad company loses 15 percent of its workforce each year. Barclay's Bank of Zambia has lost about 25 percent of its senior managers to AIDS. Forty percent of Uganda's military forces are infected with AIDS. Classrooms in Malawi are deserted because a third of the teachers have AIDS. Rural areas are also suffering. Many farmers are too sick to grow crops to feed their families, and many family members are too busy caring for those infected with AIDS to cultivate the land. Malnutrition is increasing, making more people vulnerable to contracting a variety of diseases. In 1998, for example, the production of corn by Zimbabwe's small farmers dropped by 61 percent because of illness and death from AIDS. Anti-AIDS campaigns have been launched throughout the developing world. Roughly 55 million people are expected to need anti-AIDS drugs by the year 2030.[22]

Political Instability

Political instability and violence stifle development and have forced countries into economic decline. However, the process of development itself sometimes creates instability and violence, largely by destroying old institutions and values before new ones can be built to replace them and by bringing different groups into closer physical proximity. The challenge of development is to manage the forces of change that cause instability and violence while strengthening political, social, and economic institutions to achieve economic growth and social equity.

Political instability reinforces other impediments to development. Violence and instability have forced the best-educated and most talented citizens to leave, taking with them financial resources and skills essential for development. Civil wars increase risks for investors, destroy personal and state-owned property, seriously disrupt agricultural productivity and industrial activities, make normal trading arrangements difficult, disrupt communications by destroying the infrastructure, and consume valuable scarce natural resources. Nigeria, a country with abundant natural resources, has experienced long periods of instability since its independence. In the late 1960s, it fought a civil war in which roughly 1.5 million people died. The Ibo, one of three main ethnic groups in the country, attempted to form a separate country, called **Biafra.** This part of the country, the eastern region, has large supplies of petroleum. Control over petroleum would have enabled Biafra to prosper as an independent country but would have harmed the rest of Nigeria. The government has deliberately kept the Niger Delta underdeveloped. The Delta produces about 2 million barrels of oil daily. Environmental degradation is widespread. Residents of the Niger Delta resorted to violence to change their situation. They routinely kidnapped oil workers, damaged oil pipelines, and took over oil stations. In 2009, violence ended when fighters agreed to surrender their weapons and to participate in the government's amnesty program. They were promised stipends, training, and jobs.[23] To safeguard the oil industry, Western oil companies that operate in the

Biafra ■ The eastern region of Nigeria that has large supplies of petroleum.

Delta provide electricity and water, and build roads, bridges, schools, and hospitals—services for which governments are usually responsible.

Political incompetency in India is blamed for thwarting development of the country's transportation network, particularly rail lines, at a time when India is poised in other ways to become a major source of new global economic growth.

Corruption and Economic Development

A formidable obstacle to economic growth and social equity is widespread corruption. Many societies fail to achieve high levels of development precisely because corruption drains scarce resources away from vital public services and infrastructure projects. Much of the illegally obtained money is invested abroad to protect it—money that could be invested at home. Prime ministers, presidents, civil servants, politicians, and average citizens participate in bureaucratic corruption. **Bureaucratic corruption** is the illegal use of an official position or title for private gain.[24] This may include using your office to obtain bribes, stealing state property, embezzling public money, hiring your relatives for government jobs, and selectively enforcing the law or the delivery of public services.

bureaucratic corruption ■ The illegal use of an official position or title for personal gain.

Corruption makes everything in a society more expensive for most citizens. The average person has to pay public officials just to receive basic services. Citizens also have to pay higher prices for food, construction materials, automobiles, and other consumer goods because government officials cooperate with local businesspeople to overcharge the public or demand illegal payments from merchants. Customs officials usually must be bribed for individuals and companies to conduct legal and illegal trade. Bureaucratic corruption robs the state of money directly and indirectly. In some cases, corrupt officials simply take money from various government enterprises or they pocket money that was allocated to build schools or bridges. In other cases, kickbacks and other illegal payments to officials drive up the cost of government contracts, equipment, and supplies. Roads may be poorly constructed, inferior materials may be used for building, and the state may be routinely overcharged for services. Official corruption spills over into the general population and becomes a way of life. Ultimately, costs escalate for almost everyone, cynicism grows, and political and social discourse that is essential for development is stifled because of repressive tactics that accompany corruption. A culture of secrecy, fear, dishonesty, and distrust is deeply embedded in the society from top to bottom. Social, economic, and political institutions are weakened.

There are several reasons for corruption in Africa, Asia, and Latin America: (1) Public officials are not held accountable for their actions by the people. Low levels of political participation, high levels of illiteracy, and other social and economic problems prevent the emergence of responsible governance, or **good governance.** (2) Public servants believe that employment in government is more about private gain than public service. (3) Growing economic hardship is another reason for corruption. In many developing countries, public servants have to wait several months before they are paid because the government does not have any money or paying public servants is not a priority. Many public servants engage in corrupt activities to maintain their economic status or to survive. (4) Because politicians also engage in corruption, average persons find it easy to justify their own illegal behavior. (5) Values also contribute

good governance ■ Responsible, responsive, and accountable government.

to corruption. What is usually seen as corruption in industrialized countries may be regarded as a legitimate social transaction. Loyalty to family, friends, and ethnic groups is still strong in most developing societies. (6) Finally, corruption is widespread because governments control much of the economy.[25]

Nigeria has been consistently rated as one of the most corrupt countries in the world by **Transparency International,** a Belgian-based organization that monitors corruption. Nigerians generally regard corruption as a way of life, despite repeated promises by government officials and politicians to eliminate it. Despite its abundant natural resources, Nigeria has been declining economically. South Africa also suffers from widespread corruption, especially in government. Police openly solicit bribes, criminal files often disappear from court, many public contracts are obtained through kickbacks, welfare benefits are stolen by officials, and public funds often disappear.[26] Corruption has caused gasoline shortages in a country that is a major oil producer and exporter. Because corrupt officials diverted more than $2 billion from state-owned refineries, refineries were unable to function and gas pipelines were never completed. As a result, Nigeria was forced to import refined fuels at higher costs and Nigerians waited in mile-long lines for gas.

In India, billions of dollars are stolen from the government's power stations. Customers bribe electrical company workers to slow down the meters, and bureaucrats and politicians sell jobs to supervising engineers. In Uttar Pradesh, India's most populous state and one of its poorest, more than 40 percent of the power generated is stolen. Power failures are common, leaving factories idle and retarding economic growth. The World Bank estimates that roughly $40 billion a year is plundered from developing countries.[27]

Debt, Foreign Aid, and Development

Weak economies often find themselves burdened with large external debt. Many countries borrowed heavily from commercial banks to finance development projects during the 1980s when interest rates were high. At the same time, prices for raw materials exported from the developing world declined, thereby preventing many developing countries from repaying their debts. Interest payments on their external debts deprived these countries of money that could have been used for development. The inability or unwillingness of the governments of these countries to repay their debts further eroded their access to additional credit from commercial banks. To prevent countries from defaulting on their loans, the IMF makes financing available. The IMF was created in 1944 to encourage world trade and international cooperation and to help countries with **balance of payments** problems.[28] A country's balance of payments is its record of economic transactions with other countries. If a country buys more from abroad than it sells, it has a balance of payments problem and has to find ways to finance the difference. Poor countries often rely on the IMF to help them when they face balance of payments difficulties. However, the IMF's loans are given on the condition that governments adopt economic policies determined by the IMF. These include severely reducing government spending to balance the budget, eliminating trade barriers, cutting social subsidies, encouraging exports, devaluing currencies, and removing artificial barriers to foreign investment. These policies have often resulted in increased income inequality, social strife, and poverty. Ironically, it is partly due to these strict measures imposed by the IMF that developing economies continue to grow in the global recession.

Overseas development assistance, or foreign aid, is usually designed to promote economic development. Organizations such as the United Nations and the U.S. Agency for International Development (AID) are actively supporting projects in agriculture, public health, housing, public administration, industry, trade, and many other areas. Foreign aid is transfer of resources such as money, food, and technical assistance. These transfers are often gifts. Others, such as loans, are given on very favorable terms. Despite receiving substantial amounts of foreign aid, many countries have failed to achieve significant economic development. In many cases, governments abuse foreign aid. Governments have used food aid as a weapon against their adversaries. Much of the foreign aid has also been taken by corrupt officials for private gain. Aid is also seen as encouraging economic dependence and detrimental to economic growth. For example, food aid may actually contribute to the decline of agriculture in a poor country by pushing local farmers off the market. In response to these problems, many donors have made aid conditional. To receive assistance, countries must eradicate corruption, implement economic reforms, and practice good government. Governments are also relying more on NGOs, groups that are not part of a government, to distribute aid in countries where corruption is a serious problem or where human rights and democratic practices are violated.[29] In light of the financial problems of rich countries, aid to the developing world will continue to decline.

▶ Case Study: Venezuela

When Alonso de Ojeda landed in South America in 1499, a year after Christopher Columbus had sailed to the peninsula of Paria, he observed that the indigenous population had constructed their homes on poles to raise them above the water. Their buildings reminded Ojeda of Venice, so he called the area "little Venice," or Venezuela. It remained a Spanish colony until Simon Bolivar successfully challenged Spanish rule in 1821. Similar to many Latin American countries, Venezuela experienced oppression under military strongmen and the economic elites. By 1959 the country had transitioned toward democratically elected governments.

Bordering Brazil, Colombia, and Guyana, Venezuela has abundant natural resources that provide a strong foundation for economic development. With recent oil and gas discoveries, Venezuela's oil reserves are estimated to be 500 billion barrels, the largest in the world. Oil accounts for roughly 90 percent of the country's export earnings. Almost half the oil is imported by the United States, and Venezuela's CITGO gas stations are part of the American economy. In addition to huge reserves of oil and natural gas, Venezuela has large amounts of iron ore, gold, bauxite, and diamonds. It grows corn, sorghum, sugarcane, bananas, rice, coffee, and other crops. Its strong industrial base includes food processing, mining, textiles, and motor vehicle assembly. Its per capita gross domestic product (GDP) is around $13,500. Venezuela has 27 million people, 93 percent of whom live in urban areas. Life expectancy for females is around 77 years and for males 71 years.

Almost 40 percent of the population lives below the poverty line, and income inequality remains a major challenge. Increasing global demand for petroleum, especially in emerging countries such as China and India, intertwines Venezuela with the global economy. Venezuela's heavy reliance on oil exports makes it extremely vulnerable to the forces of economic globalization.

Venezuela's economic development is strongly influenced by the values of its leaders, especially President Hugo Chavez. After leading an attempted coup against President Carlos Andrés Pérez in February 1992, Lieutenant Colonel Chavez ran for the presidency six years later on a platform of social, economic, and political changes. His Fifth Republic Movement would transform Venezuela and implement 21st Century Socialism at a time when globalization emphasizes privatization and economic liberalization. Chavez, elected president on December 6, 1998, focused on improving the lives of impoverished Venezuelans through policies that redistributed land from wealthy landowners to peasants and small farmers, expanded educational opportunities for the poor, and enhanced health care. Embracing state capitalism, Chavez increased government's control of the economy by nationalizing cement, petroleum, steel, electricity, and communications companies. While his populist programs engendered strong support among the poor, Chavez alienated many in the middle and upper classes. He is widely viewed as taking actions that undermine democracy, discourage opposition groups, diminish judicial independence, and concentrate executive power. He also uses grassroots organizations to stifle civil society. His leftist policies and harsh rhetoric against the United States, especially when George Bush was president, and his close relations with Cuba, Iran, and Russia have created friction between Venezuela and the United States. An attempted coup against Chavez in 2002 ultimately provided him with an opportunity to consolidate power by removing his opponents from government and taking measures to silence dissent.

High oil prices, which peaked at $145 a barrel in July 2008 before dropping sharply to $41 a barrel by the end of the year, enabled Chavez to achieve many of his economic development goals and social policies. Increased government spending, a rise in the minimum wage, and easier access to credit fueled economic growth.

The number of families in poverty declined by more than half, infant and child mortality dropped by more than one-third, and malnutrition-related deaths fell by roughly 50 percent. Two new programs were particularly instrumental in improving nutrition: (1) The Programa Alimenticio Escolar gives approximately 4 million students a free breakfast, lunch, and snack. (2) The Mercal network of government food stores sell food at deeply discounted prices.[30] Significant improvements also were made in providing greater access to potable water, improving sanitation, expanding access to medical care and education, and strengthening social security for the old, widowed, orphaned, and disabled.

Ongoing political instability and deepening social divisions and conflict have contributed to weakening Venezuela's economic development. The precipitous drop in petroleum prices, together with the global financial crisis and economic recession in 2008–2009, pushed the country into recession. Economic growth fell to −5.8 percent. In sharp contrast to the United States and other countries, Venezuela did not implement a spending program to keep the economy stable and growing, despite its sizeable international reserves. Another significant impediment to economic growth is Venezuela's overvalued currency (fixed at 4.3 bolivares per dollar in 2010). An overvalued exchange rate drives up the cost of exports while reducing the price of imports. This diminishes the country's ability to diversify its economy away from its heavy dependence on oil exports.[31]

Another major challenge to Venezuela's economic development is its reliance on hydropower dams for 70 percent of its electricity. Faced with the worst drought in a hundred years, the government declared an electricity emergency and rationed electricity in the first half of 2010. Cuts of up to six hours a day were imposed and there were severe water shortages. People had to purchase water at highly inflated prices. These problems also were due to the lack of economic planning and low levels of investment in energy development.

Regional problems play a significant role in Venezuela's development. Sharing a border with Colombia is an impediment to Venezuela's growth. One of the most violent countries in the world, Colombia produces 90 percent of the cocaine consumed in the United States. Its ongoing conflict with guerillas from the Revolutionary Armed Forces of Colombia (FARC) has contributed to the internal displacement of between 2.6 and 4 million Colombians. Only war-torn Sudan, with 5 million refugees, has more displaced persons. There are an estimated 140,000 displaced Colombians living along the border in Venezuela. Organized drug groups penetrate the porous border spreading violence and instability.

An agreement between the United States and Colombia in 2009 granted America access to seven military bases for joint operations against drug traffickers and guerillas. Chavez, perceiving this development to be a direct threat to his leftist regime, imposed economic sanctions against Colombia and increased his acquisition of weapons from Russia, thereby diverting attention away from economic development.[32]

SUMMARY AND REVIEW

Although change is a necessary part of life, some people often receive it negatively. Thus, development, which encompasses change, is perceived differently by different people and countries. However, with globalization and increasing interdependence, countries throughout the world are concerned with issues of development. The success or failure of development efforts depends to a large extent on changes in the broader global economic system. Numerous factors contribute to change, including a country's values, ideologies, institutions, resources, and technology. Many scholars believe that development is synonymous with industrialization and modernization. Developing an infrastructure is key to development. Even though development includes social and political aspects, the ultimate measure of the development and growth of a country is through economic changes seen in the GDP. Economic changes also are essential for social and equity changes that affect the quality of life. Governments are the major actors in development. Developing countries need social order, revenue, law enforcement, education, and health care to develop. These areas are largely in the hands of the government, although the global community has an increasing responsibility to help those countries struggling to develop.

Numerous theories have been created in order to advance development. These include (1) modernization theory, or developmentalism, (2) Marxist theory, (3) dependency theory, (4) Third World and African socialism, (5) grassroots development, and (6) sustainable development. Development theories must also take into account factors that may impede or facilitate development when forming a plan of action. Some common factors impeding development are a lack of natural resources, hostile regional or international economic environment, high or low populations, poor health care, ethnic conflict, political instability, corruption, and a lack of foreign aid. The opposite of all the aforementioned can be facilitators of development as well. Natural disasters are major impediments to development. A lack of natural resources makes self-sufficiency extremely difficult. The AIDS epidemic in the developing world also is incapacitating their populations. Foreign aid, even when provided, also can cause problems for the developing world because of stipulations the developing world must follow in order to get aid. However, the financial problems of rich countries, combined with economic growth in poor countries, are likely to reduce the flow of aid to the developing world.

KEY TERMS

development   100
growth   100
economic development   100
infrastructure   100
gross national product   100
gross domestic product   100
human development index   101
gender-related development
    index   101
government institutions   101
maquiladora program   101
North American Free Trade
    Agreement   102
law of supply and demand   102
trade barriers   102
privatization   102

International Monetary Fund   103
state capitalism   103
theory   104
development theory   104
naturalistic theories   105
Walt W. Rostow   105
Marxism   106
world systems theory   106
dependency theory   106
Group of 77   107
New International Economic
    Order (NIEO)   107
import substitution   107
Third World socialism   107
African socialism   107
Ujamaa   108

Grameen Bank   108
sustainable development   109
culture   109
Confucianism   109
ideology   111
regional economic development
    banks   111
economies of scale   112
carrying capacity   114
one child policy   114
Biafra   116
bureaucratic corruption   117
good governance   117
Transparency International   118
balance of payments   118

DISCUSSION QUESTIONS

1. How are economic and political developments linked?
2. Discuss the stages of modernization theory.
3. What is state capitalism and how is it different from free-market capitalism?
4. What are the features of Third World socialism? Is Third World socialism different from communism? Why or why not?
5. What do you think are the most important factors impeding development?

SUGGESTED READINGS

Ellner, Steve. *Rethinking Venezuelan Politics*. Boulder, CO: Lynne Rienner, 2010.

Harper, Stephan. *How China's Authoritarian Model Will Dominate the 21st Century*. New York: Basic Books, 2010.

Heineman, Ben, and Fritz Heinman. "The Long War Against Corruption." *Foreign Affairs* 85, No. 3 (May/June 2006): 75–86.

Kapstein, Ethan B. "Africa's Capitalist Revolution." *Foreign Affairs* 88, No. 4 (July/August 2009): 119–128.

Moyo, Dambisa. *Dead Aid*. New York: Farrar, Straus and Giroux, 2009.

Schwab, Klaus. "Global Corporate Citizenship." *Foreign Affairs* 87, No.1 (January/February 2008): 107–118.

Woods, Ngaire. *The Globalizers: The IMF, the World Bank, and Their Borrowers*. Ithaca, NY: Cornell University Press, 2008.

NOTES

1. Larry Rohter, "Colombia Adjust Economic Figures to Include Crops," *The New York Times*, 22 June 1999, A3; and Benjamin Powell, Ed., *Making Poor Nations Rich* (Stanford, IL: Stanford University Press, 2008).

2. David Stoesz, Charles Guzzetta, and Mark Lusk, *International Development* (Boston, MA: Allyn and Bacon, 1999), 117–118.

3. Altha J. Cravey, *Women and Work in Mexico's Maquiladores* (Lanham, MD: Rowman and Littlefield, 1998), 15.

4. Monte Palmer, *Political Development: Dilemmas and Challenges* (Itasca, IL: F. E. Peacock Publishers, 1997).

5. Harold James, "The Rise of the Chinese Model," *Foreign Affairs* 88, No. 1 (January/February 2009), 162.

6. Ngaire Woods, *The Globalizers: The IMF, The World Bank, and Their Borrowers* (Ithaca, NY: Cornell University Press, 2006), 3; Craig N. Murphy, *The United Nations Development Programme* (Cambridge, UK: Cambridge University Press, 2008), 6; and UNDP, *Capacity Development* (New York: United Nations Development Programme, 2008), 4–5.

7. Howard J. Wiarda, *Non-Western Theories of Development* (Fort Worth, TX: Harcourt Brace and Company, 1999), VII–VIII; and S. Charusheela, *Structuralism and Individualism in Economic Analysis* (New York: Routledge, 2005), 8.

8. Walt W. Rostow, *The Process of Economic Growth* (New York: W. W. Norton, 1962), 307.

9. John Rapley, *Understanding Development* (Boulder, CO: Lynne Rienner, 1996), 17; and Wiarda, *Non-Western Theories of Development*, 6–7.

10. Michael F. Lofchie, "The New Political Economy of Africa," in David Apter and Carl G. Rosberg, Eds. *Political Development and the New Realism in Sub-Saharan Africa* (Charlottesville, VA: University Press of Virginia, 1994), 147–150.

11. Muhammad Yunus, *Creating a World Without Poverty* (New York: Public Affair, 2007): 56–60.

12. Kinan Suchaovanich, "Drought Threatens Thai Rice Crop," *The Miami Herald*, 10 June 2010, 3B.

13. Richard J. Payne, *The Clash with Distant Cultures: Values, Interests, and Force in American Foreign Policy* (Albany, NY: State University of New York Press, 1995), 18.

14. David G. Victor and Linda Yueh, "The New Energy Order," *Foreign Affairs* 89, No. 1 (January/February 2010), 61–62.

15. Donald G. McNeil, "As Britain Sells Some Gold, South Africa Howls," *The New York Times*, 7 July 1999, C1.

16. Shailagh Murray, "Dems Target Jobs Moving Abroad," *The Miami Herald*, 11 June 2010, 3B.

17. Jack A. Goldstone, "The New Population Bomb," *Foreign Affairs* 89, No. 1 (January/February 2010), 37.

18. United Nations, *The World's Women 1995: Trends and Statistics* (New York: United Nations, 1995): 12–13.

19. Therese Hesketh and Wei Xing Zhu, "The One Child Family Policy," *British Medical Journal* (June 1997): 1685–1687.

20. Catherine Bertini and Dan Glickman, "Farm Futures," *Foreign Affairs* 88, No. 3 (May/June 2009), 95.

21. Laurie Garrett, "The Lessons of HIV/AIDS," *Foreign Affairs* 84, No. 4 (July/August 2005), 63.

22. Michael Fleshman, "A Crisis in Waiting for AIDS Patients," *Africa Renewal*, April 2010, 16.

23. "Former Militant Threatens to Abandon Nigerian Amnesty," *Daily Herald*, 12 June 2010, 28.

24. Kempe Ronald Hope, *Development in the Third World* (London, UK: M. E. Sharpe, 1996), 130.

25. Ibid., 134; Seth Mydans, "In Vietnam, Deep-Rooted Corruption Threatens Growth," *The New York Times*, 7 May 2006, A10.

26. "South Africa and Corruption," *The Economist*, 17 October 2009, 57.

27. "World Bank Calls for Action on Asset Plundering," *Daily Herald*, 9 June 2010, 33.

28. Ngaire Woods, *The Globalizers: The IMF, the World Bank, and Their Borrowers* (Ithaca, NY: Cornell University Press, 2008), 3.

29. Neil MacFarquhar, "Donors' Aid to Poor Nations Declines," *The New York Times*, 5 September 2008, A10; and Jagdish Bhagwati, "Banned Aid," *Foreign Affairs* 89, No. 1 (January/February 2010), 124.

30. Mark Weisbrot, Rebecca Ray, and Luis Sandoval, *The Chavez Administration at Ten Years* (Washington, DC: Center for Economic and Policy Research, 2009), 11.

31. Mark Weisbrot, "Venezuela Needs an Economic Development Strategy," http://mrzine.monthly review.org/2010.

32. "Putin Bolsters Oil, Defense Ties with Venezuela," *Daily Herald*, 3 April 2010, 26.

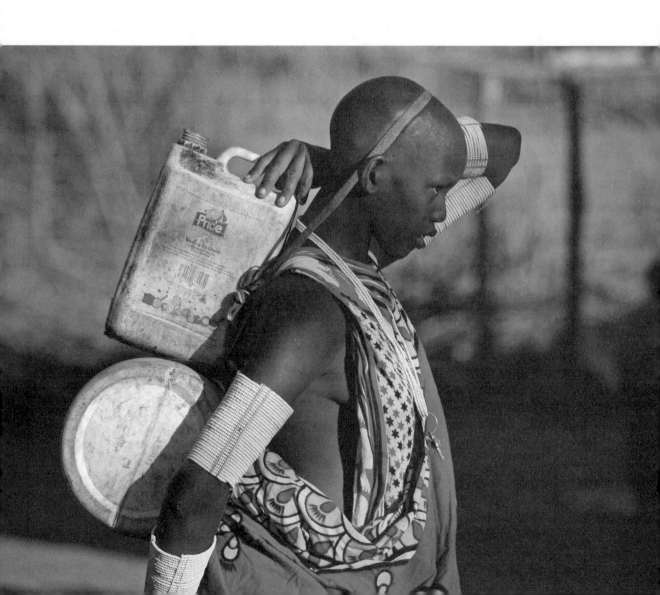

The Costs of Development

Globalization and the Costs of Development

Many costs and benefits associated with development are not caused solely by globalization. As the global recession in 2009 demonstrated, globalization contributes to some of these costs as well as to finding ways to diminish their impact. Free-market reforms that are part of globalization have contributed to high levels of unemployment and rising levels of poverty, government downsizing, failing local businesses that are unable to compete with more efficient global companies, and lower-than-expected foreign investments. It is argued that globalization leads to an inevitable "race to the bottom" in labor and environmental standards as countries compete for foreign investments by lowering their standards and allowing companies to operate freely. But the costs of development that are attributed to globalization have prompted a global effort to diminish them. Companies are pressured by advocacy groups to practice nondiscrimination in the workplace, recognize workers' rights to unionize, prohibit forced labor and exploitative child labor, and reduce environmental damage.

E conomic development, which provides many benefits, is inevitably accompanied by various costs. Students are all too familiar with the costs of obtaining a college education. Apart from allocating scarce resources to their education, they must also give up opportunities to do other things, due to limited time and money. But they pay the costs associated with getting a college education because of the many benefits that are usually derived from having a college degree. This trade-off is referred to as an **opportunity cost.** Some students, however, spend more time and money than they should on their education because of their own decisions or because of circumstances that are beyond their control. Policy makers, like students, must weigh the costs of development against the benefits of development. Equally important, they must determine if they can achieve the benefits of development at lower costs.

Given the growing interdependence of countries and increasing globalization, the costs of development often spread from one society to another. For example, pollution in China sometimes affects places as far away as the United States. Americans' demand for consumer items at low costs cannot be divorced from the growth of sweatshops in Asia and elsewhere. Many of the costs of development, however, are borne by people in the developing world. Taking into consideration the benefits of development, this chapter examines the many costs associated with economic progress, including (1) social and cultural costs, (2) economic and political costs, and (3) environmental costs.

opportunity cost
■ Passing up an opportunity to achieve a greater benefit.

SOCIAL AND CULTURAL COSTS OF DEVELOPMENT

Many small communities throughout the United States encourage companies to invest in them in order to improve their economies and the quality of life of the residents. As these communities grow, they become more aware of the loss of a sense of community; social alienation; the disintegration of families; a relentless pursuit of consumerism; a decline of their cultural identity; and an increase in drug abuse, alcoholism, and other problems that were largely confined to urban areas. Developing societies are confronted with many of these social and cultural costs. Development, by definition, involves some destruction of traditional values and cultures and the adoption of values and cultures similar to those found in industrialized societies.

As societies develop economically, they become socially and politically more complex. The old sense of community is undermined by the demands of modernization. As more industries locate in these societies, people adjust to conform to their requirements. As more time is devoted to work, less time is available for interacting with families, neighbors, and friends. As greater emphasis is placed on the individual, less attention is given to the community. People become increasingly independent and isolated. As the infrastructure develops, there are more options for moving away from tightly knit communities. Members of the community who once played essential roles now live elsewhere, thereby depriving their old communities of valuable services. As more roads, bridges, and ports are constructed, the number of automobiles increases. Instead of walking or bicycling to work and other activities, people are more likely to drive. Even though the automobile gets them to their destination faster, it also isolates them from members of their communities.

Social alienation, the pressure to make money, and the increased exposure to values of modern societies contribute to the rise of social problems. Many children, in search of meaningful connections, may engage in activities that are destructive to themselves and their communities. Even in relatively small and isolated societies, gangs begin to emerge and tear the social fabric. Parents feel they can no longer control their children, despite their growing material wealth. Elders, who were once highly respected, are ignored, as individualism replaces a sense of social and familial obligation. Drug abuse, alcoholism, and prostitution have become more widespread. For example, rapid economic growth in the United Arab Emirates has been accompanied by dramatic increases in alcohol and drug abuse. Despite earlier efforts to deny the problem, public campaigns against drug abuse and the establishment of rehabilitation centers are part of the Dubai society.

Instead of viewing development as a replacement for traditionalism, a more accurate view of development is that both modernization and traditionalism coexist in most societies. Most cultures are extremely durable, despite the adoption of new values. However, some cultures that are closely linked to location and the environment are threatened with extinction by the forces of change. Cultures of people in the Amazon rain forest, for example, are tied to the land. When the land is altered, these cultures are affected. Many are destroyed. The cost of development for indigenous peoples is often extremely high. The challenge for many traditional cultures is to balance the costs of change against the costs of maintaining the status quo.[1] As will be discussed, development of the Amazon has generally ignored the desire of indigenous people to preserve their cultures. Greater efforts are being made to improve the economic and physical well-being of indigenous peoples without destroying their traditional cultures.

One of the most important social costs of development is the escalation of criminal activities. Modernization weakens many of the social bonds that helped reduce crime. As urbanization spreads, as communities are destroyed, and as individualism, alienation, and consumerism are strengthened, crime rates tend to rise. Rising levels of prosperity, unequal distribution of benefits, the breakdown of traditional societies, and the failure of countries to establish modern institutions to replace traditional ones make developing countries particularly vulnerable to widespread crime. Mexico City is often cited as a leading example of widespread and uncontrollable crime in the developing world. The vast majority of Mexico City residents are directly affected by crime. Muggings, burglaries, and car thefts are rampant. Many police officers are often victims of crime, partly because criminals want to demonstrate the ineffectiveness of the police. It is quite common for people to be mugged and beaten even when police officers are nearby. In fact, more than 94 percent of all violent crimes reported to the police are never solved or prosecuted.

Since 2006, roughly 23,000 people were killed in drug wars. Violence became more gruesome in 2010 as the government increased military action against drug traffickers. People in Brazil and other Latin American cities routinely protest against high crime rates and personal insecurity. The Mexican government decided to enforce stricter gun-control laws, to restrict the right to carry guns, and to implement a program to buy back guns to decrease violent crimes.[2] Both Mexico and the United States agreed in 2009 to stop the flow of guns from America into Mexico in order to reduce violence related to the drug trade. In June 2010, the U.S. government seized large quantities of drugs and 141 weapons and arrested 400 people suspected of drug trafficking. Part of the problem is that some police officers actually collaborate with criminals, largely due to economic reasons.[3]

Development also facilitates crime by creating closer links among countries, by enhancing transportation and communication among them, and by enabling individuals to acquire financial resources to engage in crime. The positive side of development is that it stimulates trade among countries that is both legal and beneficial to many people. The negative side of this, however, is that illegal activities also flourish. As countries develop their infrastructure for legitimate trade, they also run the risk of having their ports, roads, airports, and telecommunications systems utilized for illegal trade. For example, the infrastructure for international trade makes it relatively easy for cars stolen in the United States to be transported to Mexico, Panama, Colombia, the Dominican Republic, China, and elsewhere in the developing world. A $70,000 Mercedes that was stolen in Miami was found a thousand miles from Florida. Its new owner was Mayra Sandoval, director of judicial affairs in Panama's Foreign Ministry. Ironically, Sandoval was responsible for negotiating an agreement between Panama and the United States to deal with the problem of stolen cars.[4] Americans who live in cities with ports or international borders are most likely to have their stolen cars shipped overseas.

Illegal drug cultivation, processing, and trafficking have emerged as one of the greatest social costs of development. Virtually all countries, large and small, are affected by illegal drugs. Development helps make economies and societies more interdependent, and it exposes developing countries to the problems generally associated with advanced industrialized societies such as the United States and Western Europe. Consumption of illegal drugs in rich countries influences poor countries with weak and corrupt governments to supply them. Suppliers usually become consumers, a development that has high social, economic, and political costs for poor countries. Even though a few individuals and groups benefit from drug trafficking, society as a whole suffers and development is often impeded. Countries involved in producing and selling illegal drugs include Colombia, Mexico, Afghanistan, and Thailand. But countries such as Jamaica, Nigeria, and South Africa also participate in the illegal drug trade as transit points, producers, and facilitators of financial transactions by international and domestic criminal organizations. Their modern communications networks, banking, and transportation systems facilitate not only drug trafficking but also the concealment of income derived from criminal activities. Eventually, banking, law enforcement, customs officials, and others in developing countries are pulled into a network of illegal activities based on the drug trade. In Jamaica, for example, criminal gangs are intricately linked to political elites and political parties. When the United States requested the extradition of Christopher Coke, leader of the brutal Shower Posse gang, for guns and drug trafficking in 2010, the Jamaican government delayed taking action on the request. Bowing to political pressure, the government launched an assault against Tivoli Gardens in Kingston, where Coke ruled "The Mother of All Garrisons." Seventy-six people were killed. Coke was captured and extradited to the United States.

Child Labor

Approximately 218 million children aged 5–14 are working in developing countries. Roughly 317.4 million children work outside the home part time. About half of them work full time, whereas the others combine work with school. Although the problem of child labor has always existed to greater or lesser degrees, economic development and the increasing globalization of the economies of various countries have served as a catalyst for the growth of child labor. Developing countries must compete for foreign investment and must produce goods at low prices to gain access to global markets. As poor countries are pressured to compete with each other for investments and markets, they look for ways to reduce labor costs. This makes child labor, the cheapest labor of all, attractive to manufacturers. Most of the children do not work in industries that are connected to international companies or multinational corporations. The vast majority of them, about 70 percent, are employed in agriculture, forestry, and fishing. Another 8.3 percent work in wholesale and retail trade, restaurants, and hotels; 8.3 percent in manufacturing; and 6.5 percent in community, social, and personal services. Most child laborers are viewed as essential contributors to their families. Without their income, many families would not survive. Countries of Asia such as India, Pakistan, Bangladesh, Thailand, Indonesia, and the Philippines employ approximately 153.5 million children. Africa, the poorest and least developed continent, has about 80 million child laborers, whereas Latin America and the Caribbean employ roughly 17 million children. But the developing countries are not the only societies with child labor problems. It is estimated that 300,000 to 1 million children are working illegally in the United States, primarily in agriculture.[5]

India, with roughly 100 million children working, has the largest number of child laborers in the world. Widespread poverty and an enduring caste system reinforce the practice of child labor. Both poverty and social attitudes make child labor acceptable to Indians, the majority of whom live in villages. Child labor on the farms and in the villages throughout India is considered part of the social and economic reality. Parents, many of whom are landless, illiterate, and hungry, worked when they were children and expect their own children to follow in their footsteps. For most parents, child labor is a way of life. With two children, ages 11 and 16, working with their father, a typical rural family in India may earn less than $1 a day. Children work in dangerous industries such as lead mining, metal manufacturing, fireworks, stone quarrying, brick kilns, brothels, and carpet weaving. Many of them work long hours. They inhale dust and chemical fumes and are exposed to other hazardous conditions. Many suffer from chronic pain and breathing problems caused by working conditions. Much of the attention has been focused on the carpet industry because it is a major source of income. Countries that import carpets from India and elsewhere find themselves under pressure from various groups that oppose child labor. Responding to such pressure, the United States passed a law in 1997 to ban imports of goods made by child laborers. But India, which has numerous laws against child labor, does not regard children working at home for free as child laborers. In Uttar Pradesh and other parts of India, much of the carpet weaving is done in mud huts that are largely hidden from investigators from the outside world. Most Indian families are too poor to abandon the system of child labor. Educational opportunities are generally not available for the poorest children.[6]

Pakistan and Bangladesh also make extensive use of child labor. Until 1999, Pakistan relied primarily on child labor for its soccer ball industry. International pressure is forcing Pakistan to take steps to eventually eliminate the use of child workers and to employ women instead. Forced by the unwillingness of importers and consumers in the United States, Western Europe, and elsewhere to purchase soccer balls made by children, Pakistan realized that it had to change in order to maintain an important industry. Reebok, which purchased soccer balls from Pakistan, established a monitoring system at a new central production facility in Pakistan. It also affixed new "Made Without Child Labor" labels to its soccer balls. The company was clearly worried about the effect of negative publicity on its image and its sales. The Pakistani soccer ball industry has largely abandoned child labor. But the carpet industry in Pakistan is the principal employer of children. Many poor families literally mortgage their children to carpet factories. Employers make it virtually impossible for child laborers to accumulate enough money to pay off the mortgages by overcharging them for food, housing, and even drugs. Bangladesh employs around 7 million children. Most of them work between 9 and 14 hours a day and give their earnings to their parents. As is the case in India, many of the children work in agriculture for their families. But as modernization has reduced the amount of land available for small farmers, many rural residents are forced to migrate to urban areas in search of employment. Many children find jobs in the garment industry, which provides Bangladesh with about 70 percent of its export earnings. Women employed in these factories earn as little as $30 a month. Such low wages perpetuate the use of child labor to supplement the family's income. Furthermore, in order to obtain international funding for economic development, Bangladesh, which is highly dependent on foreign aid, adopted a **structural adjustment program.** This program required cuts in government spending on health care, education, nutrition, and other programs that benefit the poor.[7]

structural adjustment program ■ Required cuts in government spending on programs that benefit the poor.

Reduced government expenditures forced more families to rely on their children for income.

Latin America and the Caribbean are not as dependent on child labor as Asia and Africa. However, child labor is a serious problem in countries such as Haiti and Brazil. Under Haiti's **Restavec system,** impoverished parents who cannot afford to raise their children allow them to stay with wealthier families. The children are treated as slaves, psychologically abused, and beaten. They are not educated and are forced to do domestic work and menial jobs. The Restavec system is so widely practiced that many Haitians, who are the poorest people in the Western Hemisphere, regard it as an integral part of their society. Children are also used as laborers in Brazil's agricultural industry. For example, despite **Brazil's Labor Code,** which outlaws child labor, many children are employed to pick oranges and work in citrus-processing industries. Brazil is the world's largest exporter of orange juice and a supplier of major U.S. brands such as Minute Maid. But both domestic and global pressure, mainly from labor unions, is helping to end the use of child labor in the citrus industry.[8]

Several countries have enacted legislation banning child labor. Others have allowed industries to be inspected by outside investigators. Many countries, in cooperation with international organizations, mark their products with labels indicating that they were not made with child labor. In India, for example, many carpet manufacturers use the **Kaleen** label and the **Rugmark** label to demonstrate their compliance with laws banning child labor. Inspectors carry out spot checks and fine violators. However, many manufacturers are able to circumvent the law and still obtain labels certifying that they do not use child labor. The **International Labor Organization (ILO),** a part of the United Nations, which is based in Geneva, Switzerland, adopted an agreement to abolish the worst forms of child labor. These include slavery, debt bondage, trafficking in children, prostitution, child pornography, and the recruitment of children as soldiers by militias and paramilitaries. However, in 2010, ILO's *Global Report on Child Labor* showed that global efforts to eliminate the worst forms of child labor had lost momentum.[9]

Sweatshops

Sweatshops are widely perceived as integral parts of developing economies. The connection between sweatshops and economic development is as old as the Industrial Revolution. Charles Dickens, the British novelist, wrote extensively about the horrific working conditions in industries throughout England from the middle of the eighteenth century to the middle of the nineteenth century. Many contemporary critics of factories in the developing world use the term *sweatshop* to portray the dangerous working conditions found in many of them. Characteristics of sweatshops include the dreariness of the work, the harshness of supervisors, difficult and hazardous jobs, frequent and serious accidents, long hours and low pay, few employee benefits and rights, and a generally toxic, polluted, and unsanitary working environment.

Sweatshops provide much-needed jobs. The existence of sweatshops reflects economic realities. But they also underscore the need for multinational corporations from the developed as well as the developing countries to produce low-cost

Restavec system
■   A system in Haiti that allows children of the poor to live with those who are wealthy.

Brazil's Labor Code
■   A Brazilian law that outlaws child labor.

Kaleen and Rugmark
■   Labels used by manufacturers to show compliance with child labor laws.

International Labor Organization (ILO)
■   An organization of the United Nations that deals with labor-related issues, including child labor concerns.

products for insatiable consumers throughout the world. Sweatshops are part of the global economy. The poorest countries are most likely to have the worst working conditions and lowest wages, which make them attractive to many foreign as well as domestic investors. Many of these factories are actually small businesses that are owned by local entrepreneurs who make products for various companies. Many workers earn less than $1 a day and labor 12–14 hours each day, six days a week. Work in the agricultural sector is often viewed as even more strenuous than a factory job, and the pay is lower and infrequent. The poorest of the poor often must become garbage scavengers to survive.[10]

As more Western companies have moved parts of their operations to developing countries to take advantage of inexpensive labor and lower environmental standards and working conditions, they have encountered opposition from labor unions, environmentalists, humanitarians, and other activists. The global economy, increased and rapid communications, and the willingness of the media to expose exploitative labor practices by well-known personalities and corporations have made it easier for human rights activists and others to change the companies' practices. Companies such as Wal-Mart, Gap, Reebok, Nike, Starbucks Coffee, Walt Disney, and Mattel have been criticized for taking advantage of sweatshop labor. The Walt Disney Company was exposed for contracting with suppliers in Haiti who paid their workers less than the minimum wage of $2.40 a day. Wal-Mart was accused of using child labor in Bangladesh to make inexpensive clothing, and Mattel was exposed for its production of "Sweatshop Barbies." Starbucks Coffee was picketed by activists for buying its coffee beans from Guatemalan plantations that exploit their workers.[11]

Many of these companies have attempted to protect themselves by adopting various codes and labels. The **No Sweat** label is being used to verify that clothing, shoes, toys, and other products were not made in sweatshops or by children. Perhaps Nike has embraced the most far-reaching reforms after being faced with an effective boycott of its products in the mid-1990s. Nike developed a "Memorandum of Understanding" that is signed by factories that produce Nike shoes and other products. Nike's Memorandum of Understanding calls on factories to comply with the following: (1) government regulation of business; (2) safety and health regulations; (3) local laws providing health insurance, life insurance, and worker's compensation; (4) laws forbidding the use of forced labor; (5) environmental regulations; (6) laws promoting equal employment opportunities; and (7) efforts by external groups to certify that factories are complying with Nike's rules.[12]

No Sweat ■ A label used to verify that products were not made in sweatshops or by children.

ECONOMIC AND POLITICAL COSTS OF DEVELOPMENT

Many economic costs of development are unavoidable because of the relatively weak bargaining position of poor countries. Some of these costs are not strictly economic but have significant economic implications. Overpopulation, for example, is caused by many noneconomic factors, as Chapter 6 points out. Advances in medical technology and improvements in transportation and access to food contribute to population growth by reducing death rates. A growing population imposes a heavy economic burden on the developing world. Overpopulation threatens economic progress because of the enormous amounts of resources that are needed to sustain it. Schools, hospitals, roads, airports, harbors, electricity, water, sewage treatment plants, and other infrastructure projects must be provided. Governments must also deal with rising levels of unemployment as the population shifts from rural to urban areas.

An economic cost is economic inequality. Inequality discourages investment on a wider scale and encourages the poor and their supporters to pressure governments to allocate resources to benefit those left behind by unequal economic growth. High rates of inequality may encourage some members of society to be more productive and entrepreneurial. But such inequality usually leads to a concentration of political power and the stifling of economic competition. Poor people are deprived of opportunities to become productive and the powerful are inclined to be corrupt. Ultimately, the poorest of the poor, who are usually women and children, pay the highest economic costs of growing inequality.[13]

One of the main political costs of economic development is the decline of the government's ability to control what goes on inside the country or international developments that directly affect it. This relative loss of *sovereignty*, or control over internal affairs, is part of the process of globalization and interdependence. This decline of sovereignty can also be viewed as a positive aspect of development. Communications technology and transportation have helped to weaken the ability of governments to control the activities of their citizens.

Another short-term political cost of development is instability and the violation of human rights. As people from different ethnic, regional, and religious backgrounds are brought together by the forces of modernization, the likelihood of conflict increases. Instability is often caused by government's economic policies, such as structural adjustment. Indonesia, for example, experienced political instability and violence when it agreed to demands of the International Monetary Fund to implement economic reforms that deprive the poor of various subsidies. Unstable political conditions together with insecure governments and weak institutions contribute to violations of human rights.

Consumerism and Development

One of the most obvious changes brought about by economic development is a marked increase in consumerism, along with dramatic changes in what people consume, where they acquire consumer products, and how they relate to each other and the rest of the world. A common measure of better life is usually greater access to more food, clothes, and better housing and the acquisition of various products that make life easier and more enjoyable. Many of the benefits are obvious. Yet these developments have negative consequences or costs. As discussed earlier, some of these costs are unavoidable and essential components of the overall positive nature of economic development. Economic development, by definition, implies growth and increased consumption of an ever-larger supply of products. The global recession of 2009 reduced consumerism.

Consumerism increases as countries develop, partly because many of the products are produced by them. As factories in developing societies produce electronics, appliances, automobiles, apparel, footwear, household furnishings, and other consumer items, people become more aware of these products, develop the need to acquire them, and, because of the jobs these industries create, are better able to purchase them. Industries such as tourism dramatically alter consumer tastes and desires. Tourists demand modern accommodations, restaurants, recreational facilities, and transportation. They also bring aspects of their own culture with them that influence people in the developing world to acquire a similar lifestyle. Visiting or living in developed societies often profoundly changes consumption patterns. When travelers from developing countries return home, they not only take with them new ways of living, they also help to replicate consumption patterns of rich societies in their own countries. Consumerism is also positive because it contributes to further economic growth and increased economic opportunities. However, the global financial crisis demonstrated that consumerism in developing countries has contributed to increasing credit card debt. In Asia and Latin America, credit card transactions are growing by roughly 20–30 percent a year.[14]

As more people in the developing world adopt the habits of people in developed countries, they also encounter the same problems. The consumption of fast foods and the sedentary lifestyles that characterize modern societies increase the number of overweight people, especially children, in poor countries. This rapid increase in the consumption of fast food is seen by the emphasis of McDonald's, for example, on building most of its new restaurants overseas. Children throughout Asia, Latin America, and the Caribbean are suffering from obesity. In fact, there is a growing weight gap in the developing world, as the rich grow fat and the poor suffer from malnutrition and hunger. Overweight people outnumber underweight people everywhere except in South Asia, where 553 million are underweight, compared with 115 million people who are overweight. In North America, 153 million people are overweight, compared with 13 million who are underweight. In Latin America, 152 million people are overweight and 32 million are underweight. Worldwide, there are as many overweight people, 1.1 billion, as underfed people. More than 230 million people worldwide suffer from diabetes, caused mainly by changes in lifestyle and diet.

Other costs include poor diets in general, an increase in alcohol consumption, and smoking. Even though antismoking campaigns in the United States have reduced the number of smokers, just the opposite is happening in developing countries. Advertising and marketing of cigarettes have increased as tobacco companies have attempted to gain markets in poor countries to offset their lost markets in rich countries. As people in poor countries overeat, adopt sedentary lifestyles, abuse alcohol and drugs, and smoke, they begin to suffer from the same diseases that plague affluent societies. These include heart attacks, cancers, strokes, diabetes, and high blood pressure.

Urbanization and Development

Urbanization is an integral part of economic development. Almost half of the people in the world live in urban areas. It is estimated that about 65 percent of them will live in cities by 2025. Latin America and the Caribbean will have 80 percent of their populations living in cities by 2015.[15] It is important to point out that many governments, especially those in developing countries, do not know precisely how many people are living in urban areas. There is no effective way to count them.

Furthermore, migration patterns, the tendency of people to reside in cities temporarily, and the reluctance of some people to be counted make it difficult for governments to collect accurate demographic data.

Patterns of urbanization are different in the developed countries than in the developing world. In most developed countries, there are many medium-sized and small cities and towns. By contrast, the developing countries have a few very large cities, often referred to as megalopolises. People from around the country come to these few cities, largely because of the economic, social, and political benefits they offer. Eleven of the 15 most populated cities in the world, with more than 13 million residents, are in developing countries. Four of these megacities are in Latin America, with Mexico City (19 million) and Sao Paulo in Brazil (19 million) taking the lead. Megacities in the poor countries include Jakarta in Indonesia, Seoul in South Korea, Lagos in Nigeria, Mumbai and Kolkata in India, Rio de Janeiro in Brazil, Buenos Aires in Argentina, Shanghai and Beijing in China, and Cairo in Egypt. The population density of cities in developing countries is usually higher than that in the developed world. For example, Mexico City has twice the density of New York City, three times the density of Paris, and four times that of London. But Bombay and Calcutta, for example, have higher population densities than Mexico City.[16]

A major problem is that urbanization tends to reduce responsibility and accountability. Very large cities encourage the fragmentation of environmental management. Although decentralization of authority to deal with urban problems is almost essential, decentralization can result in uncertainty about who deals with particular problems and who provides the necessary resources. Many local authorities in megacities are unable to raise revenues to build and maintain streets, collect garbage, and provide adequate sanitation services. Raw sewage is routinely discharged into rivers, streams, lakes, and throughout the urban area. India, for example, treats 18 percent of the sewage its cities produce.[17] As more people move to the city, the demand for already scarce resources grows, making it difficult for governments to improve sanitation and diminish sprawl. When governments destroy shantytowns to promote urban development and public safety, residents of the squalid settlements recreate shantytowns elsewhere, or become homeless. Many urban residents do not have adequate water supplies because the demand is too great, because much water is wasted by industries and is not recycled, and because of the inability or unwillingness of governments to repair water pipelines and storage systems.

Urban areas throughout the world have severe traffic and air pollution problems. These problems are so serious because of the rapid growth of urbanization and other changes brought about by economic development. Cairo, for example, has more than 2 million cars but only enough roads to handle a third of that number. Mexico City is probably the most obvious example of traffic congestion and air pollution caused by automobiles. Efforts have been made to restrict automobile traffic by reducing the number of cars on the streets by almost half during some air pollution emergencies. China's rapid economic growth has also contributed to a rapid increase in the use of automobiles. China alone is responsible for two-thirds of the growth of greenhouse gases and is the world's largest emitter of these gases.[18]

Unsanitary living conditions, limited access to clean water, extremely high levels of air pollution, exposure to toxic and hazardous wastes, untreated sewage, and malnutrition create serious health problems for residents in developing countries. Mosquitoes, which transmit diseases such as yellow fever, malaria, and dengue fever, breed in the unsanitary conditions in urban areas. Discarded automobile tires, drainage ditches, irrigated urban gardens, water tanks, and garbage heaps provide ideal breeding places for mosquitoes. Increasing globalization also puts residents of developed countries at risk of contracting diseases that originate in poor societies. Shipping industries, airlines, and cruise ships facilitate the transportation of diseases from one country to another. For example, untreated sewage flowing into the Bay of Bengal off Bangladesh was loaded into the bilge tanks of a freighter bound for South America. When the bilge tanks were emptied off the coast of Peru, a new strain of cholera, which was in the untreated sewage in Bangladesh, flourished in sewage from Lima, Peru. The cholera soon made its way into various cities as people ate contaminated shellfish from off the coast of Peru.[19]

The Decline of Agriculture and Economic Development

Agriculture has been given a lower priority in many poor countries as they rushed to industrialize. For example, in 2008, conflict erupted between Tata, one of India's largest corporations, and small farmers over Tata's efforts to use valuable farmland for industrial development, including automobile manufacturing. Asian countries, such as South Korea, Taiwan, and Thailand, have achieved high levels of industrialization as well as increased agricultural productivity. Latin America has also managed to balance agricultural development and industrialization. It is in Africa where agriculture has suffered most as a result of the pressures of economic development and government policies. In Asia and Latin America, the **Green Revolution** enabled farmers to produce more crops on the same amount of land by using hybrid seeds, chemical fertilizers, pesticides, herbicides, irrigation, and modern farm machinery. The Green Revolution largely bypassed Africa.

Urbanization and rapid industrialization influenced many farmers to leave the rural areas in search of a better life in the cities. Fewer farmers, in the absence of improved agricultural productivity, meant that less food was being grown. As urban populations expanded, more land was lost to urban sprawl. Infrastructural projects essential to urbanization and industrialization require large amounts of land. Shopping malls, airports, roads and highways, tourist facilities, harbors, hospitals, schools, power plants, and so on reduce the amount of land available for agriculture.

Green Revolution
■ Enabled farmers to produce more crops on the same amount of land via the use of technological advancements in the agricultural field.

urbanization
■ Takes valuable land away from agriculture.

Environmental Costs of Development

The massive oil spill in the Gulf of Mexico in 2010 is a sobering reminder that an obvious cost of economic development is environmental degradation. Urban areas throughout the developing world suffer from excessive rates of air and water pollution, toxic wastes, and the destruction of natural habitats for wildlife. Even small towns are plagued with environmental problems that result from development. Garbage is recklessly disposed of in areas that were once pristine. Discarded plastic bags are universal symbols of pollution. E-waste (discarded computers, phones, printers, televisions, and other appliances) will continue to grow as a new source of pollution in developing countries. Fragile beaches are destroyed as tourist facilities are constructed to fulfill the exotic fantasies of the rich and famous. Cruise ships routinely pollute once-crystal-clear waters in the Caribbean and elsewhere. Environmental destruction also results from the rapid and reckless exploitation of natural resources. In Indonesia, for example, mining companies have been largely exempt from complying with the relatively weak environmental laws. Consequently, mining activities have caused widespread destruction of surrounding forests and the pollution of rivers, lakes, and other water sources. The pollution of many rivers in the Philippines by wastes from copper mining has reduced fish yields by half. Oil companies have caused similar environmental damage in many oil-producing regions in Africa, Asia, and Latin America.

In Ecuador, for example, Texaco was the dominant oil company in the country until 1990. Its determination to maximize profits and its disregard for protecting the environment caused long-lasting environmental damage. Texaco poured low-grade crude oil on dirt roads it cleared to reduce dust, but the heavy rainfall in the Amazon soon carried the oil into the fields and rivers, which contaminated crops and water supplies. In addition, millions of barrels of oil were accidentally spilled over a 20-year period. Large pools of oil and other toxic wastes are everywhere in the oil-producing region of Ecuador. The environmental costs were largely overlooked by a country that depends on oil and related products for 44 percent of its national budget. Revenues from the petroleum industry financed electrification of Ecuador and contributed to its industrial development. The massive oil spill in the Gulf of Mexico is forcing policy makers and citizens around the world to rethink the costs of exploiting oil.[20]

Water pollution is a major cost of economic development. Increased fertilizer and chemical usage improved agricultural productivity. However, heavy rains washed chemicals into rivers, lakes, and groundwater supplies. Farm chemicals in China are washed into the sea, creating massive blooms of algae. In places such as Taiwan, many industrial plants are located in agricultural areas. Untreated industrial metals and wastewater contaminate some of the crops, especially rice, which requires a large amount of water to grow. Industrial development in Asia has resulted in heavily polluted rivers, lakes, and seas. For example, it is not uncommon to see many rivers and streams in China in which the water is so polluted that it is completely black and putrid.

Most of the water pollution in the developing world is caused by untreated human waste. India provides one of the best examples of how urbanization, water pollution, religious beliefs, and the contraction of dangerous diseases are intertwined. Almost half of India's 1 billion citizens live along the **Ganges River,** which stretches for 1,500 miles from the Himalayan Mountains to the Bay of Bengal. The crowded cities dump millions of gallons of untreated human and industrial waste into the sluggish river. What makes the pollution of the Ganges River even more dangerous is the belief of many Hindus that bathing in the Ganges will wash away their sins. For them, the Ganges is India's holiest river. They believe that their bodies and souls are purified by drinking its water. Hindus also believe that if their bodies are cremated on the banks of the Ganges, their souls will escape from the material world's cycle of suffering.[21]

Ganges River
■ A river in India along which almost half of the country's citizens live.

Air pollution is also a serious problem in the developing world. Economic development has resulted in making many cities in Asia, Latin America, and Africa extremely dangerous to the health of their inhabitants. Beijing, Taipei (Taiwan), New Delhi (India), and Mexico City are among the most polluted cities in the world. Most of these cities are constantly covered with air that is so polluted that visibility is drastically diminished. Automobiles are a major source of the black haze that hangs over these cities. Millions of cars now crowd the streets of New Delhi, Beijing, and Mexico City. To reduce pollution during the 2008 Olympic Games in Beijing, China closed several factories and allowed only half of the cars and trucks to operate. Another major source of air pollution is the industries that are seen as essential to economic development. In China, for example, many of these industries use coal. Coal-powered plants spew harmful particles into the air and create the haze that cannot be escaped in places such as Beijing. Adding to the problem caused by industry is the widespread use of coal by Chinese citizens to heat their homes and cook their food. Sixteen of the 20 most-polluted cities in the world are in China. Toxic chemicals and climate-changing gases from the smokestacks of China's coal-burning power plants cross the Pacific to pollute California, Oregon, Washington, and other parts of the United States. Few developing countries are willing to impose pollution restrictions on industries that fuel economic growth. China's economic growth continues to increase its carbon dioxide emissions.[22]

Pollution imposes significant economic and social costs on developing societies. Governments have to allocate more of their resources to efforts to reduce pollution levels and to pay for the health consequences of pollution. Taiwan, China, and Mexico are experiencing escalating rates of asthma and other respiratory diseases, lung and heart diseases, premature births and low birth weight, and premature deaths. The **World Health Organization (WHO),** an agency of the United Nations that attempts to improve the health of people around the world, studied the effects of contaminants in heavily polluted cities. It found that Mexico City's pollution is the most noxious for children. They are exposed to contaminants that are the equivalent of smoking two packs of cigarettes a day.[23] Some governments have taken steps to deal with the problem. China, India, Mexico, and Brazil have increased gasoline prices by as much as 121 percent to reduce emissions of carbon dioxide. India is the world's largest producer of wind energy, and Bangladesh is relying increasingly on solar energy in rural areas. Poor countries believe that rich countries should bear most of the burden of emissions that cause the greenhouse gases that are contributing to **global warming.** However, they are being pressured to change by environmental groups such as **Greenpeace** as well as by grassroots organizations that are concerned about the costs of environmental problems.

World Health Organization (WHO)
■ An agency of the United Nations that attempts to improve the health of people around the world.

global warming
■ Caused mainly by emissions of carbon dioxide.

Greenpeace
■ A nongovernmental environmental group.

Deforestation

Compared with productive agricultural land, forests are widely seen as less valuable. Destruction of forests makes the land more valuable. Population pressures help speed up the process of deforestation in many ways. As population expands, the demand for fuel for cooking increases. Most of the trees that are cut down in developing countries are used for cooking and other domestic uses. As urbanization and industrialization spread, more trees are destroyed. Land must be cleared to accommodate the growing number of urban residents. The pollution caused by industrialization and urbanization contributes to deforestation as more people use wood as fuel to boil contaminated water in an effort to purify it. Population pressures sometimes trigger ethnic conflicts. In an attempt to escape violence, many refugees live in the forests. They destroy many trees in order to obtain shelter and food.

Most of the land that is cleared of forests is used for slash-and-burn agriculture. Many people in developing countries depend on traditional agricultural methods to produce enough food for themselves and their families. Commercial agriculture also contributes to deforestation. Millions of square miles of forests are cleared each year to grow coffee, tea, cocoa, rubber, palm oil, sugarcane, citrus, bananas, soybeans, and rice. Forests are also destroyed to create pasture to expand commercial cattle production. Cattle ranching has been a main cause of deforestation in Brazil and Central America. As commercial farming expands, agricultural workers are usually replaced by machines. Unless new employment opportunities are created, many of the unemployed landless workers see moving to the rain forest in search of land as their only option. In fact, many governments have aggressively supported deforestation in an effort to relocate people to less crowded areas. **Indonesia's Transmigration Program,** for example, attempted to relocate 140 million people and convert 2.5 million acres of rain forest to rice paddies. Similarly, Brazil constructed the **Trans-Amazon Highway** and encouraged millions of landless peasants to move to the Amazon and clear the land for cultivation. Both projects received funding from the World Bank. Economic globalization contributes to the destruction of forests.[24] Deforestation is also caused by commercial logging practices that do not focus on sustainable development of forest resources. The demand for tropical hardwoods such as mahogany is contributing to the destruction of forests in Southeast Asia, Central America, and elsewhere in the developing world. The demand for furniture and construction materials in developing countries themselves makes it difficult to practice sustainable development. Indonesia signed an agreement with China that enables China to obtain wood from its forests for flooring, furniture, and construction. China has developed large palm oil plantations to replace trees destroyed in Indonesia. Many tropical woods are being harvested faster than they can be replaced. Development also creates a greater demand for paper products. This leads to more forests being exploited for pulp and paper production. The export of forest products is also viewed by many governments in the developing world as a relatively low-cost and easily accessible source of revenue for funding domestic projects and to pay down their foreign debts.

One of the most common causes of deforestation is the deliberate setting of fires by small farmers, commercial farmers, ranchers, logging companies, and others. Satellite images of Brazil, Colombia, Indonesia, Tanzania, and elsewhere show that fires caused by people are destroying many tropical forests. Burning is widely practiced to clear brush and forest regrowth. However, many people who set fires do not have effective measures to contain them. Furthermore, burning forests is not generally perceived as a serious problem in most poor countries. In fact, burning is an integral part of agriculture and farming. Fire is used because it is cheap, fast, and effective—if it can be controlled. Another factor contributing to the

Indonesia's Transmigration Program ■ A program attempting to convert rain forest land to rice paddies.

Trans-Amazon Highway ■ Encouraged millions of landless peasants to move to the Amazon and clear the land for cultivation.

increase in forest fires in the Amazon and Southeast Asia is selective logging. As forests are thinned out, humidity falls. Drier conditions facilitate the spread of human-made fires.

Numerous problems are created by deforestation. Many plant and animal species are destroyed, thereby reducing the earth's biodiversity. The preservation of biodiversity is essential to many scientific advances in industry, agriculture, and medicine. Destruction of the rain forests is also seen as contributing to climate change. Areas become hotter and drier after forests are destroyed. Deforestation may actually change an area from being moist and humid to a desert. Deforestation releases carbon dioxide stored in vegetation and in the soil. Because large rain forests, such as the Amazon, have an impact on the global climate, their destruction is seen as helping to create the problem of global warming and climate instability. Agricultural productivity declines as rainfall diminishes and as soil erosion becomes more extensive. In some areas, destructive floods become more prevalent even as groundwater reserves fall. Homes, farms, the infrastructure essential to development, and industrial plants are destroyed by extreme weather conditions. People who depend on forest products for their livelihoods must find other sources of income as deforestation expands. Forests provide a habitat for animals that help to pollinate plants and control agricultural pests. Deforestation in China facilitates the spread of dust from the Gobi Desert. Dust covers windowsills and blows under doors to cover floors and walls. Concerns about deforestation have influenced countries, non-state organizations, and individuals to plant more trees, a development that is slowing the pace of deforestation.[25] Destruction of the forests ultimately threatens human survival.

Dam Construction

Economic development requires the availability of abundant and inexpensive energy to run industries, cities, and irrigation systems. Even though many developing countries have natural gas, coal, and petroleum, others have to import the energy. Alternative sources of energy, such as wind energy, solar energy, and hydroelectric power, are attractive to poor countries that want to reduce both costs and their vulnerability to unstable global energy markets. As with other aspects of development, the construction of dams carries costs as well as benefits. The choice between constructing a dam and preserving the environment was relatively easy for Egypt, a country in which almost the entire population is concentrated in less than 5 percent of the land area. Most of Egypt is a desert. The country has always depended on the water of the Nile River for its survival. Economic development and rapid population growth influenced the British, who ruled Egypt at the time, to build the Aswan Dam, in 1902. A major objective was to store water to irrigate agricultural areas of the Nile Valley. In 1960, a hydroelectric power station was added to meet the rising demand for energy. When Gamal Abdul Nasser gained control of Egypt in 1954, he made the construction of another dam, the **Aswan High Dam,** the major component of Egypt's economic development program. The goal was to expand the amount of land for agriculture by providing relatively inexpensive water for irrigation. With the application of fertilizers and modern farming

Aswan High Dam
■ A dam built in Egypt to meet the rising demand for energy and to control flooding.

techniques, Egypt was able to plant two or three crops a year instead of just one. To build the dam, more than 90,000 people and many archaeological treasures had to be moved. Like most large infrastructure projects, construction of the Aswan High Dam generated much controversy.

One of the most controversial projects is the world's largest dam, the **Three Gorges Dam** on the Yangtze River in China. Like the Nile in Egypt, the Yangtze has played a central and often destructive role in China's history. The Yangtze flooded an area the size of New York State in 1931 and created about 14 million refugees. In 1954, the river flooded more than 6.9 million acres of land and killed more than 30,000 people. In 1998, the Yangtze flooded and nearly 14 million people were displaced and an undetermined number were killed. A principal reason for building the Three Gorges Dam is to prevent such disastrous floods, which not only take many lives but also impede China's economic development. Other reasons for building the dam are to increase electrical power for **Pudong,** a major industrial development zone not far from Shanghai, and for relatively isolated inland areas that receive electricity infrequently. The dam's construction also made it easier for ships and barges to navigate the Yangtze further into the country's underdeveloped interior. But the costs of building the Three Gorges Dam are high. Apart from the $32 billion allocated for construction, it is estimated that 1.2 million people have been removed from their homes. Hundreds of historical sites have been covered by water, and thousands of acres of fertile agricultural land have been lost. Many scenic areas that attracted tourists are now hidden. However, the Three Gorges Dam itself has become a major tourist attraction.

Three Gorges Dam
■ Located on the Yangtze River, it is the world's largest dam.

Pudong ■   A major industrial development zone in China.

Case Study: Indonesia

Indonesia, one of the childhood homes of President Barack Obama, with 240 million people, has the world's fourth-largest population and is the world's largest Muslim country. It has roughly three times the number of people in Egypt, the most populous country in the Arab world. Indonesia captured global attention due to the devastating earthquake and tsunami on December 26, 2004, which killed more than 165,000 people and left incalculable damage. Other countries in the Indian Ocean also suffered widespread death and destruction. Comprised of 17,508 islands, 6,000 of which are inhabited, Indonesia is located in one of the most dangerous places on earth. It routinely experiences earthquakes, floods, severe droughts, volcanoes, forest fires, and tsunamis.

As we saw in Chapter 3, Islam spread from the Arabian Peninsula to other parts of the world, primarily through trade. It became the dominant religion in Indonesia by the sixteenth century but did not radically alter the culture. Competition among European powers in an earlier age of globalization added Portuguese and Dutch influences. The Dutch had replaced the Portuguese as the dominant European economic power by 1750. Indonesia remained under Dutch control until Japan occupied it during World War II, from 1942 to 1945. As we saw in Chapter 4, the conflict weakened the European countries and paved the way for colonies in Africa, Asia, and the Caribbean to obtain their independence. Nationalists led by Sukarno declared Indonesia's independence. The Dutch fought the nationalists for four years before agreeing to independence in 1949. When Sukarno became president, he suspended Parliament, was named president for life, and formed close alliances with communist governments during the Cold War, which was an ideological conflict between the United States and the Soviet Union.

Following an attempted military coup in 1965, Sukarno was forced to transfer power to the army, which was led by General Suharto. Suharto became president and ruled Indonesia for 31 years. However, the Asian financial crisis in 1997 led to protests and violence in which roughly 500 people were killed. Suharto resigned in 1998 and was succeeded by his vice president, Bacharuddin Habibie. Reflecting the global trend toward democratization, Abdurrahman Wahid was elected president in 1999. However, due to pressure from the legislature, he agreed to share power with Vice President Megawati Sukarnoputri, Sukarno's daughter. Megawati became Indonesia's first female president in 2001 following the forced resignation of Wahid. She was defeated in the presidential election of 2004 by Susilo Bambang Yudhoyono, a development that marked the consolidation of democracy.

Often ranked with China, India, and Brazil as having one of the fastest-growing emerging economies, Indonesia has a per capita gross domestic product (GDP) of $4,000 and an economic growth rate of 6 percent, despite the global economic recession. Roughly two-thirds of its economic activities depend on domestic consumption, making Indonesia less vulnerable to global economic influences. Indonesia implemented policies following the Asian financial crisis in 1997 that protected it from the ravages of the global financial crisis of 2008–2009. The Asian crisis began in Indonesia and spread to Malaysia, South Korea, other parts of Asia, and to the rest of the world. Once-prosperous economies were now in deep recession, with stock markets crashing and capital flowing out of various countries at unprecedented rates. The Asian crisis was largely caused by hasty and imprudent liberalization that allowed free global flows of short-term capital without adequate attention to the potentially potent downside of such globalization.[26] Indonesia's experiences with the Asian financial crisis has made it more cautious. With Southeast Asia's largest economy and global demand for its natural resources such as coal, palm oil, coffee, and cocoa, Indonesia is attracting global capital. Compared to interest rates of close to 0 percent in some cases such as in the United States and Western Europe, Indonesia's interest rates are 6.5 percent. Fearing that the rapid inflow of investment funds could undermine financial stability and engender costs reminiscent of the Asian crisis of 1997, the Indonesian government took measures to channel money away from short-term investments.[27]

The economic globalization that contributes to Indonesia's rapid growth also challenges traditions and transforms societies. Globalization is generally equated with Westernization in general and with Americanization in particular. It is in the Islamic countries where globalization has been most violently resisted. The lack of a central religious authority, the cultural diversity of Islamic countries, and the rigidity of many interpretations of Islam make Islam more vulnerable to and threatened by the forces of globalization. Globalization engenders greater freedom, secularism, and democracy, all of which are seen as undermining traditional societies. Indonesia has historically been a moderate and tolerant society that differed significantly from the Arab world. However, terrorists and their supporters in Indonesia have embraced Islamic fundamentalism and generally perceive themselves to be in a war with the United States to rejuvenate Islam. Globalization, as we have seen, helps create winners and losers in the global economy. It widens the gap between the rich and the poor. Many Indonesian Muslims have not benefited from the country's rapid economic growth. They feel humiliated over being left behind as the rest of the world presses on into the twenty-first century.[28]

Another major cost associated with development is corruption. Indonesia has been consistently ranked near the bottom of Transparency International's yearly Corruption Perception Index. As we discussed earlier, the military exercised significant power under Suharto. They owned businesses, plantations, logging industries, hotels, and a wide range of properties. The Asian economic crisis created severe economic problems that focused public anger on nepotism, cronyism, and corruption. Responding to the public's anger, President Susilo Bambang Yudhoyono made fighting corruption a major priority. In 2002, Indonesia created an independent agency, the Corruption Eradication Commission (known as KPK) to investigate and prosecute individuals accused of involvement in corruption. Both the police and the legislature, two of the country's most corrupt institutions, routinely undermine the effectiveness of the KPK.[29]

Environmental problems are an obvious cost of Indonesia's rapid economic growth. Industrialization has contributed to climate change that is leading to further deterioration of the environment. As cities have grown larger, traffic congestion has increased, and, like China, Indonesia has high rates of water and air pollution. Industrial wastes, sewage, and forest fires also create serious environmental problems including health hazards. Demands for palm oil, hardwoods, and lumber for building, especially in China and Indonesia, have given Indonesia one of the world's highest rates of deforestation. Domestic and global pressures to address global climate change have influenced Indonesia to participate in programs designed to diminish deforestation. Increasingly, developed countries and global companies are paying people and governments in the developing world to not cut down trees and to plant more forests to reduce global carbon dioxide emissions. Trees in tropical areas like Indonesia grow much faster than trees in temperate climates and remove carbon dioxide from the atmosphere at a much faster rate.[30] In 2010, Indonesia signed an agreement with Norway and Germany that provides Indonesia with $1.5 billion to monitor and protect its forests. Indonesia is required to limit clearance of forests for two years to promote biodiversity and decrease carbon emissions. A similar agreement, the Tropical Forest Conservation Act, was made with the United States in 2009 to save Sumatran forests.

Finally, like many other developing countries, Indonesia's economic growth has been accompanied by rising rates of child labor and human trafficking. Many children work in agriculture on the palm oil, cocoa, tobacco, rubber, tea, and sugar plantations. Others work in fisheries, construction, manufacturing, footwear production, food processing, textiles, and the mining sector. Many children and women are trafficked both domestically and internationally. Increasing tourism, an important component of development, makes women and girls vulnerable to sexual exploitation and abuse. Many children also are involved in the production, trafficking, and sale of illegal drugs.

SUMMARY AND REVIEW

Economic development is accompanied by various costs. However, not all of these costs are inevitable. Sometimes countries, and particular communities within them, pay a much higher cost for economic growth than is necessary. Progress usually is achieved at a price. Developing and developed countries alike wrestle with costs of development. Many of the costs of development, however, are borne by people in the developing world as their economies are affected by rapid changes brought about by globalization. These include (1) urbanization; (2) pollution; (3) deforestation; (4) political instability and corruption; (5) the destruction of cultural artifacts and communities due to the construction of dams, airports, roads, and other infrastructure projects; (6) consumerism; and (7) the growing inequality within developing countries. These costs, even those that are obviously undesirable, are usually accompanied by many benefits. As modernization theorists argue, development, by definition, involves the destruction of traditional values and cultures and the adoption of values and cultures found in industrialized societies. One of the most important social costs of development is the escalation of criminal activities and a significant change in the nature of the crimes committed. Modernization weakens many of the social bonds that helped reduce crime. Two groups that most frequently bear the most severe negative consequences of development are women and children. Many argue that destruction of the old social fabric, degradation of the ecosystem, and high levels of exploitation are hallmarks of development. Critics of such a "no pain, no gain" approach, on the contrary, argue that development can be achieved at sustainable levels, and that the development of underdeveloped countries in Africa, Asia, and Latin America will not occur along the same destructive linear lines that were taken in case of the developed countries of Europe.

KEY TERMS

opportunity cost   125
structural adjustment programs   129
Restavec system   130
Brazil's Labor Code   130
Kaleen and Rugmark labels   130
International Labor Organization
   (ILO)   130

No Sweat   131
Green Revolution   135
urbanization   135
Ganges River   136
World Health Organization
   (WHO)   137
global warming   137

Greenpeace   137
Indonesia's Transmigration
   Program   138
Trans-Amazon Highway   138
Aswan High Dam   139
Three Gorges Dam   140
Pudong   140

DISCUSSION QUESTIONS

1. Is sustainable development an achievable goal or a hopeless utopian dream?
2. What are the negative consequences of development? Is development possible without the destruction of the old social fabric?
3. How does increased globalization place pressures on societies of Asia, Africa, and Latin America to develop?
4. Do you support development theorists in their claims that development occurs along a destructive linear path? Support your argument.
5. Does Nike set a standard for other companies to avoid exploitation of developing societies, or is its Memorandum of Understanding a pathetic, normative attempt at disguising their exploitative guilt and co-opting public opinion?

SUGGESTED READINGS

Andreas, Peter, and Kelly Greenhill. *Sex, Drugs, and Body Counts*. Ithaca, NY: Cornell University Press, 2010.

Bass, Loretta E. *Child Labor in Sub-Saharan Africa*. Boulder, CO: Lynne Rienner, 2004.

Brainard, Lael, et al. *Climate Change and Global Poverty*. Washington, DC: Brookings Institution Press, 2009.

Economy, Elizabeth C., and Adam Segal. "China's Olympic Nightmare." *Foreign Affairs* 87, No. 4 (July/August 2008): 47–56.

Esbenshade, Jill. *Monitoring Sweatshops*. Philadelphia, PA: Temple University Press, 2004.

Heymann, Jody, and Alison Earle. *Raising the Global Floor*. Stanford, IL: Stanford University Press, 2010.

Houck, Oliver A. *Taking Back Eden: Eight Environmental Cases That Changed the World*. New York: Island Press, 2010.

NOTES

1. Alfonso Gonzalez, "Introduction," in Alfonso Gonzalez and Jim Norwine, Eds., *The Third World* (Boulder, CO: Westview Press, 1998), 2.

2. Phil Gunson, "Deaths in Venezuelan Prison Spur Call for Investigation," *The Miami Herald*, 1 July 2010, 4A.

3. "U.S. Arrests Over 400 Suspects in Mexican Drug Cartel Sweep," *Daily Herald*, 11 June 2010, 29.

4. Chitra Ragavan and David Kaplan, "Why Auto Theft Is Going Global," *U.S. News and World Report*, 14 June 1999, 16; and Willem van Schendel and Itty Abraham, *Illicit Flows and Criminal Things* (Bloomington, IN: Indiana University Press, 2006).

5. Adam Nossiter, "Hundreds of Factory Workers Are Held in Immigration Raid," *The New York Times*, 26 August 2008, A12.

6. John Zubrzycki, "A Tough Buy: Child-Woven Carpets," *The Christian Science Monitor*, 30 October 1997, 1.

7. Jeremy Seabrook, "Reproach of Child Labor," *Financial Times*, 24 August 1999, 10.

8. Marc Lacey, "Children in Haiti, the Poorest of the Poor," *The New York Times*, 14 September 2008, A8.

9. "World Day Against Child Labor," *Daily Herald*, 12 June 2010, 1; and "Sex Tourism in South-East Asia," *The Economist*, 23 August 2008, 36.

10. Jodi Heymann and Alison Earle, *Raising the Global Floor* (Stanford, IL: Stanford University Press, 2010).

11. Debora L. Spar, "The Spotlight and the Bottom Line," *Foreign Affairs* 77, No. 2 (March/April 1999): 9.

12. "The Global Sweatshop," *Far Eastern Economic Review*, 19 September 1996, 5.

13. Isobel Coleman, "The Better Half: Helping Woman Help the World," *Foreign Affairs* 89, No. 1 (January/February 2010), 127.

14. Mark Landler, "Credit Cards Tighten Grip Outside U.S.," *The New York Times*, 10 August 2008, A1.

15. Jack Goldstone, "The New Population Bomb," *Foreign Affairs* 89, No. 1 (January/February 2010), 38.

16. Ibid.

17. "India and Pollution," *The Economist*, 19 July 2008, 49.

18. Elizabeth Rosenthal, "Booming China Leads the World in Emissions of Carbon Dioxide," *The New York Times*, 14 June 2008, A5; and Michael A. Levi, "Copenhagen's Inconvenient Truth," *Foreign Affairs* 88, No. 54 (September/October 2009), 96.

19. Eugene Linden, "The Exploring Cities of the Developing World," *Foreign Affairs* 75, No. 1 (January/February 1996), 57.

20. Helen Cooper and Jackie Calmes, "BP to Suspend Dividend," *The Miami Herald*, 17 June 2010, 1A.

21. "India and Pollution," *The Economist*, 19 July 2008, 49.

22. Heather Timmons, "India Offers 8 Ideas on a Climate Change Policy, But Few Details," *The New York Times*, 1 July 2008, 2008, C4; and

"China Fossil Fuel CO$_2$ Jumps," *Daily Herald*, 10 June 2010, 32.

23. Levi, "Copenhagen's Inconvenient Truth," 93.

24. "The Future of the Forest," *The Economist*, 13 June 2009, 27.

25. "Paying to Save Trees: Last Gasp for the Forest," *The Economist*, 26 September 2009, 93.

26. Jagdish Bhogwati, *In Defense of Globalization* (New York: Oxford University Press, 2004), 199.

27. "Indonesia Moves on Hot Money to Keep Financial Stability," *Daily Herald*, 17 June 2010, 36.

28. Christopher S. Bond and Lewis M. Simons, "The Forgotten Front," *Foreign Affairs* 88, No. 6 (November/December 2009), 58.

29. "Indonesia's Anti-Corruption Commission," *The Economist*, 10 October 2009, 44.

30. Joel Kurtzman, "The Low Carbon Diet," *Foreign Affairs* 88, No. 5 (September/October 2009), 121.

Women in the Developing World

Globalization and Women

The main engines of globalization—communications technology and rapid and inexpensive communications—have facilitated interactions among women and the formation of global networks. Many women from elite families who were educated in the West maintained connections with influential men and women in the United States and Western Europe. Many women in the West perceive the struggles of women in the developing world as linked to their own. Consequently, many of them pressure their governments and international organizations to make women's issues a priority in their relations with Africa, Asia, and Latin America.

One of the most potent effects of globalization is its tendency to diminish differences not only among cultures but also between men and women. Globalization has hastened the spread of the movement for gender equality by making women more aware of their status and the need to change it. Women in developing countries compare themselves with the most visible and influential women. Furthermore, global companies usually prefer to employ women in the developing world, thereby giving them a measure of financial independence. Women become more educated and are generally unwilling to accept the status quo.

Although it is common to discuss women in the developing world as a unified group, this oversimplification ignores the complexity that characterizes developing countries. Old values, challenged by new values, continue to influence relations between men and women and among women themselves. In some Islamic societies, some women insist on wearing a veil and yet others reject veiling. However, throughout the developing world, women are the principal initiators of change that will improve their lives. Modernization and globalization are eroding cultural boundaries and weakening the control that some men, the government, and some women exercise in an effort to maintain the status quo. Access to education and economic opportunities have enabled many women in Asia, Latin America, and Africa to develop a degree of social and financial independence that most women in the United States and other industrialized countries enjoy. The UN Development Programme created the gender empowerment measure (GEM) to focus on women's participation in economic and political activities. It also concentrates on gender disparities in government and economic opportunities.

Global changes have not affected all women in the same way. Development has, in some cases, helped widen the economic and social gaps among women. Rural and urban women do not necessarily have the same problems or opportunities. Furthermore, each country has its own traditions and policies relating to women. These differences make it difficult to generalize about women in developing areas. Nonetheless, there is widespread agreement that women throughout the developing world are bringing about economic, social, and political changes. This chapter discusses the roles and status of women, the practice of veiling, female genital mutilation, the sale of women, and "honor" killings. It also examines educational opportunities for women, the role of women in economic development, and women's political participation, including leadership roles.

THE ROLES OF WOMEN

People in all societies have certain perceptions of themselves and of others. How we see ourselves, and those around us, is shaped by values that we learn from parents, teachers, religious authorities, friends, and the media through the process of **socialization.** Values are widely shared beliefs and assumptions about what defines right and wrong, proper and improper, and just and unjust. These values, beliefs, and perceptions tell us how to relate to others and how they should relate to us. They tell us how to behave. In other words, values and perceptions help determine our roles in society. Many of these values and perceptions are reinforced by laws and policies made by governments. **Roles** can be defined as expectations regarding the skills, rights, and duties of individuals. Roles function as prescriptions for inter-personal behaviors that are associated with particular categories of persons.[1] But people constantly challenge prescribed roles, thereby changing societal perceptions of how men and women should behave and relate to each other.

In June 1998, the Southern Baptist Convention, America's largest Protestant denomination, issued a controversial statement that called on women to submit themselves graciously to their husbands' leadership.[2] When King Hussein of Jordan died in early 1999, his American wife, Queen Noor, did not attend the funeral. Because of Muslim teachings that discourage the mixing of unrelated men and women, female relatives of King Hussein stayed at home to accept condolences from other women.[3] It may be argued that these two examples should not be equated. However, in both cases, religion and tradition support maintaining what many regard as different and distinct roles. These examples, although not equivalent, show that developed countries also have many stereotypes. At the same time, women are helping undermine those traditional roles. Several women in leadership roles, including Rima Khalaf, a member of the Jordanian senate, Queen Beatrix of the Netherlands, and President Mary McAleese of Ireland, attended King Hussein's funeral.

Most countries in Africa, Asia, and Latin America have traditions that make women primarily responsible for domestic work. Latin American societies generally view women as moral guardians of the family. Women teach values and morality by example. Susan Tiano maintains that according to the ideology of **marianismo,** the cult of Virgin Mary, the family is seen as being held together spiritually and emotionally through the mother's steadfast devotion. Marianismo supports the gender division of labor, which confines women to the house.[4] In some Islamic societies, religion assigns domestic roles to women. The emphasis on women as guardians of the family virtue sometimes leads to extreme actions, such as honor killings, when women violate social roles. In Bangladesh, India, and other Asian societies, women are responsible for taking care of their own families and their husbands' families.

Gender roles in poor countries are shaped to some extent by colonialism and the globalization of industry and trade. Plantation agriculture in Africa, for example, weakened the role of women as farmers. Colonial authorities imposed their own values on the Africans. They strengthened the role of men as heads of families, provided education for men on a limited scale, hired men to work in agriculture, and emphasized training in domestic skills for women.[5] Many women, however, managed to continue as entrepreneurs. The decline of plantation agriculture contributed to the

---

socialization ■ The process in which values and perceptions help to determine our roles in society.

roles
■ Expectations regarding the duties, rights, and skills of individuals.

marianismo ■ An ideology in which the family is seen as being held together spiritually and emotionally through the mother's steadfast devotion.

emergence of women as the primary producers of food. As countries industrialize, more women work in labor-intensive industries. Women are the majority of workers in the apparel, footwear, and electronics industries in Asia and Latin America. Increasingly, more women are gaining major positions in areas such as law, business, higher education, finance, medicine, and government, in addition to nursing, teaching, and other traditional fields. The roles of women are closely linked to their status.

THE STATUS OF WOMEN

Women generally have a lower status than men in most societies, including those in the industrialized world. **Status** refers to one's position in the social, economic, and political hierarchies. Men are generally regarded as occupying a higher place than women in the social system. These positions are largely **socially constructed,** primarily by men. This means that societies use subjective standards to determine who will have a higher or lower status. These standards are subject to change as societies change. Tradition, religion, political and social beliefs, and economics determine status. In Saudi Arabia, for example, law and tradition impose male guardianship over women. Women are not allowed to drive. They cannot legally study, work, travel, marry, obtain medical care, and sign contracts without the consent of a male relative. Women in societies in which religion does not play a dominant role generally have a higher status than women in countries where social relations are based on religion. As societies become more industrialized and the economic position of women is strengthened, the gap in status between men and women narrows. Modernization, economic necessity, and globalization are forces that challenge notions of status based on tradition and religion.

Marriage exemplifies the differences in status between men and women. Men in some Islamic societies are permitted by law and religion to have four wives and to divorce them. On the other hand, women are allowed to have one husband and cannot easily obtain a divorce. A Muslim woman cannot marry a non-Muslim unless he becomes a Muslim. However, a Muslim man may marry a non-Muslim woman, but she too needs to convert to Islam. In Egypt, for example, the law allowed rapists to escape punishment if they married their victims. Parents and other relatives of rape victims have used the law to regain their family's honor. Parents of brides in some societies provide **dowries,** or property, given at the time of marriage. Many women are killed in India, Pakistan, and Bangladesh because their husbands are not satisfied with the size of their dowries. Women in Bangladesh who have achieved a degree of financial success to enable them to refuse marriage proposals have been victimized by the rejected men. Some have had acid splashed in their faces, to be blinded for life. Widows in India become dependent on their husbands' families, many of whom perceive them as social and economic burdens. Eventually, many Hindu widows become social outcasts, a fate they believe to be their Karma. Karma is the Hindu belief that what happens to one in this life is determined by one's good or evil deeds in a previous life. The low status of women is further demonstrated by veiling, female genital mutilation, the selling of girls, and honor killing.

status ■ One's position in the social, economic, and political hierarchies.

socially constructed ■ Subjective standards used by societies.

dowries ■ Money given to a husband for marrying a particular woman.

veiling ■ The covering of a woman's body with garments that preserve the notion of male dominance and female subservience.

Veiling symbolizes gender segregation, the unequal relationship between men and women, and the complex nature of status in some Muslim countries. It also represents a broader cultural and political defense against Western cultural influences that appear to be irresistible even in very religious and traditional societies. But the main function of veiling is to preserve male dominance and female subservience and chastity. It is in countries where Islamic fundamentalism dominates that veiling is strictly enforced. As religious groups became more powerful in Iraq, following the fall of Saddam Hussein's regime, women were coerced into wearing veils. Women have generally suffered personal, social, economic, and political setbacks under the Shiite-dominated government. Veiling varies from one Islamic society to another and covers a broad range of garments.[6] The veil in Morocco covers most of a woman's face and the rest of her body. In other countries, the veil leaves the face uncovered. Women in Afghanistan were covered from head to toe. In Turkey, Egypt, Tunisia, and other Muslim countries, the veil is used as a fashion statement, and what it covers depends on the message the wearers intend to communicate.

Taliban movement ■ Composed of extreme Islamic fundamentalists in Afghanistan.

Afghanistan, Saudi Arabia, and Iran are examples of how veiling represents maintaining or returning to Islamic traditions. These countries are concerned with preserving their identity and interpretation of Islamic heritage in the face of steady erosion of values and norms associated with a purer form of traditional Islam. All three countries have been exposed to Westernization and, in varying degrees, are resisting Western values. The Islamic **Taliban movement,** which ruled most of Afghanistan until 2002, was the most extreme of the Islamic fundamentalists. The religious police, in the General Department for the Preservation of Virtue and Prevention of Vice, came from villages in which contact between men and women who are not family members has always been forbidden. The Taliban strictly segregated men and women. Women were beaten if they allowed their faces, feet, or ankles to show beneath the mandatory head-to-toe shrouds. Women's bodies, including their ankles and feet, were seen as being sexually provocative. The veil in Afghanistan was equated with morality and female subservience. The defeat of the Taliban in 2002 by American and British forces ended many of the restrictions on women in Afghanistan. However, the resurgence of the Taliban threatens women's freedoms. Saudi Arabia is a much more complex and less extreme society than Afghanistan. However, the moral police in Saudi Arabia also enforce strict dress codes. Women are not allowed to drive automobiles, wear short sleeves in public, or appear in public without covering their heads. Iran, which experienced significant social and economic changes before Ayatollah Khomeini took control of the country, struggles with both modernization and Islamic fundamentalism. Religious authorities in Iran enforce laws requiring women to wear the Islamic **chadore,** which covers their bodies completely. Some women wear the veil for personal, political, and cultural reasons. Many women see Islamic dress as giving them both dignity and privacy in their societies. Modern women in urban areas may wear the veil in order to communicate their adherence to the Islamic moral and sexual code, while, at the same time, allowing them to interact with men. Women from traditional families and rural areas wear the veil in places such as Egypt to maintain a sense of identity. Coming from areas where men and women are segregated, women see the veil as providing security for women in sexually integrated settings.

chadore ■ A garment that women are required by law to wear in Iran and that covers the body completely.

It also allows women to maintain outward signs of traditional behavior even as they participate in modern life.[7]

Throughout the Islamic world women are challenging veiling and the values it represents. In fact, the renewed emphasis on veiling women reflects significant cultural change. Many Islamic fundamentalists adopt extreme measures precisely because they see their power eroding in the face of modernization and globalization. Practical economic concerns have always challenged the status quo. Many women in the United States, who once worked at home, now work outside the home because of economic as well as social reasons. As more women are educated, find employment, and live in urban areas, traditional forces are weakened. Veiling is at the heart of political conflict and social change. Men and women, primarily from less-privileged economic backgrounds, use religion and traditional values to assist the old order to maintain political and social control. Women who do not wear the veil are usually from the upper and middle class. These two groups clash because their interests and perceptions of women are fundamentally different.[8]

Female genital mutilation, also known as female circumcision, is an extreme form of social control. It is practiced in societies in which women are given a low social status. Even though both men and women are circumcised, female genital mutilation is largely done for the benefit of men. It enables them to control women by inflicting severe pain during sexual intercourse. There are varying degrees of female genital mutilation. It involves the removal of the clitoris in its less severe form, and all of the external female genitals in its most severe form. In extreme cases, genitals are stitched shut, with only a small opening left through which urine and menstrual fluids can pass. These crude and painful operations are usually performed with knives and razors by traditional women practitioners. The main objective of female genital mutilation is to deprive women of any sexual feelings. By so doing, men are assured of women's chastity. Some women are severely injured and many bleed to death from the procedure. Chronic urinary tract infections are common, and childbirth is dangerous and extraordinarily painful. Egypt, Nigeria, Ethiopia, Somalia, Kenya, and the Sudan account for about 75 percent of the cases.[9] Like veiling, female genital mutilation is usually seen as a religious practice as well as a cultural issue by some Islamic conservatives. Muslims in Africa believe that the circumcision of girls is as much a religious requirement as the circumcision of boys. Parents and girls who are educated are increasingly opposed to the operation. Furthermore, some governments, despite opposition from religious and traditional leaders, have banned genital mutilation.

The **sale of females** remains an important indicator of the status of women in developing countries. Like other forms of human bondage, this trafficking of young girls and women is rooted in both traditional and economic considerations. People of lower social and economic status are generally vulnerable to extreme forms of exploitation and even death. In Asia and Africa, poor girls and women are often sold by their families as brides. In some parts of Kenya, for example, mothers encourage their daughters to remain chaste so that they may obtain a higher price for them. This preoccupation with virginity influences families and others to sell very young girls, both as brides and as prostitutes. Unlike in India, where women pay dowries to men, tradition in Africa requires a man to pay a **bride price.** Girls who are educated are often sold for higher prices. Sometimes the bride's family will take her from her husband if he fails to make regular payments.[10]

female genital mutilation ■ The practice of circumcising women for the benefit of men; it is often defended on the grounds of cultural relativism.

sale of females ■ Practice of trafficking young girls and women into forced marriages and prostitution.

bride price ■ A tradition in Africa in which a man is required to pay for his bride.

Women throughout the world are forced or choose to go into prostitution primarily for economic reasons. Young girls are especially vulnerable. India, Bangladesh, Thailand, Cambodia, and other Asian countries have long traditions of family-sanctioned prostitution. In Nepal, for example, as many as 40,000 girls and women have been sold and forced into prostitution, mostly in neighboring India. Many Nepalese girls from destitute families, especially those from low castes, often see leaving their homes as their only hope for a better life. This makes them easy victims for sex traffickers. Because of the low status of women, and perceptions of prostitution as a business, not a moral issue, some families willingly sell their daughters. As in other Asian societies, Nepalese families tend to value sons more than daughters. Sons are viewed as assets, whereas daughters are viewed as liabilities. This facilitates selling daughters into prostitution. Similar practices are found in Africa and Latin America.[11]

honor killings ■ The slaughter of women who are deemed to be unchaste.

Honor killings occur in societies in which women are basically regarded as bodies over which male relatives have absolute control, including the power to destroy them. Such murders are becoming infrequent and occur primarily in rural areas and traditional societies. Sex has always been a central reason for extreme forms of control exercised by men over women. Honor killing is the slaughter of women deemed to be unchaste by male relatives. An unchaste woman is regarded as a threat to the family's honor, or **sharaf**. Honor is defined in terms of the sexual purity of women. Female chastity is equivalent to honor and respect. An unchaste woman is often perceived as being worse than a murderer, even if she is raped, because she essentially destroys her family socially. Family members are usually ostracized. Only by killing unchaste women can the family's honor be cleansed and restored. Marrying or divorcing without the family's consent may also result in honor killings. For example, five women were killed in Baluchistan Province in Pakistan in 2008 because three of them had planned to be married without the consent of male relatives. The other two victims were older female relatives who supported the young women. A provincial lawmaker defended the honor killings as societal norms. Although honor killings are generally associated with Muslims in a few Arab countries, they also occur among Arab Christians in Egypt, Jordan, and Palestine, and in non-Arab countries such as India, Pakistan, and Turkey. In Brazil and other South American countries, men often kill women to protect their honor. Many Muslims who favor the practice use Islamic teachings to justify killing their unchaste female relatives. This perception is strengthened in Jordan, where one-fourth of all murders each year are honor killings. Jordan treats premarital sex as a criminal offense, equal to adultery. A pregnant unmarried woman has no rights to her child, which is taken away at birth and raised in an orphanage. In 2009, women in the Sudan were given 10 lashes and fined $100 each for wearing pants in public.[12]

sharaf ■ A family's honor.

RAPE AS A WEAPON OF WAR

The rape of women and girls has accompanied virtually all violent conflicts throughout history. From ancient times, in Rwanda, the former Yugoslavia, the Congo, Sierra Leone, Liberia, and the Sudan, rape has been deliberately and systematically used as a weapon of war. The basic objectives of using rape as a weapon have always been to humiliate, dominate, disgrace, degrade, and terrify not only individual victims but also their families, ethnic groups, and national communities. In Zimbabwe, for example, rape was consistently used as a weapon of humiliation and political intimidation during the 2008 election. Female relatives of members of the political opposition were raped in front of their families. Many victims were deliberately infected with AIDS. Similar violence against women and girls routinely occurs in Darfur, Sudan, as an integral component of the genocide campaign that is being carried out by Arabs against black Africans. Rape as a weapon of war is widely practiced in the Congo. Rape as a weapon of war received special attention in the human rights debates following World War II. The international community explicitly stated that rape is a crime against humanity, a war crime. The International Criminal Tribunal for the former Yugoslavia, the International Criminal Tribunal for Rwanda, the Special Court for Sierra Leone, and the International Criminal Court regard rape as a gross violation of fundamental human rights and treat it as a war crime, a crime against humanity. Nobel Peace Prize laureates Shirin Ebadi of Iran and Wangari Maathi of Kenya argue that national laws must be changed to make it easier for women to prove that they are victims of gender-based crimes, especially at the International Criminal Court.[13]

WOMEN AND EDUCATION

Educating women is essential to economic and political development as well as to improving the status of women. Because educated women challenge traditional roles, men's control over their lives is weakened. Early marriages, an emphasis on childbearing, and religious beliefs have prevented women from achieving educational equality. In Afghanistan, for example, the Taliban, the Islamic movement that once controlled most of the country, outlawed education for women, closed educational institutions for women, and prevented women from teaching. The only schools that girls could attend were required to teach the Quran, the holy book for Muslims. Girls older than eight years could not legally attend school. Afghanistan represented extreme efforts to force women into inferior positions by depriving them of access to education. In the developing world, men have higher literacy rates than women, but this is changing as countries achieve greater economic growth. Literacy rates are essentially the same for women and men in rich countries. They are similar in the more industrialized societies in Asia and Latin America. Korea, Thailand, the Philippines, Mexico, Costa Rica, Brazil, and Chile have substantial gender equality in literacy. On the other hand, more traditional societies such as Saudi Arabia, India, Egypt, Pakistan, Bangladesh, and Ethiopia do not.

Many governments have made deliberate efforts to educate women because they see them as the key to development. As part of its revolutionary approach, the new government in Egypt, which overthrew King Farouk in 1952, implemented equal educational opportunities for women. Education was made compulsory and free for all students between the ages of 6 and 12. University education was opened to both men and women on a competitive basis, and the government not only made higher education free and accessible to those who qualified for admission but also guaranteed them jobs after graduation. Women in urban and less traditional areas benefited most from these changes. Improvements in education for women change women's perceptions of themselves and their status and roles in society. The empowerment of women through education has far-reaching implications for economic growth, gender equality, and social equity. The World Bank, the United Nations, and private organizations finance programs that allow women to attend literacy classes in private homes or small schools. They learn how to write their names, read at a basic level, and do simple arithmetic. The not-for-profit Sewa Project in India provides employment for women through their handicrafts. One Sewa success story is Kakuben Lalabhi Parmar, a member of the "untouchable" caste in India, married at 14 and mother of seven, who by 2010 had become a globe-trotting businesswoman and advocate for the education of women.[14] Such programs are influencing Indian women to become more self-confident, to discard the veil, to be less dependent on their husbands, and to protect themselves and their children. Many women now challenge the customs of feeding girls less than boys and waiting longer to give girls medical attention. These customs result in high rates of malnutrition among girls and women. Women who are literate better understand how depriving girls of proper nutrition ultimately contributes to the birth of weaker males.

WOMEN IN DEVELOPMENT

Women's role in the development process is shaped to a large extent by how they are perceived in their societies. Although traditional societies limit women to specific occupations, in many parts of Asia and the Middle East women are the backbone of the local economy. They gather fuel, get water, raise animals, manage local markets, and engage in business transactions in the barter economy. Several factors have caused women to become more active in all sectors of the economy. International development agencies such as the U.S. Agency for International Development (AID), the World Bank, and the United Nations have placed greater emphasis on the need to include more women in development programs. In an AID/CARE International (Cooperative for Assistance and Relief Everywhere, Inc.) project in Afghanistan in 2010, women made up half the workers in a face-lift of the Kabul Women's Garden, doing landscaping and rebuilding paths and walls, which was nontraditional for Afghan women. Economic necessity has also contributed to the participation of the growing number of women in the labor force. The most important reasons for the sharp rise in women's employment are globalization and the erosion of traditional values that rigidly defined women's roles. Global pressures have contributed to greater attention to gender responsive budgets that reflect governments' commitment to promoting gender equality through the allocation of public resources.

Many women are solely responsible for their family's economic welfare. They engage in subsistence farming as more men migrate to cities. Many reluctantly join the job market to help maintain living standards that have been undermined by economic crisis and structural adjustment policies imposed by the International Monetary Fund (IMF). Economic crises influence governments to reduce spending on social programs. As we have seen, the IMF will often require them to balance their budgets as a condition for receiving financial assistance. Latin America, with its huge debt burden, was forced to abandon cultural values that kept women at home when the region faced serious economic decline in the 1980s. This period of economic crisis is often called the **Lost Decade.** Even in Saudi Arabia, where women are strictly controlled, forbidden by law to drive, and segregated, more women are working outside the home. In 1996, the Saudi government made it legal for women to work in the private sector. The main impetus for change is economic decline. As the price of oil dropped from around $37 a barrel in 1979 and 1980 to about $10 a barrel in 1998, the Saudi per capita gross domestic product (GDP) plummeted from around $18,000 to $6,000. Similarly, the economic crisis in Asia in the late 1990s prompted more women to enter the labor markets.

Lost Decade ■ The period of economic decline in Latin America in the 1980s.

Economic development in poor countries, increased educational opportunities and achievements for women, women's greater self-confidence, declining fertility rates, and other forces of modernization contribute to the growth of the number of women in the workforce. Free trade and globalization changed not only how and where products are made, but also who makes them. Many jobs that were once performed mainly by women in the industrialized world are now done by women in developing countries for lower wages. The growth of service industries further heightened the demand for low-cost, efficient labor. Globalization and the information technologies have led to what is called the **feminization of employment** in the newly created industries.[15]

feminization of employment ■ The increasing number of women working in the new global economy.

Most women are concentrated in the labor-intensive and low-wage industries such as clothing, textiles, shoes, electronics, and communications. Most of the jobs open to women require a willingness to take orders, manual dexterity, an ability to do monotonous tasks, and a willingness to work with the public. These jobs provide limited opportunities for upward mobility or decision-making authority and are closely linked to stereotypes of women's roles. Women in factories are still seen as nurturing, docile, subservient, and responsible. In the **maquiladora industry,** for example, single, childless women who have completed secondary school are the preferred workers. Occupational segregation by sex, a situation in which men get higher-paying jobs than women, reinforces gender stereotypes.[16]

maquiladora industry ■ Prefers to hire single, childless women who graduated from high school.

WOMEN IN AGRICULTURE

Although more women are being employed in global factories, men are much more likely to be employed in the private sector than women. Men still receive most of the jobs in urban areas throughout the developing world. Many leave women behind in rural areas to engage in subsistence agriculture. Women are expected to grow enough food for their families and to produce cash crops to supplement their income. It is difficult to determine precisely how much of the agricultural production is done by women. The Food and Agriculture Organization (FAO) of the United Nations estimates that women's contribution to the production of food crops ranges from 30 percent in the Sudan to 80 percent in the Democratic Republic of the Congo. The role of women in agriculture will become even more significant as world food prices increase and there is more starvation due to population growth, drought, and natural disasters.[17] Although women play a crucial role in agriculture, many aid organizations often assume that men are the farmers and overlook or downplay women's contributions. Governments tend to give men more financial and technical assistance than women.

Economic and cultural changes are making it easier for women to become entrepreneurs. Advocates of community-based development and sustainable development tend to focus on women's economic contribution as essential to the overall development of a country. Although many efforts to include women in entrepreneurial activities occur at the grassroots level, much of the impetus for them comes from private voluntary organizations (PVOs), various nongovernmental organizations (NGOs), and individuals from outside the area. A key aspect of helping women to build their own businesses is helping them gain access to credit. Women's access to financial support assists the development process in several ways:

1. Women are able to contribute more to household expenditures and increase the value of their assets.
2. More money in the hands of women also means greater consumption, which stimulates more economic growth.
3. Women who work outside the home are likely to have lower fertility rates, greater access to health care, better nutrition, and increased self-empowerment.
4. As their financial status improves, many other aspects of their lives are likely to change.

Women not only enhance their own educational opportunities and access to new cultural values and technologies but also make sure that their children have similar advantages. Women must have access to credit to break the cycle of poverty by becoming entrepreneurs.

Women face several obstacles when they attempt to obtain credit. Major banks and other lending institutions attempt to minimize their risks by working with larger and more secure borrowers. Women are disadvantaged by their general lack of control over their financial resources and widespread cultural perceptions of women as "minors" who are dependent on men. Another problem faced by women is their role as homemaker. Throughout the world, women who work at home are not generally regarded in the same way as women who work outside the home. Women's reproductive lives are another disadvantage. Caring for large families makes it difficult to convince lenders that one can also manage a business simultaneously. Perhaps the most important barrier for women is **internal self-selection.** This refers to the tendency of individuals to decide not to apply for loans. In other words, they select themselves out of the process. Self-selection occurs for several reasons: (1) Some women believe that they do not need credit. (2) Others will not apply for loans because of their experiences with gender discrimination, which lead them to believe that they will be rejected. This creates a self-fulfilling prophecy. (3) Self-selection is often based on erroneous assumptions and information. Although women may correctly assume that their loan applications will be rejected because they lack sufficient income or collateral, they may also incorrectly assume they do not meet the criteria for financial support. Because of these reasons, many women in poor countries rely on the informal sector for their financial services.[18]

internal self-selection
■ The tendency of individuals to decide not to apply for loans.

The Grameen Bank is the best example of an informal lending program that is targeted at rural women. More than 2.3 million people in Bangladesh have received microloans to start their own businesses. More than 94 percent of the borrowers are women. More than 150 organizations around the world, including some in the United States, have replicated the Grameen model to help women escape poverty and its negative consequences. The Grameen Bank was created in Bangladesh by **Muhammad Yunus.** He believed that banks and other financial institutions, by concentrating on individuals with collateral and reliable incomes, excluded the poor from the development process. Taking a grassroots approach to development, the Grameen Bank provides credit to members of the self-selected small groups, about five to seven women. These group members are responsible for each other, and their individual access to credit depends on the group's performance. To become a member of a group, women must be poor, must not be related to others in the group, and must agree to help each other succeed in their entrepreneurial activities. This approach entails peer support as well as peer pressure. Women are required to learn the rules of the Grameen Bank and to memorize a social contract, known as the **Sixteen Decisions.** These include (1) a commitment to educating their children, (2) a refusal to take or give a dowry, (3) an emphasis on self-improvement and economic prosperity, and (4) a pledge to have small families. At the foundation of the Sixteen Decisions are **four principles:** discipline, unity, courage, and hard work. Women must pass an oral exam that tests their understanding of the bank's rules and its Sixteen Decisions. Once the group qualifies for participation in the program, only two members are allowed to apply for loans. These loans are small, ranging from $25 to $75. After the first two women make about 5 out of 50 payments, another two members qualify for microloans. The last member will receive a loan when the second two members make four payments. Members are eligible for larger loans after all of them have repaid the initial loans.[19] This program is widely viewed as being extremely successful in lifting women and their families out of poverty. In 2006, Yunus was awarded the Nobel Peace Prize for his work with the Grameen Bank.

Muhammad Yunus
■ Created the Grameen Bank.

Sixteen Decisions
■ The social contract of the Grameen Bank.

four principles
■ Discipline, unity, courage, and hard work—the foundation of the Sixteen Decisions.

WOMEN'S POLITICAL PARTICIPATION

Women's participation in politics is influenced to a large extent by a particular society's perceptions of women, their roles, their status, and the country's level of economic and political development. As societies develop, women's political participation also rises. In most political systems, however, women experience varying degrees of political marginalization. Politics is still regarded as an activity for men. Barbara Nelson and Najma Chowdhury refer to this tendency as the **maleness of politics.** They argue that politics is closely connected to the traditional fatherly connotation of patriarchy, which excludes women from power, and to fraternalism. Politics has historically been the province of a brotherhood of men.[20] The American Revolution, the French Revolution, and others focused on the equality of men and fraternity. Nonetheless, women are experiencing unprecedented participation in politics. Women, as will be discussed, occupy important political offices and leadership positions in several developing countries.

maleness of politics
■ Politics regarded as an activity for men.

Madres de la Plaza de Mayo ■ Mothers who marched in Argentina to draw attention to the "disappeared."

Women's political rights have been gradually recognized, first by the right to vote and then by the removal of barriers to their access to public office. As women exercised their right to vote, political parties, interest groups, and other political organizations were pressured to include them in various political institutions. Furthermore, as the international system changes from a preoccupation with security issues to a greater concern with social and economic issues, women are better equipped to play a greater role in politics. Influenced by a sense of justice and strong opposition to gross violations of human rights, women mobilized to bring about change. The **Madres de la Plaza de Mayo,** Argentine mothers who marched daily in Argentina, drew attention to the "disappeared," their relatives who had been killed by the government.[21] Throughout the developing world, women's involvement in politics has reached unprecedented levels. Women in Africa and the Middle East are generally not as actively involved in politics as women in other developing areas. Most African countries are still dominated by cultural values that emphasize politics primarily as a male activity and stress the subordination of women. Women in the northern parts of Africa, where Islam is strong, must also contend with religious beliefs that allow men to control their lives. Husbands and fathers determine women's political participation. Another factor limiting African women's role in politics is education. Uneducated women are less likely than educated women to vote. Women who have access to financial resources—market women in West Africa, for example—are more engaged in political life. Finally, women must often work closely with men and concentrate on men's interests to succeed in a male-dominated political system. Politically active women, usually better educated and wealthier than most women, often pursue class rather than gender issues.[22] Their interests and positions may be actually threatened by increased participation by women from lower social and economic backgrounds. All of these factors combine to diminish African women's political involvement.

Women in some parts of the Middle East, as we have seen, tend to be rigidly governed by religious and traditional beliefs that exclude them from politics. Furthermore, most countries in the Middle East are not democracies. However, women in countries such as Egypt and Iran vote. Despite restrictions imposed on women by Iran's Islamic government, women are making significant progress. In 2009, women held 3 percent of the seats in Iran's parliament. It is important to point out that women in Iran had achieved a high level of education and many were indistinguishable from women in Europe and America before the Iranian Revolution of 1979 turned the country into an Islamic state. Since 1956, women in Egypt had the right to vote and to run for public office. Throughout the Middle East, including in conservative Saudi Arabia, women are demanding more rights from governments.

Women in India, Pakistan, and Bangladesh have actively participated in politics and have become leaders in all three countries. India, known as the world's largest democracy because of its population, was ruled by Prime Minister Indira Gandhi from 1966 to 1977 and from 1980 to 1984. Although India is a democracy, traditional values, religion, widespread poverty, and the pervasive and deeply rooted caste system discourage women from fully participating in politics. However, economic progress in India is contributing to a growing number of women and men who are challenging the status quo. To bring more women into politics, India passed a constitutional amendment in 1993 that set aside a third of all **panchayat,** or village council seats, and village chief positions for women. It further allocated a percentage of those for women from the lowest rungs of the caste system, based on their percentage of the population.[23] This approach is consistent with India's policy of affirmative action for the low castes of society.

panchayat ■ Village council seats in India.

Pakistan, under Prime Minister Benazir Bhutto, attempted to bring more women and the poor into the political process. The **Pakistan People's Party (PPP)** ran on a platform that promised to eliminate barriers to women's political participation. Bhutto and the PPP wanted to (1) sign the UN Convention on the elimination of all forms of discrimination against women, (2) improve working conditions and job opportunities for women, (3) introduce maternity leave, (4) repeal laws that discriminated against women, and (5) promote female literacy.[24] These promises were not implemented because of resistance from members of Bhutto's own party who held strong patriarchal views on women's status and roles in society. Furthermore, political problems that threatened the survival of Bhutto's government diverted attention away from women's issues. Political instability remains a major impediment to implementing reforms that empower women politically. Finally, Islamic fundamentalists in Pakistan have succeeded in reinforcing values that emphasize women's inferior status and exclusion from political life.

Pakistan People's Party ■ Promised to support women's equality.

Bangladesh, one of the poorest countries in the world, recognizes women's right to vote and hold elective office. Similar to women in India and Pakistan, women in Bangladesh encounter cultural and economic constraints to political participation, despite formal constitutional guarantees of political equality. Women who engage in political activities are often accused by religious leaders and others of violating the rule of **Purdah.** Purdah requires women to wear veils, restricts their mobility and social interaction, and limits access to employment. Many poor and illiterate women have formed village associations to challenge tradition and to secure their rights. They are demanding (1) an end to the illegal but common practice of **oral divorce,** which allows a husband to divorce his wife simply by telling her that he is divorcing her, (2) the abolition of dowries, and (3) ending the sexual harassment of women.

Purdah ■ The rule that requires women to wear veils, restricts their mobility and social interaction, and limits access to employment.

oral divorce ■ Practice that allows a husband to divorce his wife simply by telling her that he is divorcing her.

Latin American women are less constrained by tradition and are generally more highly educated than women in many parts of the developing world. The revolutionary tradition in parts of Latin America and the area's geographical and cultural proximity to the United States laid the foundation for women's involvement in political life. Influenced in part by the struggle of women in the United States for political equality, Brazilian women formed their own suffragist movement. Like the suffragist movement in the United States, the Brazilian movement was led by upper-class and professional women who strongly believed that women should have the right to vote. Some of the women had participated in women's international conferences, which heightened their awareness of gains made by women in other countries. By 1932, 12 years after American women won the right to vote, Brazilian women achieved their right to vote. Shortly thereafter, in 1933, Carlota Pereira de Queiroz, a physician from Sao Paulo and a member of a traditional and wealthy family, became the first woman to be elected to Parliament.[25] On October 31, 2010, **Dilma Rousseff** was elected Brazil's first female president. In 2006, Michelle Bachelet was elected as the president of Chile and Portia Simpson-Miller was elected as the prime minister of Jamaica. In 2007, Cristina de Kirchner was elected as the president of Argentina. As educational opportunities increased for women, more of them became politically active.

Women in Mexico have also made significant gains in politics. Women are well represented in Mexico's federal government workforce. Women held 22 percent of the seats in Mexico's Congress in 2009. Women have held positions such as the Comptroller General, the Secretary of Tourism, and the Secretary of the Environment, Natural resources, and Fisheries. In mid-1999, Amalia Garcia Medina was elected to head the Party of the Democratic Revolution (PRD), one of the three main political parties in Mexico. In 1995, Maria de los Angeles Moreno was appointed to lead the Institutional Revolutionary Party (PRI). Women's political participation is rising as most countries in Latin America make a transition to democracy and embrace free trade.

Dilma Rousseff
■ First female president of Brazil, elected in 2010.

WOMEN LEADERS IN THE DEVELOPING WORLD

One of the most interesting paradoxes in the developing world is that countries that generally perceive women as inferior are often governed by women. These leaders share several characteristics: (1) They are from elite families, (2) they are usually highly educated, (3) they enter politics to continue the work of their husbands or fathers, and (4) they enter politics after their husbands or fathers have been assassinated while in political office or when they challenged the ruling elite. Women's ascent to power in countries that regard women as inferior demonstrates that gender is not the only consideration. These are cases in which families are so powerful that gender becomes a secondary factor. Many of these families played a crucial role in their countries' independence struggles. Indira Gandhi of India, Aung San Suu Kyi of Burma, and Megawati Sukarnoputri of Indonesia came from such families.

Indira Gandhi
■ India's leader from 1966 to 1977 and from 1980 to 1984.

Indira Gandhi, leader of the world's second most populous country, is perhaps the best known of all the women who rose to leadership positions. She was the only child of Jawaharlal Nehru, the head of the Indian National Congress Party, the country's dominant political party. Nehru, a leader in India's struggle for independence, became that country's first prime minister. Educated at Visva-Bharati University in India and Oxford University in Britain, Indira Gandhi served as her father's official hostess and unofficial advisor. She was elected to several leadership positions in the Congress Party before becoming prime minister in 1966, two years after her father died. Indira Gandhi ruled India for a total of 15 years, before she was assassinated by Sikh members of her security guard. Her government had implemented policies to forcefully suppress Sikh insurgents.

Benazir Bhutto
■ First woman to lead Pakistan.

Benazir Bhutto, a leader of Pakistan, was the first woman to lead a Muslim country. Pakistan, which was considered part of the British-ruled India, became a separate state when India gained its independence in 1947. As discussed in Chapter 3, Pakistan was formed for Muslims under the leadership of Ali Jinnah, a secular charismatic lawyer. India, which is predominantly Hindu, has been involved in many conflicts with Muslim Pakistan. Although India remained a democracy, despite periods of political turbulence, Pakistan has suffered from political instability, military rule, and religious extremism. Benazir Bhutto, like Indira Gandhi, grew up in a political family. Her father, Zulfiqar Ali Bhutto, belonged to one of the most important landowning families in Pakistan. He became Pakistan's leader in 1971 following his country's defeat by India and the resignation of President Yahya Khan. In 1977, he was overthrown by General Zia ul-Haq; he was hanged in 1979. Benazir Bhutto, like Indira Gandhi, learned politics from her father. In the male-dominated society of Pakistan, her father favored her over his two sons and another daughter. A Muslim, Benazir Bhutto was educated by Catholic nuns before going to Harvard University for under-graduate studies and to Oxford, which her father had attended, for graduate work. Bhutto returned to Pakistan in 1977 and protested her father's imprison-ment and the military rule. She was jailed or placed under house arrest for much of the period between 1977 and 1984, when she was allowed to leave Pakistan to receive medical treatment in London. When General ul-Haq ended martial law and permitted political parties to function as a step in a transition to democracy in 1986, Benazir Bhutto returned to Pakistan. Largely because of her father's leadership of Pakistan and his murder by the military government, Benazir Bhutto enjoyed wide popular support. She became Pakistan's prime minister in 1988, shortly after General ul-Haq was killed in a plane crash.[26] She was ousted from power in 1996. When she returned to Pakistan in 2007 to compete in elec-tions for a new president, she was restricted by Pervez Musharraf, Pakistan's president. She was assassinated in December 2007. Her widower Asif Ali Zardari became president in September 2008.

The rise to power of **Violeta Barrios de Chamorro** in Nicaragua in 1990 was similar to that of Corazon Aquino of the Philippines. Like Aquino, Chamorro came from a wealthy landowning family. Her education at Blackstone College in Virginia was interrupted by her father's death. Chamorro married a journalist, Pedro Joaquin Chamorro, from a wealthy landowning family that had been active in Nicaraguan politics. His opposition to the Somoza family that ruled Nicaragua began while he was a law student and continued when he became the editor of his family's newspaper, *La Prensa*. He supported the **Sandinistas,** the opposition to the Somoza regime. They were led by Daniel Ortega. Chamorro's support of the Sandinistas contributed to the Somoza regime's decision to assassinate him in 1978. His wife took over as *La Prensa*'s publisher. Her support of the Sandinistas, who eventually overthrew the Somoza regime in 1979, helped her gain a position in the new government. However, she soon became critical of the Sandinistas for their socialist policies and their close relationship with Cuba. When the Sandinistas allowed free elections to be held in 1990, Violeta Chamorro was elected to lead the country.

In 2006, Ellen Johnson-Sirleaf, a former economist at the World Bank, became Africa's first female head of state. She has made significant progress toward restor-ing stability, reducing poverty, and consolidating democracy in Liberia.

Violeta Barrios de Chamorro ∎ Leader of Nicaragua.

Sandinistas ∎ A movement that over-threw the Somoza regime in Nicaragua.

EMPOWERING WOMEN

Between 1975 and 1995, the United Nations held four conferences on women. The first conference, held in Mexico City, focused on documenting gender gaps in education, employment, income, legal rights, and political participation. Subsequent conferences stressed the need to reduce poverty among women and to eliminate unequal treatment of men and women. The fourth conference on women, held in Beijing, was the most ambitious and widely publicized one. Hillary Clinton attended the conference and drew attention to the need for women's empowerment. The **Beijing Conference** outlined the major concerns that women have and emphasized respect for the rights of women. It stressed the following: (1) the right of women to decide all matters related to their sexuality and child-bearing, (2) an end to the genital mutilation of girls and violence against women because their dowries are too small, (3) the right of women to have access to credit, and (4) the equal treatment of males and females. The Beijing conference reflected the growing communication among women about issues that affect them and an increase in grassroots efforts in developing countries to end discrimination against women. As U.S. Secretary of State, Hillary Clinton toured Africa in 2009 and made women's rights a critical foreign policy issue. She met with women's groups throughout her visit. Women continue to experience violations of their rights in all societies to varying degrees. They are often raped in conflict situations. Thousands of domestic workers around the world are routinely abused. Maids in countries such as Lebanon, Saudi Arabia, and the Arab Emirates endure forced confinement, are overworked, and beaten. Some commit suicide. Many are denied their wages and are often treated as slaves.

Beijing Conference
■ A conference held by the United Nations where major concerns of women and their rights were emphasized.

The forces of globalization, particularly the cultural and economic aspects of globalization, are profoundly enhancing women's empowerment. As we have seen, globalization challenges traditional values and exposes people to a vast array of ideas, knowledge, and lifestyles. Women throughout the world are affected by globalization to varying degrees. The growing power of women in the developed world has a direct impact on the self-perceptions and expectations of women in the developing world. The boundaries between them are becoming less distinct. Table 8.1 shows four important measures of gender empowerment as it applies to women throughout the world.

Economic globalization is improving the status of women and narrowing the gaps between men and women, and bringing about greater gender equality. Some of the world's largest global companies are increasing their efforts to empower women. Given the shifting economic power toward developing countries, these corporations realize that their growth depends on expanding their operations there. Women remain vital potential consumers in the developing world, where population growth will continue to surpass growth in rich countries. Companies need to work with women on all levels to improve their own profits. Companies such as Nike, Goldman Sachs, and GE are involved in activities to empower women. Goldman Sachs, for example, launched a program called 10,000 Women initiative to invest in business and management education for female entrepreneurs in developing countries.[27]

Table 8.1

Gender Empowerment Measure Components

Country	Seats in Parliament Held by Women (%)	Female Administrator and Managers (%)	Female Professional and Technical Workers (%)	Women's Share of Earned Income (%)
United States	17	43	56	62
Norway	36	31	51	77
Canada	25	37	56	65
Japan	12	9	46	45
Sweden	47	32	51	67
Netherlands	39	28	50	67
United Kingdom	20	34	47	67
Korea, Rep. of	14	9	40	52
Mexico	22	31	42	42
Venezuela	19	27	61	48
Philippines	20	57	63	58
Brazil	9	35	53	60
Turkey	9	8	33	26
United Arab Emirates	23	10	21	27
Jordan	8	0	0	19
Iran	3	13	34	32
China	21	17	52	68
South Africa	34	34	55	60
Indonesia	12	14	48	44
Egypt	4	11	32	27
India	9	0	0	32
Pakistan	21	3	25	18
Bangladesh	6	10	22	51
Zambia	15	19	31	56

Source: United Nations Development Programme, *Human Development Report 2009* (New York: Oxford University Press, 2009), 186–189.

Case Study: Turkey

Straddling Europe and Asia, Turkey has been at the center of various periods of globalization. Constantine the Great, the first Christian Roman emperor, founded Constantinople (now Istanbul), which became the capital of the Byzantine Empire. This empire was conquered by the Ottoman Turks, who expanded their control of the Balkans, Syria, Lebanon, Palestine, Iraq, Jordan, Saudi Arabia, Yemen, and islands in the Aegean Sea. Like previous empires, the Ottoman Empire gradually contracted, fragmented, and declined. The final blow came when it decided to ally itself with Germany in World War I. Countries such as Britain and France, which were allied against Germany, occupied parts of the Ottoman Empire. Modern Turkey emerged from the ruins of the Ottoman Empire. Turkey, with a population of 77 million, has a diversified economy, with the agricultural and textiles industries employing roughly two-thirds of the workers. Its per capita GDP is around $12,000, and life expectancy is 72 years. It is a member of the North Atlantic Treaty Organization (NATO) and an associate member of the European Union (EU). One of Turkey's primary objectives is to become a full member of the EU, an aspiration that entangles it in the webs of globalization.

Women in Turkey enjoy a unique position among women in the Muslim countries of the Middle East. Women's status and roles in Turkey are shaped by Turkey's historical experiences and the values and actions of **Mustafa Kemal Ataturk,** founder of the modern Turkish state in 1923. Ataturk's revolutionary changes must be seen in the context of Turkey's geographical position as the land bridge between Europe and Asia. Ataturk led a successful war of independence from 1919 to 1922. The Republic of Turkey, under Ataturk's leadership, was based on the model of parliamentary democracy. Ataturk deliberately and systematically dismantled much of the old social and political system in an effort to modernize the country. An essential part of this change was the abolition of theocratic or Islamic religious control and the imposition of some aspects of Western European culture and values.

Many of the revolutionary changes directly affected the status of women and their participation in politics. Religious laws were replaced with secular laws. The system of religious education was abolished, religious courts were eliminated, and the constitutional provision accepting Islam as the state religion was repealed. Polygamy was outlawed, women gained equal rights to divorce and have custody of their children, and the government strongly supported legal and social equality between men and women. The veil was abandoned, due in part to Ataturk's campaign against wearing it. Both men and women were strongly encouraged to dress like Europeans. However, wearing a head scarf continues to be controversial. The scarf is an integral component of arguments about Turkey's Eastern and European identities, its Islamic and secular cultures, and its embrace of tradition and modernity. The scarf is at the heart of politics in Turkey.[28]

Although traditional values continue to influence contemporary politics and society in Turkey, a country in which 98 percent of the citizens are Muslim, the separation between church and state implemented by Ataturk endures. This distinction between religious and secular practices is clearer in large cities than in small towns and rural areas, where most Turks live. Women in urban areas continue to enjoy a legal status similar to that of European women. They can travel and work outside the home without having to obtain the permission of men, they have had a right to abortion since 1988, and they can marry whom they desire and get a divorce. Their participation in various professions is similar to that of European women. Numerous women are lawyers, engineers, doctors, diplomats, and educators. In 1993, **Tansu Ciller** became the first woman to lead Turkey.

Despite significant steps toward gender equality, women continue to face barriers to equal treatment in government, the economy, and society. Since 2004, women's participation in virtually all areas has declined and Turkey ranks near the bottom of various international indexes on gender equality. According to the Human Development

Mustafa Kemal Ataturk ■ Founder of the modern Turkish state in 1923.

Tansu Ciller ■ First woman to lead Turkey.

Report, published by the UN Development Programme, in 2009 women in Turkey held 9 percent of seats in parliament, comprised 8 percent of the administrators, and earned 26 percent as much income as men.

Literacy rates for women are 79.6 percent, compared to 95.3 percent for men. Forced marriages and efforts to retain traditional roles for women continue to be an impediment to educating girls, especially in rural areas. Women continue to experience violence, including honor killings.

This trend toward diminishing gains for women is linked to the success of the Justice and Development Party (AKP), an Islamic group headed by Prime Minister Recep Tayyip Erdogan since 2003. The major beneficiaries of Turkey's economic growth of roughly 6 percent a year are rural areas where residents are generally more religious and conservative than secular urban dwellers.

The EU has postponed discussions on full membership for Turkey until it resolves various issues relating to women's rights, human rights in general, immigration, and the economy. Kurdish separatism, Turkey's invasion of Cyprus in 1974 to prevent the country from being united with Greece, and its support for Northern Cyprus remain serious impediments to Turkey's full membership in the EU.

SUMMARY AND REVIEW

Throughout the developing world, women are the principal initiators of change that will improve their lives. They have global role models and globalization is challenging traditional societies to an unprecedented degree. Access to education and economic opportunities have enabled many women in Asia, Latin America, and Africa to develop a degree of social and financial independence that most women in the United States and other industrialized countries enjoy. The fact remains, however, that women throughout the world remain the largest marginalized group. In the developing countries of Africa, Asia, and Latin America, traditions make women primarily responsible for domestic work. Such gender roles in poor countries are shaped to some extent by colonialism and the globalization of industry and trade. Even though women's status continues to improve in many developing societies, most women suffer from an inferior status. Thus, throughout the world, including in the United States, women are seen by societies as inferior beings, with many attempts at controlling them. Violating gender roles can often have serious ramifications. Gender often serves as a tool or justification for oppression. Just as in the United States, a sexual double standard exists, whereby promiscuous males are studs and promiscuous females are unchaste. Honor killings are often the result of such a gendered double standard. Throughout the developing world, women remain less educated and less nourished on the basis of their sex and perceived gender roles. However, the forces of globalization, including global companies, are helping empower women and bring about greater gender equality. Women's achievements in the developing world, however, should not be overlooked. Hence, India, Pakistan, and Bangladesh have all seen women prime ministers, and throughout the developing world women serve in leadership positions that run the gamut of public and private life.

KEY TERMS

socialization   148
roles   148
marianismo   148
status   149
socially constructed   149
dowries   149
veiling   150
Taliban movement   150
chadore   150
female genital mutilation   151
sale of females   151
bride price   151

honor killings   152
sharaf   152
Lost Decade   155
feminization of employment   155
maquiladora industry   155
internal self-selection   156
Muhammad Yunus   157
Sixteen Decisions   157
four principles   157
maleness of politics   157
Madres de la Plaza de Mayo   158
panchayat   159

Pakistan People's Party (PPP)   159
Purdah   159
oral divorce   159
Dilma Rousseff   160
Indira Gandhi   160
Benazir Bhutto   160
Violeta Barrios de Chamorro   161
Sandinistas   161
Beijing Conference   162
Mustafa Kemal Ataturk   164
Tansu Ciller   164

DISCUSSION QUESTIONS

1. What role does socialization play in determining gender roles? Compare and contrast socialization trends in different parts of the developing world.
2. How do politics often exclude women? What methods should be employed to equalize, among genders, access to political systems?
3. In what ways have women attempted to help themselves in developing countries?
4. What are some ways of punishing women for behaving inconsistently with their prescribed gender roles?
5. How does the legacy of colonialism and globalization affect the roles of women?

SUGGESTED READINGS

Ahmed, Leila. *Women and Gender in Islam*. New Haven, CT: Yale University Press, 1992.

Bernard, Cheryl. *Women and Nation-Building*. Santa Monica, CA: Center for Middle East Public Policy, 2008.

Coleman, Isobel. "The Global Glass Ceiling." *Foreign Affairs* 89, No. 3 (May/June 2010): 13–21.

Hunt, Swanee. "Let Women Rule." *Foreign Affairs* 86, No. 3 (May/June 2007): 109–121.

Kristof, Nicholas D., and Sheryl Wu Dunn. *Half the Sky: Turning Oppression into Opportunity for Women Worldwide*. New York: Knopf, 2009.

Skaine, Rosemarie. *Women Political Leaders in Africa*. London, UK: McFarland and Company, 2008.

NOTES

1. Nelly P. Stromquist, "Roles and Statuses of Women," in Nelly P. Stromquist, Ed., *Women in the Third World* (New York: Garland Publishing, 1998), 4.
2. Gustav Niebuhr, "Southern Baptists Declare Wife Should Submit to Her Husband," *The New York Times*, 10 June 1998, A1.
3. Douglas Jehl, "Following Tradition, an Affair for Men," *The New York Times*, 9 February 1999, A11.
4. Susan Tiano, "The Role of Women," in Richard S. Hillman, Ed., *Understanding Contemporary Latin America* (Boulder, CO: Lynne Rienner, 1997), 239.
5. Paul Cammack, David Pool, and William Tordoff, *Third World Politics* (Baltimore, MD: Johns Hopkins Press, 1993), 212.
6. Leila Hessini, "Wearing the Hijab in Contemporary Morocco," in Fatma Muge Gocek and Shiva Balaghi, Eds., *Reconstructing Gender in the Middle East* (New York: Columbia University Press, 1994), 41.
7. "Egypt and the Veil," *The Economist*, 17 October 2009, 60.
8. Fatima Mernissi, *Beyond the Veil: Male-Female Dynamics in Modern Muslim Society* (Bloomington, IN: Indiana University Press, 1987), XI.

9. Barbara Crossett, "Senegal Bans Gutting of Genitals of Girls," *The New York Times*, 16 January 1999, A3.

10. Lara Santoro, "Kenya Brides That Can't Be Bought," *Christian Science Monitor*, 13 October 1998, 6.

11. "The Sex Industry in Cambodia," *The Economist*, 13 June 2009, 46.

12. "Sudan's Dress-Code Row," *The Economist*, 8 August 2009, 43.

13. Salman Masood, "Pakistan in Begins Inquiry into Deaths of 5 Women Amid Dispute Over Honor Killings," *The New York Times*, 3 September 2008, A6; and "Better Laws Needed to Protect Women," *Daily Herald*, 5 June 2010, 27.

14. Guy Trebay, "From Untouchable to Businesswoman," *The New York Times*, 22 July 2010, E1.

15. Rod Nordland, "Working to Help a Haven for Afghan Women Blossom," *The New York Times*, 21 June 2010, A4; and Isobel Coleman, *Paradise Beneath Her Feet: How Women are Transforming the Middle East* (New York: Random House, 2010).

16. Richard Anker, *Gender and Jobs: Sex Segregation of Occupations in the World* (Geneva, Switzerland: International Labor Office, 1998), 411.

17. Carlisle Ford Runge and Carlisle Piehl Runge, "Against the Grain," *Foreign Affairs* 89, No. 1 (January/February 2010), 8.

18. Mayada M. Baydas, Richard L. Meyer, and Nelson Aguilera-Alfred, "Discrimination Against Women in Formal Credit Markets," *World Development* 22, No. 7 (July 1994), 1075.

19. Alex Counts, *Give Us Credit* (New York: Random House, 1996), XII.

20. Najma Chowdhury and Barbara J. Nelson, "Redefining Politics: Patterns of Women's Political Engagement from a Global Perspective," in Barbara J. Nelson and Najma Chowdhury, Eds., *Women and Politics Worldwide* (New Haven, CT: Yale University Press, 1994), 16; and Swanee Hunt, "Let Women Rule," *Foreign Affairs* 86, No. 3 (May/June 2007): 109–112.

21. Jane S. Jaquette, Ed., *Feminist Agendas and Democracy in Latin America* (Durham, NC: Duke University Press, 2009).

22. Margaret Jean Hay and Sharon Stichter, *African Women South of the Sahara* (New York: Longman, 1995), 203.

23. Celia W. Dugger, "Lower-Caste Women Turn Village Rule Upside Down," *The New York Times*, 3 May 1999, A1.

24. Anita Weiss, "The Slow Yet Steady Path to Women's Empowerment in Pakistan," in Yvonne Yazbeck Haddad and John L. Esposito, Eds., *Islam, Gender, and Social Change* (New York: Oxford University Press, 1998), 134.

25. Fanny Tabak, "Women in the Struggle for Democracy and Equal Rights in Brazil," in Barbara J. Nelson and Naoma Chowdhury, Eds., *Women and Politics Worldwide* (New Haven, CT: Yale University Press), 131.

26. Laura A. Liswood, *Women World Leaders* (London, UK: Pandora, 1995), 10.

27. Isobel Coleman, "The Global Glass Ceiling," *Foreign Affairs* 89, No. 3 (May/June 2010), 15.

28. Deniz Kandiyoti, "End of Empire: Islam, Nationalism, and Women in Turkey," in Deniz Kandiyoti, Ed., *Women, Islam, and the State* (Philadelphia, PA: Temple University Press, 1991), 23; and Farnaz Fassihi, "Scarf Standoff Splits Women," *The Wall Street Journal*, 21 August 2008, A8.

Transitions to Democracy and Human Rights

Globalization and Democracy and Human Rights

The rapid spread of communications technology, the growth of international travel, and increasing cultural globalization helped weaken undemocratic governments. This trend was significantly strengthened by the fall of communism in the Soviet Union and Eastern Europe and the end of the Cold War in the late 1980s. By creating greater interdependence among countries, globalization is instrumental in encouraging transitions to democracy and the protection of human rights. Globalization has contributed to the erosion of national boundaries and weakened the power of governments over their citizens. Concerns about democracy and human rights transcend national borders. Economic globalization creates pressures on governments to end authoritarian or totalitarian rule and embrace a more open and civil society. Some governments that fail to change face economic sanctions as well as political isolation. Globalization makes available political and financial resources to movements concerned with democracy and human rights.

Countries in Africa, Asia, and Latin America have struggled, in varying degrees, to achieve democracy and widespread respect for human rights. Their experiences with colonialism underscored the importance of instituting constitutional safeguards to protect citizens from arbitrary rule and violations of their fundamental freedoms. In some cases, such as in British India, colonization also brought Western democratic practices for a select few. To a large extent, struggles in the developing world for democracy and human rights were intertwined with movements for national independence. This was due in part to developments in Europe, especially the rise of Nazi Germany and World War II, which made it obvious that greater attention had to be paid to protecting human rights and supporting democratic governments. Despite their initial enthusiasm for democracy and human rights during their struggle for independence, most governments in Africa, Asia, and Latin America became dictatorial and oppressive. The end of the Cold War and the fall of communism in Russia and Eastern Europe strengthened democratic movements in poor countries around the world. The majority of them, with help and encouragement from the United States and Western Europe, made a concerted effort to abandon dictatorships and to implement political systems that are committed to upholding democratic freedoms and human rights. In 2003, the United States invaded Iraq, partly to promote democracy in that country and in the broader Middle East. However, U.S. violations of human rights at Abu Ghraib prison in Iraq and at Guantanamo Bay in Cuba and the controversy surrounding the release of documents in 2009 detailing America's use of torture seriously undermined U.S. efforts to promote democracy.

This chapter discusses the difficult and uneven process of transition to democracy and protection of human rights. It focuses on the importance of institutions such as constitutions, political parties, and independent judiciaries, in democratic societies. It examines the nature of democracy, the criteria for democracy, and the factors that contribute to the growth and stability of democracy, such as culture, the international and regional environment, historical experiences, and levels of economic development. This chapter shows that students and women have been instrumental in building democracy, especially in Latin America and Asia. International pressures and the forces of globalization also play critical roles in fostering the democratization of the developing world. Discussions of democratic transitions in Latin America, in particular, make it clear that many problems impede a full transition to and consolidation of democracy. Many ordinary citizens believe that democracy has failed to provide sustained economic growth or to end government corruption. Basic institutions such as courts, legislatures, and political parties are seen as ineffective. Africa and Asia face similar problems. Nevertheless, this chapter shows that significant progress is being made toward democratization. Discussions of democracy inevitably include human rights. This chapter looks at the evolution of human rights as a major international issue as well as conflicting perspectives on human rights.

DEMOCRACY

Democracy has been practiced by people throughout the world to varying degrees. However, the form of democracy found in most developed countries has its roots in ancient Greece. The word *democracy* is of Greek origin. It is derived from **demos,** meaning people or populace, and **kratia or kratis,** meaning rule. In other words, democracy is simply rule by the people. The people govern themselves. Democracy in ancient Greece was a **direct form of self-government**. This means that the people actually represented themselves and influenced decisions by voting for themselves. With the exception of small New England towns that hold town meetings, direct democracy is not practiced in modern societies. The United States and other democratic societies practice what is called representative democracy or indirect democracy. Citizens elect representatives to vote for them and to safeguard and further their interests. **Democracy** is a system of government in which the majority of the people rule but the rights of the minority are protected. It is a system of government that is based not on the use of force to gain compliance but on the consent of the citizens. Democracies allow individuals and groups to freely compete for most positions of governmental power in an orderly manner. This means that free and fair elections must be held on a regular basis and that all adult citizens have a right to participate, with a few exceptions.

Modern democratic societies have constitutions to protect the rights and freedoms of their citizens. A **constitution** may be defined as the fundamental legal framework, or basic law, of a country. A constitution assigns powers and duties to governmental institutions and agencies, indicates how decision makers are to be selected, defines the scope of governmental authority, establishes the nature of the relationship between the people and their government, and states how political leaders are to be held accountable. In essence, a constitution creates as well as limits power.

Constitutions may be written or unwritten. In either case, a constitution reflects the general agreement of a community about how it wishes to be governed. Although the American constitution is written, much of the fundamental law of the country is based on unwritten customs and traditions. The British Constitution, on the other hand, is unwritten. It is composed of traditions, customs, general understandings, legislative acts, and court decisions, but these are not compiled into a single document. The **British Constitution** is often

demos ■ Greek word meaning people or populace.

kratia or kratis ■ Greek word meaning rule.

direct form of self-government ■ A system of governance where the people represent and vote for themselves.

democracy ■ A system of government in which the majority rules but minority rights are protected.

constitution ■ The legal framework or basic law of a society.

British Constitution ■ Composed largely of customs and traditions; it is not a single document.

referred to as a *received constitution*. The constitution of a country is generally regarded as the supreme law. All other laws, no matter how popular they are with the majority of citizens, must be consistent with the constitution. The courts of a country, and ultimately the supreme or highest court, must have the final authority to interpret the constitution. In other words, the Supreme Court, or the highest court, makes the final decision on what is the law of a country. Because constitutions reflect political power and national values and priorities, they must be amended or updated through interpretation, new legislation, new customs, and formal changes in the document.

Democratic societies emphasize the political equality of all citizens and guarantee that their fundamental rights and freedoms are not only protected but are viewed as sacred. People in a democracy have the right to express their ideas freely; offer dissenting opinions; be left alone; form and join political, social, economic, and other organizations; worship or not worship as they see fit; and live their lives without unreasonable governmental interference. These freedoms are not absolute. Governments must balance the rights of one individual or group against the rights of another individual or group. A fundamental aspect of democracy is citizens' acceptance of responsibility for governing and safeguarding the rights and freedoms of society as a whole. Democratic governments are supposed to respect the dignity of all individuals and protect the civil and human rights of all citizens, especially those of minorities that suffer from racial, ethnic, religious, and other forms of discrimination.

There are many values and beliefs that are regarded as essential to the functioning of a stable and peaceful democratic society. One of the most important is the belief in the legitimacy of democracy. **Legitimacy** is the power to govern based on the consent of the majority of those who are governed. This is a fundamental principle of democracy, one that is closely related to the idea of a social contract articulated by John Locke and others. To a large extent, people's belief in the legitimacy of democracy depends on the performance of the government. The more successful the government has been in meeting the demands of the people, the more willing they will be to be ruled by it and to support it when it faces serious economic, social, or military challenges. Other beliefs that are important for maintaining democratic stability are (1) tolerance for different viewpoints, (2) willingness to compromise and cooperate with political opponents, (3) commitment to civility and pragmatism, and (4) willingness to get involved in the political process and to believe in one's ability to help achieve particular objectives.[1]

legitimacy ■ The power to govern based on the consent of the majority being governed.

Modern democratic societies have either a presidential or a parliamentary form of democracy. The best example of a presidential democracy is the United States. In countries with a **presidential form of democracy**, there is a clear separation of powers, and a system of checks and balances. The main branches of government—the executive, legislative, and judicial—are independent of each other and often in conflict with each other. The American system makes this conflict inevitable. The framers of the Constitution, James Madison in particular, believed that the best way to protect democracy and individual freedoms was to implement a system in which separate branches of government would check each other's powers. Members of Congress and the president are elected separately and independently of each other. This means that there can be divided government in the United States, with the Congress (or one house of Congress) controlled by

presidential form of democracy ■ A government with clear separation of powers and a system of checks and balances.

Republicans and the executive branch led by a Democratic president. The president, who is both the leader of the government and the leader of the country, must work with Congress to get legislation passed. The judicial branch must determine the constitutionality of the actions of both Congress and the executive branch.

parliamentary form of democracy
■ Governmental system where the legislative branch has greater powers over other branches.

In the **parliamentary form of democracy**, there is no clear division between the executive and legislative branches of government. Instead of a president as the chief executive, parliamentary systems have prime ministers. The best example of a parliamentary democracy is Britain. There is relatively little conflict between the prime minister and the legislature or parliament because the prime minister is chosen by the majority in parliament. Unlike the American president, the British prime minister is elected as a member of the legislature first and is then chosen by members of the majority party to lead the government. In other words, the prime minister is both head of government and the leader of the majority party. The symbolic head of the country is Queen Elizabeth II.

Developing countries have varying views of democracy. They do not always see democracy in the same way as most people in the United States and Britain. It could be argued that, in reality, many developing societies have a partial democracy and are moving closer to the ideal democracy. Although Latin Americans declare their commitment to democracy, they are not generally enthusiastic about practicing it. Saudi Arabia provides another example of how some developing countries view democracy. Saudi Arabia is an Islamic country in which there is no separation of religious and secular authority. Most Islamic countries, including those that are democracies, view democratic rights and freedoms within the broader context of Islamic beliefs and customs. Unlike Western democracies, which believe that the people are sovereign, Islamic societies believe that God is sovereign and has ultimate authority and political power. Saudi Arabia's religious and historical background played a major role in shaping its contemporary political system. Muhammad ibn Saud, leader of a nomadic group, made an alliance with Abd al-Wahhab, an important religious scholar in the eighteenth century, for mutual protection. This combination of political and religious power is the foundation of the modern Saudi state.

Wahhabi tradition
■ A religious tradition that is used as the basis of Saudi law and social behavior.

Saudi kings institutionalized the religious **Wahhabi tradition** as the basis of Saudi law and social behavior.[2] Although the Saudi leaders must consult with numerous princes and allow citizens to ask for favors from and express their opinions to the royal family, Saudi Arabia is not a democracy.

In sharp contrast to Saudi Arabia and Latin America, the English-speaking Caribbean countries are very democratic societies, despite occasional political problems. These islands hold free and fair elections regularly, allow the winning party to peacefully replace the governing party after elections, and protect the basic democratic freedoms of the people. Jorge I. Dominguez believes that this Caribbean achievement is far superior to that of Latin America and also to that of countries of Africa and Asia that acquired their formal independence from European powers after World War II.[3]

political participation
■ Activities that would include voting, joining an interest group, and protesting or running for a position in government.

Political Participation and Democratic Freedoms

Political participation and respect for civil liberties are basic to democracy. **Political participation** allows the people to communicate with elected officials and others in the government. Citizens must be able to express their viewpoints, make their concerns known, and demand certain actions or public policies from the government. In order to effectively communicate with and influence their representatives, people in democracies form political parties and interest groups, support freedom of the press and speech, and engage in informal activities. **Conventional political participation** includes voting, supporting particular candidates for political office, running for a position in government, writing letters to the editor of a newspaper about a particular issue, and joining an interest group or an organization that tries to influence government policies or decisions. **Unconventional forms of participation** include mass demonstrations, civil disobedience, and sometimes, even, acts of violence. In many developing countries, political parties, interest groups, and the mass media are not very strong institutions. Political participation in many developing countries is done through **patron–client systems.** The patrons are intermediaries who have connections to both the modern and traditional parts of a society. They are often powerful landowners, religious authorities, bankers, and political figures. Their clients are usually poor people, agricultural workers and small farmers, small entrepreneurs, and laborers in urban areas. These patron–client systems contribute to political participation in several ways, including (1) providing a channel for the rural and urban poor to engage in politics, (2) influencing the making and implementation of public policies or decisions, and (3) serving as a communication link between their clients and the government.[4]

Freedom of the press and freedom of speech are essential aspects of democratic society. These freedoms allow people to express their opinions, criticize government policies and behavior, offer solutions to problems, and engage in activities that may ultimately change the government and society. Freedom of the press and of speech means that there should be no prior restraint or censorship. This means that the government is not legally permitted to prevent people from writing or saying what they want. But these freedoms are not absolute. Governments may prevent speech that presents a clear and present danger to society; may outlaw fraudulent advertising, child pornography, and obscenity; and may punish those who engage in defamation of the character of others.

Political parties play a crucial role in the democratic process. Political parties are defined as a coalition of interests whose goal is to gain control of the government by winning elections. To win, political parties must appeal to a wide range of interests. Ultimately, the goal is to win the majority of the votes cast by the people, or the electorate. Some parties are organized to represent narrow interests, and sometimes to focus on a single issue. They know that they are unlikely to win enough votes to enable them to control the government. In some societies, these minor parties may join with other larger parties to influence public policy. Political parties play the essential role of helping transfer power peacefully from the losers to the winners of regularly held elections. Political parties give the electorate choices by offering competing candidates for office and competing programs for society. Political parties help mobilize public opinion, offer alternative solutions to society's problems, and link the people to the institutions of government. Finally, political parties not only provide people to run the government, they also play the role of the opposition and help keep the government accountable and responsive to the people. The concept of loyal opposition means that the party out of power criticizes the ruling majority and suggests

conventional political participation
■ Includes voting, running for office, and joining interest groups.

unconventional forms of participation
■ Includes mass demonstrations.

patron–client system
■ A system used in developing countries where patrons act as their clients' link to political participation and the government.

political party
■ A coalition of interests whose goal is to gain control of the government by winning elections.

alternative policies and programs. The loyal opposition accepts the legitimacy of the ruling majority and does not adopt unconstitutional means to undermine it.

Political parties in developing societies are usually linked to the nationalist movements that were instrumental in achieving independence. Political parties are also formed in poor countries to deal with the challenges of economic development and to provide political stability. For example, the Republican People's Party in Turkey was an important part of the whole process of the modernization and Westernization of that country under the leadership of Mustafa Kemal Ataturk. The Indian National Congress Party, created in 1885, helped achieve India's independence from Britain in 1947 and built the foundation for India's democratic society. The Indian National Congress Party served as an institution in which different viewpoints could be heard and compromises made on national objectives. The leaders of the party were strongly committed to democratic values such as respect for the rule of law, tolerance of political opposition, and reconciliation of conflicting interests.[5] Many developing societies have been dominated for a long period of time by one political party. The Institutional Revolutionary Party of Mexico (PRI) and the Indian National Congress Party are examples of dominant political parties. Both India and Mexico held elections regularly and allowed other parties to compete, although not always on a level playing field. Some developing countries instituted one-party systems. Gamal Abdel Nasser of Egypt, for example, created a one-party state and outlawed all opposition parties. Most developing countries have abandoned the idea of a single-party democracy. Many of them now face the problem of having too many political parties competing in elections.[6]

Turkey provides an example of how a society that is committed to democracy and multiple political parties can justify excluding particular political parties. From an American point of view, banning a political party because of its religious beliefs is inconsistent with democratic principles. To understand Turkey's position, we must put the issue of banning a religious party in the broader context of the creation of the modern Turkish state. Ataturk strongly committed his country to secularism and Westernization. He believed that the fall of the Ottoman Empire, from which Turkey emerged, was caused to a large extent by the leaders' misuse of Islam. When the Refah (Welfare) Party won 6 million votes, about 24 percent of all votes cast in the national election in 1997, a political crisis erupted in Turkey. The Refah Party is an Islamic party. Islamic parties in Algeria and Iran have contributed to the division in those societies. Many Turks viewed the Refah Party as a threat to Turkish society and secular values. In early 1998, the court banned it.[7]

Part of the reason for banning the Refah Party was the strong opposition of the military to what it regarded as the threat of Islamic filtration into Turkish society. Unlike in the United States, where the military is under civilian control, the military in Turkey, Indonesia, and elsewhere in the developing world is an independent institution with a political role. By law, the military in Turkey has a right to intervene in politics if it believes that Turkey's secular society is threatened. The military's power in politics also stems from the fact that it is Turkey's most powerful and respected institution.[8] Similarly, the military is the most powerful institution in Indonesia. As the country's stability was threatened owing to the serious economic crisis in 1997, the military was widely perceived as the backbone of Indonesia. The Indonesian military had 75 reserved seats in the country's parliament. Many government positions were held by military officers, including roughly half of the provincial governorships. Cabinet ministers, senior civil servants, ambassadors, and directors of state corporations were often soldiers. Military personnel were responsible for maintaining public order and monitoring political parties, nongovernmental organizations (NGOs), and religious and labor groups. Reforms in Indonesia have severely limited the power of the military, as the case study shows.[9]

Judicial systems are essential to maintaining democratic freedoms, including political participation. Democratic governments respect the **rule of law.** This means that no person is above the law and that all individuals are treated equally under the law. It also means that personal considerations are not allowed to determine how individuals are treated. The judiciary is critical to checking the power of the executive and legislative branches of government by making sure that their actions are constitutional or consistent with the constitution. A strong judiciary prevents political leaders from making arbitrary decisions and from depriving citizens of freedoms and basic human rights. It is the judiciary that determines the meaning of laws and holds political leaders accountable. The state bureaucracy or the administrative agencies also help to promote the rule of law and impartiality.

judicial systems
■ Have the responsibility for ensuring that the laws are fair and that individuals' rights are protected.

rule of law ■ The rule that no person is above the law and that all individuals are treated equally under the law.

Many developing countries have weak and ineffective judicial systems. In some cases, the judicial systems do not safeguard the rights of all individuals or treat them equally. In some cases, the judicial systems are strongly influenced by religious beliefs and customs that are inconsistent with democratic ideals. In Saudi Arabia, for example, the legal system is based on shari'a or Islamic law. Shari'a courts have jurisdiction over criminal cases and civil suits dealing with marriage, divorce, child custody, and inheritance. In a shari'a court, the testimony of one man equals that of two women, and those who commit crimes against Muslims generally receive harsher penalties than those who commit crimes against non-Muslims.[10] In Jordan and Turkey, women are not treated equally. The law allows courts to treat men who have committed "crimes of honor" leniently.[11]

Interest groups, like political parties, are critical players in societies that are becoming or are already democratic. An interest group or pressure group is composed of individuals who share common concerns. They are generally not interested in gaining political power. They organize to influence the government to make decisions that are favorable to them. Unlike political parties, which try to build broad coalitions, interest groups usually focus on narrow issues. They are policy specialists in the sense that they concern themselves only with specific policies that directly affect their group. Interest groups in both the developed and the developing world can only influence the government if they have access to it. Because most governmental institutions are located in urban areas, especially in developing countries, most interest groups are concentrated in cities.

interest groups
■ Groups composed of people who share common concerns and want to influence the government.

Membership in interest groups reflects the level of development of a particular society. As economic development becomes more widespread, labor unions and agricultural groups begin to organize to protect their interests. Agricultural groups are often less powerful than labor movements because of their location in the countryside and the difficulties they face in getting members together and traveling to the urban areas to gain access to the government. Labor unions, on the other hand, are usually connected to industries that are vitally important to the country's economic prosperity as well as its political stability. Labor unions are most likely to be located in cities, close to the nerves of government. Their organization, importance in the economy, and ability to strike give them significant political power. College students are also strongly involved in politics in developing countries. They are some of the most articulate critics of government policies, have important organizational skills, and are much less bound by traditions and customs than most citizens. Students are usually located in areas that are close to government institutions. Because they usually belong to middle- and upper-class families, they have access to power as well as some protection against punitive actions by the government. But students must also eventually graduate and get jobs. This limits their ability to sustain their political activities.[12]

Factors Conducive to Democracy

A combination of factors provides a fertile environment for the growth and stability of democratic societies. Political scientists often refer to these factors as preconditions for democracy. Countries that are democratic share certain characteristics. One of the most important prerequisites for democracy is a culture or a set of values, beliefs, and attitudes that fosters toleration, bargaining, and compromise. Democracy requires a commitment to pragmatism and flexibility. Citizens must be willing to listen to different viewpoints with which they disagree and accept the policies voted for by the majority. The culture of a society also determines, to some extent, the degree of political participation that citizens enjoy. Another factor that is conducive to democracy is the social, political, and religious **beliefs** of the ruling groups. The **international or regional environment** also facilitates or impedes the development of democratic societies. For example, Spain and Portugal became democratic societies in the 1980s because of pressure from their European neighbors and their desire to be included in the wider European community. Closely related to the international and regional environment are historical experiences with democracy. India and the English-speaking Caribbean are examples of democracies that are rooted partly in their historical experiences with European colonialism. A final factor that is conducive to democracy is economic development.

Countries such as Botswana and Nigeria in Africa demonstrate that culture plays a major role in determining if a country will be democratic. Botswana, a country with about 1.5 million people, is a stable democracy. Among the reasons given for Botswana's democratic society are its political culture of discussion, community consensus, and a tradition of nonviolence. Similarly, the political culture of Nigeria has helped make it difficult for many military regimes to gain legitimacy and institutionalize authoritarian rule. Nigerians' strong commitment to political and personal liberties has influenced military regimes to promise a transition to civilian rule and democratic government.[13] Although many of these promises were postponed by successive military regimes, Nigeria has periodically returned to democratic rule.

Cultural factors also help explain the existence of democratic governments in the Caribbean. The British brought many of their democratic institutions with them to their colonies in the Caribbean and implemented a process of decolonization that deliberately prepared the new countries for democratic government. The Westminster, or British, model of government had been in place, on a limited scale, from as early as 1639. The House of Assembly in Barbados, which began meeting

beliefs ■ A set of thoughts and values that encompass the social, political, and religious aspects of life.

international or regional environment ■ The surrounding societies that facilitate or impede the development of democratic values in other nations.

in 1639, is the third oldest legislative body in the Western Hemisphere, preceded only by Bermuda's legislature and the Virginia House of Burgess.[14] British rule helped create a culture that emphasizes the rule of law, constitutional government, civilian supremacy, bureaucratic neutrality, and respect for social, economic, and political freedoms. Democratic competition was embraced and attempts were made to use government as an instrument for promoting social welfare and economic equality.[15]

Economic development also influences the adoption of democratic values. This does not mean that poor countries cannot be democracies or that all countries that have achieved a certain degree of economic progress are democratic. However, evidence shows that poor countries are less likely to be democratic than countries that are more prosperous. Poor countries generally do not have a relatively large middle class, high rates of literacy, a vibrant and independent private sector, a well-developed infrastructure, or a large number of newspapers, radio stations, or televisions. Communication with the outside world is limited. All of these drawbacks make the growth of democracy unlikely. Africa provides a good example of how poverty stifles democracy.[16] Increased national wealth eventually expands the **middle class,** which many political scientists believe is essential to the acquisition and maintenance of democratic values. Many Asian and Latin American countries that have experienced rapid economic development, coupled with deliberate efforts by the government to reduce economic and social inequality, have adopted democratic values and practices.

middle class ■ The middle income group that is essential to the maintenance of democratic values.

Transitions to Democracy

Democratization is a process of changing from a previous authoritarian or totalitarian government to a democratic government that is widely regarded as legitimate and permanent. A democratic transition involves the negotiation and acceptance of democratic rules and procedures, the building or restructuring of political institutions, and the channeling of political competition along democratic lines.[17] An essential part of this process is deciding on a new constitution. **Constitutions** both create and limit power and help legitimize political power and unify the population. To achieve this, constitutions must be accepted by the people as a political creed. Compromises must be incorporated in constitutions for the documents to embody the values, beliefs, interests, and aspirations of the population.

constitutions ■ Create as well as limit power.

Democratic transitions often begin with **liberalization** in what remains essentially a nondemocratic setting. Liberalization may include changes such as fewer restrictions on freedom of the press, the recognition of the right of workers to form trade unions, a movement away from arbitrarily arresting citizens, the release of political prisoners, and greater tolerance of political opposition. **Democratization** includes liberalization but is a much broader concept. Democratization involves the right of citizens to compete in elections to gain control of the government. But elections alone are not an indication of democratization. Many countries in Latin America—Guatemala, for example—have had many elections but have not completed the transition to democracy. Juan J. Linz and Alfred Stepan argue that a democratic transition is complete when there is widespread agreement on how to elect a government; when a government comes to power through a free and popular vote; when the government has the authority to make decisions for the country; and when there is a legal separation

liberalization ■ Involves reducing restrictions on freedom.

democratization ■ Includes the right of citizens to compete in elections and to control the government.

of executive, legislative, and judicial powers.[18] After a country achieves a democratic transition, it faces the challenge of consolidating democracy.

consolidation of democracy
■ Involves behavioral, attitudinal, and institutional changes.

The **consolidation of democracy** is a long-term process that continues after countries have made the transition to democracy. It involves behavioral, attitudinal, and institutional changes. Behaviorally, a democratic regime is consolidated when there is no significant effort to change the government by force. Attitudinally, a democratic regime is consolidated when a strong majority of the population believes that democratic institutions and procedures are most appropriate for their society. Institutionally, a democratic regime is consolidated when society as a whole, including the government, believes that there are certain laws, procedures, and institutions that must be used to govern society.[19] For democracy to be consolidated, **four conditions** are seen as essential:

four conditions
■ Essential to consolidating democracy.

1. The conditions must exist that make it relatively easy for a civil society to develop. Individuals must be able to form organizations that are autonomous from the government to protect their interests, inform the public, and challenge the government.
2. Specific arrangements must be made for groups and individuals to compete for political power. This usually means the development and functioning of core institutions such as political parties and interest groups.
3. Society must respect and uphold the rule of law, and an independent judicial system must exist to determine what the law is.
4. There must be an institutionalized economic society or significant degree of market autonomy and the right of individuals to own property.

The free market and private ownership of property are regarded as essential to the independence and liveliness of a civil society and, ultimately, the survival of democracy itself.[20]

transitional phase of democracy ■ A phase in society that contains both democratic and nondemocratic elements.

Transitions to democracy do not occur in any specific order. What most countries that make the transition to democracy seem to have in common is a serious national crisis. The disruption of the status quo often creates rivalries within the nondemocratic government. Eventually, the government begins to disintegrate. Faced with unprecedented domestic and international pressures, most governments in these circumstances commit themselves to holding free elections and relaxing restrictions on fundamental freedoms. Elections usually change the old government and install new leaders. The **transitional phase of democracy** contains both democratic and nondemocratic elements. Several free and fair elections must be held, and there must be a general societal consensus that there is no alternative to democracy before the transition to democracy is consolidated.[21] But democracies must also deliver. They must demonstrate that they can improve the economy, maintain order, and provide a better quality of life for the people to obtain legitimacy or acceptance by the people. A **full transition to democracy** is accomplished when basic democratic rights are an integral part of life and when people believe in the superiority of democracy over the alternatives.

full transition to democracy ■ This occurs when democratic rights are an integral part of life.

managed transitions
■ Attempts to control the process of governmental change in order to protect specific interests.

Nondemocratic governments, especially those controlled by the military, attempt to manage transitions to democracy instead of making changes quickly. African governments provide many examples of **managed transitions.** They have essentially attempted to control the process of change in order to protect their own interests, to ensure stability, and to minimize concessions to the forces of change. In managed transitions, the military establishes a timetable for the return to democratic rule and determines the process for democratic elections.[22] These managed transitions occur in response to national unrest and economic crises. Some military leaders may initiate transitions to democracy because developments in the country, regionally and globally, indicate that military rule is no longer a viable option.

Whether they are managed or haphazard, transitions to democracy are influenced by pressures for change. The press, the business community, women, and students play a crucial role in bringing about political reforms. Nondemocratic countries that allow a measure of democratic freedom, such as limited freedom of the press and speech, are ultimately challenged by the press. In both Nigeria and South Africa, the press played a crucial role in creating the condition that eventually forced the government to implement democratic rule. Widespread access to information and ideas provided by a free press helps end the nondemocratic government's control of information and, eventually, its ability to control the population. Women in Latin America and Asia were instrumental in helping governments in those regions to become democratic. Women began to organize against worsening economic conditions and increased government brutality. The women's movement was led by upper- and middle-class professional women who not only were well educated but also had lived in the United States and other democratic societies. They were joined by poor urban women who were struggling to take care of their families. Women were able to play a crucial role in transitions to democracy because (1) their activities were not viewed as threatening by the military rule; (2) the Catholic Church, an extremely powerful institution in these countries, urged women to participate in various nonpolitical activities; and (3) the military regimes were forced to commit themselves to political reforms in light of their serious economic failures.[23] The Ladies in White have held protest marches weekly in Cuba since 75 political dissidents, activists, and journalists, many of them their family members, were jailed in 2003. In addition to their protests, the Catholic Church and Spanish government put pressure on Cuba that resulted in 2010 in the promised release of 52 of those prisoners. The first seven were released to Spain in July 2010.

International Pressure International pressure for democratic reform grew with the proliferation of human rights groups and NGOs. As more citizens became actively involved in international issues, their governments became more responsive to their demands. The ideological conflict that characterized the **Cold War** had imposed restrictions on the ability of Americans to criticize American allies who violated their citizens' rights. This ideological barrier was no longer in place, and groups were now less restrained in their opposition to all governments that failed to practice democracy. When Indonesian forces attacked civilian demonstrators in 1998, the United States responded by pressuring the government to refrain from using excessive force. When violence erupted in East Timor, which voted for independence from Indonesia, the United States suspended military ties with and arms sales to Indonesia until the government stopped its soldiers and their allies from destroying the lives and property of the East Timorese.[24] Indonesia had to confront intense pressure not only from domestic groups but also from the United States, a longtime ally.

Cold War ■ The end of this ideological conflict contributed to democratization.

Catholic Church
■ A non-state actor that influenced transitions to democracy.

International pressure for transitions to democracy comes not only from governments and various human rights groups but also from the **Catholic Church.** In early 1998, Pope John Paul II visited Cuba. Like other countries in Latin America, the majority of Cuba's population is Catholic. Unlike other Latin American countries, which have made a transition to democracy, Cuba continues to practice communism and to deny its citizens certain rights and freedoms found in other democratic societies. Pope John Paul II's historic visit to Cuba was designed to strengthen the role of the Catholic Church in bringing about democratic reforms in Cuba. As a result of the pope's visit, the Catholic Church in Cuba has gained greater freedom to advocate for social change. In June 2010, its negotiations with the government led to improvements in prison conditions for dissidents, including better medical care and greater access to family members.[25]

Democratic Transitions in Latin America

Latin America has experienced more dynamic political changes than Africa and Asia. Between 1978 and 1993, 15 countries made the transition from dictatorship and authoritarianism to democracy. Several factors contributed to the dramatic political changes in Latin America:

1. Economic difficulties, symbolized by the debt crisis, destroyed the already low levels of legitimacy of many governments.
2. Military conflicts and military defeats weakened dictatorships in Nicaragua, El Salvador, Panama, and Argentina.
3. Several authoritarian regimes were shaken by their inability to adequately respond to serious problems caused by natural disasters.
4. Some governments were pressured by sanctions imposed primarily by the United States.
5. The demise of communism in the Soviet Union and Eastern Europe exposed the weaknesses of that ideology and made democracy a more attractive alternative.
6. The United States withdrew its support for dictatorships in Nicaragua, Argentina, Chile, Panama, Haiti, and the Dominican Republic.[26]

These changes reinforced pressures within the various countries for a transition to democracy. Despite their progress toward democracy, many Latin American countries face several problems that weaken the democratic process. Poverty continues to be the reality for many Latin Americans, despite growing economic prosperity in most countries. Corruption continues to erode the people's confidence in political, social, and economic institutions. Nevertheless, most Latin Americans are better off economically and they have greater faith in democracy. In fact, satisfaction with democracy has increased sharply.[27]

Shining Path
■ A Peruvian rebel movement that was formed by university professors and students who subscribed to the philosophy of Mao Zedong.

Developments in Peru underscore the people's ambivalence toward democracy. Although Peru made the transition to democracy in the 1980s, the country has suffered from high levels of inflation, economic depression, and widespread violence. The most serious challenge came from the **Shining Path**, a rebel movement that was formed by university professors and students who subscribed to the philosophy of Mao Zedong (Mao Tse-tung), the first leader of China's Communist Party.

The Shining Path used extreme violence against residents of impoverished villages, banned Indian and Christian holidays, and attempted to destroy the traditional family in an effort to create a new society. More than 30,000 people were killed and about 600,000 were displaced throughout Peru. The failure of the previous democratic government to end the violence and improve the economy led to the election of Alberto Fujimori as Peru's president in 1990. Fujimori not only ended much of the violence but also weakened the democratic process by dominating the legislature and the courts. Fujimori also exercised considerable control over the media and used undercover police agents to intimidate opposition leaders. By the end of 2000, Fujimori's government had collapsed. Fujimori went to Japan, where he claimed his right to Japanese citizenship. Alejandro Toledo was elected as president of Peru in 2001. Extradited from Chile to Peru in 2007, Fujimori was convicted in many criminal trials and remains in prison. In 2006, Alan Garcia became Peru's new president.

Both Chile and Costa Rica have had relatively stable democracies for a long time. Chile's democracy was ended when **Salvador Allende**, the country's first elected Marxist president, was overthrown and killed by General Augusto Pinochet in 1973. Pinochet and the military ruled Chile until the restoration of democracy in 1990. Domestic and international pressure, as well as a growing middle class, influenced Pinochet to hold elections, which he lost. Chile returned to its democratic roots, despite retaining authoritarian tendencies and Pinochet's continuing role as a senator-for-life in the government. Political polarization diminished; there was greater national consensus of economic and social policies; and political parties, interest groups, and human rights activists were reinvigorated.[28] Ricardo Lagos from the Socialist Party won Chile's presidential election in 2000, and Michelle Bachelet (also from the Socialist Party) won the presidential election in 2006, thereby demonstrating the consolidation of democracy. Because Chile's constitution prohibits consecutive terms, Bachelet, who had a 72 percent approval rating, could not be reelected in 2010. Sebastián Piñera, a conservative businessman from the opposition party, was elected president.

Salvador Allende
■ Chile's first elected Marxist president; was killed by General Augusto Pinochet.

Costa Rica also stands out in Latin America as a country with a long history of democracy. Unlike most societies, Costa Rica does not have a military. It was abolished by the 1949 Constitution. The Ministry of Public Security and the Ministry of the Presidency share responsibility for law enforcement and national security. The Constitution and various laws prohibit arbitrary arrest and detention, cruel and unusual punishment, and inhumane treatment of prisoners. The Constitution also protects the people's right to privacy and provides for freedom of religion. However, unlike the United States, which emphasizes the clear separation of church and state, the Constitution established Catholicism as the state religion. This is similar to England, where the Anglican faith is the state religion. However, people of all denominations freely practice their religion. The press operates freely. Newspapers, television stations, and radio stations are privately owned and operate independently of the government.[29]

Mexico's democratic government has been dominated by the Institutional Revolutionary Party (PRI) since the 1920s. PRI has used its advantage of incumbency (its control over political offices) to consolidate its power. For example, PRI is often accused of systematically using state-financed aid programs to influence voters to support the party. Some voters are given groceries, scholarships, crop payments, and

pork politics ■ The name given to the activity of allocating the government's resources in such a way that it influences people to vote in a particular way.

other benefits to encourage them to vote for PRI. Incumbents in most societies use their positions to enhance their chances of being reelected. They allocate the government's resources in a way that will influence the people to vote for them. This practice is referred to as **pork politics** in the United States. In Mexico, however, there are few checks to prevent politicians from abusing the power of incumbency. On the other hand, other political parties are beginning to successfully challenge PRI's dominance. In 1999, Vincente Fox of the National Action Party (PAN) became the president of Mexico, thereby ending 71 years of political dominance by the PRI.

Mexico's judicial system is structured similarly to that of the United States. It has a system of local, state, and national courts, including a Supreme Court. Members of the Supreme Court do not serve for life. They are nominated by the president and must be approved by a two-thirds majority in the Senate. It is generally believed that the judiciary's independence is compromised by the fact that the Supreme Court judges can serve for no more than 15 years. The courts protect freedom of speech, freedom of the press, and other basic rights that are guaranteed by the Constitution. However, human rights abuses are a common problem in Mexico. There was an escalation in brutal murders connected to the illegal drug trade in 2010. State authorities do not always prevent police officers and private militias from violating the rights of particular groups and individuals. Courts continue to admit as evidence confessions that have been obtained under torture, despite the Constitution's prohibition against the use of torture. Although the Mexican government created a National Human Rights Commission in 1990, the organization has been largely ineffective. Victims are often not consulted and the commission's condemnations and recommendations are routinely ignored by government officials. It is estimated that each year the commission has received 5,000 cases. However, only between 40 and 50 nonbinding recommendations are made.[30]

The judicial system in Mexico is undermined by official corruption. Because people lack confidence in the police, about 64 percent of crime victims in Mexico City do not even bother to report crimes to law enforcement authorities. In fact, many of the robberies are committed by the police. In some cases, especially in states along the U.S.–Mexican border, judges, police, and others posing as attorneys extort large sums of money, ranging from $3,000 to $10,000, from tourists to "fix" real or fabricated violations of the law. The prison system reflects the corruption that is generally associated with the judicial system. Many detainees are able to bribe prison officials to have charges dropped before they were scheduled to appear before a judge. Many prisoners have to purchase their own food, medicine, and other necessities from prison guards. Prisoners also bribe guards to allow things they need to be brought in from relatives and friends. Endemic drug-related violence, the proliferation of weapons, the poor conditions of the prisons, widespread poverty in Mexico, and the huge income gap between the rich and the poor help to weaken the judicial system in particular and the democratic process in general.[31]

Democratic Transitions in Africa

Most African countries briefly experienced democratic rule after achieving independence from Britain and France in the early 1960s. They inherited British and French institutions. However, many of these societies soon abandoned democracy. The governments in Tanzania, Ghana, and Guinea adopted socialist policies and stifled political opposition. In Nigeria, the military seized power, and ethnic and regional rivalries plunged the country into a devastating civil war in the late 1960s. Throughout much of their existence as independent states, African countries were directly or indirectly caught up in the Cold War. Many of the military conflicts that erupted during the Cold War were fought in Africa. In many ways, several African leaders used the rivalry between the United States and the Soviet Union to consolidate their authoritarian and military rule. Transitions to democracy were a low priority for African leaders as well as their external supporters. But many Africans remained hopeful that military dictatorships would end and worked to achieve that goal. Nigeria returned to civilian rule in 1979, but reverted to military rule four years later.

The end of the Cold War and an emphasis on global free trade by the United States and Western Europe pushed African societies closer to opening their societies and embracing democratic reforms. Military dictatorships came under increased domestic and international pressure to transfer power to freely elected governments. Because Russia itself was undergoing its own transition to democracy, Africans could no longer count on Russian support for their military regimes. Namibia, Mozambique, and Zimbabwe became more democratic, whereas Zaire (now the Democratic Republic of the Congo), America's staunchest African ally during the Cold War, resisted political reforms. Poverty and corruption became the hallmarks of Zaire under the leadership of Mobutu Sese Seko. In May 1997, Laurent Kabila overthrew Africa's longest dictatorship. The change was hailed as a major step toward democracy. But the bright promise soon faded as Kabila demonstrated his own preference for repression and dictatorship.[32] In January 2001, Kabila was assassinated and his son took over the country. Following a civil war, in which more than 3 million people died, multiparty elections were held in July 2006. Congo remains unstable. Both Kenya and Zimbabwe experienced widespread violence and economic problems in 2008 following what many observers viewed as undemocratic practices by those in power. In 2010, Guinea had its first free and fair democratic election since its independence from France in 1958. However, the two most important transitions to democracy in Africa occurred in South Africa (see case study) and Nigeria.

Nigeria's transition to democracy is more uncertain than South Africa's. Nigeria's experience with democracy is limited. The rule of law has not been embedded in Nigerian society. Military rule in Nigeria impoverished the country and destroyed most of the democratic institutions. The courts were manipulated by military leaders. The press, although relatively free, was frequently intimidated and disrupted by government officials. Human rights were routinely abused, excessive force and murder were used by the government to silence political opposition, and police officers often detained relatives and friends of suspects without charge to induce suspects to surrender. Prisoners such as **Ken Saro-Wiwa** and his eight co-defendants, who protested the government's oil policies and its oppression of the Ogoni people, were executed, without receiving a fair trial by an impartial jury or judge.[33] Corruption was widely viewed as the norm, and government officials and their supporters used their positions to enrich themselves.

Ken Saro-Wiwa
■ Executed for protesting Nigeria's oil policy.

Nigeria's transition to democracy in early 1999 was influenced by many factors. Despite Nigeria's oil wealth, most Nigerians are desperately poor. Most of the revenues obtained from the country's petroleum were taken by political leaders. Widespread poverty, in such a potentially wealthy country, inspired Nigerians to try

General Sani Abacha
■ Military dictator whose oppressive rule led to Nigerian transition to democracy.

to end military rule. Another factor influencing the transition to democracy was the brutally oppressive actions of **General Sani Abacha**. General Abacha seized power after the results of Nigeria's presidential elections in 1993, which were designed to return the country to democratic rule, showed that Moshood Abiola would win. Abacha's ruthless dictatorship and unrestrained corruption resulted in Nigeria's isolation by the international community. This international pressure also contributed to political changes in Nigeria. After General Abacha's unexpected death in June 1998, his successor, General Abdulsalam Abubaker, implemented democratic reforms and promised to return Nigeria to civilian rule. Elections were held in February 1999. General Olusegun Obasanjo, a former Nigerian leader and the only general to give up power voluntarily to a civilian government (in 1979), won the presidential election. However, Obasanjo and his supporters attempted to amend the Nigerian constitution to enable him to seek another term in office. This effort was defeated in the Nigerian Senate in 2006. Umaru Musa Yar'Adua became president. The election was widely viewed as not credible. When President Yar'Adua was unable to function due to illness, presidential powers were transferred to Vice President Goodluck Johnson in April 2010. Johnson became president when Yar'Adua died later that year.[34]

Democratic Transitions in Asia

Rapid economic growth in Asia has served as a catalyst for democratic reforms. Countries such as Taiwan, South Korea, Thailand, Indonesia, and even China have been influenced to make transitions toward democracy. Although China remains a communist country, it has implemented far-reaching economic reforms and limited democratic freedoms. Taiwan and South Korea, for example, responded to pressure from pro-democracy movements and labor unions by ending authoritarian rule. Their economic prosperity and integration in the global economy weakened the old system. Unlike Latin America, which suffers from high rates of economic inequality, many Asian countries attempted to reduce inequality and provide education, health care, housing, and employment for their citizens. A strong and growing middle class, as we have seen, plays a critical role in a country's transition to democracy. The middle class, especially students, moved the largest Islamic country, **Indonesia**, toward democracy during its economic crisis in the late 1990s.

Indonesia ■ The largest Islamic country; has transitioned toward democracy.

President Suharto of Indonesia, who came to power in 1965 after he led a military takeover of government, attempted to legitimize his authoritarian rule by building a strong economy. Suharto's government insisted that people minimize their differences and work together to develop the country. Indonesians agreed to accept fewer democratic rights in exchange for rapid economic development. But economic development strengthened the forces of change. Indonesia's economic success inevitably led to increased participation in society. When Indonesia's economy collapsed, the government had not built a large enough reservoir of political legitimacy to convince people to remain loyal and to keep their side of the bargain.

Students led the struggle against Suharto and his government. They called for Suharto's resignation, withdrawal of the military from politics, respect for the rule of law, immediate elections, a free press, competitive political parties, an independent and impartial judicial system that upholds basic freedoms, a strong legislative branch, and an end to corruption. Some Indonesians believed that such democratic reforms would endanger the country's stability and contribute to its disintegration. But the economic crisis had such a devastating effect on the majority of Indonesians that support for the status quo was seriously eroded. Middle-class people became more supportive of reform as they watched their wealth disappear when the stock market and the value of the country's currency, the **rupiah**, plunged. A major catalyst for change was the slaying of four students at Trisakti University by the security forces. Their deaths signaled to Indonesia's middle class that they were also vulnerable. The murder of the students, combined with the worsening economic crisis, triggered massive rioting that left more than 1,000 people dead. The security forces decided that only Suharto's resignation could prevent an escalation of the violence. But the end of Suharto's presidency only influenced students to demand more political reforms. After two years of protests, the students saw Suharto's dictatorship collapse, the election of a new government, and a commitment by Indonesia's leaders to move forward with democratic reforms.[35]

> **rupiah** ■ The currency of Indonesia.

The 2008 Olympic Games in Beijing renewed attention on China's problems with a transition to democracy. Preoccupied with its global image and winning gold medals, China wanted to appear democratic but did not tolerate demonstrations, despite the official designation of protest zone. China's transition to democracy is carefully controlled by the Communist Party. Although China is officially a communist society, generational change, rapid economic growth, the emergence of a strong middle class, and the government's embrace of capitalism and international trade are weakening the government's control over its citizens. In many ways, China is a paradox. The Communist Party is both the initiator of major changes and the guardian of conservatism and stability. China's huge markets and its growing economic power have entangled it with the global economic system. In order to be effective in global economic organizations, like the World Trade Organization (WTO), China has to reject many of its communist policies. It has to open up the society to outside forces of modernization. Economic development and globalization, especially the influence of revolutions in communications technologies, are gradually weakening the Communist Party and its ideology.

Changes in China's judicial system demonstrate the government's cautious approach to democratic reforms. In 1997, China revised its **Criminal Procedure Law** to give defendants the right to legal counsel, right to an active legal defense, and other rights of criminal defendants that are practiced in democratic countries. However, the judicial system, which is independent in theory, is strongly influenced by the Communist Party. The government places a higher priority on maintaining political and social stability and suppressing political opposition than on safeguarding individual rights. The government often dictates the sentences in politically sensitive cases. Arbitrary arrest and detention occur routinely. Officials often ignore procedures that are designed to give defendants a fair trial. In fact, prisoners are often forced to confess, and these confessions are admitted as evidence. The conviction rate is more than 90 percent. In 2008, more than 220,000 people were serving "re-education through labor" sentences, including a woman who was 71 years old and disabled.[36]

> **Criminal Procedure Law** ■ China's revised law that granted defendants the right to legal counsel, among other rights.

The Communist Party restrains freedom of speech, press, and religion. However, it has also enacted reforms that facilitate the practice of these freedoms. Modern communications technologies connect China to the world. Many Chinese citizens in cities such as Beijing and Shanghai seem to constantly use cell phones.

The Internet is used by an increasing number of Chinese, despite the government's efforts to control the content of materials available on the Internet. This is obviously a difficult undertaking. Many Chinese citizens have access to global television networks, especially in larger cities. Most Chinese enjoy personal freedoms that would have been unthinkable only a few years ago. However, political dissent is usually repressed by the government. Religious groups, including Protestants and Catholics, are required to register with and are monitored by the government. Although 15–20 million Christians are registered, approximately 30 million more worship privately in places that are not registered with the government. Religious groups that are perceived to be a challenge to the government are banned. The **Falun Gong**, or Buddhist law, for example, was banned in 1999 because of its religious and political activities. The Falun Gong is a popular spiritual movement that is based on Buddhism and Taoism. With more than 10 million members in China, it is the largest mass movement that is not controlled by the Communist Party.[37] Falun Gong received renewed attention in 2006 when one of its members interrupted President Hu Jintao's speech during his visit to the United States.

Falun Gong
■ Buddhist law and a banned religious group in China.

Grassroots democracy is being promoted across China. Influenced in part by Russia's difficulties with democratic and economic reforms, which were imposed by Russia's leaders, China has emphasized building democracy at the village level. About 900 million people, or about 75 percent of China's population, live in villages that practice limited democracy. As part of its managed transition to democracy, the Communist Party sent people to villages to train officials in the most basic principles of democracy and democratic procedures. The process started in 1989, shortly after hundreds of students and others protested in Tiananmen Square for democratic reforms and were killed by the Chinese military. Villages nominate and vote for committee candidates, without being controlled by the government.[38] Political participation at the village level, although not a serious threat to the Communist Party's control over China, is seen as an important first step toward a transition to democracy.

Human Rights in the Developing World

Respect for human rights and fundamental freedoms are, as we have seen, an essential component of democratic societies. However, there are conflicting perspectives on human rights and disagreements on how to deal with violations of human rights. **Human rights** are often equated with natural rights or God-given rights. These are rights that everyone has. People are born with these rights. These rights include the right to minimal subsistence, security against physical violence, the ownership of property, freedom of speech and religion, and the right to justice. Human rights are claimed by individuals, religious groups, political communities, women, ethnic minorities, and those not in positions of power. **John Locke** (1632–1704) and other proponents of human rights or natural rights argue that human beings are entitled to life, liberty, and property or, as Thomas Jefferson wrote in the American Declaration of Independence, the pursuit of happiness. The function of government, in their view, is to protect these fundamental rights. As this chapter has shown, many governments fail to respect human rights. In some cases, such as in Rwanda and Burundi, extreme violations of human rights—genocide and torture—have been prevalent.

human rights
■ Equated with natural or God-given rights.

John Locke
■ Leading proponent of natural rights who influenced Thomas Jefferson.

Many homeless children are killed in urban areas throughout Latin America by police death squads. Slavery still exists in parts of North Africa, especially in the Sudan.

Tibet Riots in March 2008 against Chinese rule and violations of human rights in Tibet focused global attention on these issues. Protests before and during the 2008 Olympic Games and efforts by the Dalai Lama, Tibet's exiled spiritual leader, to gain global support made the issue of Tibet a major concern for China, which wanted to use the Olympics to demonstrate its global power. Several demonstrators were arrested and deported, including Americans who were members of Students for a Free Tibet. China, which annexed Tibet in 1951, claims that Tibet has always been part of China. In other words, China rejects Tibet's arguments for autonomy or independence. Furthermore, from China's viewpoint, granting Tibet any kind of autonomy would only encourage other areas such as Xingiang and Inner Mongolia to demand their own independence. An underlying issue in Tibet is widespread violation of human rights. China continues to repress religious activities, freedom of speech, freedom of the press, academic freedom, and freedom of movement. As is the case in China itself, the Tibetan population is subject to torture, arbitrary arrest and detention, house arrest, and surveillance. China continues to undermine Tibet's spiritual and cultural heritage by outlawing various practices, refusing to recognize the Dalai Lama, and populating Tibet with Han Chinese.[39]

Concerns about human rights can be found in all cultures, religions, and political systems, in varying degrees. Christianity, Judaism, Islam, Buddhism, Hinduism, Confucianism, and other religions have articulated rights and responsibilities of individuals and communities.[40] However, not all societies or religions have embraced the concept of individual freedom and the equality of all people. Although advocates of human rights embrace a universal or cosmopolitan view, others take a narrow and more limited view, generally referred to as relativism. **Universalists or cosmopolitans** believe that all people, no matter where they live, are entitled to basic rights simply because they are human beings. Greek and Roman philosophers, most notably **Cicero** (106–43 B.C.E.), believed in the idea of universal rights based on natural rights and natural law. Cicero articulated the view that governments as well as citizens anywhere in the world must obey the authority of the higher law of nature. All laws must be compatible with the law of nature, which can be discovered by right reasoning.

In sharp contrast to the universalists or cosmopolitans, proponents of relativism believe that rights enjoyed by individuals are determined by each society's specific culture and historical experiences. They view the government as the source of individual rights. One of the strongest proponents of relativism was Thomas Hobbes (1588–1679). An English philosopher, Hobbes believed that law was the command of the government or sovereign, and the only rights that individuals had came from government or the monarchy. Like Hobbes, Edmund Burke (1729–1797) argued that the rights of British people were derived not from abstract natural laws but from society's traditions, customs, and laws.

The rise of Nazi Germany and World War II dramatically focused the world's attention on human rights, including the rights of people living under colonialism to self-determination and independence. The debate on human rights after World War II took place within the broader context of the Cold War, symbolized by the rivalry between the United States and the Soviet Union. Countries focused on the different

universalists or cosmopolitans
■ Those who believe that people everywhere are entitled to human rights.

Cicero ■ Roman philosopher and lawyer who believed in universal natural rights.

negative rights
■ Rights of individuals and groups to be protected from the government.

positive rights
■ Rights of individuals to economic well-being, health care, and education.

areas of human rights, depending on their ideology and level of economic development. The United States, Western Europe, and Canada believed that **negative rights**, or the rights of individuals and groups against the government, should be the priority. These rights, which include freedom of speech, freedom of religion, freedom of the press, and the right to a fair trial, are found in the International Covenant on Civil and Political Rights. The Soviet Union, China, and most developing countries focused primarily on **positive rights**, or the rights of citizens to certain levels of economic well-being, health, education, and cultural amenities. Numerous human rights covenants have been passed by the United Nations. Some of them are the Universal Declaration of Human Rights; the International Convention on the Elimination of All Forms of Racial Discrimination; and the Convention against Torture and Other Cruel, Inhumane or Degrading Treatment or Punishment.

humanitarian intervention ■ The use of military force against a country that engages in gross violations of human rights.

The growing interdependence of countries and the decline of sovereignty have diminished the ability of governments to violate human rights without drawing international attention to the problems. Many governments and humanitarian organizations strongly support **humanitarian intervention**, or the use of military force against a country that engages in gross violations of human rights. As we have seen, even countries that are moving toward democratic governments continue to violate human rights. Democratic societies such as the United States and Britain are sometimes accused of violating human rights. The United States, for example, faced global condemnation for its human rights violation in Iraq, Afghanistan, and Guantanamo Bay (Cuba). Humanitarian intervention is used only in some of the most extreme cases. NGOs, such as Amnesty International, Americas Watch, Asia Watch, Africa Watch, Medecins Sans Frontieres (Doctors Without Borders), and the Women's Environment and Development Organization, monitor human rights violations worldwide.[41] **Amnesty International** is one of the best-known human rights groups. It was founded in London in 1961 by a group of writers and lawyers. It publicizes human rights abuses in different countries and encourages its members around the world to participate in letter-writing campaigns to seek the release of prisoners of conscience. These prisoners of conscience are individuals who are imprisoned because of their political, religious, social, and other beliefs. Many governments are sensitive to negative publicity, especially those that are integrated in the global economy. Human rights groups often pressure democratic governments to impose economic sanctions and other measures against countries that violate human rights.

Amnesty International
■ A leading human rights group.

▶ Case Study: South Africa

Hosting the Soccer World Cup in 2010 brought South Africa unprecedented global attention and reminded the world about the country's transition to democracy. Increasing globalization in the 1980s, especially the growth of global communications and the spread of global companies, played a pivotal role in the transition from minority rule to majority rule. Equally important was the impact of the global spread of democracy following the disintegration of the Soviet Union and the decline of Soviet–American confrontation in the developing world following the fall of communism.

South Africa was the largest economy in sub-Saharan Africa and is integrated into the global economy, largely because of its abundant natural resources and its relatively high level

FIGURE 9.1
South Africa

of industrialization. It has large amounts of gold, diamonds, chromium, coal, iron ore, platinum, nickel, and other resources essential for industries in the developed world. Although its economy continues to grow at around 3 percent, and its per capita GDP is $10,000 a year, South Africa, with a population of 49 million people, has many serious economic and social problems. Half the population lives below the poverty line and South Africa remains one of the most unequal societies in the world. Life expectancy for males is 49.6 years, and it is 48.1 years for females. These low rates are due partly to the HIV-AIDS epidemic, which affects more than 5.3 million South Africans. Violent crime rates are among the highest in the world. There is an epidemic of rape in general and child rape in particular, robbery, organized criminal gang activities, and illegal drug use. More than 3,000 white farmers and members of their families have been murdered since South Africa achieved majority rule.

Located on the southern end of Africa, South Africa was settled by the Dutch in 1652. In an earlier period of globalization, when Europeans engaged in a scramble for African territory, Britain seized the Dutch settlement on the Cape of Good Hope in 1806. The Dutch trekked north and formed two republics, Transvaal and Orange Free State. However, the discovery of diamonds in 1867 and gold in 1886 in the Dutch settlements made them attractive to the British. Between 1899 and 1922, the Anglo-Boer (Dutch) war erupted, leaving Britain in control of the Dutch colonies. In 1910, Britain created the Union of South Africa by uniting its two colonies (Cape and Natal) with Orange Free State and Transvaal. Nevertheless, the British and Dutch remained largely separate and hostile.

In 1948, the National Party (Dutch) was voted into power and implemented a system of extreme racial separation known as **apartheid.** Under apartheid, the small white

apartheid ■ Legal discrimination and racial separation.

minority, descendants of Dutch, English, French, and German settlers, maintained a democratic system for themselves and oppressed the majority black, Indian, and racially mixed South Africans. Apartheid established a racial hierarchy with whites at the top and blacks at the bottom. Through extreme oppression and the implementation of divide-and-conquer strategies, the small white minority was able to rule South Africa. On the other hand, the democratic institutions that whites developed for themselves over time served as a foundation for the expansion of democracy to all South Africans.

Oppression by the white minority government influenced the formation of the **African National Congress (ANC),** led by Nelson Mandela. After Mandela and other leaders of the ANC were imprisoned for resisting apartheid, black South Africans and their supporters believed that only a combination of armed struggle, trade union activity, mass demonstrations, various acts of resistance, and global pressure would force the minority to abandon apartheid. The global opposition to apartheid was galvanized by the Sharpeville Massacre in 1960, during which white policemen killed 69 unarmed protesters and shot another 180 as they tried to flee the violence. During the Soweto uprising by students in 1976 more than 600 people were killed. The United Nations, global media, grassroots organizations, and political and social activists around the world focused global attention on ending apartheid.

As South Africa's economy became more developed and attracted more global companies, it became more dependent on black labor and more vulnerable to global pressure. Global businesses in particular concluded that apartheid was too costly and outdated. The business community advocated ending apartheid as international sanctions against South Africa escalated. Faced with global opposition to apartheid, President P. W. Botha abolished the racial pass laws that controlled the movement of blacks and offered blacks an advisory role in government. When roughly 2 million black workers went on strike in June 1988, Botha resigned in 1989, and was replaced by **F. W. de Klerk,** just as the Soviet Union was disintegrating and when the Soviet leader, Mikhail Gorbachev, had initiated political and economic reforms that eventually led to the demise of communism. Faced with the reality that neither side could defeat the other, the National Party, under the leadership of de Klerk and the ANC, decided to negotiate an end to apartheid.[42] In 1990, the government lifted its ban against the ANC, the Pan-African Congress, and the South African Communist Party and released Nelson Mandela, who had been imprisoned for 27 years. The major pillars of apartheid were abolished. In 1993 both de Klerk and Mandela won the Nobel Peace Prize for ending apartheid and for their work on South Africa's transition to democracy. South Africa adopted a new constitution, elected a new parliament, developed a new judicial system, and established a **Truth and Reconciliation Commission,** which examined human rights violations during apartheid, tried to repair some of the damage caused by apartheid, and attempted to unite South Africans. Nelson Mandela was elected to lead South Africa. In 1999, ANC leader Thabo Mbeki became South Africa's second popularly elected president. South Africa's transition to democracy was further consolidated by Jacob Zuma's election as president in 2009.

The spotlight that South Africa enjoyed by hosting the World Soccer Cup also focused attention on ongoing problems that undermine South Africa's transition to democracy. In many ways, a new black political and economic elite has joined whites in controlling the country's wealth. Unemployment ranged from 26 percent to 42 percent. It is estimated 80 percent of blacks control about 5 percent of South Africa's wealth. Despite a growing

African National Congress
■ Opposition to apartheid, led by Nelson Mandela.

F. W. de Klerk
■ Leader of the National Party; helped end apartheid.

Truth and Reconciliation Commission
■ Instituted as an alternative to punishment by death or imprisonment for crimes against humanity.

middle class and improved access to electricity, water, and mobile phones, South Africa remains a bastion of inequality. When apartheid ended, the government adopted a plan to redistribute 30 percent of white-owned farmland to poor blacks through the free market. Only 5 percent of the land has been transferred to blacks. Violence against white farmers continues. Land reform is no longer regarded as an urgent priority.[43]

SUMMARY AND REVIEW

An important component of the current wave of globalization was the push for democracy following the disintegration of the Soviet Union and the demise of communism. It is generally assumed that greater economic growth facilitates transitions to democracy. Most developing countries struggle to achieve both economic development and democracy. Some have achieved a remarkable degree of democratic freedom and respect for basic human rights, despite their relative poverty. Many, on the other hand, have experienced significant economic growth without making major progress toward democracy. Political development may be defined as the growth of modern and effective political institutions and practices such as those that are found in the United States, Canada, Britain, France, and other democratic societies. Judicial systems are essential to maintaining democratic freedoms, including political participation. Democratic governments respect the rule of law. Many developing countries, however, have weak and ineffective judicial systems. Interest groups,

like political parties and judicial systems, are critical players in societies that are becoming or already are democratic. As economic development becomes more widespread, interest groups such as labor unions and agricultural groups begin to organize to protect their interests. Students are also strongly involved in politics in developing countries. Political scientists often refer to factors like judicial systems, interest groups, respect for the rule of law, opposition, and fair elections as preconditions for democracy. Economic development also influences the adoption of democratic values. Moreover, pressures for change influence transitions to democracy. Many of the pressures for change stem from women, international pressure, groups perceived to be marginalized in a political system, students, and many other less obvious variables. A major component of democratic societies is the respect for human rights and fundamental freedoms. Although transitions to democracy continue throughout Asia, Latin America, and Africa, they do not occur in any prioritized order.

KEY TERMS

demos   170
kratia or kratis   170
direct form of self-government   170
democracy   170
constitution   170
British Constitution   170
legitimacy   171
presidential form of
   democracy   171
parliamentary form of
   democracy   172
Wahhabi tradition   172
political participation   172

conventional political
   participation   173
unconventional forms of
   participation   173
patron–client systems   173
political party   173
judicial systems   175
rule of law   175
interest groups   175
beliefs   176
international or regional
   environment   176
middle class   176

constitutions   177
liberalization   177
democratization   177
consolidation of democracy   178
four conditions   178
transitional phase of
   democracy   178
full transition to democracy   178
managed transitions   178
Cold War   179
Catholic Church   180
Shining Path   180
Salvador Allende   181

pork politics 182
Ken Saro-Wiwa 183
General Sani Abacha 184
Indonesia 184
rupiah 185
Criminal Procedure Law 185
Falun Gong 186

human rights 186
John Locke 186
universalists or
  cosmopolitans 187
Cicero 187
negative rights 188
positive rights 188

humanitarian intervention 188
Amnesty International 188
apartheid 189
African National Congress 190
F.W. de Klerk 190
Truth and Reconciliation
  Commission 190

DISCUSSION QUESTIONS

1. Is economic development a prerequisite for democratic transition? Why or why not?
2. What are the characteristics of a patron–client relation? Could a patron–client relationship be consistent with democratic values? Why or why not?
3. Why are the freedoms of press, assembly, opposition, and speech important for democratic societies?
4. Discuss the preconditions for democracy. Are there some preconditions that are more important than others? If so, which ones?
5. Do you believe that democracy occurs from the bottom up or from the top down?

SUGGESTED READINGS

Barkan, Joel D., Ed. *Legislative Power in Emerging African Democracy*, Boulder, CO: Lynne Rienner, 2009.

Bass, Gary J. *Freedom's Battle: The Origins of Humanitarian Intervention*. New York: Knopf, 2008.

Dominique, Jorge I., and Michael Shifter, Eds. *Constructing Democratic Governance in Latin America*. Baltimore, MD: The Johns Hopkins University Press, 2008.

Gibson, James L. *Overcoming Historical Injustices: Land Reconciliation in South Africa*. Cambridge, UK: Cambridge University Press, 2009.

Haugen, Gary, and Victor Boutros, "And Justice for All: Enforcing Human Rights for World's Poor." *Foreign Affairs* 89, No. 3 (May/June 2010): 53–62.

Hunter, Shireen T., and Huma Malik. *Modernization, Democracy, and Islam*. Westport, CT: Praeger, 2004.

Thornton, John L. "Long Time Coming: The Prospects for Democracy in China." *Foreign Affairs* 87 (January/February 2008): 2–22.

NOTES

1. Larry Diamond et al., "Introduction: Comparing Experiences with Democracy," in Larry Diamond et al., Eds., *Politics in Developing Countries* (Boulder, CO: Lynne Rienner, 1990), 16.
2. Thomas M. Magstadt, *Nations and Governments* (New York: St. Martin's Press, 1994), 289.
3. Jorge I. Dominguez, *Democratic Politics in Latin America and the Caribbean* (Baltimore, MD: The Johns Hopkins University Press, 1998), 14.
4. Gary K. Bertsch et al., *Power and Policy in Three Worlds* (New York: Macmillan, 1991), 580.
5. Jyotirindra Das Gupta, "India," in Larry Diamond et al., Eds., *Politics in Developing Countries* (Boulder, CO: Lynne Reiner, 1990), 223.
6. "Despite UN Plea, Haiti Postpones Elections Indefinitely," *Chicago Tribune*, 5 March 2000, Sect. 1, 9.
7. Scott Peterson, "Struck Down in Turkey, Islam Coils," *Christian Science Monitor*, 20 January 1998, 6; and Marina Ottaway and Thomas Carothers, "Middle East Democracy," *Foreign Policy* 145 (November/December 2004), 22–28.
8. Hugh Pope, "Turkey's Military Moves to Center Stage," *The Wall Street Journal*, 23 December 1997, A11.
9. "Indonesian Army: Going Out of Business," *The Economist*, 4 October 2008, 42.

10. U.S. Department of State, *Country Reports on Human Rights Practices for 1997* (Washington, DC: U.S. Government Printing Office, 1998), 1559.
11. Ibid., 1500.
12. Monte Palmer, *Political Development: Dilemmas and Challenges* (Itasca, IL: F. E. Peacock, 1997), 202.
13. Diamond et al., "Introduction," 18.
14. Richard J. Payne, *Opportunities and Dangers of Soviet-Cuban Expansion* (Albany, NY: State University of New York Press, 1988), 125.
15. Dominguez, *Democratic Politics*, 26.
16. Ronald Inglehart and Christian Welzel, "How Development Leads to Democracy," *Foreign Affairs* 88, No. 2 (March/April 2009), 34.
17. Geoffrey Pridham et al., "The International Dimension of Democratization," in Geoffrey Pridham et al., Eds., *Building Democracy* (London, UK: Leicester University Press, 1997), 2; and Marc F. Plattner, *Democracy without Borders* (Lanham, MD: Rowman and Littlefield, 2008).
18. Juan J. Linz and Alfred Stepan, *Problems of Democratic Transitions and Consolidation* (Baltimore, MD: The Johns Hopkins University Press, 1996), 3.
19. Ibid., 6.
20. Ibid., 7–11.
21. Georg Sorensen, *Democracy and Democratization* (Boulder, CO: Westview Press, 1998), 39.
22. Bratton and van de Walle, *Democratic Experiments*, 171.
23. Sonia E. Alvarez, *Engendering Democracy in Brazil: Women's Movements in Transition Politics* (Princeton, NJ: Princeton University Press, 1990), 262.
24. Keith B. Richburg, "On Indonesia, It's Wait and See," *Washington Post National Edition*, November 1999, 16.
25. Frances Robles, "In Cuba More Political Prisoners Going on Hunger Strikes," *The Miami Herald*, 17 June 2010, 1A.
26. Robert K. Shaeffer, *Power to the People: Democratization around the World* (Boulder, CO: Westview Press, 1997), 124.
27. "The Latinobarometro Poll: A Slow Maturing of Democracy," *The Economist*, 12 December 2009, 44.
28. Felipe Aguero, "Conflicting Assessments of Democratization," in Felipe Aguero and Jeffrey Stark, Eds., *Fault Lines of Democracy in Post-Transition Latin America* (Miami, FL: North-South Center Press, 1998), 3.
29. U.S. Department of State, *Country Reports*, 476.
30. Roderic Camp, *Politics in Mexico* (New York: Oxford University Press, 1996), 163; and "Big Expensive and Weirdly Spineless," *The Economist*, 16 February 2008, 44.
31. Shannon O'Neill, "The Real War in Mexico," *Foreign Affairs* 88, No. 4 (July/August 2009), 64–65.
32. Howard W. French, "New Congo Leader's Star Steadily Loses Its Luster," *The New York Times*, 21 May 1998, A1.
33. U.S. Department of State, *Country Reports*, 262–266.
34. Jean Herskovits, "Nigeria's Rigged Democracy," *Foreign Affairs* 86, No. 4 (July/August 2007), 115; and Osasu Obayiuwana, "Nigeria: A Problematic Solution," *New African*, March 2010.
35. Seth Mydans, "Indonesia's Students Pledge to Press Democratic Agenda," *The New York Times*, 9 November 1999, A8.
36. Andrew Jacobs, "No Voice is Too Small for a China Still Nervous About Dissent," *The New York Times*, 30 August 2008, A6.
37. ohn Pomfret and Michael Laris, "A Standoff Between Falun Gong and Government," *Washington Post National Weekly Edition*, 8 November 1999, 15.
38. Daniel Duedney and G. John Ikenberry, "The Myth of the Autocratic Revival," *Foreign Affairs* 88, No. 1 (January/February 2009), 77–79.
39. U.S. Department of State, *Country Reports on Human Rights Practices for 2009* (Washington, DC: U.S. Government Printing Office, 2010); and "The Illusion of Calm in Tibet," *The Economist*, 12 July 2008, 55.
40. Seyom Brown, *Human Rights in World Politics* (New York: Addison Wesley Longman, 2000), 41–47.
41. Richard W. Mansbach, *Global Puzzle* (Boston, MA: Houghton Mifflin Company, 1997), 558.
42. Richard J. Payne, *The Nonsuperpowers and South Africa* (Bloomington, IN: Indiana University Press, 1990), 245.
43. "Land Reform in South Africa," *The Economist*, 5 December 2009, 58; and Pusch Commey, "South Africa: Change, But for Whom?" *New Africa*, March 2010, 8.

Political Leadership and State Capacity

Globalization, Leadership, and State Capacity

Leaders and states are still important, but, in this rapidly changing, technology-driven world, leaders need to be innovators. No more can the world afford old-style leaders who will continue to think in nationalist terms. The world we live in is a different world than the one our forefathers knew. Today, most of our problems are global in nature. National solutions cannot solve global problems. In this age, the forces of globalization are redefining the sovereign state. Political leadership, however, has not caught on. Nationalist leaders still thrive. Patriotism is still a force greater than humanism. Some would argue that nationalism is a form of reaction to globalization. But resistance to change cannot stop the change. It only slows it down. It also could force those who desire it into a violent reaction. President John F. Kennedy once said, "Those who make peaceful change impossible make violent change inevitable." The role of leaders is still significant even though they no longer have full control of the agenda. When an oil spill raged for months in the Gulf of Mexico in 2010, President Obama reminded people that he was unable to dive in and close the source of the spill. All he could do was to assign people to work on it.

The people President Obama could assign are bureaucrats. The capacity of a state, therefore, has to do more with bureaucracy than with leadership. After all, it is the bureaucracy that must transform the dreams of leaders into reality. Today, the bureaucracy is under serious pressure with globalization. New standards are coming into being with deregulation and privatization. The bureaucracy of the old national state had authority and control. Today, forces beyond the control of a single nation-state are undermining that authority. Regulating trade, drug traffic, health, pornography, and many other activities are now harder to address than in the past. With the global networks that have eased the flow of information, the national bureaucracies are slowly losing their grip in the area of regulation.

The new technologies could also make the work of the bureaucracy more efficient. The rapid flow of information could allow for the spread of lessons from one bureaucracy to another. Failure of a program somewhere may save similar program elsewhere as information becomes more readily available. With cellular telephones, text messaging, and iPads, bureaucrats cannot hide away from offices. With the Internet, much new information is now within reach as are individuals. We may be in control of technology, but technology also can control our lives.

It may be that people are the foot soldiers of change, but societies need leaders to direct the process of change. Some have argued that leaders are really no different from those who are led and that, although they occupy a special position, they are a mere reflection of their constituents. Others have argued that leaders are all important. They are the ones who shape society. Both arguments are probably accurate to a degree. In situations of great change, such as the current process of globalization, leaders are, perhaps, more important. It is for this reason that we have decided to devote a chapter of this book to the role of political leadership and state capacity. Africa, Asia, and Latin America are in the midst of a profound revolution. They are changing very rapidly.

In times of change, when old structures are no longer respected and new ones are not yet fully developed, people often find it easy to attach their loyalty to an individual leader. This makes leaders in such societies more important. Political leaders play a critical role in developmental policies throughout the areas under study. We could classify leadership in Africa, Asia, and Latin America into a number of types. In some societies leadership is still old-style patriarchal leadership.

PATRIARCHAL LEADERSHIP

patriarchy
■ Leadership where authority is closely related to family and kinship groups, especially to the men in those groups.

Patriarchy comes from the word *patriarch* and is at the core of all traditional systems where authority is closely related to family and kinship groups. The male head of the clan, tribe, or village acts in patriarchy as the head of a family; the group then becomes the family. In some traditional societies, the nation becomes the family and the national leader becomes the patriarch, or father, of the whole nation. In such societies, who becomes the leader is more related to an accident of birth than to qualifications or an electoral process. A patriarchal leader leads because he is perceived to have a right to lead. His followers obey because they believe that it is their duty to do so. Patriarchal societies are often referred to as premodern. But if you visit such a country, you are likely to encounter modern appearances. You are likely to see high-rise buildings, modern dress, and up-to-date cars. This is how the late Professor Hisham Sharabi distinguished between traditional patriarchy and what he termed as **neopatriarchy**.[1]

neopatriarchy ■ A patriarchal system in a society that hides under the façade of modernity.

Underneath that façade of modernity, society remains patriarchal. Government remains rooted in the family unit, extended to include the whole nation. Prior to independence, most developing countries had patriarchal systems. After some years of independence, new types of leaders began to emerge. Initially, most came about as a result of **military interventions**. Some of the new military leaders wanted revolutionary change; others wanted incremental change; yet others took over the government so as to prevent impending change. In some cases, revolutions toppled patriarchal or military leaders and put forth the revolutionaries in power. More recently, some form of democratization has taken place and some countries have moved to yet a different type of democratically elected leadership.

military intervention
■ A military takeover of government.

MILITARY LEADERSHIP

The phenomenon of intervention by military leaders in politics and their attempts to control governmental institutions is not limited to one region or area of the contemporary world. Such attempts have occurred on almost every continent. The majority of countries in Africa, Asia, and Latin America experienced one or more attempts of military intervention since independence. Even Europe and the United States did not completely escape this phenomenon of military intervention in politics in one form or another. There are examples of direct and successful interventions, as in Spain, Greece, and Portugal, as well as the unsuccessful, as in France in 1962. In the United States, indirect intervention is often indicated in the notion that the defense establishment enjoys excessive power, which is often used to influence governmental decisions and policies. Military intervention, especially in developing countries, has attracted the attention of social scientists because of its implications to stability and to international affairs. Yet, this area of study is still short of adequate theory or concepts to explain, let alone predict, such developments. Social scientists, and political scientists in particular, do not possess the proper information or the adequate analytical tools to deal confidently with events of military intervention in a certain society. Their generalizations are often not much more trustworthy than those of the journalists reporting the news according to their senses and personal preferences. Among the early scholars who investigated military intervention in the governments of the developing countries were Samuel P. Huntington and Morris Janowitz. Their work has had a major impact on later scholars in the field. Consequently, a brief look at their approaches is in order.

Huntington asserted that "military explanations do not explain military intervention"[2] because of the general politicization of all groups in the society. In an attempt to answer the question of why the military intervenes in politics, Huntington cited the "absence or weakness of effective political institutions in the society."[3] Morris Janowitz, on the other hand, attempted to relate military intervention to the organizational structure of the military establishment and the social background of the individual officers leading the intervention. In attempting to discover the causes of intervention, Janowitz pointed out the "characteristics of the military establishment" of the country and relates the capabilities of the leading officers to their "ethos of public service." He also discussed their skills "which combine managerial ability with heroic posture," their class origin from middle or lower-middle classes, and their internal cohesion.[4]

There is some evidence to support both arguments. Other theorists working on the subject either explained or employed one or both of these theoretical approaches. Others reminded us of some other factors contributing to the phenomenon of military intervention in politics. Regardless of theoretical reasons for intervention, the fact remains that many developing countries have had military intervention or are run by civilians dependent on the military. When military officers carry out a successful intervention or coup d'état, new leadership suddenly emerges. Some are revolutionary, some are moderate, and others are conservative. Let us look at an example of each.

Case Study: Egypt

As you know, Egypt represents an old civilization. Its history stretches back thousands of years. Modern Egypt, however, is a recent state. At the turn of the twentieth century, Egypt found itself under British protection, meaning a lesser form of colonialism. It had been declared a British Protectorate in 1882 after the British occupied the country. British interest in Egypt centered on the **Suez Canal**, a significant trade route that connects the Mediterranean Sea to the Red Sea. The Suez Canal was built back in 1868 with British and French help.

Suez Canal ■ A significant trade route that connects the Mediterranean Sea to the Red Sea.

capitulation system
■ System that exempted non-Egyptians from Egypt's laws.

Under British rule, the **capitulation system** allowed for many abuses in the country. The capitulation system exempted non-Egyptians from Egypt's laws. This exemption allowed British and other Western adventurers to rob the country of many artifacts. Some Hollywood movies show Western adventurers compete for Egyptian and other artifacts in developing societies. In reality, the adventurers were not heroes to those whose culture was robbed. Instead, they were seen as thieves and robbers taking away what is not theirs for profit. This is one reason so many Western museums have Egyptian mummies and other artifacts. In a way, we can be thankful that the Sphinx and the pyramids were too big and heavy to carry away; otherwise, they too would have ended up in some European or North American museum.

Internally, Egypt had a feudal system. Under this system 2 percent of the people owned more than 70 percent of all the agricultural land. Most people lived and worked on the feudal estates. The small aristocratic elite lived in luxury while the Egyptian masses labored hard under Egypt's burning sun to produce for and serve the aristocratic families. Politically, Egypt had a monarchy with a king as head of state. Although there was a constitution, in practice, the king held absolute power in consultation with the British. By the end of World War II, King Farouk had been the monarch for almost a decade. His dependence on British advisors and his loyal aristocratic elite had grown. King Farouk by then was too involved in his own hobbies to worry much about government. In 1948, Egypt lost a war with the newly founded state of Israel.

FIGURE 10.1
Egypt

It was at this juncture that Gamal Abdel Nasser and other military officers began to organize for the eventual coup d'état. Nasser, Anwar Sadat, and 10 other young army officers began to meet and discuss ways to rid Egypt of corruption and place it on the right path to creating a more just society. Known as the **Free Officers**, the group eventually carried out a bloodless military takeover on July 23, 1952. King Farouk was forced to abdicate and leave the country. A year later, the monarchy was finally dropped in favor of a constitution that put power in the hands of the military officers. Nasser emerged as the sole and all-powerful leader of the country. His charismatic style made Nasser very popular among the Egyptian masses.

Now in power, Nasser began a series of activities designed to achieve his objectives for the country. As mentioned earlier, Nasser and his colleagues in the Free Officers group wanted to end feudalism, rid Egypt of British domination, and modernize the country. Feudalism was ended by decree. The **Agrarian Reform Act** limited land ownership and redistributed land among the peasants. The British role in Egypt, however, was a different story. It required a war. If you recall, British interest in Egypt revolved around the Suez Canal. The British, French, and the government of Egypt had collaborated to build the canal back in 1868. In return, the British and French were given rights to the canal for the next 100 years. Nasser did not have the patience to wait for the end of that term to rid his country of British troops in the Canal Zone. He attempted to negotiate a British exit to no avail. Consequently, on July 26, 1956, Nasser decided to nationalize the Suez Canal Company and take sole control of the canal. In late October of the same year, Britain, France, and Israel invaded Egypt. The invasion of Egypt caused uproar throughout the Arab countries and the states of Africa, Asia, and Latin America. Other developing countries denounced the invasion as imperialist. In Britain itself, domestic opposition to the actions of the government threatened the ruling party's hold on power. The Soviet Union and the United States both opposed the invasion of Egypt and demanded the withdrawal of the invading forces. The pressure was too strong to resist. Under such global pressure, the three countries withdrew from Egypt, leaving Nasser in a much stronger position. Although Nasser may have lost the battle, he clearly won the war. He emerged from the war as a great hero, not only to his own people, but also to other Arab, African, and Asian peoples. Finally, a Third World leader was able to stand up to the former colonial powers. Nasser became an instant celebrity and one of the most charismatic leaders of his day.

Another area of interest to the military leadership of Egypt was the modernization of the country. Aside from the usual modernization projects that include education, health care, and infrastructures, Nasser decided to build the largest dam in the world, the **Aswan High Dam**, on the Nile River. As you may already know, the Nile is Egypt's mainstay. More than 90 percent of all Egyptians live around the river and depend on it for the production of their food. Every year, the Nile flooded, destroying crops in the process. By building a large dam on the river, Nasser hoped to control the floods, expand agricultural land into the desert, and generate hydroelectric power to help industrialize the country. The construction of the dam became highly publicized and internationally controversial. Loans and expertise were needed for the project. Nasser attempted to secure those from the United States, but when that failed, he went to the Soviet Union for help. Doing so at the height of the Cold War turned out to be controversial. The Aswan Dam, however, did increase Egypt's cultivable land by about 2 million acres and

Free Officers ■ The group of military officers who overthrew the government of King Farouk.

Agrarian Reform Act ■ Limited land ownership and redistributed land among the peasants in Egypt.

Aswan High Dam ■ At the time, the largest dam in the world, brought about through Nasser's efforts in Egypt.

increased its power output 10 fold. It also controlled the flooding that plagued the country's farmers. In addition, industrialization projects were created and Egypt seemed to be on the road toward modernization.

Population growth and the Arab–Israeli conflict, however, kept Egypt from joining the ranks of modern states. As productivity grew so did the population, eating up any meaningful growth. The Arab–Israeli conflict also required that the country devote much-needed resources for military buildup and occasional wars. But Nasser's charisma and his personal integrity were never questioned by his followers. When he died of a heart attack in 1970, millions of Egyptians paid their respects, and he is still remembered as a great revolutionary leader by his countrymen. Nasser's military regime continues to rule Egypt long after his death. Anwar Sadat, Nasser's vice president took over after Nasser's passing, and Husni Mubarak, Sadat's vice president became president after Sadat was assassinated in 1981. While ailing and old, Mubarak remains Egypt's president and seems to be preparing his son to succeed him. Egypt's conflict with Israel came to an end in 1979, but population growth keeps the country's development at bay.

▶ Case Study: Nigeria

As we will discuss in Chapter 11, Nigeria is Africa's most populous state and the eighth most populous country in the world. With a population of more than 150 million and endowed with a wealth of natural resources, Nigeria is also potentially one of Africa's richest countries. But ethnic problems, constant military interventions, and rampant corruption have kept the majority of Nigerians impoverished.[5] A former British colony, Nigeria achieved independence in 1960. Since then, for all but a dozen years, the country has been ruled by military regimes. One of the most notorious of those was the rule of General **Sani Abacha** from 1993 to 1998. During his reign, the country was dragged down by neglect, corruption, and mismanagement—despite its billions in oil revenues. Abacha ruled Nigeria with an iron fist that made it into an international pariah. Political opponents were imprisoned, exiled, or killed; the constitution was discarded; and violations of civil and human rights became commonplace.

On June 8, 1998, General Sani Abacha died after suffering a heart attack. He was mourned by very few. The commander of the country's armed forces and defense minister, General Abdulsalam Abubakar, took over as the new ruler. Under domestic and international pressure, Abubakar began a process to return the country to civilian rule. He invited all exiles to return home to help in rebuilding the country. He also released many political prisoners. On July 20, 1998, the new military leader of Nigeria released a plan to return power to civilian rule and to move the nation on a path of political and economic reform. May 29, 1999, was set as the date for swearing in a new civilian president.

A new constitution was adopted, political parties were chartered, and local elections were held. The presidential elections were held on February 27, 1999. With more than 60 percent of the votes, Olusegun Obasanjo was declared the winner. On May 29, 1999, the world watched as Obasanjo took over power from Abubakar. Nigeria had made its transition to civilian rule. On the eve of the inauguration, Abubakar urged the new civilian rulers to seize the opportunity to change a nation wrecked by years of

Sani Abacha ■ A notorious general who ruled Nigeria from 1993 to 1998.

dictatorship. Since then, the country has seen two new presidents sworn in peacefully. Today, Nigeria seems to be on the road to maintaining a federal democratic system modeled on that of the United States. Corruption and ethnic conflict, however, remain a serious problem.

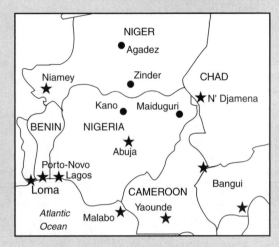

FIGURE 10.2
Nigeria

Case Study: Chile

Chile is a beautiful coastal country with a rather long history of democracy. The people inhabiting the area tell a legend about their lands. It goes like this:

> In the beginning of time, God created the world with all its wonders. Upon completion, God found that he had many pieces left. He had parts of rivers and valleys, of oceans and lakes, of glaciers and deserts, of mountains and forests, and of meadows and hills. Rather than let such wonders go to waste, God put them together and cast them onto the most remote corner of the earth. This is how Chile was born.

Looking closely at Chile, we can understand the legend. Chile is a rather long and narrow country located in the extreme southwestern part of South America. It is geographically very diverse. In the north Chile reaches the Andes Mountains and in the south, the Antarctic zone. In between it has long beaches on the Pacific Ocean; behind the Andes lies the Atacama Desert. About 80 percent of Chile's population lives in urban areas. The country is rich in mining (mainly copper), agriculture, tourism, and fishing. Born out of Spanish colonization, Chile's constitution was, until 1973, one of the oldest in Latin America. The country had a republican form of government with elected presidents and a congress for 140 years.

In 1970, **Salvador Allende,** a medical doctor who led the Popular Unity Coalition, won the election for the presidency. With many Chileans suffering from malnutrition, and the country facing shortages of food, housing, health care, and education, Allende

Salvador Allende
■ The elected president of Chile in 1970 who was overthrown by Pinochet's coup d'etat in 1973.

International
Telephone & Telegraph
(IT&T) ■ The U.S.
corporation that owned
Chile's copper mines.

pursued a socialist policy designed to redistribute the wealth of the nation. He began a land distribution program. He nationalized many industries and took over the foreign-owned copper mines and other natural resources. Such actions put him on a collision course with the United States, whose companies were severely affected. One major U.S. company that was affected was **International Telephone & Telegraph (IT&T)**, which operated Chile's telephone system and owned copper mines there. In the 1972 U.S. presidential campaign, IT&T contributed $1 million to Richard Nixon's campaign. But the United States was moved more by Allende's perceived "Marxism" than by campaign donations. Allende's close relationship to Cuba and other communist countries further angered the U.S. government.

Augusto Pinochet
■ The military
dictator who ruled
Chile from 1973
until 1990.

Aided by training and financing from the U.S. Central Intelligence Agency (CIA), a faction of the Chilean military, led by General **Augusto Pinochet**, carried out a coup d'état on September 11, 1973. Allende lost not only his job as president but also his life. In the process, democracy in Chile came to an abrupt end, ironically with the help of the United States. A military regime was set up and the constitution was suspended.

Under Pinochet, Chile became an international outlaw state. To suppress the supporters of the previous government, Pinochet waged a campaign of terror that included raids, executions, disappearances, imprisonment, and torture of his opponents. In the four months following the coup, Amnesty International and the United Nations Human Rights Commission reported that 250,000 people were detained for political reasons. The government also halted the distribution of land and reversed many of Allende's policy decisions. Naturally, as in the case of all oppressive regimes, oppression did not end the opposition, it only strengthened it. Labor uprisings and nonviolent resistance by the Chilean masses continued, as did international pressure.

In 1980 Pinochet, under pressure, proposed a new constitution for the country. It provided that Pinochet would remain president until 1989 or possibly 1997. The proposed constitution allowed for the gradual return to some democratic forms of governance and restored a limited, and appointed, National Congress in 1990 and an elected president in 1997. But when the country went into an economic recession in the mid-1980s, opposition grew. Street protests, strikes, and symbolic resistance, such as people banging on pots, became commonplace. Consequently, Pinochet decided to hold a referendum on his presidency. The question voters were asked was whether Pinochet should remain president until 1997. The voters turned out in large numbers to defeat the proposition. Pinochet then made arrangements to step down as president but to remain head of the armed forces until 1998. After that time, he was to become senator-for-life.

In 1990, the people of Chile voted for Patricio Aylwin to be president, and Chile was on its way back to democracy after 17 years of oppressive military rule. Pinochet, of course, remained head of the military until 1998, when he became senator-for-life. Life did not go smoothly for the new senator, however. In October 1998, Pinochet was arrested in the United Kingdom when he was hospitalized for back surgery. His arrest was based on a Spanish request to extradite him to Spain for trial for the death of Spanish citizens killed in Chile under Pinochet's leadership. The Chilean government asked for his release, arguing that foreign courts have no jurisdiction for trying crimes committed on Chilean soil. The Spanish prosecutors argued that Pinochet's actions constituted crimes against humanity. Although the

British eventually let Pinochet go back to his homeland, it took 15 months of agonizing house arrest while British courts were looking into the matter.

Shortly after returning to his homeland, Pinochet learned that Chilean courts were stripping him of his congressional immunity as a senator-for-life, a privilege he granted himself in the constitution as a condition of his stepping down from the presidency. Pinochet's failing health prevented him from facing dozens of criminal cases involving the death and disappearance of many Chileans during his 17-year military rule over the country. His legacy of military dictatorship and reversal of change will remain for a long time.

Not all states in Africa, Asia, and Latin America have military regimes. Some are still monarchies, others have democratic systems, and a few have communist systems. Each has a different type of leadership and politics. Let us now take a look at some of those.

CaseStudy: Nonmilitary leadership

Many countries in Africa, Asia, and Latin America have civilian governments. In some cases, the civilian leadership is still dependent upon the military establishment to maintain its power. In other cases, the civilian leadership has the consent of the governed through a constitutional system that is supported by the people. In a few cases, the civilian leadership is accepted because of traditions and customs that the population seems to continue to tolerate. Saudi Arabia has such a system. In this part of the chapter, we will take a look at leadership in a monarchy, a communist system, and a democratic system.

The Monarch as Leader: Saudi Arabia

> *I will be father to the young, brother to the elderly,*
> *I am but one of you; whatever troubles you, troubles me;*
> *Whatever pleases you, pleases me.*

THE LATE KING FAHD

The Kingdom of Saudi Arabia is the largest political unit in the Arabian Peninsula. A country that is almost entirely a desert, it has about one-fourth of the world's known oil reserves. The kingdom's founder was **Abd al-Aziz Ibn Saud**, who fought other tribal leaders to unite the country by 1927 under the name of the Kingdom of Hijaz and Najd and Its Dependencies. The country was renamed the Kingdom of Saudi Arabia in reference to Ibn Saud in 1932. Since that time, the country has been ruled by the descendents of Ibn Saud.

During the days of its founder, the person of the king combined executive, legislative, and administrative functions. Each tribal chief was responsible for the behavior of his people, and the Royal Army was ready to aid him if needed. In March 1958, legislative and executive powers were transferred to the crown prince, who also served as deputy prime minister. The king maintained veto powers. In May of the same year, a royal decree established a cabinet system with administrative powers. The cabinet, however, serves at the wishes of the king. Even today, Saudi Arabia has no constitution and maintains that the Islamic holy book, the Quran, is the guiding law of the land. The king still has absolute

Abd al-Aziz Ibn Saud
■ Founder of Saudi Arabia.

FIGURE 10.3
Saudi Arabia

power and all government action is done by decree in the name of the king. No elections take place for any central government positions. Political parties are nonexistent.

Because no official census figures are available, the Saudi Arabian population is estimated. Latest estimates put that population at more than 28 million. That figure includes about one-fourth of the population who are non-nationals, or foreigners. Until recently, nearly all Saudis were nomadic or seminomadic. Today, however, about 80 percent of the population is urban, the rest live in rural areas, and very few are still nomadic. Saudi cities look modern. High-rise buildings dot the landscape. Modern facilities shock first-time visitors.

The considerable influx of money from oil sales, especially in the 1960s and 1970s, generated many plans for development. Roads were built, universities were established, and industrialization was begun. Even agricultural projects were put in place, and this desert country became an exporter of wheat and other agricultural products. Industrialization targeted petrochemical products such as plastics, fertilizers, fiberglass, and other goods. Socially, the story is very different. Saudi Arabia is a rather conservative kingdom that attempts to maintain social cohesion through the application of Islamic principles. As such, even though visitors may be impressed with modern buildings and amenities, they soon discover a society that is inward looking and very traditional. It was fitting then that, in 1992, when the country celebrated its sixtieth anniversary, the Ministry of Information adopted the slogan of "Sixty years of progress without change."

Since its creation in 1932, Saudi Arabia had a total of five kings. The first was the country's founder, Ibn Saud. The rest were all his sons. An inner circle of his male descendants determines succession to power. When a king dies, the crown prince assumes the throne. King Fahd was the ruler until he died in 2005. The current monarch, King Abdallah, is the half-brother of the late king, and had acted on his behalf as crown prince owing to King Fahd's health problems that had prevented him from carrying out the duties of ruling the country.

The person of the king combines legislative, executive, and administrative authority. Law is clearly guided by Islamic teachings as interpreted by the **ulema**, or learned religious men. The king and the crown prince normally lead the Council of Ministers. The Council of Ministers is an appointed body that is vested with most powers with the king holding the right to veto their decisions. In sum, Saudi Arabia has a system of absolute monarchy supported by a patriarchal leader who acts as the father of the nation.

ulema ■ Islamic learned religious men.

CaseStudy: Communist Leaders: The Case of Cuba's Castro

Cuba is the Caribbean's largest island. It is also the only communist state in the Western Hemisphere. With 11 million inhabitants, Cuba has a long history that goes back to 3500 B.C.E. Europeans arrived only in the late fifteenth century. As in other parts of the Americas, the arrival of the Europeans brought with it slavery, wars, and misery to the inhabitants of the island.

Although Christopher Columbus sighted Cuba in 1492, he did not land there. It was Diego Velazquez de Cuellar who led an expedition to the island to claim it for the Spanish Crown in 1512. The Spanish slaughtered thousands of the native Taino-speaking **Arawaks**. Cuba was later used as the base from which expeditions to conquer Mexico were launched. As such, the island became Spain's gateway to South America.

Arawaks ■ Original inhabitants of Cuba.

The Spanish created large estates on the island, where the local population was essentially enslaved under the pretext of teaching them Christianity. Exploitation, oppression, and European illnesses that the locals were not immune to led to the disappearance of the native population. Imported African slaves replaced the natives on the plantations. Tobacco was the major product of the island until sugar production became its major industry about a hundred years later. By 1820, Cuba became the world's largest sugar producer.

By 1825, Cuba and Puerto Rico were the only remaining Spanish colonies in the Western Hemisphere. As other Spanish colonies were freed, Cuba became a haven for Spanish loyalists escaping the victorious rebels. In October 1868, an attempt at independence from Spain took the lives of 200,000 people only to fail. In 1895, a similar attempt was made by a group of exiles led by a poet, Jose Marti. Marti was killed soon after he landed in Cuba, and his followers eventually were defeated.

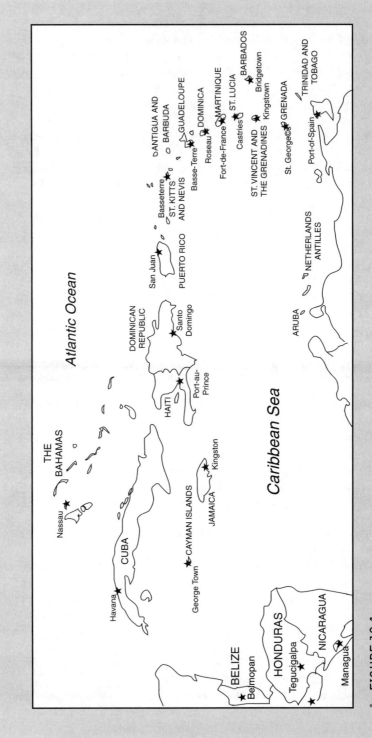

FIGURE 10.4
The Caribbean

In January 1898, an explosion destroyed a U.S. warship anchored at the Havana harbor. The U.S. government used this incident to achieve the eventual annexation of the Spanish colony. The United States declared war on Spain, and hostilities lasted for three months before the Spanish surrendered. By then Cuba had become a U.S.-occupied territory. An American governor was appointed, and a military base was created on Cuba's Guantanamo Bay. The U.S. naval base on Guantanamo Bay remains until today, reminding Cubans of the occupation of more than a hundred years ago. Cubans view the base as an insult to their nation.

Within two decades, U.S. companies came to dominate Cuba. American corporations gained ownership of two-thirds of the country's farmland, and tourism became a major industry run mostly by U.S. companies. Tourism was based on gambling and prostitution. In time, the country became known as the whorehouse of the United States. This was a time when the United States had a prohibition on alcohol.

A sergeant called Fulgencio Batista carried out a coup d'état that overthrew the government in August 1933. Over the next two decades, Batista ran a very corrupt government that left the country's assets in the hands of foreign interests. The Batista dictatorship is known as an era of corruption and social injustice for many Cubans today. That sad era in Cuba's history ended when a young lawyer named **Fidel Castro** overthrew Batista after a three-year rebellion. Batista escaped the country, taking with him a reported $40 million.

Fidel Castro
■ Cuba's revolutionary leader from 1959 until his resignation in 2008.

The son of a plantation owner, Fidel Castro worked in the sugarcane fields as a boy. He went to Jesuit schools and later to law school, where he received a law degree. Castro practiced law in Havana, where he devoted his work to helping the poor. His opposition to the Batista dictatorship landed him in prison for a brief period. Eventually, he went to Mexico, where he began to organize the Cuban exiles into a fighting force, which he called the **26th of July Revolutionary Movement**. This movement of 82 men tried to overthrow Batista in an attack on December 2, 1956. They landed in eastern Cuba on the famous Granma yacht to launch their armed struggle. Most of the attackers were killed or captured in a devastating defeat for Castro. He did not give up. Castro and 11 followers retreated to the mountains, where they established a stronghold from which they waged guerilla warfare against the Batista government.

The 26th of July Revolutionary Movement
■ Castro's group of 82 men who landed in Cuba in 1956.

Castro's movement grew after each attack. Numbering about 800, the movement scored many victories in small hit-and-run battles with government forces. Continuously growing, Castro's movement eventually became a serious threat to Batista. On January 1, 1959, Batista fled the country and Castro entered Havana as a liberating hero.

Soon after assuming power, Castro began to reform the economy. Decrees were passed cutting rents down, slashing electric rates, and nationalizing landholdings of more than 400 hectares. The United States was outraged at the nationalization of U.S. corporate interests. Telephone, electric, oil, and sugar companies were taken over by the government from U.S. corporate owners. Castro's offer of compensation did little to ease the tensions with the United States over Cuban actions. Castro simply wanted to take charge of his country's affairs to serve the poor and needy Cubans. Cuba's small elite, which included upper- and middle-class businesspeople and plantation owners, was similarly outraged. Most of them fled to Miami, where they have since orchestrated anti-Castro campaigns and influenced U.S. policy toward Cuba. The U.S. government imposed an **embargo** against trade with and travel to Cuba, which is still in place until this day.

embargo ■ Decision that restricts or bars some or all trade with certain countries.

Bay of Pigs ■ Failed
invasion of Cuba by
Miami exiles.

The U.S. government also armed and trained a group of Cuban exiles to overthrow Castro's government. On April 17, 1961, this force of 1,300 exiles attempted an invasion of Cuba from the **Bay of Pigs** on the southern coast of the island. The invaders were defeated. But Cuban–U.S. relations worsened when Castro sought help and support from the Soviet Union in his confrontation with the United States. In a speech honoring the Cuban forces that defeated the invaders in April of that year, Castro said for the first time that the Cuban Revolution was socialist. Cuba's international behavior became more and more anti-American, as Castro supported revolutionary forces in Central America and Africa. The Soviet Union also responded to Castro positively by giving Cuba massive amounts of aid.

The close Soviet–Cuban relations alarmed the U.S. government. In October 1962, a major crisis took place that brought the United States and the Soviet Union close to a nuclear holocaust. The United States discovered that the Soviet Union was setting up long-range ballistic missiles in Cuba. The U.S. president, John Kennedy, ordered a blockade of the island and demanded the removal of the missiles. Initially, the Soviet Union threatened to break the blockade, and a nuclear confrontation seemed imminent. That confrontation was averted when the Soviet Union decided to remove the missiles. If you have seen the movie *Thirteen Days*, you already have an idea about the crisis. For a long time after that, U.S.–Cuban relations remained hostile. In the early 1990s, however, Cuba began to soften its anti-U.S. rhetoric and actually changed its constitution to drop any references to Marxism–Leninism. Relations with the United States remain cool, and the embargo against Cuba remains in place.

The Cuban society under the Castro regime has done relatively well. Through a state-supported agricultural system and ration program for basic nutrients, Cuba became the first underdeveloped economy to wipe out hunger and malnutrition. Cuba's public health system is so advanced that the World Health Organization recommended it as a "model for the world." Cuba was successful in wiping out epidemics that infect most developing countries. Among Latin American countries, Cuba ranks best in life expectancy, infant mortality rate, literacy, and the number of doctors per thousand people. In sum, even though Castro's government had to deal with a harsh embargo, it was able to move Cuba in a direction that serves its people, especially the poor ones. Today, Castro is ill and has handed power to his brother Raul, but his legacy still dominates the country. Cuba's relations with the United States remain strained. There are expectations that such relations will change with the current Obama administration.

▶ CaseStudy: Leaders in Democracies: The Case of India

Few countries in the world have such an ancient and diverse culture as India's. Stretching back 5,000 years, India's culture has been enriched by successive waves of migration that were absorbed into India's way of life. It is the physical, religious, linguistic, and racial variety that is the hallmark of India. As discussed in Chapter 3, India became independent in 1947 after centuries of British domination. The leaders who struggled for independence chose to remain within the British Commonwealth and retained many of the features of the British administration. India also adopted the British system of parliamentary democracy, making it the largest democracy on earth.

The Indian Constitution, adopted in 1950, safeguards all people from all forms of discrimination. Given the long history of the caste system in the country, this was a major break from tradition. It also caused severe hardships for the new government. The constitution also guaranteed freedom of speech, expression, and belief. The political system created a parliamentary democracy, where the House of Representatives decides on the prime minister, who holds executive power. The Indian Parliament consists of two houses: the Rajya Sabha or the Council of States, and the Lok Sabha or the House of Representatives. The Council of States has 250 members, and the House of Representatives has 543 members. All legislation requires the approval of both houses. India has a ceremonial president elected by an electoral college drawn from both houses of parliament. The judiciary is independent and is headed by a Supreme Court. The country is set up as a federal state with 25 states and seven union territories represented in the federal system.

The achievement of independence in 1947 was just the first step for India's progress toward the creation of a modern state. The constitution set forth a number of goals for India's democracy. Economic growth, social justice, and self-reliance are most significant among them. To achieve such objectives, the country embarked on the promotion of five-year plans for development. Since then, India has come a long way in its progress toward development, but the process still has a long way to go. One thing is certain, however—India has created a democratic political system that could serve as a model for other countries in Africa, Asia, and Latin America. In Latin America, democracy has been on the rise. Sometimes, it has resulted in the rise of nationalist and revolutionary individuals to the top. Venezuela's Hugo Chavez and Evo Morales of Bolivia are such leaders.

FIGURE 10.5
India

Leadership and Change

Africa, Asia, and Latin America are in the midst of a profound revolution. They are changing very rapidly. In times of change, when old structures are no longer respected and new ones are not yet fully developed, people often find it easy to attach their loyalty to an individual leader. This makes leaders in such societies more important. Political leaders play a critical role in developmental policies throughout the areas under study. We could classify leadership in Africa, Asia, and Latin America into a number of types. In many societies leadership is still patriarchal. Patriarchy is at the core of all traditional systems where authority is closely related to family and kinship groups. Prior to independence, most developing countries had patriarchal systems. After some years of independence, new types of leaders began to emerge. Initially, most came about as a result of military interventions. The phenomenon of intervention by military leaders in politics and their attempts to control governmental institutions is not limited to one region or area of the contemporary world. Such attempts have occurred on almost every continent. This chapter focused on military interventions in the cases of Egypt, Nigeria, and Chile. In all of these countries, the military has served, for the most part, as a largely patriarchal authority that uses its powers to bring "order" to the society in which it operates. Countries in Africa, Asia, and Latin America—and all over the world—have varying degrees of patriarchal leadership. This, however, may stem from a communist background, as is the case in Cuba, or from democratic institutions, as is the case in India. Although not homogeneous in character or styles, leaders throughout Africa, Asia, and Latin America claim to represent their people's traditions, values, and political cultures. But leadership needs a sound state capacity to affect real change.

STATE CAPACITY

Let us say that the U.S. Congress passed a bill to construct a new interstate highway linking New York and California. The bill allocates $10 billion for the project. The president signs the bill and it becomes a national government decision. Who is going to plan, design, and oversee the actual construction of the interstate? Surely, it will not be Congress or the president. It is likely to be the U.S. Department of Transportation. Who works there? It is civil servants or bureaucrats. They are the ones who administer government decisions.

bureaucracy ■ The administrative arm of government.

The importance of administration is almost universally recognized. The **bureaucracy** is, in essence, the administrative arm of government. Political and economic development cannot be achieved without a competent bureaucracy. Policy decisions are not self-enforcing. The bureaucracy carries them out. Decisions by policy makers represent hope. It is the bureaucracy that must transform the hope or the dream into reality. Although bureaucrats are less visible than political leaders, their power usually is much greater in that it extends to every area of citizens' lives. If you need a driver's license, a passport, a birth certificate, a permit to add to a home, or a tax auditor, you will see a bureaucrat.

Bureaucrats also do much more than simply carry out orders of decision makers. They are the ones with information and expertise that is essential for policy makers. In essence, they are partners with the decision makers on issues of policy. In the countries of Africa, Asia, and Latin America, they not only administer laws but, in the absence of parliamentary institutions, usually also fashion them. They not only license, tax, and supervise, but often also organize and manage major financial, industrial, and agricultural enterprises. In order to modernize, the bureaucracy, therefore, ought to be the most permanent, the most expert, and the most efficient institution in the state.

As the core of the modern state, bureaucracy is very important in the process of modernization. The task of a modernizing bureaucracy involves not only running an ongoing system but also developing new modes of operations, refining old norms, and building the new modern state. In all societies, the bureaucracy has the tasks of **implementation** and **regulation**. Let us take a look at such tasks.

Implementation
■ The stage between decision and its consequences.

Regulation
■ Government mandates on processes in society.

IMPLEMENTATION

Implementation is the stage in between the making of a policy decision and the consequences of the decision upon those people who are supposed to be affected by that decision. As already mentioned, policy decisions, such as the passage of a legislative act, are not self-executing. They need to be executed or carried out by someone else. As we saw earlier, a new interstate decision is likely to go to the U.S. Department of Transportation for implementation. Implementation involves the creation of a new agency or the assignment of responsibility to an existing one. It also takes the development of plans and guidelines for carrying out policy goals and the coordination of resources and personnel to achieve such goals.[6]

Implementation is not as simple as it may sound. It is a complicated process that involves the potential for policy failure. Planning, for example, does not always lead to success. The best-laid plans sometimes flunk the implementation test. Lack of clarity in the policy itself may contribute to differing interpretations and contrary results. Resources are not always readily available to carry out policies. Administrators may also be disposed to defeat a policy decision through inadequate implementation.

REGULATION

Government regulates all sorts of activities in society. Government regulates universities, hospitals, gambling casinos, businesses, environmental hazards, the sale of alcohol, and all types of activities. Regulation is often a controversial function of the bureaucracy. Policy makers usually give government agencies broad mandates to regulate industries, businesses, and a host of activities in society. Such regulations reach us on a continuous basis. When we discussed the role of government in Chapter 1, we saw that government is with us from the moment we are born to the moment we are buried or cremated. Any time we discuss government, we are, in essence, discussing the bureaucracy.

Government regulates in order to protect us. But some people argue that too much regulation is not healthy for society. Such individuals want less regulation and less government in our lives. They advocate **deregulation**. The argument for deregulation is a popular one in many parts of the United States. The idea behind deregulation is that too much regulation raises prices, distorts market forces, and does not work. Consequently, the cry "get government off our backs" gets receptive audiences during national elections in many parts of the country. Popularity, however, does not necessarily equal accuracy. Regulation of society is very important to its own well-being. Some regulations have not worked and have created problems; others have done a good service to society. It is because of regulations that we now breathe cleaner air, have lower lead content in our blood, and have children who are more likely to survive infancy.

deregulation ■ The desire for less government regulation of the market.

THE BUREAUCRACY IN AFRICA, ASIA, AND LATIN AMERICA

As we have seen so far, bureaucracy is the core of the state. For the states of Africa, Asia, and Latin America, the bureaucracy is most important as they attempt to modernize their societies. Without a competent bureaucracy, modernization is destined to fail. In many of their states, the bureaucracy has gone a long way toward competency and efficiency; in others, it still has a long way to go. It is therefore difficult to make generalizations about the bureaucracy in so many countries. Instead, we will take a look at some common characteristics of the modern bureaucracies in Africa, Asia, and Latin America.

Some of the common characteristics that may be typical of administration in Africa, Asia, and Latin America include **structural uniformity**, **cultural variations**, shortage of skilled staff, corruption, formalism, and operational autonomy. Let us now take a look at each.

structural uniformity ■ Similarities in bureaucratic structures.

cultural variations ■ Differences in cultures as they relate to the bureaucracy.

Structural Uniformity

A basic pattern of the bureaucracy in Africa, Asia, and Latin America is imitative rather than indigenous. Modern bureaucracy in the states of Africa, Asia, and Latin America developed as they came in contact with the Europeans. That contact came in the form of colonial rule. The colonial powers established a new system of administration similar to those of the colonial motherland. The colonial administration was suited to the requirements of the colonial government rather than to the needs of the indigenous population. It was more elitist, more authoritarian, more aloof, and more paternalistic. The task of the colonial administration was to subvert the society to serve the needs of the dominant colonial power, not to serve the masses of people in the society. Remnants of these bureaucratic traits have inevitably carried over to the successor administration.

The transition from colonial administration to the new independent state was not an easy one. The colonial structure remained almost intact. The function, however, changed. Once independence was achieved, the function was not to subvert the society to the needs of a ruling foreign government but to mobilize society for national development. With independence also came the loss of top executive officials. Those who ran the colonial bureaucracy were foreign officials who were nationals of the colonial motherland. With independence, those expert managers were reassigned back home or into some other colony. The new independent bureaucracy, therefore, had a colonial structure that was alien in origin, contradictory to native culture, and lacked trained and experienced managers to run the system.

Cultural Variations

Few bureaucracies in the world have been in existence as long as those of Asia, the Middle East, or Africa. In fact, the bureaucracy was born somewhere there. Historians trace the earliest bureaucracy to Mesopotamia (today's Iraq). Others say it started in China, and some say it began in India. Europeans were left behind and developed their bureaucracies much later.

Although the inherited European system emphasized control and productivity, most African, Asian, and Latin American cultures put greater emphasis on values. In such cultures, being fair is more important than abiding by rigid bureaucratic rules. Often, rules are subverted to help an old person, someone in need, or a close friend or relative. There, bureaucracies tend to emphasize orientations that are not necessarily production directed. Status based on ascription rather than achievement is common. In some countries, the cultural norms dominate, whereas in others, the legal-structural ones do. In Japan, for example, the bureaucracy benefited from the nation's strong sense of unity and ancient traditions of political centralization.[7] While employing European-based structures for its bureaucracy, and improving them, Japan was able to make major strides toward the advancement of its people. In the process, Japan created an economy that is stronger than that of France, Italy, Spain, or many other European countries. Some countries in Africa, Asia, and Latin America, on the other hand, found their societies hindered by a burdensome bureaucratic structure that is essentially alien to their cultures.

Shortage of Skilled Staff

Bureaucracies in Africa, Asia, and Latin America have to deal with many problems when it comes to staffing. Often, they have a deficit in skilled staff necessary for carrying out the programs designed by their leaders. This shortage is not in employable individuals but rather in trained administrators with management capabilities, developmental skills, and technical competence. As the era of colonialism ended, the European powers withdrew their nationals to other assignments at home or in other colonies. Consequently, the newly independent states had to contend with training their own nationals to carry out the tasks of administration. As political instability occurred, so did instability in the

brain drain
■ Migration of technically competent individuals from poorer states to wealthier ones.

bureaucracy. Top bureaucrats are replaced with new regimes, often by individuals who need time to develop the necessary experience to carry out their tasks. Technically competent bureaucrats often find opportunities to work in more technologically advanced and wealthier countries. When experience and know-how migrate, the bureaucracy suffers. This process of migration of technically competent individuals from poorer states to wealthier ones is called the **brain drain**.

Corruption

bureaucratic
corruption ■ The illegal use of an official position or title for private gain.

In Chapter 5 you read about corruption as a formidable obstacle to economic growth and social equity. You may remember that corruption is endemic in Africa, Asia, and Latin America, with the poorest states having the most serious problems. Corruption, of course, is not limited to the bureaucracy in any region or state on earth. It occurs in all states, including the wealthiest ones. The consequences of corruption, however, are greater in poorer societies lacking in resources. **Bureaucratic corruption** is the illegal use of an official position or title for private gain.[8] This could take place in many forms, including taking bribes, embezzlement, nepotism, patronage, or the selective enforcement of the law. Bribes are common in many societies. Often, bureaucrats are not paid a meaningful salary for survival. Bribes become a supplemental salary to allow public servants to make a living wage. This notion is generally accepted in some societies, in which bribes are expected just like a tip for an airport or hotel baggage carrier. In the wealthier states too bribery takes place. But the consequences are often grave for the perpetrators.

Some states in Africa, Asia, and Latin America are starting to take tough measures against corrupt officials. The People's Republic of China, for example, executed a senior parliament official on September 14, 2000, for taking bribes. Cheng Kejie was the highest Chinese official to be executed for bribery in more than 50 years of communist rule.[9]

Formalism

formalism ■ A concept used to remind people of the widespread discrepancy between form and reality, such as false reporting.

A prominent scholar on developing administrations, Fred W. Riggs, used the concept of **formalism** to remind us of the widespread discrepancy between form and reality.[10] It is often the case in many countries that bureaucrats attempt to make things look as they ought to be rather than as they actually are. False reporting is, perhaps, the most common method of formalism. State Department official Roger Hilsman reported on such a practice during the Vietnam War. The United States was interested in developing statistical indicators to measure progress in that war. Once the request for such indicators reached a Vietnamese official, he responded, "Ah, les statistiques! Your Secretary of Defense loves statistics. We Vietnamese can give him all he wants. If you want them to go up, they will go up. If you want them to go down, they will go down."[11] Although very few bureaucrats will admit to that, it is nevertheless a common practice in some countries to fabricate statistics when necessary. Formalism could also take the shape of false reporting by electing to disregard personnel regulations.

Operational Autonomy

Colonialism was essentially the rule of the bureaucrats with policy guidance from abroad. After independence, this pattern persisted in many societies—bureaucrats having a monopoly over decision making with guidance from their new masters at home. This pattern of operational autonomy is strengthened by the reality that the bureaucracy is usually the most permanent institution in the state. Government leaders usually make the major decisions, whereas bureaucrats determine the details and manage the day-to-day workings of the government.

The bureaucracy in the postcolonial states has many other problems. Some view these problems differently. For example, writing about democracy and political development in India, Walter L. Weisberg asserts that "corruption helps the stability of society by allowing many individuals access to an otherwise impersonal bureaucratic machine. Greasing the wheels of the machine helps it work more quickly and smoothly."[12] Many experts have told us that cultural variations are wonderful and ought to be celebrated. Formalism could also help the poorer states receive low-interest loans and grants from wealthier countries or institutions. Operational autonomy could also be viewed as a form of participation and representation in authoritarian states. To better understand the bureaucracy in so many countries is not a simple task. Just generalizations will not do. A study of a few of those bureaucracies may give us a better understanding of how such societies work.

▶ CaseStudy: Bureaucracy in the People's Republic of China

As you already learned, China is a single-party state where the Communist Party is in command. When the communists took over in 1949, there were only 700,000 state employees in administrative and other posts. Within 10 years, that number had jumped to more than 7 million.[13] Although administrative growth creates new problems, it also indicates the emphasis of the government on development. After all, it is the bureaucracy that transforms the dreams of political leaders into reality.

Control of policy at all levels in China rests with the Communist Party. The party makes policy and the bureaucracy carries it out. Although formally the State Council and the National People's Congress are the official bodies making policy, the reality is that the Communist Party dominates those and directs them. The way the whole Chinese system is organized revolves around the Chinese Communist Party (CCP). Significant government officials are CCP members. All levels of government have parallel party levels. Party committees watch over government decisions and operations all the way from the smallest community to the national government. The CCP also maintains control over every government organization through its members who are employed by such organizations.[14]

One interesting feature of China's bureaucracy is the periodic rotation that occurs. Top administrative officials are occasionally rotated down to the basic level where they have to handle matters that deal directly with the people. This serves as a reminder of the needs of the people the bureaucrats are supposed to serve. Although this approach is innovative and useful, China's bureaucracy is still plagued with occasional corruption, red tape, nepotism, and a host of other common problems of the bureaucracy.

CaseStudy: Bureaucracy in Mexico

Mexico is a country that has been in the shadow of its neighbor to the north, the United States. Its economic problems have contributed to constant migration, legal and illegal, to the United States. Even though Mexico is an oil-producing state, it is a country that has accumulated huge external debts. Its economy has improved with the country's entry into the North American Free Trade Agreement (NAFTA) in 1993 but problems remain. Most important is the problem of drug trafficking. Drug cartels often fight with each other and almost always fight against the authorities.

From a colonial economy based largely on mining, especially silver, Mexico now has a diversified economy that includes strong agriculture, industry, and petroleum sectors. The Mexican bureaucracy is divided along federal lines into 31 states and a federal district. Historically, a single political party, the Institutional Revolutionary Party (PRI), dominated the bureaucracy, just like the federal government. The election of 2000, however, brought in a new party, the National Action Party (PAN), to power. On July 2, 2000, the PRI lost the presidency to Vicente Fox Queseda of the PAN, ending 71 years of PRI rule. The new president promised to improve the economy, reform taxes, overhaul the justice system, and give states more power. With Queseda in power, Mexico now has a government dominated by the PAN and an entrenched bureaucracy from the PRI. Many argue that the failure of the PAN government to improve the lives of its people is due to an entrenched bureaucracy.

Although the leadership had promised more honest government, even prior to its assumption of powers news broke out of less-than-honest dealings by the president-elect. On September 1, 2000, news reports surfaced about a scandal involving the president-elect using child labor to work on his ranch and freezing plant. The newly elected president conceded that he and his family had illegally used children as young as 11 years old and promptly fired those children after the story broke. In 2006 Philipe Calderon of the PAN won election, but has faced a fierce battle with drug cartels since often called the Mexican Drug War. Today, Mexico's government is caught in the midst of a serious conflict with competing drug groups and a potentially corrupt police force. Drug cartels still control large portions of the country and rule in a number of regions. Corruption among officials including police and drug enforcement agencies is rampant and the security situation there continues to deteriorate.

CaseStudy: Bureaucracy in South Africa

You learned about South Africa earlier. You may remember that South Africa began as a colony. White settlers created the system of apartheid, which enforced racial segregation and kept the white minority in a dominant political and economic position.[15] The struggle led by the African National Congress (ANC) eventually brought about an end to apartheid.[16] Even though apartheid officially ended and black leaders like Nelson Mandela, Thabo Mbeki, Kgalema Motlanthe, and Jacob Zuma became presidents, the economic reality remains one of a dominant white minority and a poverty-stricken black majority.

With so much frustration, and a political and economic system dominated by a minority for so long, the new leaders had to find ways to reward their loyal supporters and party members. The easiest way to reward them was to hire them into the bureaucracy. This is called patronage. Common in many parts of the world, including the United States, **patronage** is the use of political office to hire supporters. Patronage, however, can be

patronage j The use of political office to hire supporters.

harmful to the work of government. It often contributes to corruption. After all, it is a form of corruption in which the loyal supporters of leaders are hired rather than those best qualified to carry out the tasks of the bureaucracy. Patronage can also create a bloated bureaucracy with many unneeded civil servants on the payroll. Those civil servants, on the payroll but without much to do, contribute to lowering the morale of those actually needed to get the job done. Another way in which patronage can hurt is by creating a new class of civil servants who fear change. To them, change could mean that they lose their jobs. Therefore, a new class of civil servants would now do its best to block change.[17]

CaseStudy:Bureaucracy in Egypt

As you have already learned, most states in Africa, Asia, and Latin America have no provisions for unemployment insurance. Their socialist programs do not even include a welfare provision. Egypt is one of those states. Its leaders, since the overthrow of the monarchy in 1952, have opted for a mild form of socialism that remains in place despite the many modifications over the years. To make up for the lack of unemployment insurance in their program, leaders have often resorted to using the bureaucracy as the dumping ground for the unemployed. During the days of Nasser, as many as one-third of all high school graduates ended up employed in the bureaucracy.

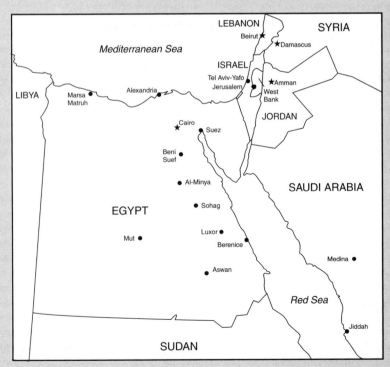

FIGURE 10.6
Egypt

In 1950 about 2.2 percent of Egypt's population was employed in the country's civil service.[18] This figure jumped from 350,000 in 1952 to 1.2 million by the time Nasser died in 1970. By 1986, 4.6 million Egyptians were employed in the bureaucracy, almost 10 percent of the entire population at the time. What impact do a large number of civil servants have on productivity or on politics? When the numbers go up, productivity normally goes down. This is because of the lower morale that results when you have a few who really work and many in the same office who do not even have tasks to do. They have their job instead of an unemployment check. The officials in charge also enhance their own power by granting the favor of a job to those desperate for one. The ones employed become loyal supporters of those who did them the favor.

SUMMARY AND REVIEW

The entity that is responsible for administering governmental decisions is known as the bureaucracy. Decisions are made by leaders but carried out by bureaucrats. Although it is this governmental arm that transforms hope into reality, its powers extend far beyond administering public policy; this is because the bureaucracy also holds valuable knowledge that other officials need in order to form policies and ultimately modernize the country. The bureaucracy is therefore inextricably linked to a country's modernization process, which involves not only running an ongoing system but also developing new modes of operations, refining old norms, and building the new modern state. Without the bureaucratic tasks of implementation and regulation, the country would most likely advance slowly, if it advanced at all.

KEY TERMS

patriarchy   196
neopatriarchy   196
military intervention   196
Suez Canal   197
capitulation system   198
free officers   199
Agrarian Reform Act   199
Aswan High Dam   199
Sani Abacha   200
Salvador
   Allende   201

International Telephone &
   Telegraph (IT&T)   202
Augusto Pinochet   202
Abd al-Aziz Ibn Saud   203
ulema   204
Arawaks   205
Fidel Castro   206
26th of July Revolutionary
   Movement   206
embargo   208
Bay of Pigs   208

bureaucracy   210
implementation   211
regulation   211
deregulation   212
structural uniformity   212
cultural variations   212
brain drain   214
bureaucratic
   corruption   214
formalism   214
patronage   217

DISCUSSION QUESTIONS

1. What impact has rapid change had on governments and leaders in Africa, Asia, and Latin America?
2. Why are leaders important throughout the developing world? Is this importance similar to or different from the developed world?
3. What exactly is bureaucracy? Do all governments have some sort of a bureaucratic body?

4. Why is it that governments are involved in the regulation of activities and institutions? Are governments too regulated?
5. Discuss how colonialism has affected bureaucratic structures in Africa, Asia, and Latin America.

SUGGESTED READINGS

Bakshi, S. R., Sudanshu R. Sharma, and Susheel Gajrani, Eds. *Contemporary Political Leadership in India*. New Delhi, India: APH Publishing, 1998.

Barlow, Max, Ed. *New Challenges in Local and Regional Administration*. Burlington, VT: Ashgate Press, 2004.

Dibua, Jeremiah I. *Modernization and the Crisis of Development in Africa: The Nigerian Experience*. Burlington, VT: Ashgate Press, 2006.

Farazmand, Ali, Ed. *Handbook of Comparative and Development Public Administration*. Switzerland: Marcel Dekker, 1991.

Heady, Ferrel. *Public Administration: A Comparative Perspective*. 3rd Ed. New York: Marcel Dekker, 1984.

Ladeur, Karl-Heinz. *Public Governance in the Age of Globalization*. Burlington, VT: Ashgate Press, 2004.

Moens, Alexander. *The Foreign Policy of George W. Bush: Values, Strategy, and Loyalty*. Burlington, VT: Ashgate Press, 2004.

Riggs, Fred. *Administration in Developing Countries*. Boston, MA: Houghton Mifflin, 1964.

Santiso, Javier. *Latin America's Political Economy of the Possible: Beyond Good Revolutionaries and Free Marketers*. Cambridge, MA: MIT Press, 2006.

Shevtsova, Lilia. *Putin's Russia*. Washington, DC: Brookings Institution Press, 2005.

Theakston, Kevin, Ed. *Bureaucrats and Leadership*. New York: St. Martin's Press, 2000.

Westlake, Martin, Ed. *Leaders of Transition*. New York: St. Martin's Press, 2000.

NOTES

1. Hisham Sharabi, *Neopatriarchy: A Theory of Distorted Change in Arab Society* (New York: Oxford University Press, 1988).
2. Samuel P. Huntington, *Political Order in Changing Societies* (New Haven, CT: Yale University Press, 1968), 194.
3. Ibid., 196.
4. Morris Janowitz, *The Military in the Political Development of New Nations* (Chicago, IL: University of Chicago Press, 1964), 27–29.
5. For further reading on Nigeria, see Oladimeji Aborisade and Robert J. Mundt, *Politics in Nigeria* (New York: Longman, 1999).
6. For an additional reading on the bureaucracy in the United States, see Michael E. Milakovich and George J. Gordon, *Public Administration in America*, 8th Ed. (New York: St. Martin's Press, 2003).
7. See Rolf H. W. Theen and Frank L. Wilson, *Comparative Politics: An Introduction to Seven Countries*, 4th Ed. (Upper Saddle River, NJ: Prentice Hall, 2001), 341–343.
8. For a good discussion of the bureaucracy in the developing countries, see Fred W. Riggs, "Bureaucrats and Political Development: A Paradoxical View," in Joseph La Palombara, Ed., *Bureaucracy and Political Development* (Princeton, NJ: Princeton University Press, 1963).
9. CNN reported the execution after the Supreme People's Court issued the death sentence. The execution was carried out the next day with a single bullet to the back of the head.
10. See Fred Riggs, *Administration in Developing Countries* (Boston, MA: Houghton Mifflin, 1964).
11. Roger Hilsman, *To Move a Nation* (Garden City, NY: Doubleday, 1967), 523.
12. Walter L. Weisberg, "Democracy and Development," in David E. Schmitt, Ed., *Dynamics of the Third World: Political and Social Change* (Cambridge, MA: Winthrop Publishers, 1974), 57.
13. Victor C. Falkenheim, "The Politics of Revolution and Mobilization," in David E. Schmitt, Ed., *Dynamics of the Third World: Political and Social Change* (Cambridge, MA: Winthrop Publishers, 1974), 288.
14. For a good introduction to China's political system, see William A. Joseph, "China," in Mark Kesselman, et al., *Introduction to Comparative Politics* (Boston, MA: Houghton Mifflin, 2000), 485–544.
15. See Christopher Alden, *Apartheid's Last Stand: The Rise and Fall of the South African Security State* (New York: St. Martin's Press, 1996).
16. For a good study of how apartheid ended, see Patti Waldmeir, *Anatomy of a Miracle: The End of Apartheid and the Birth of the New South Africa* (New York: Norton, 1997).
17. For a good discussion of the impact of patronage in the United States, see Milakovich and Gordon, *Public Administration in America* (Belmont, CA: Wadsworth Publishing Co., 2007).
18. Robert Springborg, *Mubarak's Egypt: Fragmentation of the Political Order* (Boulder, CO: Westview Press), 137.

Ethnicity, Ethnic Conflict, and Conflict Resolution

Globalization and Ethnic Conflict

Increased globalization, especially migration, has brought ethnic conflicts in distant places into American cities. The connectedness and interdependence that characterize globalization allow problems in one area to spill over into other areas. Inexpensive communications and travel make it very easy for ethnic groups to organize across national boundaries, implement their plans, and maintain strong ethnic identities.

Globalization also weakens ethnic identities by exposing people to different ideas, behavior, and material goods. Furthermore, economic globalization sometimes gives those ethnic groups with education and skills an advantage over those who maintained their culture. Those ethnic groups that are disadvantaged by change often turn against the successful minority, as is the case with the Tamils in Sri Lanka. Military globalization has contributed to the spread of lethal weapons that are used in some ethnic conflicts.

Ethnic conflicts in the developing world have received increased attention since the end of the Cold War. Many of these conflicts developed independently of the East–West rivalry but were often held in check by the superpowers. American involvement in ethnic conflicts in Somalia, Bosnia, and Kosovo reinforces concerns about the dangers of ethnic conflicts, not just for the societies directly involved but also for neighboring countries, the United States, and Western Europe. The conflict in Kyrgyzstan in 2010 between Kyrgyz and Uzbeks left at least 100 dead and more than 100,000 Uzbek refugees who fled to neighboring Uzbekistan. Russia, the United States, China, and other countries are directly affected by the violence. For one thing, Kyrgyzstan is the site of an American military base important to the Afghanistan mission. Conflicts are extremely difficult to contain in one country in a world that is characterized by growing levels of interdependence and globalization. Americans are paying greater attention to ethnic conflicts because of major demographic changes in the United States that are altering its ethnic and racial balance.[1] Ethnic diversity within the developing world or in the rich countries does not automatically result in violence or conflict.

This chapter discusses the nature of ethnicity and ethnic identity, and the causes and costs of ethnic conflicts. In addition to direct casualties of ethnic wars, thousands of civilians are killed each year by land mines that are deliberately deployed to cause maximum physical damage and psychological terror. Many countries that experience severe food shortages and famine, such as the Sudan and Ethiopia, are also ravaged by ethnic wars. Conflict is clearly detrimental to both economic development and the consolidation of democracy. Although reference is made to several ethnic conflicts, this chapter focuses on recent and ongoing problems, including those in Rwanda, the Sudan, and Liberia in Africa; Sri Lanka and Kurdistan in Asia; and Chiapas in Latin America. This chapter also examines efforts to resolve these conflicts peacefully.

ETHNICITY AND ETHNIC IDENTITY

tribalism ■ An outdated term used by Westerners to refer to groups of indigenous peoples in Africa, Asia, and Latin America.

The terms *ethnicity*, *tribalism*, and *nationalism* are often used interchangeably. **Tribalism** is usually regarded as an outdated term used by some Westerners to refer to small groups of indigenous people in Africa, Asia, and Latin America. Very large groups, some of them with millions of members, are also called tribes, both by some Westerners and by people in the developing world. Most scholars prefer to refer to these groups as ethnic groups. Sometimes ethnic groups are large and their members are spread across the boundaries of many different countries. These groups may aspire to have their own country. To achieve this, they develop a strong sense of nationalism and a nationalist movement. The Kurds are an ethnic group, some of whom have nationalistic aspirations. The Kurds live in Turkey, Iraq, Iran, Syria, and parts of the former Soviet Union. But most ethnic groups do not seek to form a separate nation. Some groups, such as the Tamils of Sri Lanka, want more autonomy within the established boundaries of their country.

ethnic group ■ A group composed of individuals who generally share a sense of common identity based on factors such as a common culture, geographic location, and religious beliefs.

An **ethnic group** is composed of individuals who generally share a sense of common identity based on a common set of historical experiences, national sentiments, religious beliefs, geographic location, a common language and culture, and, in countries such as the United States, arbitrary racial categories. Ethnicity is a subjective perception of those who belong to a particular group. Ethnic group members often have their own social organizations, support a particular political party, live in specific areas of the country, attend the same schools, develop business partnerships, and are associated with the same religious organizations. Ethnicity serves as a rallying point for mobilizing the members of an ethnic group to compete effectively for economic resources, positions in government and other social and economic institutions, government contracts and benefits, constitutional protections, and social and religious status.[2]

identity ■ A conception of the self; a selection of physical, psychological, emotional, or social attributes of particular individuals.

An essential component of ethnicity is a strong sense of identity or solidarity by individuals who perceive themselves as part of an ethnic group. **Identity** may be defined as a conception of the self, or a selection of physical, psychological, emotional, or social attributes of particular individuals.[3] The self is shaped by many different social, cultural, economic, and political factors. Identity provides a framework within which people can determine their positions on various issues. This means that prejudice or prejudgment is an important part of identity. We make judgments based not so much on objective criteria but on a belief about how we should react or what we should feel in a given situation. Our sense of identity influences our thought and behavior. **Ethnic pluralism**, or the presence of many different groups within a specific geographical boundary, can be attributed to several factors. Ethnic diversity often results from conquest and annexation, when one distinct group of people is defeated by another and forced to live under the control of the conquerors. Another reason for ethnic pluralism was the decision by European colonial powers to put many different groups together in the same country. Some of these groups had been at war with each other and continued to be hostile toward each other in the countries created by the colonial rulers. Another factor contributing to the emergence of ethnic consciousness, or ethnicity, is the deliberate attempt by the European colonizers to divide people in order to control them. By emphasizing the differences among groups instead of their similarities, Europeans eventually convinced particular groups that they were

ethnic pluralism ■ The presence of many different groups within a specific geographical boundary.

indeed different. Finally, population movement or migration, whether forced or voluntary, contributes to ethnic pluralism.[4]

THE CAUSES OF ETHNIC CONFLICT

Although conflicts between ethnic groups are often seen as the result of "ancient hatreds," most ethnic conflicts are very complex and have very little to do with ancient animosities. Few ethnic conflicts are just about ethnicity. In many cases, ethnic divisions are complicated by the fact that they are inseparable from other divisions, such as skin color, religious affiliation, regional ties, and socioeconomic status. These divisions are increasingly difficult to maintain when economic development and globalization help to create a greater degree of interdependence among groups within countries as well as among countries.

The most obvious cause of ethnic conflict is the geographic proximity of different groups. By bringing many different groups together to form countries, the European colonizers set the stage for ethnic conflict. But Africa's large number of ethnic groups found themselves in conflict with each other even without outside interference.

When a group's identity is based largely on adversarial relationships—on the basis of us versus them—conflict is almost inevitable. The adversarial approach influences members of different groups to expect only the worst from each other, put the worst interpretation on each other's words and behavior, and strongly distrust each other. The creation of an ethnic identity requires that group members be susceptible to viewing people not as individuals but as stereotypes. This refusal or inability to see obvious similarities helps strengthen ethnic boundaries and the group's view of itself as pure and uncomplicated by outside influences. Ethnic conflict is often caused by deliberate action by ethnic group leaders to preserve and reinforce group identity. Conflict helps strengthen the boundaries between the group and the outside world.

Another cause of ethnic conflict is the deliberate manipulation of negative perceptions by leaders to mobilize group support for their own political, economic, and social objectives. Leaders count on the emotional intensity and loyalty of the members of an ethnic group. They know that distrust can be used to fuel fears. Such fears usually override logical thinking. Consequently, despite misgivings individuals may have about engaging in or condoning violence against another group, their fears, sense of loyalty, and emotional commitment to their own group influence them to follow their leaders. Competition among groups for scarce economic resources is a major cause of violent ethnic conflict. As discussed in Chapter 6, economic development often results in the unequal distribution of resources among individuals, groups, and regions within a country. Growing economic disparities may increase the fears of those ethnic groups that are disadvantaged.

Modernization is another cause of ethnic conflict. Groups that participate in the development of the country acquire new values, have access to modern ways of life, and often have less tolerance for traditional cultures. Modernization tends to homogenize cultures, at least on the surface. The standardization of architecture, fast food, consumer items, automobiles, clothing, religion, education, and music threatens those groups that stress the uniqueness or purity of their own culture.[5]

Modernization helps destroy the boundaries that are essential to ethnic solidarity and a sense of identity. Modernization creates new identities and rearranges the boundaries. These changes are threatening to many groups. Their leaders are usually unsure of their role in the new world created by industrialization and globalization. Ethnic conflict sometimes erupts from this sense of fear and uncertainty.

Closely related to modernization as a cause of ethnic conflict is the inability of political institutions to effectively manage differences that ultimately result in violence. Political leaders often respond to demands for political participation and economic opportunities by marginalized ethnic groups with excessive force, indifference, or ineffective policies. Afraid that strong ethnic identities could undermine national cohesion and stability, many leaders attempt to eliminate these differences, often with brute force. This approach often leads to ethnic conflict. Transitions to democracy also contribute to ethnic conflicts. Change creates anxieties and threatens ethnic identities. Democratic transitions represent a major change in the status quo. Although equality is widely viewed as a positive democratic value, some groups lose their privileges and advantages in a system of government that is based on impartiality and the rule of law. Many ethnic groups are reluctant to compromise and respect different viewpoints, beliefs, and cultural practices. Finally, the proliferation of automatic weapons in developing countries is a significant cause of ethnic conflict. The availability of weapons increases the chances for conflicts among groups to escalate into violence. Conflicts are fueled by the willingness of countries as well as private groups to supply weapons to combatants. Many of these weapons were obtained from the Soviet Union, the United States, France, Britain, and other Western countries during the Cold War. When the Cold War ended, many ethnic conflicts intensified. Southern and Central Africa, for example, where many Cold War conflicts were waged, continued to be plagued by widespread warfare.

THE COSTS OF ETHNIC CONFLICT

Ethnic conflicts are extremely costly to developing countries. The poor not only get poorer but also are the most vulnerable to physical danger and psychological distress. Ethnic wars throughout the world have cost millions of lives. The exact number of lives lost will never be known because many poor countries have difficulty keeping an accurate count of the population. The conditions of war make it highly unlikely that the government, which is often preoccupied with its own survival, can keep an accurate count of the dead. Furthermore, many governments and their armed opponents use casualty figures for their own political purposes. However, estimates of the number of deaths from ethnic wars portray the devastating nature of these conflicts. For example, by 2009, more than 4 million people were killed in ethnic conflicts in the Congo.[6]

In addition to the direct casualties of ethnic wars, about 26,000 civilians are killed or wounded by land mines each year. The land mines are deliberately deployed to cause maximum physical damage and psychological terror. More than 100 million mines have been laid in about 62 countries, many of them in civilian and commercial areas. Land mines claim a new victim every 22 minutes. It is increasingly common to see people who are handicapped as a result of accidentally walking on a land mine. Advances in technology have made land mines cheaper to produce but harder to find and remove. The cost of getting rid of a land mine ranges from $300 to $1,000. However, the cost of the mine itself is less than $25.[7]

Economic costs of ethnic conflicts are especially severe for developing societies. These wars often destroy the country's best educated, best trained, and most valuable human resources. Individuals who are essential to the development process usually flee the conflict, leaving the country with decreased prospects of economic development. Instead of using scarce resources for economic development, governments are forced to spend money just to repair destroyed infrastructure projects. Industries are destroyed or cannot operate efficiently, and agricultural activities decline, as working in the fields becomes too dangerous. Foreign investments are lost and trade declines. Overall, the economy is devastated from civil strife and the insecurity that arises from it.

Transitions to democracy are difficult to accomplish in a violent environment. In fact, many ethnic conflicts occur because of the lack of effective political institutions and democratic processes for resolving disputes peacefully. Democracy implies that citizens are willing to compromise on difficult issues and are willing to respect differences. The belief in fairness, tolerance, and trust enables democratic societies to avoid violence. Human rights, an important aspect of democracy, are clearly disregarded in ethnic conflicts. Most conflicts dehumanize individuals, which makes it easier to justify killing them. Conflicts force millions of people to become refugees. Many of them remain in refugee camps long after the conflict has ended.

Neighboring countries as well as countries in which members of particular ethnic groups live are often negatively affected by ethnic conflicts in an age of globalization. Many countries throughout Africa have suffered as a result of the conflicts in Liberia, Rwanda, the Congo, Angola, and the Sudan. An entire region is affected as conflicts spill across borders or as ethnic groups, divided by national boundaries, become involved in the fighting to support members of their group. Because of global migration, ethnic conflicts in developing countries sometimes create violence in rich countries. When Abdullah Ocalan, leader of the Kurds, was captured in Kenya by Turkish agents in early 1999, Kurds living in Europe and Canada engaged in violent protests to demonstrate their outrage. Kurds occupied the Greek Embassy in London for three days. Three Kurdish demonstrators were shot and killed for trying to occupy the Israeli consulate in Berlin. Violence erupted in Vancouver, Montreal, and Ottawa when Kurdish protestors demonstrated outside offices belonging to countries they believed had participated in the capture of Ocalan.

Those regions of the world that suffer most from malnutrition and starvation are also very violent and politically unstable. Most countries in Africa, where most ethnic conflicts occur, have an abundance of rich agricultural land that has the potential to feed the continent's population. However, the worst famines and cases of malnutrition occur in Africa. Ethnic factions use food as a weapon against each other and unarmed civilians. Conflict destroys agricultural productivity and other basic industries, such as oil and mineral production. The disruption of trade, as a result of war, makes it difficult for people to obtain food supplies. The Sudan is an example of a country where ethnic conflict has caused widespread starvation. The government encouraged militiamen on horseback, known as **murahaleen,** to not

murahaleen
■ Militiamen on horseback.

only kill civilians but also burn their crops and steal their cattle and other animals.[8] Environmental destruction is another major cost of ethnic conflict. Starving populations are unlikely to make environmental protection their priority. Large numbers of refugees take shelter in the forests and use the available resources to survive. Trees as well as animals are destroyed. Forests are cleared to plant crops and animals are killed for food. Ethnic conflicts in Rwanda and the Congo have destroyed much of the region's wildlife and the tourism industry that depended on it. More than 250 eastern lowland gorillas in Kahuzi-Biega National Park have been killed, and as many as 300 forest elephants have been slaughtered. The elephants are killed for meat and the ivory is shipped out of Africa to the Middle East and elsewhere. Gorillas are also slaughtered for meat. It was estimated that most of the 500 lowland gorillas in the Congo, as well as many in neighboring Rwanda, had been killed.[9] However, many gorillas have been discovered in safe areas.

Drug problems are often made worse by ethnic conflicts. Ethnic conflicts are costly, and a way must be found to finance them. In Somalia's ethnic conflicts, drug use among armed young men escalated. Drugs are often used to induce young men and boys to join groups involved in ethnic warfare. In fact, some of the worst atrocities in ethnic conflicts are carried out by boys who use drugs. The war in Afghanistan and the ongoing violence among various ethnic groups in that country have directly contributed to the escalating drug problems in Iran. Iran, a very conservative Islamic country, accounts for as much as 85 percent of the worldwide seizures of opium. It has become the major area through which much of the world's supplies of opium, heroin, and hashish flows to markets in Iran itself and in the West. More than two decades of war has made Afghanistan a haven for drug smugglers, who are linked to various armed factions. The United Nations estimated that 3,500 tons of opium is produced each year in Afghanistan. Despite the U.S. invasion of Afghanistan, drug production increased and continues to be a major problem. The Iranian government is ill-equipped to control the flow of drugs, largely because of the 1,200-mile border and the rugged terrain. But the drug smugglers are also well armed. Many of their weapons, including American-made Stinger antiaircraft missiles, were originally obtained by the Mujahedeen from Arab countries and the United States when Afghanistan was fighting the Soviet Union. Vehicles are packed with opium and heroin and driven across the border areas at night. The drivers travel in darkness, using night-vision goggles to see their way. Drug smugglers also use camels to transport drugs. They separate a female camel from its newborn, leaving the offspring in Iran and taking the mother to Afghanistan. The smugglers use the mother as the lead camel for a camel caravan that is loaded with drugs because the mother will not stop until she reaches her young. The caravan is watched by the drug traffickers from a safe distance. The cost to Iranian society is high: Roughly 1.2 million Iranians are addicts. Some estimates are as high as 10 million.[10]

ETHNIC CONFLICTS IN AFRICA

No continent is more consumed by ethnic conflicts than Africa. From the South Atlantic to the Red Sea, African countries are at war. The conflict in Africa is so extensive that it has been called Africa's first world war. The Congo crisis, which began when Laurent Kabila's forces launched a successful war that overthrew Mobutu Sese Seko in 1997, has dragged in about eight countries and numerous ethnic groups. Many of the ethnic groups involved in the Congo war are supported by governments. Some governments seem to support one side or the other, based on the view that the enemy of an enemy is a friend. For example, the Ugandan government supports the **Sudan People's Liberation Army (SPLA)**, which has been fighting the Sudanese government since 1983. Uganda supported the ethnic groups that fought against Kabila. In light of these alliances, the Sudanese government helped Kabila. Ethnic rivalries in Rwanda and Burundi spilled over into the Congo.[11]

Sudan People's Liberation Army (SPLA) ■ Sudan People's Liberation Army; formed to achieve a secular democratic Sudan.

Nigeria

Nigeria is one of the most ethnically complex countries in the world, with more than 300 ethnic groups. With a population of more than 149 million, it is also Africa's most populous country. Once highly dependent on agriculture for its revenues, Nigeria's oil exports now account for 95 percent of its exports. This huge country, more than twice the size of California, is potentially one of Africa's richest states. But ethnic problems, together with years of military rule and "rampant" corruption, have kept the majority of Nigerians impoverished. Nigeria's ethnic problems are closely linked with other divisions in the country. The four main ethnic groups are the Hausa (21 percent), the Yoruba (21 percent), the Ibo (18 percent), and the Fulani (11 percent). These ethnic groups dominate different parts of the country, creating a regional divide as well as an ethnic divide. The Hausa and the Fulani are in the north, the Yoruba are concentrated in the west, and the Ibo live in the east. Each ethnic group has its own dominant language, although English is Nigeria's official language. Further complicating ethnicity in Nigeria is religion. The northern part of the country is dominated by Muslims and the southern and eastern regions are populated mainly by Christians. The country's petroleum wealth is located in the Ibo region, the southeast. Northerners, primarily the Hausas, have ruled the country for most of its history. They have controlled the military regimes.

indirect rule ■ A governmental system, often implemented by colonists, that allows the people to maintain their institutions, language, culture, and economic systems.

FIGURE 11.1
Nigeria

Nigeria's most serious ethnic conflict, the Biafran war, was rooted in the ethnic, religious, economic, regional, political, linguistic, and military divisions in the country. The British implemented a policy of **indirect rule** in the north that allowed the Muslims to maintain their institutions, religion, language, culture, and economic and educational systems. The rest of the country came under greater British control or direct rule. The traditional institutions were challenged by Westernization, and many people adopted Western cultures. British religious, educational, political, and social institutions competed with traditional ways. The different approaches used by Britain reinforced the regional differences.

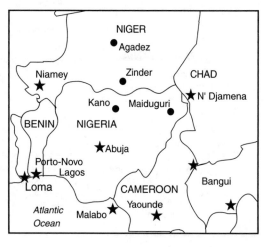

The discovery of petroleum heightened competition among the regions. With their new wealth, the Ibo believed that the independence of their region would protect their interests. In 1966, the Ibo region declared its independence, calling itself **Biafra**. After four years of warfare, during which more than a million people died, Biafra was crushed by Nigeria. Nigeria imposed a food blockade that resulted in hundreds of thousands of deaths. In early 2000, ethnic violence erupted when Muslim leaders attempted to impose shari'a, or Islamic law, on Christians living in the northern part of the country. More than 54,000 people have been killed in conflicts between Muslims and Christians. Violence continues, especially in the central Nigerian city of Jos.

Biafra ■ The Ibo region that declared its independence from Nigeria.

Liberia

Ethnic conflicts in Liberia are rooted, to some extent, in America's institution of slavery and its preoccupation with racial purity. Many leaders in the United States believed that the growing number of freed slaves threatened the institution of slavery and the practice of racial separation. Others believed that slavery was inhumane and incompatible with America's fundamental values and constitutional democracy. Both groups agreed that sending Americans with African ancestry to Africa was the solution to the problem. With the support of the **American Colonization Society**, the first group of freed American slaves landed in Liberia. They settled in an area called Monrovia, named for President James Monroe, in 1822. The American settlers called themselves **Americo-Liberians**. They maintained their American values and discriminated against Africans who lived in the area they colonized with the assistance of the American Colonization Society. In fact, as late as the 1930s, the Americo-Liberians enslaved some of the Africans from the interior of the country. Despite intermarriage between the Americo-Liberians and the Africans, the former remained a separate group. Comprising about 5 percent of Liberia's population, they ruled the country until 1980.

American Colonization Society ■ An American group that supported Africans' return to Africa.

Americo-Liberians ■ The name free slaves gave themselves once they landed in Liberia.

William Tolbert ■ The Americo-Liberian president who was overthrown by Samuel K. Doe.

In 1980, **William Tolbert**, the Americo-Liberian president, was overthrown and murdered by a group of soldiers led by Samuel K. Doe, from the Krahn group. Once in power, Doe allowed the Krahn to dominate the country, just as the Americo-Liberians had done before he overthrew them. The Krahn were soon challenged by an alliance composed of the Gio and Mano groups. In late 1990, Doe was captured and tortured to death by Prince Johnson and members of the Gio group.[12] The war continued after Doe's death, as different factions struggled for power. Liberia,

FIGURE 11.2
Sierra Leone and Liberia

one of Africa's most prosperous countries and a close ally of the United States, descended into chaos and brutality. More than 150,000 people (out of a population of 3 million) were killed, 800,000 fled to neighboring countries, and starvation was widespread. Former Liberian President Charles Taylor, who was responsible for much of the brutality, was imprisoned in Sierra Leone in 2006, after attempting to flee Nigeria, where he was living. He was transferred to The Hague to face an international trial for war crimes. His trial, which began in January 2008, continues.

The Sudan

When Britain ruled the Sudan, it allowed the northern part of the country to maintain its Islamic religion and customs. The southern part of the Sudan was treated differently. Christian missionaries were allowed to convert the region's inhabitants. Many southern Sudanese continue to practice their traditional religion, or **animism**. Differences between the north and south are rooted in history. Just as there was a trans-Atlantic slave trade, there was a **trans-Sahara slave trade**. The Arab countries of the Middle East and North Africa enslaved as many as 10 million Africans from south of the Sahara. Although the Africans were ultimately integrated into the Arab societies, Arabs and Africans remain distrustful of each other. Religious cleavages in the Sudan are reinforced by ethnic divisions. Many northern Sudanese, who are mainly Arab, are unwilling to treat southern Sudanese as equal citizens because of the legacy of slavery. In fact, some people in the northern part of the Sudan still refer to a person from the south as **abed,** or slave. This ethnic and religious conflict is complicated by the claims of both sides to territory that may contain huge oil reserves.

> **animism** ■ The religious practice of worshiping animals, rocks, plants, and other similar objects.

> **trans-Sahara slave trade** ■ A trade in which Arab countries enslaved Africans from the south of the Sahara.

> **abed** ■ A term meaning slave.

Britain granted Sudan its independence in 1956. The north and the south fought each other with varying levels of intensity from 1956 to 1972, when an uneasy truce was reached. In 1983, the Muslim government in the capital, Khartoum, declared that the entire country would be ruled by shari'a, or Islamic law. The Christians and animists in the southern part of the Sudan strongly resisted Islamic rule. They formed the SPLA to achieve a secular democratic Sudan. If that could not be done, their more radical goal was to make the south an independent country. The war has raged on. Many northern fighters use their religion to justify their own deaths. They believe that the highest aspiration of a Muslim is to die a martyr, or a **shaheed**. The government has prevented food supplies from reaching the starving people in the south and has bombed international relief centers. More than 2.6 million people have faced starvation, and more than 2.5 million people have died from famine and war. An estimated 4.5 million people were displaced or became refugees. Both sides have committed gross violations of human rights. The north continues to enslave people from the south. The stakes in the conflict have increased with the export of petroleum. Both the north and south claim the oil fields.[13] Although the conflict continued in the Darfur region of Sudan, in January 2005 the Sudanese government and southern rebel leaders signed a peace agreement to end the civil war. The conflict in Darfur, seen as genocide, left more than 300,000 dead and created 2.5 million refugees. Despite the signing of a peace agreement between

> **shaheed** ■ An Arabic term for martyr.

Sudan's government and the main rebel groups in 2008, fighting continues. Faced with growing global pressure to respond forcefully to genocide in Darfur, the International Criminal Court charged Sudan's president Omar Hassan al-Bashir with committing war crimes and crimes against humanity and issued a warrant for his arrest.

Rwanda

Tutsis and Hutus
■ Two main ethnic groups in Rwanda.

When the Europeans made contact with Rwanda, the area was ruled by a small group of cattle herders, who were predominantly **Tutsi**. The largest group was composed mainly of **Hutus**. They spoke the same language, shared the same culture, and practiced the same religion. Years of intermarriage made it difficult to neatly separate them into distinct ethnic groups. All groups supplied soldiers for their common ruler.[14] When the Germans colonized Rwanda (as well as Burundi) in 1899, they used indirect rule, relying primarily on the Tutsis to help them control the territory. The Tutsis made up 14 percent of the population, while the Hutus formed the majority, 85 percent. The Germans brought with them **racial theories** that were common in Europe and the United States and believed that the Tutsis were superior to the Hutus. This racial thinking permeated Belgian policy in Rwanda when it took over both Rwanda and Burundi in 1916, following Germany's defeat in World War I.

racial theories ■ The theories that people are superior based on their race or what skin color they have.

It was difficult to distinguish Hutus from Tutsis. The Belgians solved this problem by issuing mandatory identity cards to all Rwandans. The social mobility that was common among the groups ended. The Tutsis cooperated with the Belgians because of the privileges they received. Eventually, the Tutsis believed that they were indeed superior to the Hutus. To reinforce their belief in their superiority, the Belgians educated them while denying the Hutus equal access to education. The Belgians then blamed the low social standing of the Hutus on Hutu inferiority and passivity. The Belgians had created a superior and an inferior group. The Tutsis were allowed to exploit the Hutus. The Belgians reorganized the Rwandan society and deposed most of the Hutu chiefs. Most Hutus were placed under Tutsi control.[15]

FIGURE 11.3
Rwanda and Burundi

Belgian missionaries helped the disadvantaged Hutus obtain an education. Although educated Hutus were qualified to work in the colonial administration, they faced systematic discrimination that kept them out of the government. As their numbers grew, the educated Hutus began to challenge the system that gave the Tutsis significant advantages. They began to advocate for ethnic separation. In 1959, the Hutus rebelled and killed more than 20,000 Tutsis. When Rwanda became independent in 1962, a step for which Belgium did not prepare the country, Rwanda's Hutu majority gained control. The Tutsis in neighboring Burundi, also a minority, began to worry about developments in Rwanda. They feared that the Hutu majority would also gain control of Burundi.

Their solution was to massacre every Hutu with an education, a government position, or financial resources. More than 250,000 Hutus were slaughtered in three months in 1972.

Ethnic rivalries in Rwanda escalated in 1990, when the power of the Hutus was challenged by the army of the Rwandan Patriotic Front. To restore a measure of peace and stability, moderate Hutus agreed to share power with the Tutsi minority in 1993. Hutu extremists began to kill both Tutsis and moderate Hutus. When a plane carrying Rwanda's president Juvenal Habyarimana, a Hutu, unexpectedly crashed on April 6, 1994, violence erupted with a force that stunned the world. The Hutus blamed the Tutsis for destroying the plane and its passengers. The Hutus circulated lists of the names of people who favored a democratic transition and national reconciliation. They also set up roadblocks and demanded identity cards. Hutu militia leaders systematically searched each house and forced neighbors to turn against each other. Their goal was to eliminate every single Tutsi. Students were killed by their teachers, neighbors killed neighbors, and churches where Tutsis sought sanctuary became the scenes of some of the worst massacres. Several clergymen participated in the bloodshed. In some cases, husbands killed their wives, and then themselves, to save them from a more terrible death.[16] Almost 1 million people were slaughtered in 13 weeks of fighting in Rwanda.

ETHNIC CONFLICTS IN ASIA

The fact that Asia is more economically developed and also has fewer ethnic groups and more logical national boundaries than Africa seems to limit the number and destructiveness of ethnic conflicts in that region of the world. Nonetheless, many parts of Asia suffer from ethnic violence. The conflict in Sri Lanka is an example. Countries with large and ethnically and religiously diverse populations, such as India and China, often experience periodic outbursts of ethnic violence. In the case of the Kurds, ethnic conflict stems in part from the desire of a people who share common political aspirations and culture to form a separate country or to be given a meaningful degree of autonomy.

India

Despite its diversity, India has managed to avoid prolonged and large-scale ethnic strife. Its strong commitment to democracy and secularism undoubtedly plays an important role in reducing extremist tendencies in the society. Group competition can take place at the ballot box instead of through violence. India's political culture and its political system allow even the most disadvantaged groups to have equal voting power. This reality induces political leaders to compromise, moderate their positions on issues, and build coalitions in order to gain power. Although other democracies, such as Sri Lanka, experienced prolonged periods of ethnic violence, the Indian case shows that, generally speaking, democratic societies are more capable than nondemocratic ones of effectively managing differences and avoiding open warfare among rival groups.

Jawaharlal Nehru
■ Leader of the Congress Party in India.

Ali Jinnah ■ Leader of the Muslim League that founded Pakistan.

India's worst ethnic violence occurred as British rule ended. Although India, under the leadership of **Jawaharlal Nehru** and the Congress Party, strongly embraced secularism, many Muslims felt threatened by the Hindu majority. Led by **Ali Jinnah**, head of the Muslim League, the Muslims decided to form their own separate state in Pakistan. The creation of two countries out of what was British India was rooted in deep religious differences that erupted in horrific violence. When the Muslims living in India tried to get to Pakistan, where Muslims were the dominant majority, they encountered Hindus who had been living in Pakistan and were trying to get to India, where the Hindus were the dominant majority. Their encounter resulted in a slaughter that left more than 1 million people dead. More than 12 million became refugees. This horrifying violence shaped relations between India and Pakistan. Unlike 1947, when each side used crude weapons to butcher each other, both countries now have nuclear weapons.

Sikhs' Golden Temple
■ The place most sacred to the Sikhs.

Conflicts among the various religious, ethnic, and social groups continue, but have not escalated into widespread fighting. The Sikhs and Jains have clashed with the government over religious issues. In fact, India's prime minister Indira Gandhi was assassinated in 1984 by her Sikh bodyguards in retaliation for the government's repression of the Sikhs in Punjab, for placing the Punjab under martial law, and for desecrating the **Sikhs' Golden Temple** in Amritsar. The Golden Temple, regarded as most sacred to Sikhs, became the center of controversy when Sikh rebels used it as a refuge from Indian security forces. Tamil separatists have also challenged the Indian government. In 1991, they assassinated Rajiv Gandhi, who became prime minister after his mother, Indira Gandhi, was killed. The rise of Hindu fundamentalism and nationalism has led to greater intolerance of other religious groups. Christians are often the victims of many attacks by Hindu extremists. Nuns have been raped, missionaries killed, and religious institutions destroyed. Violence between Muslims and Hindus occurs frequently.

China

Uighur separatists
■ A minority group in China.

Although Han Chinese comprise about 93 percent of China's population, China has many different ethnic minorities. These minorities live in regions of China that contain a large proportion of the country's natural resources, such as oil, coal, copper, gold, iron, lumber, and water. China recognizes its ethnic minorities and allocates significant resources to them. However, China has taken extreme measures to ensure that ethnic groups do not threaten the country's unity and stability. For example, China stationed almost 1 million troops in its western province of Xinjiang to suppress **Uighur separatists**. China brought the Uighurs and their territory under its control in 1949 and populated the area with Han Chinese, members of the majority group. Xinjiang, once known as East Turkestan, was regarded as geographically and culturally part of Turkic Central Asia. The Uighurs are Muslims and are perceived by China to be linked to foreign Islamic extremists. China is sensitive to the influence of Islamic fundamentalism not only in the Middle East but also in parts of the former Soviet Union. Uighur separatists have attacked oil refineries, railroads, and bridges and planted bombs on buses, which have killed several people. They have engaged in numerous hit-and-run raids on Chinese institutions. Violence escalated during the 2008 Olympic Games in Beijing. Chinese authorities implemented many measures to prevent the Uighurs from threatening the Games. Apart from the Chinese policy of reserving the best jobs for Han Chinese, China has responded to the separatist movement with excessive force. More than 1,000 Uighurs have been executed and about 10,000 have been arrested.[17] Violent clashes continue. The Uighurs' goal of independence is strongly resisted by China.

The Kurds

The Kurds established a separate identity as early as the fifth century B.C.E. As empires rose and fell in the Middle East, the Kurds came under the control of different powers. The rivalry between the Ottomans (Turkey) and the Persians (Iran) led to the division of Kurdistan (the Kurdish homeland) between Turkey and Iran. Like most groups in history, the Kurds were forced to change or modify their ethnic identity to survive. However, the Kurds have remained relatively cohesive culturally and politically. Although some have demanded a separate state, most of them have attempted to integrate into the various countries in which they live. For the last 500 years or more, the Kurdish population has been spread across Turkey, Iraq, Iran, Syria, and parts of the former Soviet Union. Turkey is home to the largest number of Kurds. It is estimated that as many as 15 million Kurds live in an area that covers 30 percent of Turkey, or 80,000 square miles. Iran has the second largest Kurdish population, followed by Iraq and Syria. The Kurds tend to live in the rural and mountainous regions of these countries. Although the Kurds are Muslims, they are Sunnis. In Iran, where the majority of Muslims are Shi'ite, Sunni Kurds are a religious minority.[18] As non-Arabs, the Kurds are an ethnic minority in predominately Arab Iraq.

Because the Kurds live in different countries, they have adopted different strategies to deal with their problems. Some have struggled to gain greater political autonomy within the various countries, whereas others are committed to establishing an independent country. Iran, Iraq, and Turkey, for example, have violently suppressed them at one time or another. In some cases, Iran, Iraq, and Turkey have used the Kurds to achieve their own objectives. Iran supported Iraqi Kurds against Saddam Hussein's government, while treating its own Kurds harshly. Iraq also attempted to use Iranian Kurds against Iran. Iraqi Kurds were ruthlessly suppressed by Saddam Hussein. In 1988, during the Iran–Iraq War, Saddam Hussein's government used poisonous gas against the Kurds in **Halabja**, in northern Iraq, killing about 1,000 people. Following the Persian Gulf War in 1991, which forced Iraq out of Kuwait, Saddam Hussein launched a military attack against the Kurds and Shi'ites. As many as 30,000 Kurds and Shi'ites were killed. About half a million Kurds were forced from their homes and villages. Many died of cold and starvation in the hills along the Turkish border before the international community decided to give them humanitarian assistance and prevent further attacks by Iraq.[19] Following America's invasion of Iraq in 2003, the Kurds gained greater autonomy in northern Iraq. However, as

Halabja ■ A Kurdish village against which Saddam Hussein used poisonous gas.

FIGURE 11.4
Kurdish Areas of
Turkey, Iraq,
Iran, and Syria

the United States reduced its military forces in 2009, the Arabs challenged
Kurdish autonomy.

Turkey does not recognize the Kurds as a national, racial, or ethnic minority.
There are no legal barriers against Kurdish participation in Turkish society and
politics. Some Kurds have prominent positions in the society. Many members of
parliament, senior officials, and professionals are ethnic Kurds. There has been
a high rate of intermarriage between the Kurds and others in Turkey, and Kurds
who live in the urban and industrial areas of the country have been generally
assimilated into the Turkish society. But many Kurds want to maintain a separate identity. Others support the establishment of an independent state. The
Kurdish movement for independence is led by the **Kurdish Workers Party**,
known by its Turkish initials as the PKK. Turkey's 15 million Kurds are caught
between the Turkish government and the PKK, which has used violent methods
to achieve an independent Kurdish state. Turkey responded forcefully to the
actions of the PKK. Since 1984, when the guerrilla activities of the PKK intensified and grew more ruthless, Turkey has killed almost 37,000 Kurds. More than
3,000 Kurdish villages have been destroyed, and Turkey relocated at least
560,000 Kurds in order to depopulate rural villages that might harbor PKK
supporters. Many Kurds fled the violence and poverty of the rural areas to live
in urban areas in Turkey. Others migrated to Germany and other European
countries. Turkey's war against Turkish Kurds was expanded to the Kurdish
areas of Iraq, where PKK forces often hid. The growing autonomy of Kurdish
areas inside Iraq, due to American and European protection of the Kurds,

Kurdish Workers Party
■ Movement for
Kurdish independence.

encouraged Turkish Kurds to seek refuge with Iraqi Kurds. Turkey had also imposed severe restrictions against the use of minority languages, including Kurdish, in the schools, by the media, and by political parties. However, responding to pressure from the European Union, Turkey pledged to respect minority rights and allow limited Kurdish language broadcasts on state television and released well-known Kurdish activists in 2004.[20] With the capture of **Abdullah Ocalan**, the leader of the PKK, in 1998, the Kurdish conflict with Turkey has been calmed. However, influenced partly by greater autonomy enjoyed by Kurds in Iraq, the PKK renewed the conflict in Turkey in 2006. In March 2008, Turkish forces invaded northern Iraq, which is controlled by Kurds, to fight members of the PKK. Turkey views the PKK in Iraq as a major source of support for Kurdish rebels in Turkey. The conflict escalated in June 2010 when Kurdish fighters killed 11 Turkish soldiers. Turkey responded by bombing Kurdish areas in northern Iraq.

Abdullah Ocalan
■ Leader of the Kurdish Workers Party.

ETHNIC CONFLICTS IN LATIN AMERICA

Latin America has experienced relatively few ethnic conflicts, despite widespread violence in the region. Historical influences in Latin America have helped shape contemporary relations among ethnic groups. Brazil, Cuba, Mexico, Colombia, and other countries in Latin America were strongly influenced by their colonial rulers. Portugal, which colonized Brazil, and Spain, which ruled most of Latin America, maintained a system of slavery long after the rest of Western Europe had abolished the practice. Neither Spain nor Portugal emphasized racial or ethnic differences to justify human bondage. Jews, Moors, black Africans, and even Spaniards themselves were enslaved both in Spain and in the New World. The institution of slavery was supervised by both the Catholic Church and the Crown. The general consensus was that the status of the slave was not permanent, and the distinction between slavery and freedom was perceived to be a result of misfortune. From the Catholic viewpoint, slaves were free and equal in God's sight, and their souls were as important as those of free people. The Catholic Church helped moderate ethnic relations in Brazil and established a foundation of tolerance. High rates of interracial and interethnic marriages have diminished the significance of both race and ethnicity in Latin America, especially when compared with the United States.

The Caribbean nations of Cuba, Trinidad and Tobago, and Guyana, despite their ethnic diversity, have not had serious violent ethnic conflicts. These countries, for various reasons, have not made ethnicity an overriding concern. People recognize their racial and ethnic mixture and stress the importance of their national identities and common cultures.[21] Latin American countries in which Native Americans are a significant proportion of the population, such as Peru, Guatemala, and Ecuador, have had conflicts erupt, but not strictly along ethnic lines. The **Shining Path** in Peru, as discussed in Chapter 9, represents the Indian population to some extent. However, Indians have also been its main targets.

Shining Path ■ A Peruvian rebel movement that was formed by university professors and students who subscribed to the philosophy of Mao Zedong.

Huge economic disparities between the relatively prosperous northern and central parts of Mexico and the poor southern areas of the country have contributed to ethnic violence. The southern state of **Chiapas,** where entire Indian communities do not have electricity or running water, has been left in the preindustrial age. Although the northern and central parts of Mexico have benefited from the economic prosperity created by the North American Free Trade Agreement (NAFTA), the southern part of the country has not. In fact, many Indian communities in Chiapas and other parts of southern Mexico believed that NAFTA threatened their survival. The peasants and small farmers of the region felt that their corn and beans would be unable to compete with corn and beans produced on America's technologically advanced and highly productive farms. On January 1, 1994, the date after NAFTA went into effect, the Zapatista National Liberation Front (Zapatistas) launched attacks on the Mexican government in the state of Chiapas. The Zapatistas wanted the Mexican government to withdraw from NAFTA, ensure the fair treatment for Mexico's indigenous groups, and promote economic development of Chiapas. At least 500 people were killed between 1994 and 2000. The Mexican government negotiated with the Zapatistas and signed the **San Andres Accords,** which granted land and legal rights to the indigenous population.[22]

Chiapas ■ A southern state in Mexico.

San Andres Accords ■ An agreement that granted land and legal rights to the indigenous population of Mexico.

RESOLVING ETHNIC CONFLICTS

When ethnic groups disagree in democratic societies, they have the opportunity to compete for power and punish governments that mistreat them by participating in the electoral process. They have access to the courts. In the case of Chiapas in Mexico, the Institutional Revolutionary Party (PRI) government negotiated with the Zapatistas because it realized that rival political parties would take advantage of the government's inability to maintain stability. Democratic societies offer ethnic groups a chance to form coalitions with other groups with similar interests and problems.

As countries develop economically, most groups are able to meet their basic needs and are encouraged to work within the various institutions to achieve their goals. Governments also have more resources to allocate to ethnic groups with grievances. However, if ethnic groups do not believe that the government is concerned about them, economic disparities brought about by economic growth may fuel ethnic conflict. Some ethnic conflicts can be resolved if the ethnic group is large and lives in separate parts of the country. In cases where the population is dominated by one group, such as in British India, a solution to ethnic conflict is to allow the ethnic group to form its own country. By drawing new boundaries, ethnic groups can become new nations, as was the case with India and Pakistan. India is predominantly Hindu and Pakistan is overwhelmingly Muslim. But many states are unwilling to redraw their national boundaries, especially if they have many different ethnic groups that want to be independent countries. In that case, military force is often used to crush the ethnic group, as the Nigerian government did when the Ibos formed Biafra.

A common solution to ethnic conflicts is to create **power-sharing arrangements.** Essentially, these arrangements divide political power among the different ethnic groups. However, unless periodic adjustments are made to reflect the changing demographics of the various groups, these arrangements tend to disintegrate, and ethnic conflict erupts. In Lebanon, for example, government positions and political power were divided between the country's Maronite Christians and Sunni Muslims. But the power-sharing arrangement was not changed to reflect the rapid increase in the Muslim population. Failure to do so plunged Lebanon into a civil war that lasted from 1975 to 1990. The solution to this conflict included adjusting the division of power. **Federalism,** or the sharing of power between the central government and the states or provinces, also helps solve ethnic conflicts. Despite the continuing ethnic problems in Nigeria, India, and Mexico, the federal systems allow regions to have autonomy and flexibility to address ethnic conflicts.

power-sharing arrangements ■ Arrangements that divide political power among different ethnic groups.

federalism ■ The sharing of power between the central government and the states or provinces.

▶ Case Study: Sri Lanka

Sri Lanka, formerly known as Ceylon, was partially controlled by the Portuguese in 1505 and by the Dutch in 1658. The British conquered the island in 1796. Sri Lanka gained its independence from Britain in 1948. With a population of 21 million, Sri Lanka is largely a rural country. Only 15 percent of the population is urbanized. Its per capita GDP is roughly $4,300, and life expectancy is 73 years for males and 77 years for females. Sri Lanka's economy benefits significantly from globalization. The manufacture of textiles and garments for the global market accounts for more than 40 percent of its exports. It is extremely dependent on remittances from approximately 1.5 million Sri Lankans who work in other countries, primarily in the Middle East. They contribute more than $2.5 billion a year to Sri Lanka's economy. This makes it very vulnerable to the forces of globalization.

Like other countries in Southern Asia, Sri Lanka is ethnically complex. The most significant ethnic division is between the **Sinhalese,** who make up 74 percent of the population, and the **Tamils,** who comprise about 22 percent. The Tamils are equally divided between Ceylon Tamils, whose ancestors lived in Sri Lanka for many generations, and the Indian Tamils, whose ancestors arrived in Sri Lanka as agricultural workers in the late nineteenth century. Both the Sinhalese and the Tamils originally came from India, but the Tamils arrived more recently to the island and many still have connections with the Tamils of south India. The rest of the population is composed of Moors, Europeans, and the native people of Sri Lanka, known as **Veddah.** Similar to Nigeria, Sri Lanka is divided along religious, political, linguistic, regional, and economic lines as well. The Sinhalese are Buddhists and the Tamils are Hindus. About 8 percent of the population is Christian and 7 percent is Muslim. The Sinhalese speak Sinhala and the Tamils speak English and Tamil. The Tamils are concentrated in the northern part of the island country and the Sinhalese dominate the south. The Tamils were more exposed to Western influences than the Sinhalese majority. Missionary societies were allowed to function in Sri Lanka. These included the London Missionary Society, the Baptists, Wesleyan Methodists, and the American

Sinhalese and Tamils ■ Two main ethnic groups in Sri Lanka.

Veddah ■ The native people of Sri Lanka.

FIGURE 11.5
Sri Lanka

Missionary Society. All of them used English as the language of instruction. The American Missionary Society was extremely successful in educating a large number of Tamils. Education in English gave the Tamils an advantage in the British colonial government. Many migrated to the south, dominated by the Sinhalese, and successfully competed for jobs.[23]

Competition between the Sinhalese and Tamils intensified as Sri Lanka moved closer to independence. The Sinhalese used their majority status to determine the design of the national flag (always an emotional issue) and to deprive all Indian Tamils of Sri Lankan citizenship, even though they were born in Sri Lanka or had lived there for many years. Shortly after independence, the study of Sinhala was made a compulsory part of secondary education. Sinhalese nationalism grew when W. R. D. Bandaranaike left the **United National Party (UNP)**, which united the Sinhalese and Tamils, to form the **Sri Lanka Freedom Party (SLFP)**, which stressed Sinhalese separation and making Buddhism the national religion. Sinhalese nationalism was built to a large extent by leaders who mobilized feelings of resentment and fear against the Tamils. Although the Sinhalese were the majority, most of the important jobs were held by Ceylon Tamils. Furthermore, the Sinhalese perceived the Tamils in southern India, in the state of Tamil Nadu, as a threat because of their association with the Tamils of Sri Lanka. By 1958, riots broke out, in which Sinhalese nationalists killed hundreds of Tamils.[24]

The government, controlled by the Sinhalese majority, implemented a system of preferential university admissions for the Sinhalese students. Although only 22 percent of the population, the Tamils comprised 50 percent of the admissions to the engineering and medical schools. Their exposure to missionary education had given them a distinct advantage over the Sinhalese. Government policies led to a sharp reduction in the number of Tamil students in professional schools. By 1980, the number of Tamils with college degrees was one-fourth of the number of Tamils who had earned college degrees a decade earlier. The Sinhalese reinforced their attack on the Tamils by using their majority to implement constitutional reforms, which essentially reduced the status of Tamils to second-class citizenship. The government committed itself to protecting and fostering Buddhism as the dominant religion. Sinhalese Buddhist culture was supported, whereas Tamil culture was systematically

United National Party
■ United the Sinhalese and Tamils.

Sri Lanka Freedom Party ■ Stressed Sinhalese separatism.

undermined. The government banned the importation of literature and films from Tamil Nadu in India. Security forces attacked Tamil civilians who were attending the Fourth International Conference of Tamil Studies in 1974.[25] Violence escalated, leaving many people dead.

In 1978, Tamil separatists began to attack the Sri Lankan government. The government responded like most governments, with increased violence, arbitrary arrests and detention, and a general disregard for fundamental democratic rights and protections. The underlying causes of the conflict were ignored. These actions helped sharpen distinctions between the Sinhalese and the Tamils and helped intensify adversarial feelings and behavior. In 1983, groups of Sinhalese, like the Hutus of Rwanda, obtained information about the location of Tamil homes, businesses, factories, and educational institutions. Armed with this information, they brutally attacked the Tamils. About 2,000 to 3,000 people were killed, thousands of homes were burned or damaged, and more than 100,000 Tamils were forced to leave their homes in Colombo, the country's capital. Approximately 175,000 refugees left Sri Lanka. The government did little to prevent the violence or to punish those involved. No gesture of empathy for the Tamils was given by government officials.[26] Under these circumstances, ethnic identities hardened, and moderates on both sides were either marginalized or killed. The Tamil rebels were led by Vellupillai Prabhakaran.

India, which had provided military assistance to the Tamil guerrillas, worried about the increasing number of Tamils who were taking refuge in India. Prime Minister Indira Gandhi decided to help the Tamils and seek a settlement with the Sri Lankan government that would protect Tamil interests in Sri Lanka. The **Indo-Sri Lankan Agreement to Establish Peace and Normality in Sri Lanka** was signed on July 27, 1987. It called for the introduction of Indian troops into Sri Lanka to enforce a negotiated end to the violence. The Indian Peace-Keeping Force would be stationed in the Tamil areas to establish order. Sri Lanka would be officially a multiethnic and multilingual country, meaning that the government would not promote one group or its culture over the others. Tamil, English, and Sinhalese would be the official languages. Finally, it called on the Tamil fighters to accept the cease-fire and to disarm. The Indian Peace-Keeping Force soon found itself at war with the Tamil guerrillas in northern Sri Lanka. Growing Indian casualties eventually forced India to withdraw from Sri Lanka in 1990.[27]

Indo-Sri Lankan Agreement ■ An effort to end the conflict.

As the fighting escalated and the costs to the government climbed, Sri Lanka searched for a peaceful end to the ethnic strife. **Chandrika Bandaranaike Kumaratunga,** whose father had fanned the flames of ethnic violence shortly after the country gained its independence, promised to end the violence if elected as the country's president. She became Sri Lanka's president in 1994, a position held by her father and later by her mother after her father was assassinated. Both her father and her husband had been killed as a result of the ethnic conflict. She initiated talks with the Tamil Tigers, which resulted in a truce. The Tamil fighters made four demands that needed to be met for the truce to continue:

Chandrika Bandaranaike Kumaratunga ■ Sri Lanka's president.

1. An immediate end to the embargo on food, gas, and other supplies to the areas under Tamil control.
2. Access to northern coastal waters for the Tamil fishing industry.

3. The removal of a government military camp from a strategic area in the Tamil territory.

4. Permission for the Tamil Tigers to carry their guns when in government-controlled territory.

The government rejected the last two demands. Fighting erupted after the government was unable or unwilling to allow food and other supplies to get to the Tamils. Although the embargo had been lifted, military distrust and hostility prevented making ending the embargo a reality.[28]

President Kumaratunga, realizing that the government could not defeat the Tamil guerrillas, unilaterally offered a peace agreement to the Tamils. She offered them regional autonomy in a federal system of government. The change from a **unitary system** of government, in which power is centralized, to a **federal system** of government, in which power is shared among different levels of government, required a constitutional amendment. The UNP, which had been committed to reconciliation between the Sinhalese and the Tamils when Sri Lanka became independent, opposed changing the constitution to create a federal system of government. President Kumaratunga's People's Alliance coalition had a slim majority in the parliament and was unable to change the constitution without support from the UNP. Proposed constitutional changes in Sri Lanka require a two-thirds majority of the legislature to be passed. These changes must be ratified by a simple majority of the Sri Lankan electorate. Many Sinhalese believed that federalism would eventually lead to creating a separate country for Tamils on the island nation.[29] In February 2002 the government signed a cease-fire agreement with the Tamil rebel leader, Velupillai Prabhakaran. Although the Tamil Tigers withdrew from talks with the government in April 2003, the cease-fire remained in effect until 2006, when fighting escalated. The European Union responded by listing the Tamil Tigers as a terrorist organization. As the conflict intensified from 2007 to 2009, the Tamil Tigers suffered several defeats and were confined to a very small area. An estimated 50,000 civilians were trapped in the combat area. More than 6,500 civilians were killed in early 2009. On May 19, 2009, Sri Lanka president, Mahindra Rajapaksa, declared an end to the conflict. Vellupilai Prabhakaran was killed in the final battle of 25 years of war. In an effort to restore its image as a serene, sun-drenched Indian Ocean island to attract tourism, Sri Lanka hosted the International Indian Film Academy awards (Bollywood's Oscars) in June 2010.

unitary system ■ A system of government in which power is centralized.

federal system ■ A system of government in which power is shared among different levels of government.

SUMMARY AND REVIEW

Ethnic issues and ethnic conflicts in the developing world have received increased attention since the end of the Cold War. Increased globalization, especially the growth of telecommunications, has brought ethnic conflicts in areas that were once thought of as being extremely remote into American homes. Despite the proliferation of media attention to ethnic conflict, ethnic diversity within the developing world or in the rich countries does not automatically result in conflict. Hence, even though Canada and the United States are two of the most ethnically diverse countries in the world, they are extremely stable politically and avoid serious racial and ethnic violence, despite past and present problems with race and ethnicity. Ethnic group members often have their own social organizations, support a particular political party, live in specific areas of the country, attend the same schools, develop business partnerships, and are associated with the same religious organizations. Ethnic identity often functions to draw sharp distinctions among groups to promote group solidarity. Because of those distinctions, the most obvious cause of ethnic conflict is the geographic proximity of different groups. In addition, when a group's identity is based largely on adversarial relationships—on the basis of us versus them—conflict is almost inevitable. Other causes of ethnic conflict include the deliberate manipulation of negative perceptions by leaders, competition for scarce resources, modernization, governmental mismanagement, and proliferation of weapons along ethnic lines. Ethnic conflicts and warfare result in outrageous economic, political, and human costs to any society. Neighboring countries as well as countries in which members of particular ethnic groups live are often negatively affected by ethnic conflicts.

KEY TERMS

tribalism 222
ethnic group 222
identity 222
ethnic pluralism 222
murahaleen 225
Sudan People's Liberation Army (SPLA) 227
indirect rule 227
Biafra 228
American Colonization Society 228
Americo-Liberians 228
William Tolbert 228
animism 229

trans-Sahara slave trade 229
abed 229
shaheed 229
Tutsis and Hutus 230
racial theories 230
Jawaharlal Nehru 232
Ali Jinnah 232
Sikhs' Golden Temple 232
Uighur separatists 232
Halabja 233
Kurdish Workers Party 234
Abdullah Ocalan 235
Shining Path 235
Chiapas 236

San Andres Accords 236
power-sharing arrangements 237
federalism 237
Sinhalese and Tamils 237
Veddah 237
United National Party (UNP) 238
Sri Lanka Freedom Party (SLFP) 238
Indo-Sri Lankan Agreement 239
Chandrika Bandaranaike Kumaratunga 239
unitary system 240
federal system 240

DISCUSSION QUESTIONS

1. Distinguish between ethnic conflicts and state conflicts. Why have ethnic conflicts been so prevalent since the end of the Cold War?
2. Discuss the causes and costs of ethnic conflicts.
3. Name the different ethnic groups in Nigeria. Discuss the reasons behind the Biafran war.
4. How have European-imposed racial theories exacerbated ethnic conflicts in Africa?
5. What can be done to resolve and prevent ethnic conflict?

SUGGESTED READINGS

Brancati, Dawn. *Peace by Design: Managing Intrastate Conflict through Decentralization.* New York: Oxford University Press, 2009.

Gberie, Lansana. *A Dirty War in West Africa.* Bloomington: Indiana University Press, 2006.

Habyarimana, James, et al. "Is Ethnic Conflict Inevitable?" *Foreign Affairs* 87, No. 4 (July/August 2008): 138–150.

Lemarchand, René. *The Dynamics of Violence in Central Africa*. Philadelphia: University of Pennsylvania Press, 2009.

Mittleman, James H. *Hyperconflict: Globalization and Insecurity*. New York: Oxford University Press, 2010.

Natsios, Andrew S. "Beyond Darfur," *Foreign Affairs* 87, No. 3 (May/June 2008): 77–93.

Power, Samantha. *A Problem from Hell: America and the Age of Genocide*. New York: Basic Books, 2002.

NOTES

1. Richard J. Payne, *Getting Beyond Race: The Changing American Culture* (Boulder, CO: Westview Press, 1998), 78.

2. Donald Rothchild, *Managing Ethnic Conflict in Africa* (Washington, DC: Brookings Institution Press, 1997), 4.

3. Virginia R. Dominguez, *White by Definition* (New Brunswick, NJ: Rutgers University Press, 1986), 266.

4. Milton J. Esman, *Ethnic Politics* (Ithaca, NY: Cornell University Press, 1994), 3.

5. Robin Wright, "Ethnic Conflict: An Overview," in Charles P. Cozic, Ed., *National and Ethnic Conflict* (San Diego, CA: Greenhaven Press, 1994), 158.

6. Séverine Autesserre, "The Trouble with Congo," *Foreign Affairs* 87, No. 3 (May/June 2008), 94.

7. Boutros Boutros-Ghali, "The Land Mine Crisis," *Foreign Affairs* 73, No. 5 (September/October 1994), 8–11.

8. Ilene R. Prusher, "Inside an African Famine," *Christian Science Monitor*, 9 October 1998, 7; and Jean Clement, *Postconflict Economics in Sub-Saharan Africa* (Washington, DC: International Monetary Fund, 2005).

9. Ian Fisher, "In Congo War's Wake, a Massacre of the Wildlife," *The New York Times*, 28 July 1999, A10; and Somini Sengupta, "In Sudan, No Clear Difference Between Arab and African," *The New York Times*, 3 October 2004, A3.

10. Colin Barraclough, "Iran Confronts a Long-Hidden Problem: Drugs," *The New York Times*, 29 August 1999, A10; and Nazila Fathi, "Iran Fights Upsurge of Addiction," *The New York Times*, 27 June 2008, A6.

11. Ian Fisher, "Many Armies Ravage Rich Land in the First World War of Africa," *The New York Times*, 6 February 2000, A1.

12. Eghosa E. Osaghae, *Ethnicity, Class, and the Struggle for State Power in Liberia* (Dakar, Senegal: Codesia, 1996), 82; and Lansana Gberie, *A Dirty War in West Africa* (Bloomington, IN: Indiana University Press, 2006).

13. Andrew S. Natsios, "Beyond Darfur," *Foreign Affairs* 87, No. 3 (May/June 2008), 83.

14. Yahya Sadowski, "Ethnic Conflict," *Foreign Policy* 111 (Summer 1998), 13; and Richard F. Nyrop, *Rwanda: A Country Study* (Washington, DC: U.S. Government Printing Office, 1985), 1.

15. Alain Destexhe, *Rwanda and Genocide in the Twentieth Century* (New York: New York University Press, 1995), 40; Michael Ignatieff, *The Warrior's Honor: Ethnic War and the Modern Conscience* (New York: Metropolitan Books, 1997), 62; and Catherine Newbury, "Ethnicity and the Politics of History in Rwanda," *Africa Today* 45, No. 1 (January–March 1998), 7–25.

16. Destexhe, *Rwanda and Genocide*, 31.

17. Jake Hooker, "China Steps UP Scrutiny of a Minority," *The New York Times*, 14 August 2008, A16.

18. Bill Bowring, "The Kurds in Turkey," in Kirsten E. Schulze et al., Eds., *Nationalism, Minorities, and Diasporas* (London, UK: I. B. Tauris, 1996), 25; and Eller, *From Culture to Ethnicity to Conflict*, 177.

19. Richard J. Payne, *The Clash with Distant Cultures: Values, Interests, and Force in American Foreign Policy* (Albany, NY: State University of

New York Press, 1995), 127; and Ted Robert Gurr, *Minorities at Risk: A Global View of Ethnopolitical Conflicts* (Washington, DC: U.S. Institute of Peace Press, 1993), 228.

20. Susan Sachs, "Rebel Violence in Turkey Could Erode Kurds' Gains," *The New York Times*, 1 October 2004, A8.

21. Payne, *Getting Beyond Race*, 40–41.

22. Paul de la Garza, "Mexico Trying Again to Resolve Chiapas Muddle," *Chicago Tribune*, 12 September 1999, sect. 1, 6.

23. Jack D. Eller, *From Culture to Ethnicity to Conflict* (Ann Arbor, MI: The University of Michigan Press, 1999), 120.

24. Marshall R. Singer, "Sri Lanka's Ethnic Conflict," *Asian Survey* 36, No. 11 (November 1996), 1146; and "Monitor Says Sri Lanka Is at War," *The New York Times*, 14 May 2006, A4.

25. Eller, *From Culture to Ethnicity to Conflict*, 133.

26. Neelam Tiruchelvam, "Sri Lanka's Ethnic Conflict and Preventive Action," in Robert I. Rotberg, Ed., *Vigilance and Vengeance* (Washington, DC: Brookings Institution Press, 1996), 150.

27. Eller, *From Culture to Ethnicity to Conflict*, 139.

28. Singer, "Sri Lanka's Ethnic Conflict," 1146.

29. Nilan Fernando, "Sri Lanka in 1997: Inching Toward a Durable Peace," *Asian Survey* 38, No. 2 (February 1998), 142–145.

Migration

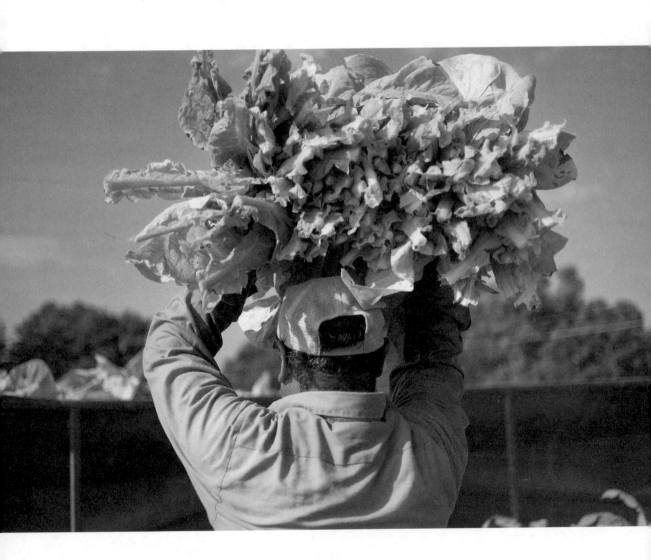

Globalization and Migration

An outstanding feature of globalization is the increased movement of people within and among countries. Globalization stimulates migration in many ways. The porousness of national borders, the availability of information about economic opportunities, easy access to relatively inexpensive transportation, and existing migrant communities in various countries make migration a part of the reality of globalization. Images of economic prosperity and freedom in Western societies or in urban areas of developing countries are made readily available through the instruments of cultural globalization, such as television, movies, the Internet, and tourism.

An earlier period of globalization is a significant contributor to migration. Colonial powers encouraged mass migration to relieve population pressures and to settle Latin America, North America, Australia, and elsewhere. The current period of globalization is creating reverse migration, or the movement of people from former colonies to former colonial powers. The former colonial powers are very wealthy, their citizens are having smaller families and are getting older, and they face a labor shortage. These influence greater migration from overpopulated and poorer developing countries. However, the global financial and economic crises of 2008–2009 slowed migration.

Migration, the movement from one place to another, is an integral part of human behavior. People have always moved from one area to another for a variety of reasons. Our ancestors moved to find the best agricultural lands, better protection from potential enemies, and water and grass for their animals; to engage in religious conversions; to conquer land for new settlements; and in response to seasonal changes. The rich ethnic, religious, and cultural diversity of most countries, especially Canada and the United States, demonstrates the strong human tendency to leave one place and to go to another. Migration is strongly influenced by social, economic, military, and political developments. The poorest countries have the most problems with migration, primarily because they are, by definition, unable to provide economic opportunities for their citizens and are often politically unstable, abusive of human rights, and victims of natural disasters.

The dominant pattern of migration in the developing world is the movement from the countryside to urban areas. This chapter shows that the demand for labor in rich countries is a major cause of migration. In fact, the prosperity of the United States, for example, is dependent to some extent on the abundant and inexpensive labor provided by migrants. This is particularly true of the agricultural and building sectors of the economy. When the United States expanded westward and acquired territories from Mexico, the relationship between American farmers and agricultural workers from Mexico was established. This chapter also examines the gains and losses, the advantages and disadvantages, that result when large numbers of people cross national boundaries or move from one part of a country to another.

migration ■ The movement from one place to another.

WHAT IS MIGRATION?

migrant ■   A person who moves from one country or area to another country or location.

refugee ■   A migrant who lives outside of his or her country but is unable or unwilling to return because of persecution.

displaced person ■   Someone who has been forced to leave his or her home because of violence, conflict, persecution, or natural disaster, but has not crossed an international border.

immigrant ■   Someone who goes to a foreign country to become a permanent resident.

transcontinental migration ■   The movement of persons from one continent to another.

The term *migration* is used in a general sense. It applies to both the movement of people within a country's geographical boundaries and the movement across national boundaries. A **migrant** is a person who moves from one country or area to another country or location. Migrants may move from one part of a country to another location within that country or they may move to another country. Migrants can be refugees, displaced persons, or immigrants. **Refugees** are essentially migrants who live outside of their country but are unable or unwilling to return because of persecution or a well-founded fear of persecution. The previous chapter gave several examples of ethnic conflicts that created refugees. Refugees who attempt to get permanent residence in the country to which they fled, usually because of a well-founded fear of persecution, are referred to as asylum seekers. The immigration laws of most countries make distinctions among asylum seekers, refugees, and other types of immigrants. A **displaced person** is someone who has been forced to leave his or her home because of violence, conflict, persecution, or natural disaster but has not crossed an international border. Displaced persons usually become refugees. Generally speaking, an **immigrant** is someone who goes to a foreign country to become a permanent resident. But many immigrants, both legal and illegal, tend to cross national boundaries frequently and do not view themselves as permanent residents in the foreign country.

Most migration occurs in a relatively limited geographical area, despite the increased **transcontinental migration,** or the movement of persons from one continent to another. People in search of physical security, economic opportunities, and education usually go to neighboring countries. Rwandan refugees go to Tanzania, and Mexicans go across the border into the United States. Africa is the continent with the highest number of migrants (33 percent), followed by North America (21 percent), Europe (17 percent), Asia (15 percent), and Latin America (11 percent).

Men are more likely to migrate than women under ordinary circumstances. There are several reasons for this. Who migrates is determined to a large extent by the requirements imposed by countries, companies, or individuals who need labor. Many countries that recruit laborers often specify the need for male workers. Much of the work to be performed is culturally defined as work for men. Large numbers of men from Turkey, North Africa, and the Caribbean migrated to Germany, France, and Britain, respectively, after World War II to help rebuild these European countries that had been devastated by war. Men have also been recruited by companies involved in mining, construction, and industry. Cultural norms and sex roles within the sending countries also help determine if men are more likely to migrate than women. Gender roles in North Africa and the Middle East, for example, restrict women's mobility. Gender roles also influence men to move in search of employment. Men are generally perceived as breadwinners in most countries, whereas women are seen as being responsible for raising the children and taking care of the home. Economic development and greater access to education for women continue to change cultural views of what men and women are allowed to do and provide more employment opportunities for women. These changes are also influencing more women to migrate. Almost half of the international migrants are women. More women tend to migrate from Europe, sub-Saharan Africa, the

Caribbean, and East Asia. Increasingly, immigration laws in many countries encourage family reunification, a development that allows more women to migrate. Many women are involved in domestic work, nursing, and teaching.[1]

Employment opportunities in neighboring countries often attract workers from other developing countries. Gold mining in South Africa, for example, attracted laborers from Lesotho, Mozambique, and Botswana. It is estimated that there are as many as 5 million African migrants from neighboring countries in South Africa. In June 2008, tensions between South Africans and the migrants erupted into widespread bloodshed and the destruction of property. At least 60 people were killed and tens of thousands were left homeless. Many returned to their countries.[2] There is also **rural-to-rural migration**. Many people leave one rural area to live and work in another rural area. India, with most of its population living in small towns and villages, has a very high rate of rural-to-rural migration. Economic development creates many opportunities in urban areas. Many people move from rural areas to go to cities to search for employment and a better life. This **rural-to-urban migration** is the dominant pattern in the developing world. However, there is also **urban-to-rural migration.** In some countries, such as Brazil, China, Indonesia, and Tanzania, governments encourage (and sometimes force) people to leave the cities to settle new areas. Urban-to-rural migration is usually designed to encourage the economic development of the interior or the countryside and to redistribute people to relieve population pressures on the major urban centers. Another type of migration is **seasonal migration**. People often move from one area to another because of seasonal demand for labor. Agricultural industries often demand more labor at certain times of the year than at others. Harvesting fruit, sugarcane, coffee, bananas, and other crops requires intensive labor for a short time. Seasonal migration is also driven by industries such as tourism. Tourism usually requires the employment of a large number of temporary workers during particular times of the year. Workers in seasonal industries come from both rural and urban areas. Finally, migration may be voluntary or involuntary. Refugees, displaced persons, and enslaved persons are involuntary migrants. Most Americans with African ancestry were involuntary migrants. Voluntary migration, which involves mainly young men and women, occurs when people move to find better jobs, health care, educational opportunities, and an improved quality of life.

CAUSES OF MIGRATION

Migration is influenced by **push factors** as well as by **pull factors**.[3] Push factors are generally negative developments and circumstances that motivate people to leave their homes. These include human rights violations, forced resettlement programs, poverty, natural and environmental disasters, and the lack of educational and cultural opportunities. Many Mexicans migrate to the United States because they cannot compete with highly subsidized U.S. grain exports to Mexico under the North American Free Trade Agreement (NAFTA). Pull factors, which also attract people away from their homes, include employment opportunities, political and social stability, and family reunification.

rural-to-rural migration ■ The movement of people from one rural area to another.

rural-to-urban migration ■ The movement of people from rural areas to urban areas; the most dominant pattern of migration.

urban-to-rural migration ■ The movement of people from urban areas to rural areas.

seasonal migration ■ The movement of people from one area to another because of a seasonal demand for labor.

push factors ■ The factors that motivate people to leave their homes, such as human rights violations, violence, and political instability.

pull factors ■ The factors that motivate people to leave their homes, such as employment opportunities, higher wages, and educational opportunities.

PUSH FACTORS

The United States was settled by people who sought religious and political freedom. During the Cold War, many Europeans came to the United States to escape oppressive governments. The large influx of Cuban immigrants to Florida and other parts of America resulted from Cuba's system of communism under the leadership of Fidel Castro. Dictatorships in Africa, Asia, and Latin America pushed people away from those societies to democratic societies in North America, Western Europe, and parts of the developing world. Ethnic violence and civil wars, as we will discuss later, continue to create some of the most horrible violations of human rights and contribute to mass migration and refugee problems. Transitions to democracy, although reducing the flow of people seeking protection from human rights abuses, have contributed to an increase in migration for economic and social reasons. The fall of dictatorships and authoritarian governments removed many political obstacles to emigration. A common characteristic of authoritarian regimes is their tendency to control the movement of people, both within the country and internationally.

overpopulation
■ Extreme population growth that threatens resources and causes overcrowding.

underpopulation
■ Occurs when there is a strong decline in the population growth rate.

Overpopulation has been a major cause of migration. People move from overcrowded areas when economic opportunities decline to places that offer better opportunities. As population growth puts pressure on the land available for agriculture, people leave the countryside and move to urban areas in search of employment. Revolutions in communication and transportation have made it easier for people to migrate across national boundaries when their societies become too overcrowded. This trend is strengthened by the fact that even though the population of developing countries is increasing, rich countries in North America, Europe, and Asia are experiencing the aging and decline of their populations. In other words, overpopulation in poor countries is occurring at a time when rich countries are faced with **underpopulation**. Prosperity in rich countries influences women to stay in school longer, put more emphasis on work, marry later, and have fewer children, if any. As fertility drops, life expectancy increases. The net result is that industrialized societies are having fewer young people to support the larger numbers of elderly citizens. Italy, Germany, Greece, and Spain have more people over the age of 60 than there are people under the age of 20.[4]

Natural disasters, environmental problems, famines, and competitive exclusion push people away from their homelands or force them to relocate within their countries. Many of the world's displaced people are casualties of earthquakes, hurricanes, floods, volcanic eruption, environmental degradation, deforestation, soil erosion, and famine. Many of these disasters are caused by or made worse because of human activities, overpopulation, and a disregard for sustainable development. As we have seen, many of the world's worst famines are

FIGURE 12.1
China and Tibet

the result of deliberate policies of governments and warring ethnic groups. Volcanic eruptions on the Caribbean island of Montserrat in the late 1990s caused the evacuation of most of the population and their migration to neighboring islands and Britain. The destruction left behind by Hurricane Mitch in Central America in late 1998 led to a huge increase in the number of people from Honduras, Nicaragua, El Salvador, and Guatemala who migrated to the United States. **Competitive exclusion** is a major cause of both rural-to-urban migration and international migration. This occurs when more land is taken by large agro-export companies, which increases land prices and decreases the land available to small subsistence farmers, who are forced to migrate. As Chapter 7 showed, this process of competitive exclusion was a consequence of the Green Revolution. It is quite common in Latin America and Asia.

competitive exclusion
■ A major cause of migration; occurs when land is taken by large agro-export companies.

Several governments have both forced and encouraged people to migrate. China, for example, has sent millions of Han Chinese to settle areas in which ethnic groups challenge China's authority. This practice of subduing troubled regions through migration has been used by China's communist government and its imperial predecessors. When Chinese troops occupied Tibet in 1950, they began to change that country's Buddhist culture. During China's **Cultural Revolution** (from 1966 to 1976), in a systematic effort to destroy everything that challenged communist ideology, Mao Zedong's Red Guard storm troopers detained Tibetan monks, destroyed temples, desecrated Buddhist sacred objects and scriptures, and punished those who practiced religion. China has encouraged many Chinese to move to Tibet. The migration of Chinese settlers has transformed virtually all aspects of Tibetan society, from music to architecture. The low, humming chants of Tibetan monks now compete with loud Chinese disco music. China perceives Tibet and its resources as essential to its territorial self-conception and its security.[5]

Cultural Revolution
■ A systematic effort to destroy everything that challenged communism in China.

Forced migration is used to evict those who are hostile to the government or who disagree with fundamental or revolutionary social and political changes adopted by a new government. Large-scale emigration of certain segments or classes is viewed as an essential step to facilitate the economic, social, and political transformation of society. Forced migration is also used to achieve certain foreign policy objectives. Fidel Castro's leadership of Cuba influenced almost a million people to leave the country, especially those from the upper class. Castro's goal in evicting them or strongly encouraging them to leave was to more easily build a communist society. Castro has also used emigration as an instrument of his foreign policy toward the United States. Allowing a large number of Cubans to migrate to the United States was one way in which Castro could pressure the United States to take (or not to take) certain actions. Many other governments have forced people to leave for different reasons.[6]

forced migration
■ The act of evicting those who are hostile to the government.

China routinely uses forced migration to achieve economic and national security objectives. The Chinese government has forcibly removed people from urban to rural areas, from developed coastal areas to underdeveloped regions of the country's interior, and from its huge urban centers to remote border regions. China's historical concerns about security have influenced it to settle people in border areas where Han Chinese are the minority or to settle in areas that are sparsely populated and vulnerable to foreign invasion. The most ambitious forced removal program started in 1957 and intensified during the Cultural Revolution. An estimated 17 million young people from urban centers were sent to rural areas and border regions to reduce population pressures in the cities. The government also attempted to spread China's communist ideology and develop the remote areas of the country. These efforts were abandoned by the late 1970s.[7]

Violence and economic problems often combine to force people out of their country. Colombia is an example of a country in which widespread domestic violence has created a serious refugee problem. Four decades of conflict between the government and various guerrilla groups and the proliferation of guns and drugs have made Colombia one of the most violent countries in the world. Its murder rate is 10 times that of the United States. It also has the highest number of kidnappings in the world. As the government escalated its war on cocaine producers, with American support, violence in civilian areas also increased, especially in Cali, home of many drug cartels. As is generally the case in countries plagued by violence, many of those leaving Colombia are young and highly educated. But many poor Colombians migrate to neighboring countries.[8]

Numerous ethnic conflicts and civil wars in Africa have left that continent with more than 4 million refugees. Violence against the Kurds has not only led to the growth of Kurdish refugees in the Middle East but also influenced many Kurds to seek refuge in Europe and North America. There are more than 500,000 Kurds in Western Europe. Germany and France are home to most of them (Germany has about 400,000 and France has 60,000). The Vietnam War and economic problems produced a mass exodus of Vietnamese. More than 132,000 people left Vietnam shortly after the communists defeated the South Vietnamese army, which was supported by the United States. Most of the Vietnamese refugees came to America. As economic conditions worsened and the communist government consolidated its power in the country, many Vietnamese sought refuge in neighboring countries. Another 70,000 Vietnamese arrived in Hong Kong in small boats, or were rescued from small boats by ocean-going ships on their way to Hong Kong. By 2008, there were more than 2 million Iraqi refugees living in Syria, Jordan, and elsewhere. There were roughly 2 million internally displaced Iraqis as a result of America's invasion and occupation of the country.[9]

Women and children make up the majority of the world's refugees. They are the most vulnerable to violence. Although women leave for the same reasons as men, women are often victims of human rights abuses and violence directed primarily at them. In most wars and ethnic conflicts around the world, women are victims of rape. In some cases, such as in Bosnia and Kosovo, rape was used to intimidate people and force them to leave their homes. Women also flee because of their fear of persecution in countries that practice honor killings or abuse women who violate traditions and religious beliefs. An increasing number of women from Africa and the Middle East have fled their societies to avoid practices such as female genital mutilation. However, women refugees often experience sexual violence when they try to escape from war and ethnic conflicts. Many women who are raped are shunned by their families and are punished socially and economically by their communities.[10]

Palestinian Refugees

The creation of the state of Israel in 1948 and wars between the Israelis and the Arabs led to a serious Palestinian refugee problem. Between 1947 and 1948, approximately 800,000 Palestinians became refugees from areas of Palestine that were occupied by Israel. Even though many Israelis claim the Palestinians left more or less voluntarily, most Palestinians regard this exodus as the result of Israel's strategy to force the Palestinians out of Palestine. There are roughly 3.5 million Palestinian refugees. More than a million of them live in refugee camps throughout the Arab world. Many of the refugees have lived in these camps for more than half a century. Their children and grandchildren were born and raised in refugee camps. The 1967 War, during which all of historic Palestine came under Israeli control, led to a second wave of Palestinian refugees. About 400,000 Palestinians, out of a population of 2.5 million, left Palestine for Jordan, Lebanon, and other Arab countries. The civil war in Lebanon and Israel's invasion of Lebanon in 1982 forced more Palestinians to become refugees again. Some of them left for Europe and the United States. There are more than 200,000 Palestinians living in the United States and Canada, and about 200,000 are living in Europe. Many Palestinian refugees migrated to oil-producing Arab countries that needed both skilled and unskilled labor. However, when Iraq invaded Kuwait, many Palestinians were perceived as being sympathetic to Iraq. The politics of the Gulf War in 1991 contributed to the expulsion of about 350,000 Palestinians from Kuwait alone. Palestinians also left Iraq and Saudi Arabia. Most of the Palestinians who were expelled from Kuwait became refugees in Jordan. An estimated 6 million Palestinians are living in the diaspora.[11] Although many Palestinian refugees hope to return to Palestine, the Palestinian refugee problem is likely to remain unresolved for a long time.

PULL FACTORS

The availability of economic opportunities has influenced people to migrate. People leave rural areas to work in the growing manufacturing and service industries in urban areas, to improve their education, and to gain greater access to health care, consumer services, and a modern way of life. This rural-to-urban migration, the movement of people away from agricultural activities and into industries, is an integral part of modernization. However, as cities become overcrowded, many governments implement policies that encourage the development of rural areas. Brazil and China, for example, have attempted to reduce urban population pressures by promoting the urbanization of the countryside. In 1985, the Chinese government implemented a **Spark Plan**, which was designed to modernize rural industries through technological innovations. It adopted an export-oriented development strategy in 1987 that facilitated the export of products made in rural areas.[12] These policies stimulated economic development and job growth. People migrated from rural areas to the small towns that were built around these new industries. Infrastructure projects often influence people to migrate. The construction of large dams in China and elsewhere in the developing world has forced many people to leave their homes. The building of industrial factories, airports, highways, and power stations and various public works projects uproot an estimated 10 million people in the developing world every year.[13]

Spark Plan ■ An effort to modernize rural Chinese industries through technological innovations.

The need for inexpensive and reliable labor to work in the gold and diamond mines in South Africa led to the systematic recruitment of workers from Mozambique, Lesotho, Botswana, and Swaziland. Petroleum producers in the Middle East and the Persian Gulf have depended on hundreds of thousands of workers from the region and from other countries to meet the demand for labor in the oil and natural gas industries. Singapore and Malaysia have relied on China, Indonesia, India, and other countries for inexpensive migrant labor to fuel their economic boom. Japan's "foreign trainee" program had brought nearly 200,000 migrant workers by 2010, many from rural China, to work at such things as assembling cell phones. That program has been criticized as a form of indentured servitude.[14]

Globalization is increasingly one of the most significant pull factors. Globalization erodes national borders and strengthens the interdependence of countries, non-state actors, and individuals. When people travel to distant places, they take with them important aspects of their culture. Westerners who go to developing countries project an image of prosperity that poor people in those countries tend to associate with all Westerners. The images obtained through inter-action with Western tourists are reinforced by images on television. Furthermore, the global system of communication provides individuals with information about economic and social opportunities in rich countries and how to get there. Low-cost transportation and the increasing flow of people across national boundaries facilitate movement from one part of the world to another. Distances are no longer an insurmountable barrier to migration.[15] **Global cities** like Los Angeles, New York, Miami, Chicago, Houston, London, Paris, Shanghai, and Hong Kong enable immigrants to blend in and become low-wage workers in hotels, restaurants, sweatshops, and homes. This demand for labor and the strong desire of people from the developing world to escape poverty have enabled labor recruiters to serve as a link between employers in rich countries and rich areas of developing countries and migrant workers.

An important cause of increased migration is the proliferation of groups that recruit laborers from poor countries and often smuggle them into the United States, Canada, and Western Europe. Labor recruiters and smugglers charge substantial sums of money to transport migrants to labor markets and to secure employment for them. Labor recruiters and smugglers are well organized and take advantage of global communication and transportation to engage in trafficking in human beings. Leaders of smuggling operations employ several subcontractors—people who find migrants as well as those who transport them or arrange their transportation to countries that provide employment opportunities. Many smuggling operations are linked to various illegal activities, including drug trafficking and prostitution. Weak governments, widespread corruption, and poverty create an environment that is conducive to human trafficking.

Asia is the area of the developing world that has the most organized and sophisticated network involved in recruiting and smuggling laborers. Overseas Chinese organizations cooperate with mainland Chinese organizations. Many illegal Chinese immigrants come to the United States by plane, ship, and automobile to work for sweatshops, slumlords, and gang bosses. Smugglers in Indonesia and other parts of Asia work with corrupt government officials to obtain the

global cities
■ Cities such as New York and Chicago that enable immigrants to blend in and become low-wage workers.

necessary permits and documentation to enable them to send large numbers of young women to work as domestic servants in Saudi Arabia and the Gulf states.[16] Smugglers in Italy, for example, engage in a lucrative business of transporting illegal immigrants from Turkey into Europe. Because Italy is part of a group of the European Union, which has eliminated border checks, illegal immigrants, once they have entered Italy, often go to Germany and France, countries that already have large immigrant populations. Migrants are recruited in Mexico, guided across the border by "fence jumpers," and driven to safe houses in border towns in Arizona, Texas, New Mexico, and California, where they are held until smugglers are paid. Once in the United States, migrants take advantage of the country's openness and transportation systems to locate in cities and towns throughout America.[17] The construction of a combination of walls and fences and stationing more border guards and troops along the U.S.–Mexican border by the United States are measures designed to reduce the flow of illegal immigrants.

The United States

The demand for labor in the United States, together with poverty, conflict, and oppression in Europe, led to the migration of large numbers of Europeans to America. The first and most significant groups of workers to come to the United States from what is now called the developing world were enslaved Africans. Chinese immigrants came to California in the 1850s to work in the gold mines, on the railroads, and in the agricultural industry. Japanese laborers also immigrated to Hawaii and California to work in agriculture. Many Mexicans were already living in territories that became part of the United States following the **Mexican–American War**, which lasted from 1846 to 1848. More than 100,000 Mexicans decided to remain in Texas, California, Arizona, New Mexico, Utah, Nevada, and Colorado—parts of Mexico that were conquered by the United States. The need for inexpensive and reliable labor continues to draw migrants from Latin America, Asia, and Africa to the United States.

Mexican–American War ■ Lasted from 1846 to 1848.

From Oregon to Massachusetts, from California to Florida, farmers depend on migrant workers to harvest most agricultural produce. Although many of the laborers on the East Coast come from Jamaica and other parts of the Caribbean, farmers on the West Coast and in the Southwest depend on workers from Mexico and other Latin American countries to harvest the crops. Immigrants from the developing world are an important part of the labor force throughout the United States. Most taxi drivers in cities such as Washington, DC, New York, Chicago, Boston, Miami, Houston, and Los Angeles are immigrants from Asia, Africa, and Latin America. Restaurants, hotels, hospitals, universities, and various industries rely on immigrants from developing countries.

France

The influx of large numbers of immigrants from the developing countries into France must be seen in the broader context of French colonialism and the demand for labor in France. France adopted a **policy of assimilation** toward its colonies in Africa, Asia, the Caribbean, and the Pacific. Under this policy, many residents of

policy of assimilation ■ A French policy that allowed residents of French colonies to gain citizenship and migrate freely to France.

French colonies gained French citizenship and were free to migrate to France. Many Africans and Asians found employment in France, especially after World War I, which had such a devastating impact on the French population that the country had to import labor for its industries. Even after Algeria, Tunisia, Morocco, and other French colonies gained their independence in the 1950s and early 1960s, the status of these former "citizens" was not changed. Many of them continued to arrive in France. The largest number of immigrants came from North Africa until the 1980s. After that time, immigration from Senegal, the Ivory Coast, and other West African countries increased.[18] Despite significant opposition to immigrants from the developing world from politicians such as **Jean-Marie Le Pen**, France continues to attract migrants from poor countries.

Jean-Marie Le Pen
■ French politician who strongly opposes immigration from the developing world to France.

Germany

Prior to the 1950s, Germany encouraged its citizens to emigrate to North America, Eastern Europe, Latin America, and elsewhere. Between 1920 and 1950, almost 7 million German immigrants settled in the United States. Germany's need for labor from the developing world was due to the destruction Germany experienced in World War II. When West Germany began to rebuild its industries, the demand for manual labor could not be met by the domestic labor force, especially after the flow of migrants from East Germany ended due to the construction of the **Berlin Wall** (by the Soviet Union) between the two countries. The growing domestic and international market for West Germany's cars, machine tools, appliances, and other manufactured products influenced the government to recruit foreign workers, mostly from Spain, Greece, Turkey, and Portugal. The government and the unions agreed that Germans and foreigners would receive equal wages. Under the **Gastarbeiter rotation system**, foreign workers, or guest workers, would stay in Germany for one to three years and then return to their home countries. But many guest workers did not go home. Instead, many made Germany their home and brought their families to join them. Employers wanted these temporary workers to stay because of the economic benefits they derived from them. By 2008, Germany was home to about 2.5 million Turks, some of the poorest and most visible migrants in the country. Outbreaks of violence against them occur frequently.[19]

Berlin Wall ■
A wall that formerly separated East Germany from West Germany.

Gastarbeiter rotation system ■ A German system that allowed foreign workers or guest workers to stay in Germany for one to three years and then return to their home countries.

THE IMPACT OF MIGRATION ON POOR COUNTRIES

Migration, by its very nature, usually deprives a region or a country of some of its valuable human resources. However, staying in a poor country often stifles the development of human capital and only helps perpetuate poverty and other problems. In other words, the impact of migration on poor countries is not always straightforward and uncomplicated. There are both gains and losses, advantages and disadvantages that result when large numbers of individuals cross national borders or move from one part of the country to another to improve their lives.

brain drain ■ The migration of highly educated and trained people from poor countries to rich countries.

Brain drain, or the migration of highly educated and trained people, is viewed as a serious problem in many parts of the developing world. Many European countries, especially after World War II, worried about the loss of talented individuals who were attracted to better opportunities in the United States. However, most European countries had the ability to train others to lessen the problems caused by brain drain. Many developing countries had relatively few educated individuals at the time of independence. As political instability and economic problems increased, doctors, lawyers, engineers, scientists, and people with valuable technological skills emigrated to the United States, Canada, France, and other developed countries. Many students from poor countries who were educated in rich countries did not return, thereby contributing to the brain drain. The lack of political stability, a general disinterest in or poor understanding of what educated persons did, and the unavailability of proper equipment, research facilities, and a supportive environment influenced many of them to remain where they received advanced education and technical training.[20] Economic opportunities were also a powerful inducement to stay in rich countries. Although the loss of expertise owing to migration remains an important concern, most developing countries have become better equipped to train a large number of people to contribute to economic, social, and political development. The brain drain issue is now more complicated.

It is estimated that half of the recent graduates from the prestigious Indian Institute of Technology leave for the United States. They are driven out of India by overregulation, high taxes, stagnant career paths, and numerous entrepreneurial impediments. Many are attracted to the United States by greater economic opportunities and an environment that is conducive to economic success and personal growth.[21] But this migration of talented individuals is seen as detrimental to India. India is deprived of innovative individuals, the economic benefits that they could provide, and role models for younger Indians. Brain drain also costs poor countries. The money they invested in these individuals' education, training, and general development is essentially lost. On the other hand, many poor countries are unable to absorb the available skilled labor. What is usually perceived as brain drain is often **brain overflow**. Poor countries, such as the Philippines and Egypt, become exporters of highly trained individuals because of their inability to use them. Many skilled migrants, in an increasingly global society, maintain contacts with their home countries and often return to them. In effect, they take back much-needed capital for investment and advanced technologies and technical knowledge they acquired in rich countries. The computer chip industry in Taiwan is an example of how migrants eventually transfer technology from rich countries to their homeland. China, India, and other developing societies systematically encourage migrants to invest in and transfer technology to their country of origin.[22] Migrants also make valuable contacts in rich countries that enable them to raise money for investments back home. They often manage to encourage experts from rich countries to help with development projects in poor countries. Many migrants become valuable assets to their homelands.

brain overflow
■ Inability of poor countries to use highly trained individuals.

Remittances from migrants play a crucial role in the economic development of many poor countries. Migrants throughout the world tend to send money to their families. In some cases, poor countries make arrangements with rich countries to recruit migrants for temporary work. Part of the migrant's pay is sent directly to the governments of poor countries. Money sent to families is used to buy food and clothes, build houses, purchase agricultural land, and help educate family members. Many Mexicans who live in the United States send money to Mexico. Remittances from migrants have transformed many parts of Mexico. For example, Mexicans

remittances
■ Money that migrant workers send back to their families or countries.

who left the state of Guanajuato in search of jobs in Chicago, Atlanta, Houston, Dallas, Los Angeles, Phoenix, and other U.S. cities invest their money in Guanajuato to create jobs. Many, with the help of the Mexican government, invest in **maquiladoras**, or export factories, to enable other Mexicans to find employment in their communities. More than 1,000 jobs were created by 1998, just one year after the program started.[23] Many migrants invest their money in building homes. In fact, constructing a house is a major incentive for emigration. These investments generate employment for Mexicans who remain in their communities and provide revenues for the Mexican government. Remittances are now seen as an important component of many countries' economies. They play a crucial role in economic development.[24]

maquiladoras
■ Export factories in which the Mexican government invests.

THE IMPACT OF MIGRATION ON RICH COUNTRIES

Migrants provide inexpensive labor that contributes to economic growth and prosperity in rich countries. As the populations of developed countries grow older and decline, migrants from poor countries are increasingly supporting an aging population. Migrants also help keep inflation low by keeping wages from rising rapidly. Most rich countries are concerned about the social and political impact of immigration. France, which is predominately Catholic, worries about the large number of Muslims from North Africa who, unlike earlier generations of migrants that adopted French culture, are maintaining their own distinct ethnic identities. Many children of migrants, who were born in France, reject much of French culture, view Islam as being incompatible with French morality, and separate themselves from the larger French society. France, which has stressed the separation of church and state and the importance of a secular society, has reacted strongly to symbols of Islam, such as the scarf, in public schools.

Germany is also facing cultural problems because of the large number of Turkish guest workers in the country. Although Turks make up one-fourth of Germany's immigrants, their relative poverty, lack of education, and practice of Islam make them the focal point of Germany's concern about migration. Germany regarded the Turks as temporary residents. Even though many of them were raised in Germany, they were not given German citizenship. Germany's refusal to see itself as a country of immigration has contributed to the Turks' reluctance to fully integrate into German society. Christian churches and labor unions have consistently urged the government to treat guest workers the same as German citizens. In 1996, Germany changed its policy on citizenship for the Turks, and made 46,300 Turks German citizens. Despite progress in this area, frictions between Turkish migrants and Germans often erupt in violence. Germany is also concerned about the impact of the large influx of Turks on German culture and society.

Migration is rapidly changing the American society. While immigrants came from Germany, Canada, Poland, the Soviet Union, and other European countries prior to 1965, most now come from Mexico, the Philippines, China, Cuba, India, Vietnam, and other developing countries. The large number of Latinos or Hispanics in the United States, estimated at 34 million, is profoundly altering American political and social institutions. Politicians are aware of the growing political power of Latinos and have begun focusing on their interests and concerns. Latinos have great potential political power because they are concentrated in states with the most **electoral votes**,

electoral votes
■ The votes that actually elect the president of the United States.

the votes needed to elect the president of the United States. These states include California, Texas, Florida, New York, and Illinois. Spanish is widely perceived to be America's second language, and the border town of El Cenizo in Texas adopted Spanish as its official language in 1999. It also declared the community to be a safe haven for illegal immigrants. The growing power of Latinos and other immigrants from the developing world is often viewed by some U.S. citizens as a threat to American culture.[25] Several groups in the United States advocate limiting immigration and making English the country's official language. Following massive demonstrations by immigrants and their supporters in 2006, the U.S. Congress passed resolutions supporting English as the official language. President George W. Bush increased the number of National Guard units along the border. Building additional walls and fences to keep Mexican migrants out of the United States was also approved by Congress. Congress allocated $2.7 billion for a secure border initiative.

Case Study: Mexico

Mexico's geographic proximity to the United States and the forces of globalization combined to influence the massive migration of Mexicans to America. Mexico is the site of ancient Indian civilizations, primarily the Mayans and the Aztecs. The Spanish, under the leadership of Hernán Cortés, destroyed the Aztec Empire between 1519 and 1521 and established colonial rule. Three hundred years later, in 1823, Mexico gained its independence. During a period of American expansionism, Mexico lost California, Colorado, New Mexico, Texas, Arizona, and other areas of the present American Southwest to the United States.

Mexico has a large population—roughly 112 million—and a relatively low per capita GDP of $14,200 (compared to $47,000 for the United States). Urbanization, especially along the border with the United States, is high and continues to grow. Life expectancy is 80 years for women and 73 years for men. A relatively high birth rate in Mexico provides a young population that faces unemployment.

Natural disasters, such as hurricanes on the Pacific Coast and in the Gulf of Mexico, growing air and water pollution, and other environmental problems force many Mexicans to migrate to the United States. Widespread drug violence also is driving people out. More than 14,000 Mexicans were murdered between 2006 and 2010. Ciudad Juárez is widely known as the murder capital of the world. In fact, drug cartels control many areas of the country and are threatening its political stability. Philip Caputo argues, "the drug bosses and their organizations have come integrated into Mexican society, corrupting every aspect of the nation's life."[26] This epidemic of violence is facilitated by the easy flow of automatic weapons from America into Mexico and America's demand for illegal drugs. Globalization contributed to Mexico's rapid economic growth in the late 1990s, while simultaneously making it more vulnerable to the global financial crisis and economic recession. As a member of the NAFTA, Mexico benefited from U.S. investments in manufacturing plants across the border. Mexico's economy became closely intertwined with America's. The automobile industry, construction, and tourism declined sharply in the United States during the recession. The impact on Mexico was severe. These problems were made worse by the outbreak of Swine Flu in 2009 and the inflow of thousands of Central Americans and others into

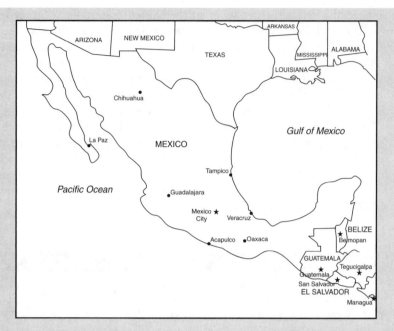

FIGURE 12.2
Mexico

Mexico. Migrants from China, Sri Lanka, Bangladesh, Lebanon, and elsewhere use Mexico as a transport point to gain entry into the United States and Canada.

Mexican migration to the United States has been largely influenced by the economic opportunities in America and difficult economic circumstances in Mexico. The annexation of Mexican territory by the United States did not significantly alter migration across the newly established borders. The Mexican Revolution of 1910 forced many Mexicans out of Mexico and into the United States. The economic and political problems in Mexico at the time served as push factors, and the need for labor in agriculture and on the railroads in the Western United States functioned as pull factors. Demand for labor in the United States during World War I drew more Mexicans to the country.[27] This demand lasted until 1923, when European immigrants began to replace Mexican immigrants. Although many employers began to see European immigrants as troublemakers and preferred the more cooperative Mexican workers, the economic devastation of the **Great Depression** of the 1930s led to the deportation of thousands of Mexican workers and their families. But the demand for labor in the United States during World War II brought Mexicans back under the **Bracero Program.** The Bracero Program was a set of agreements between the United States and Mexico that facilitated the migration of Mexican workers, on a temporary basis, to work primarily in agriculture in the United States. The increase in legal migration under the Bracero Program was accompanied by the growth of illegal immigration. From 1942 to 1952, roughly 900,000 Mexican workers entered the United States under the Bracero Program, compared with more than 2 million illegal workers over the same period. In response to economic competition and fears about

Great Depression
■ Led to the deportation of Mexican workers.

Bracero Program
■ Allowed Mexican workers to temporarily migrate to the United States.

communists entering the country through Mexico, the United States launched **Operation Wetback,** in which hundreds of thousands of Mexicans were rounded up and deported. However, by the time the Bracero Program ended in 1964, the relationship between Mexican workers and American employers was so well established that controlling the flow of migrants across the U.S.–Mexican border was extremely difficult.[28] Immigration from Mexico, both legal and illegal, became a reality of American life. Immigrant laborers in Houston, Los Angeles, and other cities in the West and Southwest wait each morning to be offered employment. Employers and their agents hire them to paint houses, repair roofs, dig ditches, hang drywall, build houses, cook, do gardening and yard work, work in the fields, clean houses, and perform many other jobs that most Americans may not want to do themselves. Immigrants provide most of the labor in dangerous meatpacking plants. In Storm Lake, Iowa, meatpacking plants attract so many immigrants from Mexico that the town has been transformed. Although most Americans regard jobs in meatpacking plants as dangerous, most immigrants often disregard the danger in order to make $7 to $10 an hour. Although the pay is low by American standards, it is very high compared with the $4 a day many unskilled laborers earn in Mexico. Because of the economic benefits of cheap labor, employers hired recruiters to find workers for them in Mexico. They also paid workers bonuses of up to $150 for finding immigrants to work in the meatpacking plants. Growing anti-immigrant sentiment and high unemployment in the United States influenced both state and federal officials to arrest illegal immigrants. Migrant workers at a meatpacking plan in Iowa were detained.[29] In 2010, Arizona passed a law allowing local police to arrest anyone suspected of being an illegal resident, but days before it went into effect, a federal judge blocked the most controversial parts of it and it appeared to be headed for a long battle and possibly to the Supreme Court of the United States.[30]

Operation Wetback
■ An American initiative that rounded up and deported Mexican workers.

SUMMARY AND REVIEW

Migration, the movement from one place to another, is an integral part of human behavior. People have always moved from one area to another for a variety of reasons. Our ancestors moved to find the best agricultural lands, better protection from potential enemies, and water and grass for their animals; to engage in religious conversions; to conquer land for new settlements; and in response to seasonal changes. People have moved with each wave of globalization, thereby transforming the world. The current period of globalization makes migration both more appealing and easier.

There are many different types of migration and migrants. The latter can include internally displaced people, refugees, and migrants, and the former includes transcontinental migration, rural-to-rural migration, urban-to-rural migration, and seasonal migration. Two broad reasons behind migration are known as push and pull factors. Push factors motivate people to leave their homes and include human rights violations, political oppression, forced resettlement programs, violence and political instability, overpopulation, unemployment, poverty, natural and environmental disasters, and the lack of educational and cultural opportunities. Pull factors include employment opportunities, higher wages, political and social stability, a healthy environment, educational and cultural opportunities, and family reunification. Most refugees and internally displaced people in the world are in Africa and Asia.

KEY TERMS

migration 245
migrant 246
refugee 246
displaced person 246
immigrant 246
transcontinental migration 246
rural-to-rural migration 247
rural-to-urban migration 247
urban-to-rural migration 247
seasonal migration 247
push factors 247

pull factors 247
overpopulation 248
underpopulation 248
competitive exclusion 249
Cultural Revolution 249
forced migration 249
Spark Plan 251
global cities 252
Mexican–American War 253
policy of assimilation 253
Jean-Marie Le Pen 254

Berlin Wall 254
Gastarbeiter rotation system 254
brain drain 254
brain overflow 255
remittances 255
maquiladoras 256
electoral votes 256
Great Depression 258
Bracero Program 258
Operation Wetback 259

DISCUSSION QUESTIONS

1. Discuss the reasons for migration.
2. What are the effects of migration on the developed and the underdeveloped worlds?
3. How has globalization contributed to migration?
4. Discuss the reasons behind China's forced migration policies.
5. Is it possible to have a world without migration? Discuss.

SUGGESTED READINGS

Chami, Ralph, et al. *Macroeconomic Consequences of Remittances*. Washington, DC: IMF, 2008.

Goldstone, Jack A. "The New Population Bomb." *Foreign Affairs* 89, No. 1 (January–February 2010): 31–43.

Greenhill, Kelly M. *Weapons of Mass Migration*. Ithaca, NY: Cornell University Press, 2010.

Martin, Phillip, et al. *Managing Labor Migration in the Twenty-first Century*. New Haven, CT: Yale University Press, 2006.

Morrison, Andrew R., et al., Eds. *The International Migration of Women*. Washington, DC: The World Bank, 2008.

Schiff, Maurice, and Caglar Ogden, Eds. *International Migration, Remittances, and the Brain Drain*. London, UK: Palgrave Macmillan, 2005.

NOTES

1. Andrew R. Morrison, et al., Eds., *The International Migration of Women* (Washington, DC: The World Bank, 2008), 8.
2. "South Africa: After the Storm," *The Economist*, 14 June 2008, 62.
3. Kimberly A. Hamilton and Kate Holder, "International Migration and Foreign Policy," The Washington Quarterly (Spring 1991), 196.
4. Jack A. Goldstone, "The New Population Bomb," Foreign Affairs 89, No. 1 (January/February 2010), 32.
5. Robert D. Kaplan, "The Geography of Chinese Power," *Foreign Affairs* 89, No. 3 (May/June 2010), 2.
6. Myron Weiner, *The Global Migration Crisis* (New York: HarperCollins, 1995), 30; and Jane McAdam, *Forced Migration, Human Rights, and Security* (Oxford, UK: Hart, 2008).
7. Lin You Su, "Migration and Urbanization in China," in Gavin W. Jones and Pravin Visaria, Eds., *Urbanization in Large Developing Countries* (Oxford, UK: Clarendon Press, 1997), 71.

8. Kris Kraul, "Colombian Migrants Seeking Refuge in Ecuador," *The Miami Herald*, 23 February 2010, 1A.

9. Ronald Skeldon, "Hong Kong's Response to the Indochinese Influx, 1975–1993," *Annals of the American Academy of Political and Social Science* 534 (July 1994): 92; and "Refugees From Iraq: Less Than Generous," *The Economist*, 23 February 2008, 78.

10. Amnesty International, *Amnesty International Report 1997* (London, UK: Amnesty International, 1997), 2.

11. Ehud Yaari, "Armistice Now," *Foreign Affairs* 89, No. 2 (March/April 2010), 56.

12. Gabe T. Wang and Xiaobo Hu, "Small Town Development and Rural Urbanization in China," *Journal of Contemporary Asia* 29, No. 1 (1999), 80.

13. Kane, "Leaving Home," 137.

14. Ben Dolven, "The China Factor," *Far Eastern Economic Review*, 18 March 1999, 54; and Hiroko Tabuchi, "Indentured Workers in Distress: Job Program in Japan Brings Migrants and Problems," *The New York Times*, 21 July 2010, B1.

15. Joel Trachtman, *The International Law of Economic Migration* (New York: Upjohn Institute, 2009).

16. Ozay Mehmet, et al. *Towards a Fair Global Labor Market* (London, UK: Routledge, 1999), 27–28.

17. Alan Zarembo, "People Smugglers Inc.," *Newsweek*, 13 September 1999, 36; and Jennifer Lee, "Human Smuggling, for a Hefty Fee," *The New York Times*, 28 May 2006, sect. 3, 2.

18. James F. Hollifield, "Immigration and Republicanism in France," in Cornelius et al., Eds., *Controlling Immigration*, 153.

19. "Two Unamalgamated Worlds," *The Economist*, 5 April 2008, 31.

20. Laurie Goering, "WHO: 57 Nations Short of Skilled Health Workers," *Chicago Tribune*, 8 April 2006, sect. 1, 6.

21. Stephan-Gotz Richter, "The Immigration Safety Valve," *Foreign Affairs* 79, No. 2 (March–April 2000), 15.

22. Weiner, *The Global Migration Crisis*, 39.

23. Paul de la Garza, "Emigrants Help Out Back Home," *Chicago Tribune*, 23 March 1998, sect. 1, 1.

24. "Migration and Development," *The Economist*, 10 October 2009, 61.

25. "Texas Town Approves Spanish As Its Language," *Chicago Tribune*, 15 August 1999, sect. 1, 7; Samuel P. Huntington, "The Hispanic Challenge," *Foreign Policy* 141 (March/April 2004), 30–45; and Dahleen Glanton, "Migrants Brace for State Laws," *Chicago Tribune*, 10 April, 2006, sect. 1, 1.

26. Philip Caputo, "The Border Madness," *The Atlantic*, December 2009, 69.

27. David M. Reimers, *Still the Golden Door: The Third World Comes to America* (New York: Colombia University Press, 1992), 2.

28. Kitty Calavita, "U.S. Immigration and Policy Responses," in Wayne A. Cornelius et al., Eds., *Controlling Immigration: A Global Perspective* (Stanford, CA: Stanford University Press, 1994), 59.

29. Adam Nossiter, "Hundred of Factory Workers Are Held in Immigration Raid," *The New York Times*, 26 August 2008, A12.

30. Randal C. Archibold, "Arizona Blocked from Enforcing Immigration Law: Federal Judge's Ruling; Injunction Against Key Parts of Measure—Appeal Is Vowed," *The New York Times*, 29 July 2010, A1.

Foreign Relations of the Developing Countries

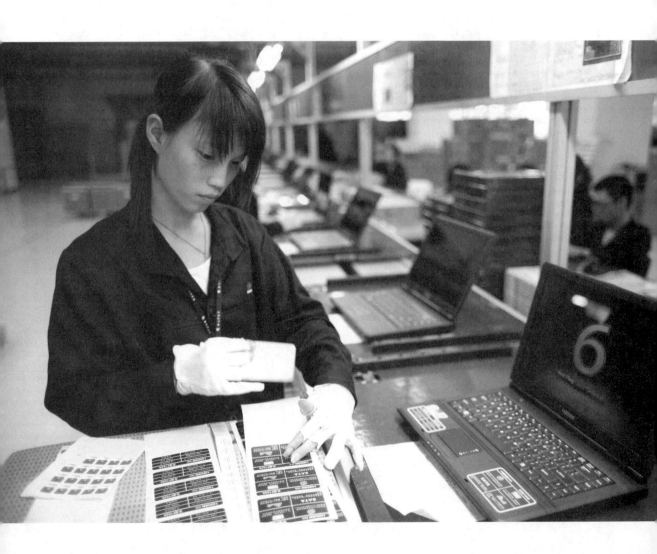

Globalization and Foreign Relations

As globalization increases, the fate of rich countries is increasingly linked to that of poor countries, to varying degrees. This is particularly the case in the area of economic globalization. China, India, Brazil, and other deveoloping countries are profoundly challenging American foreign policy, in particular, and the global power distribution primarily owing to their rapid economic growth and America's financial and economic problems. China, for example, effectively used the 2008 Olympic Games and the Shanghai World Expo in 2010 to demonstrate not only its athletic, economic, and technological prowess but, more importantly, its rise as a great power competing with the United States for global leadership and for access to the world's resources, especially petroleum. China's economic influence in relation to the United States is significant. China has also expanded both its economic and diplomatic ties with resource-rich developing countries. Roughly half of its exports go to them. Companies from the developing world are increasing their investments in the United States and Europe. Indian-based Mittal and Tata Steel purchased the two largest steel producers in Europe, Arcelor and Corus. The government of Abu Dhabi bought a 75 percent share of the Chrysler building, a New York landmark. To enhance their power in multinational forums, China, India, and Brazil joined Russia to form an organization known as BRIC. The foreign policies of developing countries are intertwined with their growing power in the global economy. Terrorist groups based in Afghanistan used the instruments of globalization to inflict a devastating blow on the United States on September 11, 2001. The United States found itself fighting the first war of the twenty-first century in Afghanistan, one of the poorest countries in the world.

The **study of international relations** is primarily about the interactions of countries or states. Just as individuals have relations with other individuals, states have to deal with each other. Their relationships are characterized by cooperation as well as conflict.

An important characteristic of all states is **sovereignty**, or control over their internal affairs and external relations. But the degree of control a state has depends on many factors, including its level of economic development, its geographic location, and the quality of its leadership and political institutions. The concept of sovereignty emerged with the rise of the modern state at the end of the Thirty Years' War, which concluded with the **Peace of Westphalia** in 1648.

The rise of non-state actors and transnational organizations changed how states interact with each other. Revolutions in technology and transportation have contributed to the creation of what is becoming a borderless world. Developing countries conduct their foreign relations in an increasingly interdependent world. Given their level of economic development, poor countries are as concerned with the activities of multinational corporations, humanitarian organizations, and nongovernmental organizations (NGOs) as they are with other countries. This chapter discusses the process of foreign policy making in developing societies, factors shaping these policies, the relationship between the developing world and the United States, and conflict as well as cooperation among developing countries. The chapter focuses on the foreign relations of specific countries, such as China, India, Brazil, Egypt, Mexico, and Cuba. Special emphasis is placed on their relations with the United States.

study of international relations ■ The study of the interactions among countries or states.

sovereignty ■ A country's control over its internal affairs and external relations.

Peace of Westphalia ■ Ended the Thirty Years' War in 1648.

MAKING FOREIGN POLICY IN DEVELOPING COUNTRIES

Foreign policy deals with efforts on the part of one country to influence the behavior and attitudes of other countries, NGOs, transnational actors, and international institutions. The foreign policies of developing countries are expressions of what governments, groups, and individuals determine to be national interests. **National interests** may be defined as a set of goals essential or beneficial to a country's survival, its economic prosperity, the psychological well-being of its population, and its status and prestige in the region and in the larger international community.[1] This definition implies that foreign policy issues are often difficult to distinguish from domestic concerns. In fact, most foreign policies are designed to achieve domestic policies through interaction with other states as well as non-state actors. Efficient foreign policies are usually based on an objective analysis of a hierarchy of interests or national priorities.[2]

national interests
■ A set of goals essential or beneficial to a country's survival, status, and economic prosperity.

Richer countries tend to have more interests and the resources necessary to pursue and protect themselves. Poorer countries are usually more dependent and subservient in their relations with rich countries. The cost of developing independent foreign policies is often too high for poor states. However, some states resist efforts by stronger countries to control their international behavior.[3] Many of these countries are ruled by authoritarian regimes. Their leaders often use confrontation with powerful states to consolidate their power over their societies. Fidel Castro, for example, maintained his control over Cuba by defiantly resisting efforts of the United States to influence Cuba's foreign policies and its internal affairs. He voluntarily relinquished power to his brother, Raul Castro, in 2008.

Foreign policies are shaped by the nature of a country's political system and the quality of its leadership. Most developing countries, despite their transitions toward democracy, are ruled by a small group of individuals. In countries where one individual dominates, foreign policy is often determined by the personal preferences and interests of that individual and his or her supporters. The military capabilities of a country shape its foreign policy objectives and how it attempts to accomplish them. Both South Africa and Nigeria have used their military superiority in their respective regions to try to end ethnic conflicts and restore order. Egypt's military might allowed it to play a leading role in the Arab–Israeli conflict.

In many cases, the foreign policies of developing countries are strongly influenced by the priorities of major countries and non-state actors. Colombia, Mexico, and Jamaica, for example, have made fighting drug trafficking a major foreign policy objective, largely because the war on drugs is a primary interest of the United States. The foreign policies of Afghanistan, for example, were widely perceived as being strongly influenced by Al Qaeda, a terrorist group based in Afghanistan and headed by Osama bin Laden.

cultural ties
■ Common values, family ties, and historical experiences shape foreign policy.

Cultural ties with other countries often help shape a country's foreign policy. Countries that share common values, beliefs, attitudes, and historical experiences tend to develop close relationships. These relationships are often cemented by family ties, cultural activities, and frequent interaction between people from the various countries.[4]

Developing countries are primarily concerned with economic issues. These concerns are reflected in their foreign policies. Developing countries' foreign policies attempt to promote economic development by attracting foreign investments and international assistance. They also try to pursue policies that are designed to narrow the economic and technological gap between themselves and the developed countries. An important part of this effort is to gain access to the markets of rich countries for their primary and manufactured products. Many poor countries make sustainable development and protection of the environment foreign policy priorities. Costa Rica is an example of a country whose foreign policy is directly linked to conservation efforts. Developing countries' foreign policies also deal with debt relief and gaining access to and sharing water supplies. Many landlocked countries develop relations with their neighbors to gain access to the oceans. Finally, as we have seen, foreign policy in developing countries often involves dealing with ethnic conflicts, refugees, migration issues, famine, and humanitarian intervention.

Developing countries use several **foreign policy instruments** to influence others. The instruments of foreign policy that are available to any country depend on a particular country's capabilities. The relative military weakness of developing countries induces them to rely less on military power and more on diplomacy when dealing with other countries. During the Cold War, several developing countries allied themselves with either the Soviet Union or the United States. However, most poor countries opted for a **policy of nonalignment**. This meant that they were not formally allied with either the Soviet Union or the United States. Theoretically, they were independent of both superpowers. Another instrument of foreign policy used by developing countries is regional, political, and economic integration. Military alliances have also been formed by several countries to deal with external as well as domestic threats.

foreign policy instruments ■ A combination of military power, diplomacy, and economic might.

policy of nonalignment ■ Policy of not being formally allied with the United States or the Soviet Union during the Cold War.

THE DEVELOPING WORLD AND THE UNITED STATES

Relations between developing countries and the United States demonstrate the growth of global interdependence in world politics and economics. As the following example of Afghanistan shows, some developing countries' actions have significant implications for the United States. America's behavior is often even more consequential for poor countries. The United States' position as the world's leading economic, military, and political power draws it into the major foreign policies of developing countries. Increasing migration of people from the developing world to the United States reinforces U.S. concerns about poor societies. Poor countries as well as developed societies expect the United States to get involved in the affairs of other countries, especially when these countries' actions threaten global peace and stability or constitute gross violations of human rights. As the discussion of specific countries' foreign policies shows, the United States is often directly or indirectly involved in most regional conflicts.

Afghanistan

On September 11, 2001, terrorists from the **Al Qaeda** organization, based in Afghanistan and headed by the Saudi Arabian exile Osama bin Laden, hijacked four American passenger jets loaded with fuel and used them as missiles to bomb the World Trade Center in New York and the Pentagon in Arlington, Virginia, just outside of Washington, DC. The terrorists took flying lessons in the United States.

Al Qaeda ■ Terrorist group headed by Osama bin Laden.

Then, relying on the Internet, telephones, and fax machines to communicate with each other, and armed with box cutters, they seized control of American planes to inflict the greatest damage the United States has ever experienced on its territory. Almost 3,000 people were killed; the World Trade Center and many other buildings were destroyed; the Pentagon was badly damaged; and the economy, already weak, was pushed into a recession. That attack on the United States demonstrated America's vulnerability to problems and violence in other parts of the world in an age of globalization. Conflicts in the developing world in which the United States is or has been involved, such as those in Iraq, Afghanistan, and the Middle East, are widely perceived in the developing world as factors contributing to terrorism against America. The September 11 attack and America's response to it also showed that the United States needs the cooperation of developed countries to achieve some of its foreign policy and national security objectives.

Afghanistan is one of the least developed countries in the world. One in every four children dies before the age of five; life expectancy is about 44 years; only 12 percent of the population has access to clean drinking water; and barely 43 percent of the men and 12 percent of the women are literate. Afghanistan's infrastructure was almost destroyed by more than two decades of war—first the war against the occupation by the Soviet Union and then the conflicts among various ethnic groups within the country. Afghanistan's population, estimated at 33 million, is made up of a large number of ethnic groups. These include the Pashtun (38 percent), Tajik (25 percent), Hazaral (19 percent), and Uzbek (6 percent). The ethnic diversity is reinforced by significant language barriers. Most of the population speaks Dari, an Afghan form of Persian. Others speak Pashto or one of more than 30 different minor languages. Only 24 percent of the population lives in urban areas, a reality that makes effective control of Afghanistan difficult, if not impossible.

Mujahedeen ■ Holy warriors.

U.S. involvement in Afghanistan is an outgrowth of its interest in maintaining access to Persian Gulf oil and its commitment to containing communism in South Asia as well as the Middle East following World War II. Although America's main concern was its relationship with Pakistan, it provided financial assistance to Pakistan's neighbor, Afghanistan, to promote political stability and minimize the ability of the former Soviet Union to dominate Afghanistan or use it as a base from which it could spread communism to South Asia. When the Soviet Union invaded Afghanistan in 1979, the United States increased its support to Pakistan and implemented largely ineffective sanctions against the Soviet Union. The United States also gave military aid to Afghan resistance movements, known as the **Mujahedeen** (holy warriors), to strengthen resistance

FIGURE 13.1
Afghanistan

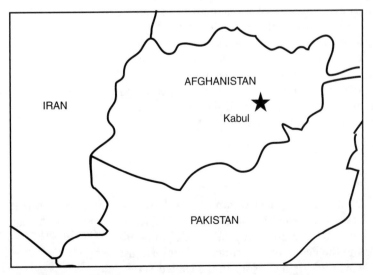

to Soviet occupation. America's Central Intelligence Agency (CIA) trained Islamic freedom fighters to resist the Soviets. Many of the leaders of the Taliban emerged from the Islamic freedom fighters. Muslims from other countries, including Osama bin Laden, went to Afghanistan to join the Mujahedeen. When the Soviet Union withdrew its troops in 1989, Afghanistan disintegrated into a civil war.

Pakistan, under Prime Minister Benazir Bhutto, supported the Taliban, enabling it to gain control of roughly 90 percent of Afghanistan. Osama bin Laden, the son of a Saudi Arabian construction magnate, opposed America's stationing of its troops in Saudi Arabia as well as the U.S.-led coalition that went to war in 1991 against Iraq to force it to end its military invasion of neighboring Kuwait. Because of opposition to the Saudi government, Bin Laden was stripped of his Saudi citizenship and forced to go into exile, first in the Sudan and later (1996) in Afghanistan. In return for the safe haven provided by Afghanistan, bin Laden provided the Taliban with thousands of fighters and millions of dollars. Bin Laden eventually gained enough influence over the Taliban to allow him to transform Afghanistan into his own personal training center for global terrorists. America's war against terrorism began with the bombing of Afghanistan in October 2001. The U.S. invasion and occupation of Iraq were also linked to fighting terrorism. America found itself deeply engaged in the developing world. The United States' "global war on terrorism" made Iraq the focus of American foreign policy. However, the resurgence of the Taliban influenced the United States to shift its focus to Afghanistan and to escalate its military activities. Despite the deployment of an additional 30,000 troops by President Barack Obama in 2010, violence has escalated and many Americans are growing doubtful about U.S. success in Afghanistan.

ECONOMIC GLOBALIZATION AND FOREIGN POLICIES

The Asian economic crisis, which began in late 1997, shows how developments in poor countries ultimately affect America's economy and its foreign policy. The United States decided to play the leading role in preventing the financial turmoil in Asia from spreading. Several parts of the U.S. economy were affected by the Asian crisis. American agricultural exports declined because Asian countries could not afford to purchase American beef, corn, pork, and other products. **Devaluation of the currencies** of Thailand, the Philippines, South Korea, Malaysia, and Indonesia meant that U.S. farm products became too expensive to purchase. These countries had to spend more of their money to purchase the same amount of corn, beef, and pork. Livestock and poultry producers in Asia that imported feed grain from the United States were faced with higher costs as the exchange rates plummeted. Severe economic problems in these societies prevented producers from passing on increased costs to consumers, many of whom were unemployed. U.S. airlines were forced to cancel flights, reduce operations, lay off employees, cancel aircraft orders, and delay aircraft deliveries. The Asian crisis severely reduced the number of Asian tourists who visited the United States. As the U.S. dollar increased in value in relation to South Korea's won, Indonesia's rupiah, Thailand's baht, and the Philippine peso, it became more expensive for travelers from those countries to come to the United States. Hawaii, with an economy that is dependent on tourism, lost substantial revenues.[5]

> devaluation of the currency
> ■ Devaluation occurs when a country's currency loses monetary value and its people have to spend more money to purchase the same amounts of products.

Organization of Petroleum Exporting Countries (OPEC)
■ Formed in 1960 to counteract the power of the oil companies.

The economic decisions of developing countries and the U.S. use of economic sanctions as an instrument of foreign policy have important consequences for American consumers. For example, when the **Organization of Petroleum Exporting Countries (OPEC)** reduced oil production in early 2000, oil prices climbed from $10 to $30 a barrel. The war in Iraq, growing instability in the Middle East, and Hurricane Katrina helped push the price of a barrel of oil above $70 in 2006. By July 2008, oil was $147 a barrel. Soaring oil prices affected many areas of the U.S. economy and demonstrated the country's vulnerability to foreign policies of oil-exporting countries. Rising gasoline prices, which are the most visible prices in a society that depends on automobiles, became both an economic concern and a political issue as America and most of the world experienced an economic recession.[6] Political leaders attempted to persuade the oil exporters to increase production in order to lower gasoline and heating oil prices. However, when Brazil exported low-priced steel to the United States, the Clinton administration imposed restrictions on steel imports. The lower steel prices, although beneficial to the consumer, were opposed by labor unions whose members' employment was threatened by cheaper steel imports from Brazil, South Korea, Japan, and Russia. The United States negotiated an agreement with Brazil that enabled Brazil to avoid tariffs of about 50 percent on its steel by "voluntarily" reducing steel exports to the United States.

To achieve specific foreign policy objectives, the United States often imposes economic sanctions against other countries. For example, following the destruction of Pan Am Flight 103 over Lockerbie, Scotland, in 1988, the United States imposed sanctions against Libya for its alleged role in the bombing. Libya's leader Muammar Qaddafi was believed to be involved in a number of attacks against the United States and its allies. Although the sanctions hurt Libya, they were also costly for the United States. American policy deprived American companies of access to Libya. U.S. farmers, who were suffering from low grain prices, could not export grain to Libya. Boeing, based in Seattle, could not compete with **Airbus**, the European consortium, to sell Libya passenger jets. These examples show how U.S. relations with developing countries affect American consumers and workers. In 2004, the United States lifted sanctions against Libya following Qaddafi's decision to abandon developing weapons of mass destruction and offer compensation to families of the Lockerbie tragedy. In 2006, America restored diplomatic relations with Libya and in September 2008 U.S. Secretary of State Condoleezza Rice visited Libya and met with Qaddafi.[7] The two countries now have normal relations.

Airbus ■ A European consortium that sold passenger jets to Libya.

CONFLICT AND COOPERATION AMONG DEVELOPING COUNTRIES

Relations among developing countries are characterized by both conflict and cooperation. Despite their many similarities, poor countries have many different interests and different approaches to achieving their foreign policy goals. Their geographic location, level of development, and degree of economic interdependence ultimately influence the extent to which they work together. There are many examples of conflict between poor countries. India and Pakistan, as we discuss later, have had hostile relations since they gained their independence from Britain in 1947. China and India have clashed over boundary disputes and ideological differences.

In fact, China has supported Pakistan and Russia has sided with India. China fought Vietnam, after supporting North Vietnam during its war with the United States. Vietnam invaded Cambodia. Many poor countries in Asia are faced with direct or indirect threats from each other. Peru has a history of strained relations with Chile and a border dispute with Ecuador, which erupted into hostilities in early 1981. Guyana and Venezuela have clashed over a territorial dispute, despite efforts to settle the conflict peacefully. Chile has had a lengthy dispute with Argentina over the ownership of three islands in the Beagle Channel.

Territorial claims led to war between Ethiopia and Somalia in 1977. Both Ethiopia and Somalia claimed the Ogaden region, where many Somalis live. Although the boundaries drawn by Britain and Italy, the colonial powers in the region known as the Horn of Africa, were accepted by Ethiopia, Somalia persisted in claiming territory within the boundaries of Ethiopia. Boundary problems also caused military conflicts between Ethiopia and Eritrea. After losing a war that was designed to conquer Ethiopia, the defeated Italians managed to carve out a colony along the Red Sea, called it Eritrea, and governed it as a separate entity from 1890 until World War II. After Italy was defeated in World War II, **Haile Selassie,** Ethiopia's leader, attempted to annex Eritrea in order for Ethiopia to have access to the Red Sea and avoid being landlocked. By 1962, Ethiopia had annexed Eritrea. This marked the beginning of the Ethiopian–Eritrean conflict.[8] After Eritrea gained its independence from Ethiopia in 1993, the two countries became allies. However, unresolved territorial disputes led to renewed conflict in 1998. In early 2000, Ethiopia faced massive starvation, but continued fighting with Eritrea. In 2007, Ethiopian forces invaded Somalia to support their allies in that country's civil war.

Haile Selassie
■ Ethiopia's leader.

Developing countries in the Middle East have also fought each other. Despite their many similarities, these countries have serious disagreements about territorial boundaries. There are also religious and ethnic differences between them. For example, although Iran and Iraq are both predominantly Islamic countries, they represent two different branches of Islam. Iran's population is largely Shi'ite, whereas Iraqis are Sunnis. Iraq is much more secular than Iran. Iraq's population is Arab and Iran's is Persian. Conflicting territorial claims along their 750-mile border led to war in 1980, when Saddam Hussein, Iraq's leader, invaded Iran. More than any other issue, Iraq's determination to maintain control over the Shatt al Arab waterway generated serious confrontation with Iran. Territorial disputes, as well as Iraq's claim to all of Kuwait, led to Iraq's invasion of Kuwait in 1990 and the Gulf War. The United States and West European states have been involved in most of the conflicts between developing countries.[9]

Conflicts among developing countries are generally overshadowed by the level of cooperation among them. Many poor countries attempted to maintain their newly won independence during the early days of the Cold War by joining the Nonaligned Movement, as discussed earlier. Because economic development is of paramount importance to developing countries, cooperation among them has focused on common needs such as access to export markets, higher prices for their products, and greater access to foreign investment and technology. Economic cooperation among poor countries, also known as South–South cooperation, grows out of the realization that they can enhance their chances to develop by pooling their limited resources and building political coalitions. As early as 1967

Group of 77 ■ A political and economic coalition formed by developing countries.

developing countries formed the **Group of 77** at the United Nations, which is now composed of about 133 countries, to promote South–South cooperation and to strengthen the bargaining position of poor countries in their negotiations with rich societies. Increased economic competition and globalization underscore the need for South–South cooperation. They discuss the implications of the globalization of the world economy, technology in developing countries, ways to increase cooperation among poor countries, and improving relations between the rich and poor societies.

REGIONAL ECONOMIC AND POLITICAL INTEGRATION

The Treaty of Rome ■ Fostered European economic and political integration.

Widespread destruction caused by World War II prompted European leaders to consider economic and political integration as part of their larger effort to create a lasting peace on the continent. The formation of the European Economic Community, established by **The Treaty of Rome** in 1957, brought European countries into an economic alliance that has also strengthened their political ties. As the Europeans moved closer to unification, other countries were also promoting economic and political integration as an essential component of economic development. The North American Free Trade Agreement (NAFTA) was created partly to enable the United States to counterbalance the growing economic power of the European Union (EU). Many poor countries were influenced to form regional economic groups by their close relationship with several European states during colonialism. The fall of communism and the spread of free markets as a path to economic development facilitate the growth of regional integration in the developing world. In this sense, regional integration is, in part, a product of globalization. Globalization influences poor countries to form trading blocs to avoid economic marginalization. A major goal of economic integration in the developing world is to achieve **economies of scale**. By combining their resources to build industries that serve a large number of people, poor countries not only lower prices for their consumers but also conserve more of their scarce resources. Economic integration is also perceived as a way of helping poor countries improve their bargaining power with respect to industrialized societies and to compete more effectively.[10]

economies of scale ■ The relationship between output and costs.

regional economic development banks ■ Regional banks and loan institutions that are modeled after the World Bank.

An important component of economic integration in the developing world is the creation of **regional economic development banks**, which are modeled after the World Bank. Each region has its own bank. There is an African Development Bank, an Asian Development Bank, the Inter-American Development Bank, and a Caribbean Development Bank. They all share similar objectives, including providing capital to governments to stimulate economic development, promoting regional economic integration, and providing policy and technical assistance. Membership in these banks is not limited to developing countries. For example, the United States is a founding member of the Washington-based Inter-American Development Bank. Britain and Canada are members of the Caribbean Development Bank. These banks give poor countries access to vital financial resources. Like the World Bank, regional development banks raise money through the contributions of their members and by borrowing from international financial institutions.[11]

Regional economic and political integration is inseparable from international relations. The OPEC is perhaps the best example of how developing countries have employed economic collaboration to achieve both economic development and greater political power in the international system. The Southern Cone Common Market (Mercosur), the **Organization of American States (OAS)**, the African Union, the **Association of South East Asian Nations (ASEAN)**, the League of Arab States, the Economic Community of West African States (ECOWAS), and the **South Asian Association for Regional Cooperation (SAARC)** share the common goals of economic development, political, cultural, and technological cooperation, and enhanced bargaining power in their relations with the industrial world.

OPEC was created in response to the power of large oil companies in relation to oil-producing states. Until the mid-1950s, most of the world's petroleum was controlled by seven large oil companies, known as the **Seven Sisters**. Five of them—Esso, Mobil, Standard of California, Gulf, and Texaco—were American companies, one (British Petroleum) was British, and one (Shell) was jointly owned by the British and the Dutch. The major oil-producing countries were extremely poor. Few of them had the technical expertise to develop an oil industry on their own or to transport the oil to markets in societies that needed petroleum. They were completely dependent on the oil companies for the extraction, transportation, refining, marketing, and pricing of petroleum. Under agreements worked out between poor countries and oil companies, the oil companies owned the petroleum. The power of the Seven Sisters was reinforced by their practice of making decisions about petroleum together. In other words, the oil companies exercised monopoly power. Oil-producing countries were clearly at a severe disadvantage.

Significant change in the relationship between the Seven Sisters and petroleum-producing states occurred as these countries became more economically developed and an educated elite began to grow. As part of their agreement with oil producers, the Seven Sisters provided technical training and education for a small number of citizens from oil states. Economic and educational progress gave these countries greater confidence to challenge the oil companies' dominance. The step toward the formation of OPEC took place when Iran and Venezuela participated in the first Arab Oil Congress in Cairo in early 1959. These two non-Arab countries strengthened the oil producer's opposition to price reductions (determined by the oil companies). They also initiated discussion about the possibility of creating an organization that would be composed of all oil-producing countries, not just the Arab states.[12] OPEC was formed in Baghdad, Iraq, in September 1960 by Iran, Iraq, Kuwait, Saudi Arabia, and Venezuela. Algeria, Indonesia, Libya, Nigeria, Qatar, and the United Arab Emirates joined OPEC in the late 1960s. Oil-producing countries such as Mexico and Norway, although not members of OPEC, work closely with the organization to prevent oil prices from falling too low.

The **Southern Cone Common Market** or the **South American Free Trade Area**, known as **Mercosur**, was formed by the Treaty of Asuncion in 1991. Composed of Brazil, Argentina, Uruguay, and Paraguay, Mercosur is the world's third largest trading bloc (Chile and Bolivia are associate members of Mercosur). The main objective of Mercosur is to reduce trade barriers among its members. Brazil and

Organization of American States (OAS) ■ Created in 1948 and composed of Latin American and Caribbean countries, the United States, and Canada.

Association of South East Asian Nations (ASEAN) ■ Founded in 1967 to promote economic and cultural cooperation in Southeast Asia.

South Asian Association for Regional Cooperation (SAARC) ■ Formed in 1985 to promote regional economic development in South Asia.

Seven Sisters ■ The name given to seven large oil companies that controlled most of the world's oil until the mid-1950s.

Mercosur ■ Economic bloc in South America.

Argentina are by far the largest countries in Mercosur, and also the most antagonistic toward each other. Brazil and Argentina fought a war against each other (1827), and as late as the 1980s Brazil was still constructing its railroads with wider tracks than Argentina's to impede potential invaders. But just as Germany and France were able to overcome their historical antagonism to play a leading role in promoting European economic integration, Brazil and Argentina are downplaying their historic rivalry to further their economic development. Mercosur is cooperating with the EU to build a counterweight to the U.S. global economic power. Historical ties between South America and Europe, especially Portugal, Spain, Britain, and Germany, are facilitating greater economic cooperation between the two regions.[13]

ASEAN was founded in 1967 by Thailand, Indonesia, the Philippines, Malaysia, and Singapore. Brunei, Burma, Vietnam, Laos, China, Japan, South Korea, India, and other countries joined later. The major purpose of ASEAN is the promotion of economic, social, and cultural progress through international cooperation. Most of the members of ASEAN have achieved significant economic growth, especially when compared with countries in Latin America and Africa. Rapid economic development in Asia has influenced the growth of democratic movements. These forces of democracy believe that ASEAN members should move beyond their focus on economic development and concentrate on creating democratic societies. ASEAN has avoided dealing with political issues because its members believed in a policy of noninterference in each other's internal affairs. ASEAN was created during the Vietnam War, and the member countries were not only concerned about the spread of communism but also preoccupied with insurgencies and ethnic conflicts at home. Their emphasis on economic growth would have been undermined if they had attempted to address broader political issues. China, India, and Japan are determined to increase their involvement in ASEAN. Japan is generally admired by ASEAN for its economic success, its management strategies, and its advances in technology. Further integration has been impeded by the failure of China and Japan to agree on certain issues, such as the formation of an Asian currency union.[14]

The OAS was established on April 30, 1948, in Bogota, Colombia. Composed of the Latin American countries, the Caribbean, the United States, and Canada, the OAS attempts to (1) promote solidarity among the member countries; (2) strengthen their collaboration and defend their independence and territorial integrity; (3) promote the economic, social, and cultural development of member states; and (4) work toward regional economic integration. The OAS, supported by funding from international organizations, deals with a wide range of issues. These include river basin management, biodiversity, conservation, planning for natural disasters, removal of land mines, prevention of drug trafficking, and addressing threats from international terrorism. The management of natural resources and sustainable development are major concerns of the OAS. Because of the power of the United States, the OAS has focused on issues in which the United States is involved. The United States' relationship with Cuba, for example, has created division and tension within the OAS. The conflicts in Central America in the late 1970s and most of the 1980s, and the United States' handling of them, resulted in serious disagreements within the OAS. During the Falkland or Malvinas Islands crisis, the United States was perceived to have supported Britain against Argentina, a member of the OAS. Despite these tensions, the OAS has strengthened relations among the Latin American countries.

African countries relied primarily on the **Organization of African Unity (OAU)** to achieve many of their foreign policy objectives. Founded in Addis Ababa, Ethiopia, on May 25, 1963, the OAU committed itself to (1) promoting the unity and solidarity of the newly independent African countries, (2) coordinating the efforts of member states to improve the standard of living for Africans, (3) defending the independence and territorial integrity of African states, and (4) ending colonial and white minority rule in Africa. From its inception, the OAU formulated a general strategy for undermining white minority rule in southern Africa. This strategy contained three interrelated components. The first involved isolating South Africa and other countries ruled by a white minority on the African continent. The second part of the strategy called for mobilizing international support to isolate minority-ruled countries economically, politically, culturally, and militarily. The final component focused on assisting the armed struggle against minority rule in Africa by providing support for various groups or liberation movements that were resisting minority governments.[15] In 2002, the OAU was replaced with the **African Union,** which emphasizes integrating Africa into the global economy. Since 2008, the African Union has been primarily responsible for trying to prevent the spread of violence in Darfur in the Sudan.

Organization of African Unity (OAU)
■ Founded in 1963 to promote African solidarity and independence.

African Union
■ Replaced the OAU in 2002.

FOREIGN RELATIONS OF DEVELOPING COUNTRIES

A discussion of the foreign policies of specific developing countries shows that each region has at least one major country that attempts to influence developments in the area. Because the United States is a global power with global interests, major developing countries often find that their pursuit of their foreign policy objectives in their regions collides with the interests of the United States. Sometimes developing countries have the same interests as those of the United States and find it advantageous to cooperate with it. The policies of all the countries discussed have implications for American foreign policy.

India

India, like China and Brazil, is using its growing economic power to profoundly shape the global economic system and international relations. India's companies compete globally, and several American, Japanese, and European multinational firms are expanding their activities in India, just as they did in China earlier. India competes with other major countries for access to raw resources, especially petroleum, to fuel its economic growth. It is also attempting to counter growing Chinese influence in Africa and elsewhere. In April 2008, India's prime minister Manmohan Singh met with leaders from 14 African countries of the first India–Africa Forum Summit in New Delhi to discuss trade, investment, and economic assistance. India promised to invest roughly $500 million in development projects in Africa and to provide $5.4 billion in credit to various countries and regional organizations. India also cooperates with China and Brazil in trade negotiations with the developed world. For example, India, China, and Brazil directly challenged the United States

FIGURE 13.2
Kashmir

on global trade in 2008 in Geneva. Although their main objective was to protect their own farmers, their ability to counter American influence demonstrates their increasing power in global affairs and the relative decline of America's ability to act unilaterally.

The world's largest democracy and the second most populous country, India has a foreign policy that reflects its concerns with its position as the leading country in South Asia and in the Nonaligned Movement. As one of the earliest countries in Asia and Africa to gain independence after World War II, India perceived itself as a model for other developing countries that also had experienced colonialism. India's early leaders believed that their country should play a prominent role in world politics, especially in relation to the developing nations and international organizations. India's geographical proximity to China and the Soviet Union, plus its strong commitment to democracy, complicated its foreign policy. On the one hand, India adopted many socialist economic policies and established close relations with the Soviet Union, partly to protect itself from China. On the other hand, despite its many economic and social problems, India remained a secular and democratic society. India's socialist policies and its ties to the Soviet Union created tensions in its relations with the United States. However, India and the United States shared a commitment to values that brought them together at a time when there were few democratic societies in the developing world.

India has traditionally focused on the security of its area of the world, the South Asian subcontinent. In addition to strengthening its military power, which now includes nuclear weapons, India has attempted to consolidate its position in the region through cooperation with the neighboring states. India also realizes that only through cooperation with other countries can it reduce widespread poverty at home and in the region. The economic success of ASEAN is also a motivating factor in India's decision to promote regional cooperation. However, ongoing tensions between Pakistan and India, which have existed since the Indian subcontinent was partitioned to form India and Pakistan in 1947, make cooperation difficult. Despite these problems, the SAARC was formed in 1985. Composed of India, Pakistan, Sri Lanka, Bangladesh, Bhutan, Nepal, and the Maldives, the organization focuses on trade, development, and stability in order to overcome regional challenges of poverty, underdevelopment, low production levels, and overpopulation. India views economic and political development as essential prerequisites for projecting its power beyond South Asia, and for an enhanced international role.[16]

One of India's most important foreign policy achievements was its role in ending apartheid, or racial separation, in South Africa. India's interest in South Africa predates its own independence. In fact, the quest for racial equality in South Africa was connected to India's struggle for independence through the activities of **Mahatma Gandhi** in both countries. For more than 20 years Gandhi had attempted to influence the white minority government in South Africa to end discrimination against

Mahatma Gandhi
■ Used nonviolent strategies in both South Africa and India to effectuate change.

nonwhite South Africans, particularly those of Indian descent. Gandhi's strategy of nonviolence, which he used to achieve change in South Africa, was also used in India during his efforts to gain India's independence from Britain. Gandhi's pivotal role in India's fight for independence and the fact that Indians in South Africa were victims of discrimination influenced the Indian government to initiate an international campaign to end apartheid. When the UN General Assembly met for the first time in October 1946, India, a self-governing territory within the British Empire, introduced the issue of the unjust treatment of Indians in South Africa. India's actions put the white minority government's racial practices on the international agenda. India continued to support efforts to end apartheid until 1994, when South Africans voted to end white minority rule. By championing a cause supported throughout the developing world, India strengthened its position in international relations and among the developing countries.[17]

India's relations with Pakistan have dominated its foreign policy. The process by which India and Pakistan were created has shaped how the two countries deal with each other and the problems that keep them in a state of conflict. The violence that erupted between mostly Hindu India and Muslim Pakistan when both countries became independent has a profound impact on how they relate to each other. Central to the conflict between them is the issue of Kashmir. As Barry Bearak put it, "for a half century, India and Pakistan have fought over this land (Kashmir), sustaining a hatred so venomous as to rival any in the world. For each, possessing Kashmir is a matter of life and death, with both persistently willing to forsake the former for the latter."[18] However, tensions have de-escalated and several efforts have been made to improve relations between India and Pakistan.

The Kashmir problem grows out of the partitioning of British India. Like India and Pakistan, Kashmir (also known as the princely state of Jammu and Kashmir) wanted to become a separate, independent, country. However, the Hindu leader of Kashmir made an agreement with India in 1948 to protect Kashmir from invaders from Pakistan. The agreement, known as the **Instrument of Accession**, gave India jurisdiction over Kashmir's external affairs, defense, and communications. This agreement was to be voted on by the people of Kashmir, but Kashmir's ethnic and religious diversity created a problem. Muslims, Hindus, Sikhs, and Buddhists dominate different parts of Kashmir. India's first prime minister, Jawaharlal Nehru, believed that Kashmir's future should be determined by the majority. However, Pakistan invaded Kashmir before the Kashmiris were allowed to vote on the future of their territory. This invasion led to the first war between India and Pakistan. The UN Security Council called for the withdrawal of Pakistan's troops, to be followed by an election that would allow Kashmiris to decide their future. India and Pakistan refused to give up the territory they controlled. Roughly two-thirds of Kashmir is controlled by India, one-third by Pakistan, and a small area (known as Aksia Chin) is claimed by China. Both India and Pakistan have stationed troops along the "line of control," which divides Kashmir into Pakistani and Indian sections. Tensions along the line of control remain high. India and Pakistan have fought three wars over Kashmir. Both countries view Kashmir as part of their own territory. China continues to maintain control over its part of Kashmir.[19]

Conflict over Kashmir has heightened the insecurity of both Pakistan and India. Their fears motivated both countries to acquire nuclear weapons in 1998.

Instrument of Accession ■ An agreement between India and the leader of Kashmir that gave India jurisdiction over Kashmir's external affairs, defense, and communications.

Given the unwillingness of India and Pakistan to engage in sustained negotiations over problems that have lasted more than 50 years, a nuclear arms race between them is extremely dangerous. The United States imposed economic sanctions against India and Pakistan in 1998 to persuade them not to engage in nuclear proliferation. These sanctions were lifted in 2001 as a part of America's effort to build a global coalition against terrorism. India accused the United States, the leading nuclear power, of hypocrisy. India believes that its security can only be protected either by global nuclear disarmament or by the exercise of the principle of equal and legitimate security for all countries.[20] Concerns about nuclear proliferation on the Indian subcontinent may have influenced President Bill Clinton to visit India, Pakistan, and Bangladesh in March 2000. Clinton urged closer economic and technological cooperation between India and the United States, focusing on finding ways to encourage Indian Americans, who had more than 750 companies in the Silicon Valley, to help develop India's growing software industry. In 2006, President George W. Bush also attempted to consolidate relations between India and the United States. During his visit to India, President Bush signed an agreement that gave India greater access to U.S. nuclear technology. This agreement was opposed by Pakistan as well as by countries and groups concerned about nuclear proliferation.[21] In November 2010, President Barack Obama visited India with the stated purpose of deepening the alliance of the two nations. On that visit, Obama announced the lifting of longstanding export controls on sensitive technologies. He also announced U.S. support for a seat for India on the UN Security Council.

Egypt

Like China, Egypt sees itself within the broader context of its powerful ancient civilization. Egypt's foreign policy is influenced by its self-perception as the unchallenged leader of the Arabs. It is also shaped by widespread poverty, overpopulation, high rates of unemployment, and the Arab–Israeli conflict. Geography has profoundly affected Egypt's relations with other countries. It lacks a large amount of arable land. About 96 percent of the population lives on 5 percent of its land. With a population that has grown by about 380 percent since 1900 and cultivated land that has expanded by only about 25 percent in the same period, Egypt is forced to look to other countries for employment opportunities for its citizens.[22]

Arab League ■ An organization that was created to promote cultural and economic cooperation.

Egypt attempted to promote cultural and economic cooperation among Arabs by forming the **Arab League** in 1945. The influx of large numbers of Jews into Palestine, largely to escape the horrors of the Holocaust in Germany and elsewhere in Europe, prompted Egypt to coordinate Arab efforts to prevent the establishment of a Jewish state in Palestine. The creation of Israel in 1948 led to the first war between the Arabs and the Israelis. As leader of the Arab League, Egypt was influential in determining the Arab response to Israel. In fact, given Egypt's military power and its geographic proximity to Israel, the other Arab countries depended on Egypt's support to carry out their own policies against Israel. Israel's seizure of Egyptian and Syrian territory during the **Six Day War** in 1967 strengthened Arab opposition to Israel. When Israeli forces took Gaza and the West Bank from the Palestinians, the city of Jerusalem and other holy places of great significance to Jews, Muslims, and Christians came under Jewish control. Arab nationalism increased after the Six Day War, and countries such as Saudi Arabia, Iraq, Kuwait,

Six Day War
■ Israel seized Arab territories in 1967.

Syria, and Jordan saw Egypt as an indispensable ally in their struggle against Israel. The Six Day War also brought the Middle East into the broader rivalry between the United States and the Soviet Union. Egypt grew closer to the Soviet Union. Israel gained increased support from the United States.[23] The Arab attack on Israel in 1973 led to a closer alliance between Egypt and the other Arab countries. The Arabs imposed an oil embargo against the United States and other supporters of Israel, which quadrupled the price of petroleum.

Egypt's leader **Anwar Sadat** believed that the cost of war with Israel was too high, despite the support Egypt received from the Arab world. In 1977, Sadat took the risky step of visiting Israel and addressing the **Knesset**, the Israeli parliament. With the strong support of President Jimmy Carter, Sadat and Menachem Begin, Israel's prime minister, met at Camp David in Maryland to negotiate an end to the conflict. Egypt and Israel signed the **Camp David Accords** in 1978, which ended hostilities between them and provided for the return of Egyptian land seized by Israel. But peace between Egypt and Israel did not end the Palestinian–Israeli conflict and the broader Arab–Israeli dispute. Egypt's actions led to its temporary expulsion from the Arab League, which moved its headquarters from Cairo, Egypt, to Tunis, Tunisia. The withdrawal of Arab financial support was offset by a large amount of foreign aid that Egypt received from the United States for making peace with Israel.

Progress in negotiations between the Palestinians and the Israelis culminated in the Palestine Liberation Organization's recognition of Israel in 1993. This development helped strengthen Egypt's position in the Arab world. Egypt had continued to work for a negotiated settlement of the Arab–Israeli conflict even after it got its territory back from Israel. The main development that helped restore Egypt's position as leader of the Arab world was Iraq's occupation of Kuwait and the Gulf War. Egypt committed troops to defend Saudi Arabia and the Gulf States from Iraq and to end Iraq's occupation of Kuwait. Conflict in the Gulf had a devastating economic impact on Egypt. Hundreds of thousands of Egyptians lost their jobs in Iraq and Kuwait. However, Egypt's support of Saudi Arabia as well as its willingness to protect Libya from what many Arabs saw as unfair treatment by Western countries enhanced Egypt's position. The Egyptian workforce in Saudi Arabia, the Gulf, and Libya increased dramatically.[24]

Anwar Sadat
■ Egyptian leader who made peace with Israel.

Knesset ■ The Israeli parliament.

Camp David Accords
■ An agreement between Egypt and Israel that ended their hostilities and granted the return of seized Egyptian land.

Mexico

History and geography have shaped Mexico's foreign relations. Mexico's relative weakness and the United States' strength have created a lopsided and unequal relationship between them. The United States used its superior strength not only to prevent Mexico from posing a security threat but also to take a large part of Mexico's territory. The power of the United States is a constant reminder to Mexico of its own weakness. Although Mexico is forced to pay attention to the United States, Mexico is often ignored by the United States on many issues. Nonetheless, the geographical proximity of the two countries has contributed to the development of an interdependent relationship. However, the unequal relationship between the two countries has heightened Mexican nationalism and influenced Mexico to adopt foreign policies that are sometimes in conflict with U.S. foreign policies, partly to demonstrate its independence and sense of identity.[25] For example, Mexico strongly opposed America's decision to invade Iraq.

Mexico's desire to play a greater role in world politics has often complicated U.S. policy in Latin America. For example, despite disagreements with Cuba's leader Fidel Castro, Mexico has not supported the United States' attempts to isolate Cuba. Instead, Mexico agreed not to ostracize Cuba in exchange for Cuba's nonintervention in Mexican affairs. Major steps toward a more assertive foreign policy were taken by President Luis Echeverria (1970–1976). Mexico strongly supported the developing countries in their effort to create a **New International Economic Order (NIEO)**. To project its power beyond the region, Mexico decided to build closer relations with the other Latin American countries and emphasize its commitment to a policy of nonalignment in international affairs. One of the major differences between the United States and Mexico arose concerning the conflict in Central America in the 1980s. The United States stressed the need for military force to counter Soviet–Cuban activities in the region, whereas Mexico focused on a negotiated settlement. Under Mexico's leadership, Panama, Colombia, and Venezuela formed the **Contadora Group** in January 1983 to find a peaceful solution to the conflicts in Nicaragua, El Salvador, and Honduras. Mexico was concerned about the growing militarization of Central America and U.S. policies, which it believed would eventually be a threat. Despite its reservations, the United States supported the Contadora peace process.[26]

Mexico has concentrated on economic development in its relations with other countries, especially United States. By signing the NAFTA in 1993, under the leadership of Carlos Salinas de Gortari, Mexico consolidated its economic relationship with the United States. Most of Mexico's exports go to the United States. In fact, Mexico is one of the United States' leading trading partners. But this dependence on the United States has influenced Mexico to find ways to diversify its commercial and political partnerships. One of the most important foreign policy initiatives taken by President Ernesto Zedillo was his decision to pursue a free-trade agreement with the EU to reduce Mexico's economic dependence on America. Despite Mexico's geographic proximity to the United States, many Mexican leaders perceive European economic and social policies as being similar to their own.

Mexico's relations with the United States have concentrated on immigration issues. The influx of Mexicans into the United States brought the two countries closer together economically and culturally. Just as important as immigration issues is the problem of drug trafficking. Drug smugglers take advantage of Mexico's proximity to the United States, the world's largest market for illegal drugs. Drug trafficking has created serious tensions in U.S.–Mexican relations. Many American politicians blame Mexico for America's drug problems. The **war on drugs**, launched by President Ronald Reagan in the early 1980s, aims at reducing the importation of drugs in an effort to solve the drug problem. The United States concentrates on diminishing supplies as the solution, but Mexico emphasizes reducing the demand for illegal drugs in the United States as the best way to eliminate drug trafficking. Mexico also focuses on the easy access that drug smugglers have to weapons from the United States as a major cause of the problem. Roughly 95 percent of the weapons used in drug violence in Mexico come from the United States. In August 2008, U.S. Secretary of Homeland Security Michael Cherloff met with Mexican officials to address this problem. Drug-related murders received greater emphasis in 2009, when U.S. Secretary of State Hillary Clinton acknowledged America's role in the growing violence. Although Mexico cooperates with the United States to solve the drug problem, it is concerned

New International Economic Order (NIEO) ■ Alliance of Latin American countries to project their power beyond the region.

Contadora Group ■ A group formed in 1983 to find a peaceful solution to the conflicts in Nicaragua, El Salvador, and Honduras.

war on drugs ■ Launched by President Ronald Reagan to keep illegal drugs out of the United States.

about the implications of America's war on drugs for Mexico's sovereignty. Escalating drug-related murders in Mexico are contributing to increased tensions between the two countries.[27]

Cuba

The dispute over the fate of a little Cuban boy, Elian Gonzalez, in early 2000 encapsulated broader issues in Cuban foreign policy in general and with the United States in particular. Cuban Americans in Miami have influenced U.S. policy toward Cuba since Fidel Castro seized power in 1959. The dispute about whether Elian should stay in the United States with his Cuban American relatives in Miami or be reunited with his father, half-brother, stepmother, and other relatives and friends in Cuba was more about U.S.–Cuban relations than about Elian. Cuba's adoption of communism and its close alliance with the Soviet Union created strong anti-Castro feelings in the United States. American foreign policy toward Cuba aimed at ending communism in that country. Cuba's decision to send more than 25,000 troops to Angola to support the Popular Movement for the Liberation of Angola against groups that were backed by the United States hardened American opposition to Cuba. Working closely with the Soviet Union, America's enemy during the Cold War, Cuba became militarily involved in Ethiopia, Central America, and the Caribbean.

From the beginning, in 1962, the United States imposed sanctions against Cuba to induce political and economic changes. Many European countries and Canada, close allies of the United States, believed that isolating Cuba was counterproductive. They established diplomatic relations with Cuba and refused to participate in economic sanctions against it. In response, the United States passed the **Helms–Burton law**, which provides for American sanctions against any foreign companies deemed to be using property that U.S. citizens claim was confiscated from them by the Cuban government. Cuba's foreign policies during the Cold War concentrated on countering American efforts to isolate Cuba diplomatically, especially in Latin America. Cuba also wanted to play a leadership role in the developing world. This was accomplished by supporting the Nonaligned Movement, calls for the establishment of a NIEO, educational and technical assistance to Caribbean countries such as Grenada and Jamaica, and military support for liberation groups in Southern Africa and Central America. Cuba's foreign policy objectives changed with the end of the Cold War. Its major foreign policy goals include attracting foreign investment to the island, building international support against American sanctions, and implementing economic reforms that would allow it to play a greater role in the regional and global economy. Similar to China, Cuba is attempting to join the world economy even while it maintains its communist system of government. Changes implemented by Raul Castro in 2008, such as encouraging cell phone use and agricultural reforms that strengthen private investment to increase productivity, are evidence of a shift in Cuba's economic policies. In late 2010, in what analysts called the country's greatest shift toward the private sector since the revolution, Cuba announced it would lay off more than 1 million state employees and encouraged them to find employment in private enterprise. The United States embarked on a new policy toward Cuba in 2009, beginning with removing restrictions on travel to Cuba for Cuban Americans and facilitating the flow of remittances to their relatives in Cuba. The unprecedented oil spill in April 2010 by

Helms–Burton law
■ A law that called for American sanctions against foreign companies deemed to be using property that U.S. citizens claimed was confiscated by Cuba.

British Petroleum (BP) in the Gulf of Mexico focused the attention of American and Cuban leaders on the need for increased cooperation. As the oil spill headed toward Florida, it became obvious that an oil spill in Cuban waters would be disastrous for the United States. Cuba discovered more than 5 billion barrels of oil offshore and will be a major oil producer.[28]

Brazil

Although Brazil's rapid economic growth, size, abundance of natural resources, and its emergence as a regional and global power have profound implications for American foreign policy in particular and global politics and economics in general, Brazil, unlike China and India, is not usually perceived as an immediate threat to America's global leadership. In terms of natural resources, Brazil is much richer than China or India. Its geographic location and good relations with neighboring countries enhance its ability to experience continued economic growth and stability. As America's influence declined in South America, Brazil assumed a greater leadership role in the region.

Like China and India, Brazil is a major player in the global economy. It is rapidly industrializing and investing in other countries. It is second only to China in terms of its investments in the developing world. Brazil dominates in the area of commodities just as China is a leader in manufacturing. It produces a large share of the world's beef, soybeans, iron ore, sugar-based ethanol, and other raw materials. In 2007, Brazil's oil company, Petrobas, discovered between 5 billion and 8 billion barrels of oil in the Tupi field. Another 33 billion barrels were found in 2008, making Brazil a leading global petroleum producer. Rising commodity prices strengthened Brazil's economy. Trade and investments between Brazil and China have been increasing, with China exporting manufactured goods and Brazil exporting commodities. Like China, Brazil is strengthening its commercial and diplomatic ties with Africa. Brazilian companies are involved in mining, oil production, and construction. Brazil's president Luiz Lula da Silva used diplomacy as well as his country's growing economic power to strengthen ties with neighboring states, especially Venezuela, Columbia, Argentina, and Cuba, and to reinforce regional/economic integration. In May 2008, Brazil hosted leaders of 12 South American countries to form the Union of South American Nations (*Unión de Naciones Suramericanas*—UNASUR), which combines the region's two main trading groups, Mercosur and the Andean Community.[29] In 2010, da Silva was actively involved, with Turkey, in diplomatic efforts to prevent an escalation of tensions between Iran and the West, primarily the United States, over Iran's nuclear weapons program. In November 2010, after he had served the allowed two terms, da Silva's hand-picked successor, Dilma Rousseff, was elected president and expected to continue his policies.

▶ Case Study: China

The world's most populous country, China also has one of the world's oldest and greatest civilizations. China was the world's leading military and economic power many years ago, more than a century before Western Europe conquered much of Asia, Africa, and Latin America. China was severely weakened by internal divisions and foreign military interventions

FIGURE 13.3
China

for much of its history. As a major economic power with nuclear weapons and one of the five permanent members of the UN Security Council, China sees itself as a leading world power. With a population of 1.3 billion, China has attracted investments from around the world. It has a per capita GDP of $6,000, a growth rate of roughly 9 percent, and reserves of $2.5 trillion. Life expectancy is 75 years for females and 71 years for males. China's growing economic power enables it to invest in many countries and to be a leading lender to the United States. China's rapid rise is widely perceived as a challenge to American power and the global system. China believes that it is entitled to the international respect and recognition that many major countries enjoy. This quest for international prominence and its growing demand for natural resources motivate China to establish relations with other developing countries and to compete with the United States and other countries for access to resources, especially petroleum. China's economic interests in Africa, the Middle East, Latin America, and Asia have influenced it to pursue diplomatic solutions that directly conflict with American interests. China's support of the Sudan and Zimbabwe undermined U.S. efforts to end the violence in Darfur and to impose effective sanctions against Zimbabwe.[30] China also refused to condemn North Korea for sinking a South Korean warship in 2010.

An overriding objective of China's foreign and domestic policies is the restoration of its dynastic borders. Unlike the European powers, which colonized much of Asia, Africa, and Latin America, China did not acquire overseas colonies. This historical fact strengthens China's determination not to give up any of its territory. In 1997, China regained control of Hong Kong, part of China that had been ruled by the British since 1842. Britain had

Opium Wars
■ Britain fought China to maintain the lucrative British trade in opium (1839–1842).

occupied Hong Kong during the **Opium Wars** of 1839 to 1842, in which Britain fought China to maintain the lucrative British trade in opium. Preventing Taiwan's independence is one of the most important goals of China's foreign policy. China has systematically and vigorously opposed Taiwan's efforts to become an independent country. China warned the Taiwanese in early 2000 that if they elected Chen Shui-bian, who had advocated Taiwan's independence, such a development could provoke a war between Taiwan and China. Chen Shui-bian was elected. However, he backed down on calls for Taiwan's independence and China backed away from its threat to invade Taiwan.[31] China opposed U.S. arms sales to Taiwan in 2010 and the visit of Tibet's Dalai Lama with President Barack Obama in Washington. In June 2010, China and Taiwan signed an unprecedented trade agreement to reduce tariffs and bring the two countries closer together both economically and politically. China also has territorial disputes with several countries over Mischief Reef, the Spratly Islands, and the Paracel Islands in the South China Sea. These islands are also claimed by the Philippines, Taiwan, Malaysia, Vietnam, and Brunei. Although China emphasizes economic cooperation with these countries, which are members of ASEAN, Chinese leaders are unwilling to compromise on the issue of sovereignty over areas believed to be part of China. Chinese ownership of these islands gives it access to valuable fishing grounds and oil and gas deposits. Conflict between China and other countries that claim the islands would undermine regional stability. Consequently, China has emphasized cooperation, and Chinese, Vietnamese, and Philippine oil companies decided to engage in focused exploration of the Spratlys.[32]

China's leaders view Chinese nationalism as an organizing principle of the country's domestic and foreign policies. China's nationalism is utilized to strengthen the increasingly uncertain legitimacy of the **Chinese Communist Party (CCP)**, which controls the country. China's rapid economic growth and growing exposure to Western ideas and international developments have weakened communism. Nationalism is being used as an alternative to communism to unify the Chinese people. Conflict with Taiwan and Tibet is often used by the CCP to promote Chinese solidarity and a national sense of common purpose. Many Chinese perceive an independent Taiwan as posing a threat to their country's security.[33]

China's relations with the United States are shaped, to a large extent, by its adoption of communism under the leadership of **Mao Zedong** in 1949. China was allied with the United States against Japan and Germany during World War II. When the communist forces defeated the Nationalists, led by Chiang Kai-Shek, the United States recognized the Nationalists, who retreated to Taiwan, as China's legitimate government. America's support of Taiwan was reinforced during the Korean conflict (1951–1953), the first major conflict of the Cold War. Communist North Korean troops invaded South Korea, which brought China and the United States into direct conflict in Asia. Although the United States insisted that Taiwan, with less than 20 million people, represented China, it could not ignore the 1.2 billion people on mainland China.

President Richard M. Nixon and Henry Kissinger, the national security adviser, saw improved U.S. relations with China as a way of diminishing the power of the Soviet Union. They also wanted to pave the way for American companies to compete with the Japanese and the Europeans for markets in China. China's prime minister Zhou Enlai invited an American table tennis team to China in 1971, a development that was called **ping-pong diplomacy**. This was followed by a secret visit to China by Kissinger. With the support of the developing countries, the Soviet Union, and many European nations, China took over Taiwan's seat in the United Nations, thereby strengthening its claim as the

Chinese Communist Party ■ Controls China.

Mao Zedong ■ Founder of Chinese communism and leader of China.

ping-pong diplomacy ■ A diplomatic initiative that sent an American ping-pong team to China in 1971.

legitimate representative of the Chinese people. President Nixon visited China in 1972 and signed the **Shanghai Joint Communiqué** with China, which declared that there is one China and that Taiwan is part of China. This was a major victory for China. This development paved the way for the establishment of diplomatic relations between China and the United States in 1979. But the passage of the **Taiwan Relations Act** by Congress in 1979 reaffirmed the U.S. commitment to Taiwan's security.

America's relations with Taiwan, and China's determination not to allow Taiwan to become independent, often lead to tensions between the United States and China. China's violations of human rights and its decision to use troops to crush pro-democracy demonstrations in Tiananmen Square in Beijing in 1989 further strained relations between the United States and China. In an effort to gain China's support for the U.S.-led coalition against terrorism following the attack on New York and Washington on September 11, 2001, America tried to improve its relations with China, and President George W. Bush went to China. While challenging China on the value of its currency, selling arms to Taiwan, and meeting with the Dalai Lama, President Obama has avoided direct confrontations, partly because of the economic interdependence of China and America.

Partly because of growing disenchantment with America, many Middle Eastern oil producers view China as an alternative to their reliance on the United States and have signed various agreements that strengthen cooperation with China. Of increasing concern to the United States is China's active growing involvement in Latin America. Latin America is now a significant source of raw materials. Furthermore, many Latin Americans perceive China as potential check on U.S. power in the region.[34]

Shanghai Joint Communiqué ■ A 1972 declaration of a single China.

Taiwan Relations Act ■ An act passed by Congress that reaffirmed the U.S. commitment to Taiwan's security.

foreign policies ■ Decisions influenced by a combination of factors.

SUMMARY AND REVIEW

As globalization increases, the fate of rich countries is increasingly linked to that of poor countries, to varying degrees. Although much of the discussion of foreign policy and international relations is focused on developed countries, especially the United States and members of the European Union, foreign relations are also extremely important to many developing countries. The poverty of developing countries heightens their vulnerability to events beyond their borders, events over which they have relatively little control. Foreign policy making is essentially decision making by countries about their national interests. It involves setting priorities and deciding how to accomplish them. In a general sense, foreign policy deals with efforts on the part of one country to influence the behavior and attitudes of other countries, NGOs, transnational actors, and international institutions. The foreign policies of developing countries are expressions of what governments, groups, and individuals determine to be national interests. The **foreign policies**

of developing countries are influenced by many factors, including (1) the country's geographical location, (2) the level of economic development of the country, (3) the nature of the country's political system and the quality of its leadership, (4) the military capabilities of the country, (5) the nature of international public opinion and the priorities of major countries and non-state actors, and (6) cultural ties with other countries. Despite many similarities among poor countries and their efforts to work together, each region has at least one major country that attempts to influence developments in the area. Because America is a global power with global interests, major developing countries often find that their pursuit of their foreign policy objectives in their regions collides with the interests of the United States. The global financial crisis has enhanced the power of China, India, Brazil, and other developing countries, a development that challenges both America's dominance and its relations with the developing world.

KEY TERMS

study of international
  relations 265
sovereignty 265
Peace of Westphalia 265
national interests 266
cultural ties 266
foreign policy instruments 267
policy of nonalignment 267
Al Qaeda 267
Mujahedeen 269
devaluation of the
  currency 269
Organization of Petroleum
  Exporting Countries
  (OPEC) 270
Airbus 270
Haile Salassie 271
Group of 77 272
The Treaty of Rome 272
economies of scale 272

regional economic development
  banks 272
Organization of American States
  (OAS) 273
Association of South East Asian
  Nations (ASEAN) 273
South Asian Association for
  Regional Cooperation
  (SAARC) 273
Seven Sisters 273
Southern Cone Common
  Market or the South American
  Free Trade Area
  (Mercosur) 274
Organization of African Unity
  (OAU) 275
African Union 275
Mahatma Gandhi 277
Instrument of Accession 277
Arab League 278

Six Day War 279
Anwar Sadat 279
Knesset 279
Camp David Accords
  (1978) 279
New International Economic
  Order (NIEO) 280
Contadora Group 280
war on drugs 280
Helms–Burton law 281
Opium Wars 283
Chinese Communist Party
  (CCP) 284
Mao Zedong 284
ping-pong diplomacy 284
Shanghai Joint
  Communiqué 285
Taiwan Relations Act 285
foreign policies 285

DISCUSSION QUESTIONS

1. As globalizing trends and bureaucratic governmental failure in the developing world render
the nation-state to an ever-shrinking role in
human affairs, what actors or alignments have
emerged to fill the void left by decreasing state
power?
2. How do regional organizations fit into the emergence of globalization? Are they beneficial or
harmful to globalization? Explain.

3. What impact has the Six Day War had on
Arab–Israeli relations?
4. What are the reasons underlying India and
Pakistan's dispute over Kashmir? Are the two sides'
aims irreconcilable, or can they mutually benefit
from a peaceful resolution? Explain.
5. Do sanctions ever achieve peaceful political aims, or
are they just another form of coercion that prolongs
conflict and poverty?

SUGGESTED READINGS

Berman, Sheri, "From the Sun King to Karzai."
Foreign Affairs 89, No. 2 (March/April 2010):
2–9.
Cooper, Andrew F., and Jorge Heine, Eds., *Which Way
Latin America? Hemispheric Politics Meets
Globalization*, New York: United Nations University
Press, 2009.
Eichengreen, Barry, et al., Eds. *China, Asia, and the
New World Economy*. Oxford, UK: Oxford
University Press, 2008.

Feigenbaum, Evan. "India's Rise, America's Interest."
Foreign Affairs 89, No. 2 (March/April 2010): 2–9.
Gilley, Bruce. "Not So Dire Straits." *Foreign Affairs* 89,
No. 1 (January/February 2010): 44–60.
Jones, Seth. "It Takes the Villages: Bringing Change
From Below in Afghanistan." *Foreign Affairs* 89,
No. 3 (May/June 2010): 120–127.
Kaplan, Robert D. "The Geography of Chinese
Power." *Foreign Affairs* 89, No. 3 (May/June
2010): 22–41.

NOTES

1. Richard J. Payne, *The Third World and South Africa* (Westport, CT: Greenwood Press, 1992), 3.

2. Donald Nuechterlein, *America Overcommitted: U.S. National Interests in the 1980s* (Lexington, KY: University of Kentucky Press, 1985), 10; and Richard J. Payne, *The Nonsuperpowers and South Africa* (Bloomington, IN: Indiana University Press, 1990), 3.

3. Stephen S. Cohen and J. Bradford deLong, *The End of Influence* (New York: Basic Books, 2010), 176

4. Richard J. Payne, *The Clash with Distant Cultures: Values, Interests, and Force in American Foreign Policy* (Albany, NY: State University of New York Press, 1995), XVI.

5. John Schmeltzer, "Asia's Travail Trips Up Travel," *Chicago Tribune*, 11 January 1998, Sect. 5, 1.

6. "Emerging Markets," *The Economist*, 8 March 2008, 79.

7. Helen Cooper, "Isolation over Qaddati Meets with Rice," *The New York Times*, 6 September 2008, A5.

8. Richard J. Payne, *Opportunities and Dangers of Soviet-Cuban Expansion* (Albany, NY: State University of New York Press, 1988), 29.

9. Richard J. Payne, *The West European Allies, The Third World, and U.S. Foreign Policy* (New York: Praeger, 1991), 122.

10. James Lee Ray, *Global Politics* (Boston, MA: Houghton Mifflin Company, 1998), 380.

11. Robert Glenn Hubbard and William Duggan, *The Aid Trap* (New York: Columbia Business School Publishing, 2009), 198.

12. Shireen Hunter, *OPEC and the Third World* (Bloomington, IN: Indiana University Press, 1984), 123–144

13. Sean W. Burges, *Brazilian Foreign Policy after the Cold War* (Gainesville, FL: University Press of Florida, 2009), xiii+229

14. Richard Rosecrance, "Bigger is Better," *Foreign Affairs* 89, No. 3 (May/June 2010), 45.

15. Payne, *The Third World and South Africa*, 25.

16. Payne, *The Third World and South Africa*, 67.

17. Ibid., 66.

18. Barry Bearak, "Kashmir a Crushed Jewel Caught in a Vise of Hatred," *The New York Times*, 12 August 1999, A1.

19. Howard B. Schaffer, *The Limits of Influence: America's Role in Kashmir* (Washington, DC: Brookings Institution Press, 2009), 47; and Somini Sengupta, "Kashmir Rumbles, Rattling Old Rivals," *The New York Times*, 22 August 2008, A5.

20. Jaswant Singh, "Against Nuclear Apartheid," *Foreign Affairs* 77, No. 5 (September/October; 1998), 41; and Dennis Kux, *India-Pakistan Negotiations: Is Past Still Prologue?* (Washington, DC: U.S. Institute of Peace, 2006), 71–72.

21. Charles D. Ferguson, "The Long Road to Zero," *Foreign Affairs* 89, No. 1 (January/February 2010), 90.

22. Gregory L. Aftandilian, *Egypt's Bid for Arab Leadership* (New York: Council on Foreign Relations, 1993), 46.

23. Payne, *The West European Allies*, 79.

24. Aftandilian, *Egypt's Bid*, 54.

25. Roderic Camp, *Politics in Mexico* (New York: Oxford University Press, 1996), 195.

26. Payne, *Opportunities and Dangers*, 108.

27. Randal C. Archibald, "Two-Nation Border Conference Discusses Gun Trafficking," *The New York Times*, 16 August 2008, A11; and Christopher Sherman and Olivia Torres, "Mexicans Chase Away U.S. Agents After Shooting," *The Miami Herald*, 11 June 2010, 1A.

28. Andres Oppenheimer, "Gulf Oil Spill Could Help Bring U.S., Cuba Closer," *The Miami Herald*, 11 June 2010, 4A.

29. Alexei Barrionuevo, "Strong Economy Propels Brazil to World Stage," *The New York Times*, 31 July 2008, A1; and Lael Brainard and Leonardo Martinez-Diaz, *Brazil as an Economic Superpower?* (Washington, DC: Brookings Institution Press, 2009), 256.

30. Nicholas D. Kristof, "China's Rise Goes Beyond Gold Medals," *The New York Times*, 21 August 2008, A23.

31. Graham Bowley, "China's Economic Might Used in Diplomatic Deal," *The New York Times*, 13 September 2008, A8.

32. David C. Kang, *China Rising* (New York: Columbia University Press, 2008), 6.

33. Robert S. Ross, "Beijing as a Conservative Power," *Foreign Affairs* 76, No. 2 (March–April 1997), 39.

34. Hassan Fatah, "Chinese Leader Increases Trade with Saudi Arabia," *The New York Times*, 23 April 2006, A12; Riordan Roett and Guadalupe Paz, Eds. *China's Expansion into the Western Hemisphere* (Washington, DC: Brookings, 2008), 93; and Peter Hakim, "Is Washington Losing Latin America?" *Foreign Affairs* 85, No. 1 (January/February 2006), 45.

INDEX

Abacha, Sani, 184, 200
Abed, 229
Abiola, Moshood, 184
Absolute monarchy, 6
Absolute poverty, 82
Abu Ghraib prison (Iraq), 169
Abubaker, Abdulsalam, 184, 200
Afghanistan
    females in, 150, 153
    foreign relations and, 265–267
    illegal drugs and, 226
    Taliban in, 150, 153
    U.S. troops in, 57
Africa. *See also specific countries*
    agriculture in, 148, 155
    Ashanti, 73
    British in, 36
    cultural diversity in, 11–12
    democratic transitions in,
        182–184
    economic development in,
        111–112
    ethnic conflict in, 226–231,
        250
    European colonialism in,
        12–13, 35–36, 65, 70–74,
        182–183
    HIV/AIDS in, 115–116
    income in, 80
    language use in, 11, 65
    overview of, 11–13
    population growth in, 112–113
    poverty in, 12, 82–83
    religion in, 11
    resistance movement in, 12–13
    role of females in, 148,
        149–152, 158
African National Congress
    (ANC), 190, 216
African socialism, 107–108
Agrarian Reform Act (Egypt),
    199

Agriculture
    deforestation and, 137–139
    economic development and,
        135
    effects of natural disasters on,
        110–111
    Green Revolution and, 91–92,
        249
    pollution and, 136
    slash-and-burn, 138
    technological advances in,
        91–92, 105, 115
    women in, 155–157
AID/CARE International, 154
AIDS. *See* HIV/AIDS
Air pollution, 137. *See also*
        Environmental issues
Airbus, 268
Al Qaeda, 265
Al Yaqubi, 72
Algeria
    case study, 70–72
    National Liberation Front
        (FLN) and, 71
Allende, Salvador, 181–201
Amnesty International, 188
Anan, Kofi, 37
Angola, 85
Animists, 90, 229
Apartheid, 86, 189–190, 191,
        216, 275
Arab-Israeli conflict, 200, 264
Arab League, 276
Arabs, 18–19, 44
Arawaks, 205
Argentina
    disappearances in, 158
Aristide, Jean-Bertrand, 53
Ariyamagga, 51
Arusha Declaration, 107–108
Ashanti, 73
Asia. *See also specific countries*

democratic transitions in,
        184–186
development of governments
        in, 15
economic crisis in, 112
economic development in, 110
ethnic conflicts in, 231–235
HIV/AIDS in, 115–116
natural disasters in, 110–111
overview of, 13–15
population growth in, 112–113
poverty in, 82
prostitution in, 151
religion in, 14–15
role of females in, 148
urbanization in, 134
Assimilation policy, 253
Association of Southeast
        Asian Nations (ASEAN),
        271, 272, 282
Aswan High Dam, 139, 199
Ataturk, Mustafa Kemal,
        164, 174
Autonomy, operational, 215
Axis of Evil, 57
Aylwin, Patricio, 202

Bachelet, Michelle, 160
Balance of payments, 118
Bangladesh background of, 14
    child labor in, 129
    Grameen Bank in, 108, 157
    microloans in, 157
    political participation in, 158
    solar energy in, 137
    untreated sewage in, 135
Bani-Sadr, Abulhassan, 57
Barber, Benjamin, 33
Batista, Fulgencio, 207
Bay of Pigs, 208
Beatrix, Queen of the
        Netherlands, 148

Beaudoin, Cindy Marie, 28
Beijing Conference, 162
Belgium, Rwanda and, 230–231
Beliefs, 176
Ben Bella, Ahmed, 71
Berlin Conference of
    1884–1885, 12
Berlin Wall, 254
Bermuda, 177
Bhutto, Benazir, 159, 160–161
Biafra, 116, 227–228
Bin Laden, Osama, 265
Biodiversity, 139
Bolivar, Simon, 74
Bonded Labor Liberation Front
    (BLLF), 33–34
Botswana, 87, 110, 111, 176
Bracero Program, 258
Brahmin, 50
Brain drain, 214, 254
Brain overflow, 255
Brazil
    background of, 16
    Bolsa Familia in, 94
    carbon dioxide emission
        in, 138
    case studies, 74–75, 93–94
    deforestation in, 138
    economic inequality in, 93–94
    foreign relations of, 280
    HIV/AIDS in, 115–116
    independence movement in, 74
    political participation in,
        159–160
Bride price, 151
British African Company of
    Merchants, 73
British Constitution, 170–171
British Petroleum (BP), 280–281
British West Africa Council, 73
Buddhism
    overview of, 50–52
    politics and, 52, 58
    similarities between Hinduism
        and, 50
Buhrayd, Jamila, 71–72
Bureaucracy
    in China, 215
    corruption in, 214
    cultural variations in, 212
    in Egypt, 217–218

explanation of, 210
formalism in, 214
globalization and, 195
implementation of, 211
in Mexico, 216
operational autonomy in, 215
purpose of, 195–210
regulation as function of, 195,
    211–212
shortage of skilled staff in,
    213–214
in South Africa, 216–217
structural uniformity in, 212
Bureaucratic corruption, 117–118
Burke, Edmund, 187
Burundi, 230
Bush, George H.W., 23
Bush, George W., 34, 57, 276

Camp David Accords, 277
Capitalism
    free-market, 102, 107
    at global level, 33
    Marxist view of, 106
    state, 103–104
Caribbean. See also specific
        countries
    case study, 75–76
    child labor in, 130
    democracy in, 176–177, 181
    effects of hurricanes in, 110
    urbanization in, 133
Carrying capacity, 114
Caste system
    child labor and, 128–130
    in India, 48, 88, 128–130
Castro, Fidel, 207–208, 248–251,
    264, 279
Castro, Raul, 264, 279
Catholic Church, 179–180
Catholics, in Latin America, 16,
    179, 180
Cattle ranching, 137
Central Intelligence Agency
    (CIA), 55, 267
Ceylon. See Sri Lanka
Chamorro, Violeta Barrios de,
    161
Charles II, King of England, 69
Chen Shui-bian, 282
Chiapas, 236

Child labor
    in Bangladesh, 129
    in dangerous industries, 129
    efforts to eradicate, 130
    in India, 128–130
    in Latin America and
        Caribbean, 130
    in Pakistan, 33–34, 129
    statistics regarding, 128–130
Children
    malnutrition in, 82, 89
    as refugees, 250
Chile
    democracy in, 181
    military leadership in, 201–203
China
    Buddhism in, 52
    bureaucracy in, 215
    Cultural Revolution in, 249
    democratic freedoms in,
        185–186
    economic development
        in, 89, 110
    energy use in, 137
    environmental issues in, 136
    ethnic conflict in, 232–233
    foreign relations and, 280–283
    income in, 81
    migration in, 251
    palm oil plantation agreement
        with Indonesia, 138
    population growth in,
        114–115
    Three Gorges Dam in, 139
Chinese Communist Party (CCP),
    185, 215, 282
Chloroflurocarbons (CFCs), 29
Christianity
    in Africa, 11
    in developing world, 52–53
    liberation theology and, 53
    politics and, 53
Cicero, 187
Ciller, Tansu, 164
Classical economic
    model, 102
Clinton, Bill, 276
Clinton, Hillary, 162, 278
Coke, Christopher, 128
Cold War, 17, 111, 183
Colombia, 100, 250

Colonialism
Africa and, 67, 12–13, 70–74, 183
democracy and, 176–177
inequality and, 89
Latin America and, 17, 74–76
legacy of, 65–66, 169
Middle East and, 19
nationalism and, 65
Columbus, Christopher, 16, 70, 205
Communication technology, 25, 146
Community development, 108
Competition, 64
Competitive exclusion, 249
Confucianism, 109
Congo, 152–153, 183, 224, 225, 226, 227
Consolidation of democracy, 178
Constitutional monarchy, 6
Constitutions
British, 170–171
explanation of, 170–171, 177
in Latin America, 182
U.S., 170–172
Consumerism, 132–133
Contadora Group, 278
Conventional political participation, 173
Corruption
bureaucratic, 214
economic development and, 117–118
Cosmopolitans, 187
Costa Rica, democracy in, 181
Coup d'etats, 14
Crime, 126–128
Criminal Procedure Law (China), 185
Crusades, 68
Cuba
background of, 205
Batista government in, 207
Catholic Church and, 179, 180
Communist government in, 208
embargo, 207–208
foreign relations and, 279–280
government in, 7
relations with, 264
women's movement in, 179

Cultural interdependence, 30–32
Cultural Revolution (China), 249
Cultural ties, 264
Culture
democracy and, 176–177
development theories and, 109
explanation of, 7–8, 109, 176–177
nationalism and, 62
political, 7–8
Currency devaluation, 267
Cyrus the Great, 54

Dalai Lama, 52, 187, 282
Dam construction, 139
da Silva, Luiz Lula, 94, 280
Debt reduction, 92
Decentralized systems, 7
Declaration of Independence, 64
Deforestation, 137–139
de Klerk, F. W., 190
Democracy
consolidation of, 178
in developing countries, 172
economic development and, 177, 178
explanation of, 7
factors conducive to, 176–177
four conditions for, 178
globalization and, 169–170
human rights and, 186–188
inequality reduction and, 91
in Islamic countries, 172
overview of, 170–172
parliamentary form of, 172
political participation and, 172–176
presidential form of, 171
values and beliefs of, 176
Democratic transitions
in Africa, 182–184
in Asia, 184–186
ethnic conflict and, 225
in Latin America, 180–182, 212
overview of, 177–180
Demos, 170
Deng Xiao Ping, 114
Dependency theory, 87, 106–107
Deprivation, relative, 32
Deregulation, 212
Devaluation of currencies, 267

Developing countries
child labor in, 128–130
democracy in, 172
females in, 146–167 (See also Females)
foreign policy in, 264–265
health issues in, 115–116
human rights in, 186–188
judicial system in, 175
natural disasters in, 110–111
natural resources in, 110–111
overview of, 10–11
political parties in, 173–175
pollution in, 136–137
population growth in, 112–115
sweatshops in, 33, 130–131
trade in, 87–88
urbanization in, 133–135
Development. See also Economic development
corruption and, 117–118
culture and, 109
debt and foreign aid and, 118–119
demographic trends and, 113
economic environment and, 111–112
education and health care and, 115
explanation of, 100–101
globalization and, 112
natural resources and natural disasters and, 110–111
political instability and, 116–117
role of government in, 101–102
Development theories
community and grassroots, 108
dependency, 106
explanation of, 104, 121
feminist, 108
Marxist, 106
modernization theory or developmentalism, 105
sustainable development and, 108–109
Third World and African socialism and, 107–108
Developmentalism, 105
Dey, Husayn, 72
Dickens, Charles, 130

Dictatorship, 6
Direct form of self-government, 170
Displaced person, 246
Diversity, 11–12
Dowries, 149
Drugs. *See* Illegal drugs

Earth Summit (Rio de Janeiro, 1992), 29
East India Company, 71
East Timor, 179
Economic aid, 93
Economic Community of West African States (ECOWAS), 237
Economic development. *See also* Development
  agricultural decline and, 135
  child labor and, 128–130
  consumerism and, 132–133
  corruption and, 117–118
  dam construction and, 139
  deforestation and, 137–139
  democracy and, 177
  economic and political costs of, 131–132
  education and health care and, 115
  environmental degradation and, 29, 136–137
  explanation of, 100–101
  females and, 108, 154–155
  global interdependence and, 26–28
  globalization and, 32–34, 99, 111–112, 124
  inequality and, 80–84
  overpopulation and, 131
  role of government in, 101–102
  social and cultural costs of, 125–128
  sweatshops and, 130–131
  theories of, 104–109
  urbanization and, 133–135
Economic globalization
  economic environment and, 111–112
  explanation of, 88–89
  foreign policies and, 267–268
Economic inequalities, 131–132

Economies of scale, 112, 270
Ecuador, 136
Education
  development in, 115
  females and, 82, 91, 112–115, 153–154
  inequality reduction and, 91
  population growth and, 112–115
  poverty and, 82
Egypt
  bureaucracy in, 217–218
  case study, 197–200
  Coptic Christians in, 11
  education in, 153–154
  foreign relations and, 276–277
  as Islamic state, 46
  military leadership in, 197–200
Electoral votes, 256
Elizabeth, Queen of England, 68
El Salvador, 87
Empowerment
  of females, 147, 162
  feminist theory and, 108
Engels, Friedrich, 106
Environment
  democracy and, 177
  economic development and, 31
Environmental issues
  deforestation and, 137–139
  ethnic conflict and, 225–226
  global interdependence and, 29–30
  pollution as an, 29–30, 136–137
  urbanization and, 133–135
Eritrea, 269
Ethiopia, 83, 269
Ethnic conflict
  in Africa, 226–231, 250
  in Asia, 231–235
  causes of, 223–224
  costs of, 224–226
  famine and, 83, 225–226
  globalization and, 221
  inequality and, 89–90
  in Latin America, 235–236
  solutions to, 236–237
Ethnic groups, 222
Ethnic identity

  emergence of, 222–223
  explanation of, 222–223
Ethnic pluralism, 222
Ethnicity, 222–223
Europe. *See also specific countries*
  economic and political integration and, 270–273
  population in, 113–114
  refugees in, 250
European Union (EU), 270–272

Falun Gong, 186
Family planning, 91, 112–115
Famine
  ethnic conflict and, 83, 225
Farouk, King of Egypt, 153, 198
Federal structures, 7
Federal system, 240
Federalism, 237
Female genital mutilation, 151
Females
  in agriculture, 155–157
  in China, 114–115
  in developing world, 147
  diverse roles of, 148–149
  economic development and, 108, 154–155
  education and, 82, 91, 114–115, 153–154
  empowerment of, 147–162
  genital mutilation and, 151
  globalization and, 146
  honor killings and, 152
  in Islamic societies, 149–152
  as leaders, 160–161
  political participation by, 157–160
  as refugees, 250
  sale of, 151
  status of, 149–152
  in Turkey, 163–165
Feminist theory, 108
Feminization of employment, 155
Fertility rates, 120–121
Flags, 63
Food and Agriculture Organization (United Nations), 155
Forced migration, 248–251
Foreign aid, 118–119

Foreign investment
  economic development and, 90
  global interdependence
    and, 28
Foreign policy instruments, 265
Foreign relations
  conflict and cooperation and,
    268–270
  developing countries and,
    264–265, 273–280
  explanation of, 263
  globalization and, 263,
    267–268
  regional economic and political
    integration and, 270–273
  United States and, 265–267
Formalism, 214
Four conditions for democracy,
  178
Four Noble Truths (Buddhism),
  50–51
Four Permissible Goals in Life
  (Hinduism), 47–48
Four principles (Grameen Bank),
  157
Fox, Vicente, 182, 216
France
  Algerian independence and,
    70–72
  interests in Middle East, 19
  migration and, 253–254
  Suez Canal and, 199
Free-market capitalism, 102, 105
Free trade policies, 88, 92–93, 95.
  See also Trade.
Freedom of press, 173
Freedom of speech, 173
Fujimori, Alberto K., 181
Full transition to democracy, 178

Gandhi, Indira, 115,
  160–161, 158
Gandhi, Mohandas K., 49–50,
  69–70, 274–275
Gandhi, Rajiv, 232
Ganges River, 136
The Gap, 131
Garcia Medina, Amalia, 160
Gastarbeiter rotation system
  (Germany), 254
GE, 162

Gender empowerment measure
  (GEM) (United Nations
  Development Program),
  147, 163
Gender-related development
  index (GDI), 101
Gender roles. *See also* Females
  in developing world, 148–149
  migration and, 250
Germany
  migration and, 254
  Nazis in, 66, 187
  Rwanda and, 230
Ghana
  case studies, 35–37, 72–74
  government in, 182
  historical background of, 12
  independence movement in,
    72–74
  international environment
    and, 112 United Gold Coast
    Convention (UGCC), 74
Global cities, 252
Global interdependence cultural
    issues and, 30–32
  economic development and,
    26–28
  effects on individuals of, 26
  environment and, 29–30
  overview of, 26
Global warming
  deforestation and, 137–139
  efforts to control, 29
  explanation of, 137
Globalization
  bureaucracy and, 195
  cultural, 30–32
  in developing countries, 3–4
  economic, 88, 111–112
  economic development and,
    26–28, 99–100, 111–112,
    124–140 (*See also* Economic
    development)
  ethnic conflict and, 221
  explanation of, 4, 32–34
  females and, 147
  foreign relations and, 263
  inequality and, 79–80
  leadership and, 195
  migration and, 245,
    251–254, 259

politics and, 4–5
  terrorism and, 34–35
  trends in, 33–34
Gold Coast, 75
Golden Temple (India), 232
Goldman Sachs, 162
Gonzalez, Elian, 279
Good governance, 118
Government
  explanation of, 5
  forms of, 6–7
Government policies
  development and, 101–102
  inequality and, 89
  population control and,
    112–115
  poverty reduction through, 92
Governmental institutions, 101
Grameen Bank, 108, 157
Grassroots development, 108
Great Britain
  Africa and, 74–76
  constitution in, 170–171
  Egypt and, 197–199
  government in, 6
  India and, 49, 68–70, 208
  Iran and, 55
  Middle East and, 19
  parliamentary democracy
    in, 172
Great Depression, 258
Green Revolution, 91–92,
  135, 249
Greenpeace, 137
Gross domestic product (GDP)
  in Asia, 14
  aspects of determining,
    100–101
  explanation of, 100–101
Gross national product (GNP),
  100–101
Grotius, Hugo, 9
Group of 77, 107, 270
Growth, aspect of, 100–101
Guantanamo Bay, Cuba, 169,
  207
Guardian Council, 57
Guinea, 183
Gulf War (1991), 26, 233–234,
  251
Gutierrez, Gustavo, 53

Haiti
    child labor in, 130
    liberation theology in, 53
    literacy rates in, 82
    natural disasters in, 110
Hajirans, 49
Halabja, 233
Hanselman, Marge, 29
Health
    development and, 115
    malnutrition and, 82–83
    obesity and, 133
    pollution and, 136–137
    poverty and, 83
    urbanization and, 133–135
Helms-Burton law, 279
Henry the Navigator, 75
Heterogenous states, 9, 76
Hijrah, 18
Hinduism
    caste system in, 48–49
    Indian politics and, 49–50
    overview of, 48–51
    similarities between Buddhism
        and, 50
HIV/AIDS
    economic development and, 115
    inequality and, 83–84
    rape and, 153
Hobbes, Thomas, 187
Homogeneous states, 9, 64
Honduras, 111
Hong Kong, 281
Honor killings, 152
Human development index (HDI)
    (UNDP), 101
Human rights
    in developing world, 186–188
    explanation of, 186
Humanitarian intervention, 188
Hunger. *See* Malnutrition
Huns, 65
Hurricanes, 110
Hussein, King of Jordan, 148
Hussein, Saddam, 233, 269
Hutus, 230–231

Identity, ethnic, 222
Ideology, 111
Illegal drugs
    ethnic conflict and, 226

foreign policy and, 264
Mexico and, 278–279
as social cost of development,
    126–128
Immigrants. *See also* Migrants;
    Migration
Immigration, 246, 253. *See also*
    Migrants; Migration
Import substitution, 107
Independence
    explanation of, 64
    nationalism and, 64–65
India
    agriculture in, 92
    case studies, 68–70, 273–276
    caste system in, 50, 86
    child labor in, 128–130
    conflict with Pakistan, 70, 232,
        275–276
    Congress Party in, 69
    corruption in, 118
    democracy in, 176, 208–209
    environmental issues in, 136
    ethnic conflict in, 231–232
    foreign relations and, 273–276
    Great Britain and, 49, 68–70,
        208
    Hinduism in, 49–50, 58
    income in, 81
    independence movement in,
        68–70, 208–209
    leadership in, 208–209
    literacy rates in, 82
    Muslims in, 70
    political participation in,
        158–159
    political parties in, 174
    population growth in, 114
    Sewa Project in, 154
    skilled workers in, 88
    Sri Lanka and, 239–240
    trade with, 68–69
Indirect democracy, 170
Indo-Sri Lankan Agreement to
        Establish Peace and
        Normality in Sri Lanka, 239
Indonesia
    case study, 140–142
    corruption in, 142
    crime in, 142
    deforestation in, 138, 142

democratic transitions in,
    184–185
Islamic fundamentalism in,
    141–142
as Islamic state, 46
military in, 141
Muslims in, 44
natural disasters in, 110, 140
Industrialization
    agriculture and, 135
    environmental issues
        and, 135
    through import substitution, 107
Inequality. *See also* Poverty
    attempts to decrease, 90–93
    background of, 79–80
    causes of, 86–90
    globalization and, 79
    regional, 85
    between rich and poor
        countries, 80–82, 86–90
    within rich countries, 84–85
    in South, 82–84, 85–86
Infrastructure, 100
Instrument of Accession
    (India), 275
Interdependence. *See* Global
    interdependence
Interest groups, 175–176
Internal self-selection, 156
International environment, 176
International Labor Organization
    (United Nations), 130
International Monetary Fund
    (IMF), 103, 154
International relations, 263
International wars, 64
Iran
    case study, 54–58
    constitutional compromise, 57
    development in pre-
        revolutionary, 109
    historical background of,
        54–55
    illegal drugs in, 226
    as Islamist state, 46
    political participation in, 158
    revolution in, 56–57, 163
    Tudeh Party in, 56
    United States and, 55–56
    veiling of females in, 150

Iraq
  Gulf War and, 26, 233–234
  invasion of Kuwait, 26, 269
Islam. *See also* Muslims
  Crusades and, 70
  democracy and, 172
  females in, 149–152,
    158–159
  human rights and, 187
  in Iran, 54–58
  oral divorce in, 159
  origins of, 18–19, 44–46
  overview of, 44–46
  politics and, 45–46
  status of females in,
    149–152, 164
  stereotypes of, 42
  teachings of, 44–45
  veiling in, 150
Islamic civilization
  background of, 18–19
  Iran and, 54
Islamic fundamentalism, chal-
    lenges to, 151
  China and, 232–233
  explanation of, 56
  role of women and, 158
  Taliban movement and, 150
Islamic law, 45, 174
Islamic Revolution (Iran),
    56–57
Islamic states, 46
Islamist states, 46
Israel
  Egypt and, 200
  origins of, 19
  Palestinian refugees and, 251
  Six Day War, 276

Japan
  economic development
    in, 14, 109
  government in, 13
Jefferson, Thomas, 186
John Paul II, Pope, 180
Johnson-Sirleaf, Ellen, 161
Jordan, 152
Judicial systems, 175
Justice and Development Party
    (AKP), 165
Junta, 7

Kabila, Laurent, 183, 227
Kabul Women's Garden, 154
Kahn, Shah Reza, 55
Kaleen carpet label, 130
Karma, 47, 150
Kashmir, 72, 275–276
Kennedy, John F., 195, 208
Khalaf, Rima, 148
Khomeini, Ayatollah, 57, 109
King, Martin Luther, Jr.,
    49–50
King, Sue, 29
Knesset, 277
Kratia, 170
Ksatriya, 48
Kumaratunga, Chandrika
  Bandaranaike, 239
Kurdish Workers Party (PKK),
    234–235
Kurds, 19, 222, 233–235, 250
Kuwait
  income in, 82–83, 87
  Iraqi invasion of, 26, 269

Labor Code (Brazil), 130
Labor force, 154–155
Labor unions, 175–176
Ladies in White, 179
Language
  in Africa, 11, 65
  colonialism and, 65–66
  nationalism and, 62
  in United States, 257
Latin America. *See also specific
    countries*
  child labor in, 130
  Christianity in, 52–53
  colonialism and, 17, 74–76
  deforestation in, 138–139
  democratic transitions in,
    180–182, 210
  ethnic conflict in, 235–236
  overview of, 15–17
  population growth in, 113
  poverty in, 80
  regional inequalities
    in, 85
  role of females in, 148–149,
    160, 179
  urbanization in, 133–135
  U.S. policies toward, 17

Law
  Buddhist, 186
  Islamic, 45, 174
  rule of, 175
Law of supply and demand, 102
Leadership
  globalization and, 195
  military, 196–197
  nonmilitary, 203–205
  overview of, 195–196
  patriarchal, 196
Lebanon, 237
Legends, 65
Legitimacy, 171
Le Pen, Jean-Marie, 254
Lesotho, 111
Liberalization, 177
Liberation theology
  explanation of, 53
  in Haiti, 53
Liberia, 228–229
Libya, 268
Limited monarchy, 6
Literacy rates
  gender and, 153
  poverty and, 84
Loans, for women, 156–157
Locke, John, 186–171
Lost Decade, 155

Madison, James, 171
Madres de la Plaza de Mayo, 158
Majlis (Iran), 57
Malawi, HIV/AIDS in, 116
Maleness of politics, 157
Mali, 12, 112
Malnutrition
  in children, 84, 92
  females and, 153–154
  poverty and, 84–85
Mandela, Nelson, 190
Maquiladoras, 101, 155, 256
Marianismo, 148
Marriage, 149
Marx, Karl, 106
Marxism, 106
Masih, Iqbal, 35–36
Mattel, 131
Mbeke, Thabo, 190
McAleese, Mary, 148
McNamara, Robert S., 61

McWorld, 33
Mecca, 18, 43
Mestizos, 15
Mexican-American War, 253
Mexico
    bureaucracy in, 216
    case study, 257–259
    economic development in, 111
    foreign relations and, 277–279
    government in, 181–182
    maquiladora program in,
        101, 256
    migration and, 256, 257–259
    political participation in, 160
    political parties in, 174
    relocation of U.S. jobs to, 88
Mexico City, Mexico,
    134, 137, 182
Microloans, 157
Middle class, 177
Middle East. *See also specific*
        countries
    economic development in, 20
    oil reserves in, 110
    overview of, 18–20
    political participation in,
        158–159
    regional inequalities
        in, 85
    religion in, 18–19
    urbanization in, 133–135
Migrants, 246
Migration
    causes of, 247
    explanation of, 246–257
    forced, 249
    globalization and, 245, 259
    Palestinian refugees
        and, 251
    in poor countries, 254–256
    pull factors and, 251–254
    push factors and, 248–251
    in rich countries, 256–257
    rural-to-rural, 247
    rural-to-urban, 247
    seasonal, 247
    transcontinental, 246
    urban-to-rural, 247
Migration of dreams, 33
Military interventions,
    196–197

Military leaders in Africa,
    183–184
    in Chile, 201–203
    in Egypt, 197–200
    explanation of, 196–197
    in Nigeria, 200–201
Military service, 26
Millennium Declaration
    (United Nations), 90
Millennium Development Goals,
    99
Modernization theory, 105
Mohammad, 18–19, 42–44, 54
Monarchy
    absolute, 6
    constitutional, 6
    explanation of, 6
    limited, 6
    in Saudi Arabia, 203–205
Mongols, 67
Morales, Evo, 289
Morena, Maria de los
    Angeles, 160
Mossadeg, Muhammad, 55
Mozambique, 183
Mujahedeen, 266
Multinational corporations
    (MNCs), 28, 87
Murahaleen, 225
Muslim states, 48
Muslims. *See also* Islam; Islamic
        fundamentalism, challenges
        to in Africa, 11
    explanation of, 44–47
    in Middle East, 18–19
    against Muslims, 72

Nasser, Gamal Abdul, 139, 174,
    199–200, 217–218
Nation-states
    explanation of, 9
    nationalism and, 64–65
National anthems, 63
National interests, 264
National Liberation Front (FLN)
    (Algeria), 73
National Rifle Association
    (NRA), 29
Nationalism
    bonds of, 62
    ethnic, 64

    explanation of, 9–10,
        61–63
    independence and, 64
    in India, 232
    negative aspects of, 64–65
    symbols of, 63
Nations, 61
Natural disasters
    development and, 110–111
    economic inequality and, 90
Natural resources
    development and, 110–111
    global interdependence and,
        24–25
    Venezuela, in, 119
Naturalistic theories, 105
Nazis
    human rights and, 187
    nationalism and, 64
Negative rights, 188
Nehru, Jawahar Lal, 232
Neopatriarchy, 196
Nepal, prostitution in, 151–152
New International Economic
    Order (NIEO), 107,
    278, 289
New World Information and
    Communciation Order
    (UNESCO), 31
Nicaragua, 53
Nigeria
    civil war in, 183–184
    corruption in, 118
    democratic transition in,
        183–184
    ethnic conflict in, 227–228
    internal conflict in, 64
    military leadership in, 200–201
    natural resources in, 110–118
    privatization in, 102
Nike, 131, 162
Nirvana, 51
Nixon, Richard M., 282
Nkrumah, Kwame, 74
No Sweat label, 131
Nonaligned Movement,
    273, 269, 279
Nonalignment policy, 265
Nongovernmental organizations
    (NGOs), 90, 156, 175
Nonviolent resistance, 49, 70

Noor, Queen of Jordan, 148
North
 causes of inequality between South and, 86–90
 economic inequalities within countries in, 84–85
 explanation of, 80
 inequality between South and, 80–82
North American Free Trade Agreement (NAFTA), 102, 216, 236, 270, 278
North Korea, 89
Nyerere, Julius K., 107

Obama, Barack, 34, 195, 282, 267, 276
Obasanjo, Olusegun, 184, 200
Obesity, 133
Ocalan, Abdullah, 225, 235
Oil industry, 135–136, 278–279
Oil prices, 155
Oil spill (2010), 195
One child policy (China), 114–115
Operation Wetback, 259
Operational autonomy, 215
Opium Wars, 282
Opportunity costs, 125
Oral divorce, 159
Organization of African Unity (OAU), 273
Organization of American States (OAS), 271–272
Organization of Petroleum Exporting Countries (OPEC), 268
Ottoman Empire, 163, 174
Outcastes, 48
Overpopulation
 child labor and, 128–130
 economic development and, 131
 inequality and, 88–89
 migration and, 248–249
 poverty and, 112–115

Pakistan
 child labor in, 33–34, 129
 conflict with India, 70, 232, 284–285

creation of, 70
 ethnic conflict in, 232
 political participation in, 159
Pakistan People's Party (PPP), 159
Palestinian refugees, 251
Palestinians, 19
Panchayat (India), 159
Parliamentary form of democracy, 172
Patriarchal leadership, 196
Patronage, 216–217
Patron-client systems, 173
Peace of Westphalia, 263
Pereira de Queiroz, Carlota, 160
Persia, 54. See also Iran
Peru
 democratic transitions in, 180–181
 Shining Path in, 181, 235
Pilgrimage, to Mecca, 44
Pillars of Islam, 44
Ping-pong diplomacy, 282
Pinochet, Augusto, 181, 202–203
Pizzaro, Francisco, 17
Political culture, 7–8
Political instability, 116–117
Political participation
 conventional, 173
 democracy and, 172–176
 in developing countries, 174–175
 explanation of, 172–176
 unconventional, 173
 by women, 157–160
Political parties
 in developing countries, 173
 role of, 173–175
Politics
 Buddhism and, 52, 58
 explanation of, 4–5
 globalization and, 4
 Hinduism and Indian, 49–50, 58
 Islam and, 45–46, 58
 study of, 4–5, 20
Pollution. See Environmental issues
Population
 development and, 112–115
 education and, 114
 inequality and, 88–89

Portugal
 in Africa, 73
 Brazilian independence and, 74
 democracy in, 176
 India and, 68–69
Positive rights, 188
Poverty. See also Inequality
 in Africa, 13, 82–84
 attempts to decrease, 90–93
 education and, 153–154
 ethnic conflict and, 224–225
 literacy rates and, 82
 malnutrition and, 82–83
 migration and, 254–256
 overpopulation and, 88–89
 in South, 82–84
Power-sharing arrangements, 237
Presidential form of democracy, 171
Private Voluntary Organizations (PVOs), 156
Privatization, 102
Prostitution, 151–152
Public opinion, 4
Pudong (China), 140
Pull factors in migration, 251–254
Purdah, 159
Push factors in migration, 248–251

Qaddafi, Muammar, 268
Quran, 44, 153

Racial theories, 230
Ramadan, 44
Rape, 152–153
Reagan, Ronald, 278
Reebok, 131
Refah Party (Turkey), 174
Refugees
 explanation of, 246
 Palestinian, 251
 women and children as, 250
Regional economic development banks, 111, 270
Relative deprivation, 32
Religion. See also specific religions
 in Africa, 11
 in Asia, 13
 gender roles and, 148

globalization and, 43
  in Latin America, 16
  in Middle East, 18–19
  politics and, 45–46, 49–50,
    52, 58
  revival of, 23, 43–44, 52
Remittances, 255
Representative democracy, 170
Republic, 6–7
Restavec system (Haiti), 130
Reza, Muhammad, 55
Rhodes, Cecil, 67
Rockefeller Foundation, 91
Roles, 148
Romero, Oscar, 53
Roosevelt, Kermit, 55
Rostow, Walt W., 105
Rousseff, Dilma, 95, 160, 280
Rugmark carpet label, 130
Rule of law, 175
Rural-to-rural migration, 247
Rural-to-urban migration, 247
Rwanda, 66, 152–153, 230–231

Sadat, Anwar, 200, 277
Sale of females, 151
Samsara, 47
San Andreas Accords, 236
San Suu Kyi, 52
Sandinista Revolution, 53
Sandoval, Mayra, 127
Sanitation, health and, 83
Sao Paulo, Brazil, 134
Saro-Wiwa, Ken, 183
Satyagraha, 69
Saudi Arabia
  economic growth and, 87
  as Islamist state, 46
  monarchy in, 203–205
  oil reserves in, 110
  political system in, 6, 172
  role of women in, 158
  veiling of females in, 150
Savak (Iran), 56
Seasonal migration, 247
Seko, Mobutu Sese, 183
Selassie, Haile, 269
Senegal, 11
Sepoy Mutiny, 69
Seven Sisters, 55, 278
Sex traffickers, 151–152

Shaheed, 229
Shang Dynasty, 15
Shanghi Joint Communiqué,
  283
Sharaf, 152
Shari'a, 45, 175
Shi'ites, 54, 233–235, 269
Shining Path (Peru),
  181, 235
Shower Posse Gang, 128
Shudra, 48
Siddhartha Gautama, 50–52
Sierra Club, 29
Sikhs, 232
Simpson-Millia, Portia, 160
Singapore, 82–83, 87
Sinhalese, 237–240
Six Day War, 276
Sixteen Decisions (Grameen
  Bank), 157
Slash-and-burn agriculture, 138
Slogans, 63
Smith, Adam, 87
Smugglers, 252–253
Social costs of development
  child labor as, 128–130
  crime as, 127–128
  overview of, 125–128
  sweatshops as, 130–131
Socialism, 107–108
Socialization, 148
Socially constructed positions,
  149
Somalia, 83, 226, 269
South
  explanation of, 80
  gulf between rich and poor in,
    85–86
  inequality between North and,
    80–82, 86–90
  poverty in, 82–84
South Africa
  African National Congress
    (ANC), 190, 216
  apartheid in, 86, 189–190,
    191, 216, 275
  bureaucracy in, 216–217
  case study, 188–191
  democracy in, 188–191
  economic development
    in, 111

natural resources in, 110,
  111, 189
Soccer World Cup host in
  2010, 188
South Asian Association for
  Regional Cooperation
  (SAARC), 274
South Korea, economic
  development in, 87,
  89, 111
Southern Baptist Convention, 148
Southern Cone Common Market
  (Mercosur), 271
Sovereignty
  economic development
    and, 132
  explanation of, 9, 264
Soviet Union
  Cold War and, 19, 111
  Cuba and, 208
  India and, 274
Spain, 176
Spark Plan (China), 251
Sri Lanka
  case study, 237–240
  ethnic conflict in, 237–240
Sri Lanka Freedom Party
  (SLFP), 238
Starbucks, 131
State capitalism, 103–104
States, 8–9, 61
Status, of females, 149–152
Steger, Manfred, 33
Stereotypes, of Islam, 42
Structural adjustment
  program, 130
Subsistence living, 24
Sudan
  agriculture in, 155
  ethnic conflict in, 90, 227,
    229–230
Sudan People's Liberation Army
  (SPLA), 227
Suez Canal, 197, 199
Suharto, President, 184
Sunnites, 54
Sustainable development,
  108–109
Swaziland, 86
Sweatshops, 33–34,
  130–131

Taiwan
  cultural values in, 109
  development in, 111
  education in, 115
  environmental issues in, 136
Taiwan Relations Act, 283
Taliban, 150, 153, 267
Tamils, 228, 237–240
Tanzania, 112, 182
Technological advances
  in agriculture, 91–92,
    105, 115
  education and, 115
  global interdependence
    and, 25
Ten Thousand Women Initiative,
    162
Territory, common, 62
Terrorism, 34–35
Terrorist attacks of September 11,
    2001, 34, 63, 265–266
Texaco, 136
Theories, 104–109
Third World, 17
Third World socialism, 107–108
Three Gorges Dam, 139
Tianenmen Square massacre, 186
Tibet, 187
Toledo, Alejandro, 181
Totalitarian systems, 7
Trade, 87–88. *See also* Free trade
    policies
  economic interdependence and,
    27–28
  illegal, 127–128
  rise of Islam and, 70
Trade barriers, 102
Trans-Amazon Highway, 138
Transcontinental migration, 246
Transition to democracy, 177–180
Transmigration Program
    (Indonesia), 138
Transparency International,
    117–118
Treaty of Rome, 270
Tribalism, 222
Tripitaka, 51
Truth and Reconciliation
    Commission (South Africa),
    190
Tudeh Party (Iran), 56

Turkey
  case study, 163–165
  females in, 164–165
  invasion of Cyprus, 8
  as Muslim state, 46
  political parties in, 174
Turkish Federated State of Cyprus
    (TFSC), 8
Turks, 67, 256–257
Tutsis, 230–231
26th of July Revolutionary
    Movement (Cuba), 207

Uganda, 112
Uighur separatists, 232
Ujamaa, 108
Ulema, 205
Unconventional political
    participation, 173
Underpopulation, 248
Unión de Naciones Suramericanas
    (UNASUR), 280
Unitary system, 240
United Gold Coast Convention
    (UGCC), 74
United National Party (UNP)
    (Sri Lanka), 238
United Nations, 119
  conferences on
    women, 162
  development programs and,
    154
  Food and Agriculture
    Organization, 155
  International Labor
    Organization, 130
  World Health Organization,
    137
United Nations Development
    Program (UNDP), 101,
    147, 163
United Nations Educational,
    Scientific, and Cultural
    Organization (UNESCO),
    7, 31
United Nations Environmental
    Programme (UNEP), 29
United States
  child labor and, 128
  Cuba and, 207–208
  democracy in, 171

  developing world and,
    265–267
  economic inequalities in, 84–85
  English language resolutions in,
    257
  government in, 5
  Iran and, 55–56
  migration and, 253, 256–257,
    251–254
  policies toward Latin
    America, 17
  religious revivalism in, 41–42
  secure border initiative, 257
Universalists, 187
Untouchables, 48
Urban-to-rural migration, 247
Urbanization
  agriculture and, 135
  benefits of, 134
  drawbacks of, 133–135
  statistics regarding, 133–134
Uruguay, 16
U.S. Agency for International
    Development (AID),
    119, 154

Vaisya, 50
Veddah, 237
Veiling, 147, 150
Velazquez de Cuellar,
    Diego, 205
Venezuela
  case study, 119–121
  economic development, 120
  hydropower dams, 121
  natural resources, 119
Vertical diversity, 12
Vietnam War, 61, 250
Violence
  migration and, 250
  relative deprivation
    and, 32

al- Wahhab, Abd, 172
Wahhabi tradition, 172
Wal-Mart, 131
The Walt Disney Company,
    131
War on drugs, 278–279. *See also*
    Illegal drugs
War crime, rape as, 152–153

War on terrorism, 34–35
Wars, 64
Washington, George, 63
Water pollution, 136.
    See also Environmental
    issues
Weber, Max, 105
West Indies, 16
Women. *See* Females
World Bank, 154

World Health Organization
    (WHO), 137
World systems theory, 106
World Trade Organization
    (WTO), 30
World War I, 54–55, 64
World War II
    effects of, 19, 70
    Iran and, 57
    origins of, 64

Yunus, Muhammad, 157

Zaire, 187
Zambia, 110, 115
Zapatista National Liberation
    Front, 236
Zedong, Mao, 181, 282
Zimbabwe, 115, 153, 183
Zuma, Jacob, 190